聖 經 故 事 一 百 篇

100 BIBLE STORIES

一百叢書

英漢對照 English-Chinese

劉意青・馮國忠・白曉冬譯

聖經故事一百篇
100
BIBLE
STORIES

商 務 印 書 館

叢書編輯：羅　斯
執行編輯：袁志超

《 一百叢書 》
聖經故事一百篇
100 Bible Stories
劉意青　馮國忠　白曉冬譯

出版：商務印書館（香港）有限公司
　　　香港鰂魚涌芬尼街 2 號 D 僑英大廈
印刷：美雅印刷製本有限公司
　　　九龍官塘榮業街 6 號海濱工業大廈 4 樓 B1
版次：1988 年 11 月第 1 版
　　　1993 年 5 月第 2 次印刷
　　　ⓒ 1988 商務印書館（香港）有限公司
　　　ISBN 962 07 1097 5

《一百叢書》總序

　　本館出版英漢(或漢英)對照《一百叢書》的目的，是希望憑藉着英、漢兩種語言的對譯，把中國和世界各類著名作品的精華部分介紹給中外讀者。

　　本叢書的涉及面很廣。題材包括了寓言、詩歌、散文、短篇小說、書信、演說、語錄、神話故事、聖經故事、成語故事、名著選段等等。

　　顧名思義，《一百叢書》中的每一種都由一百個單元組成。以一百爲單位，主要是讓編譯者在浩瀚的名著的海洋中作挑選時有一個取捨的最低和最高限額。至於取捨的標準，則是見仁見智，各有心得。

　　由於各種書中被選用的篇章節段，都是以原文或已被認定的範本作藍本，而譯文又經專家學者們精雕細琢，千錘百煉，故本叢書除可作爲各種題材的精選讀本外，也是研習英漢兩種語言對譯的理想參考書，部分更可用作朗誦教材。外國學者如要研習漢語，本叢書亦不失爲理想工具。

商務印書館(香港)有限公司

編輯部

前　言

　　《聖經》是基督教的經典，也是一部具有重要地位的世界文學著作。作爲宣揚教義的經典，它不可避免地包含着宗教傳説和説教；但是，它却可以幫助我們了解西方文明的發展和社會演變。這裏我們用英漢對照形式選譯了一百個聖經故事，其目的就是爲了幫助更多人熟悉西方文化，同時也想通過英漢對照，使有意學習英文的讀者，在獲取知識的同時，提高英語閲讀能力。而這後者，也正是我們這本聖經故事不同於其他許多版本的地方。

　　《聖經》(The Bible 或 The Holy Scriptures) 由《舊約》(The Old Testament)和《新約》(The New Testament) 兩部分組成。《舊約》最早是用希伯來語(Hebrew)寫成的，《新約》則是用希臘文，又稱猶太希臘文 (Judæo-Greek) 寫成。由於公元四世紀時，羅馬帝國的君主君士坦丁把基督教定爲國教，因此《聖經》很早就有了拉丁文譯本，叫做The Vulgate，意爲通行本。從此基督教便向歐洲各地傳播開來。在英國，中世紀時只有寺院僧侣能讀拉丁文，《聖經》都是由他們講給老百姓聽，他們還選擇了其中一些篇章，陸續出了一些譯文版本。到了十七世紀初，英王詹姆斯一世指令四十七位高僧，在大主教蘭斯洛特、安德魯斯 (Lancelot Andrewes) 主持下，參考以前若干譯本，編譯並於1611年正式出版了英文聖經。這就是後來世界通用的、最有權威的《欽定聖經》(The Authorized Version, 又稱 The King James Version)。這個譯本歷來被認爲是最佳譯本，它集合了以前諸譯本之大成，略去和替換了原譯文中某些古老、生僻的字詞；但同時又注意保持其文字古樸優美，反映出那個時代的特點，因而獨樹一幟，形成了後人稱道的 "聖經文體" (the biblical language)。《欽定聖經》雖然有近千頁之多，全書所用語滙却沒有超過六千單詞。這充分顯示了它那文筆洗煉，深入淺出，語言精湛的特點。

為了便於讀者學習英語，我們以在《欽定聖經》基礎上進行了修改的牛津學習版《新英文聖經》(The New English Bible——Oxford Study Edition) 作為我們選譯的英文依據。這是由於《欽定聖經》在二十世紀的今天已出現了詞語老化問題。1946年5月，蘇格蘭教會會員大會發起了修改《欽定聖經》的倡議。許多有名的學者和教會人士先後做了大量的、細緻的工作，直到六十年代才大功告成。《新英文聖經》既保留了原《欽定聖經》的優點，其英語又更能為現代的讀者所接受，而且通過許多學者的嚴格審閱，進一步校正了原來本子裏的一些錯誤和相互矛盾的地方。因此，以它來做我們英漢對照一百個聖經故事的英文依據是比較合適的。

　　在一百個故事裏，選自《舊約》的有六十二個，選自《新約》的有三十八個。為了方便讀者，每個故事都加了一個小標題。

　　在選擇故事時，我們力求照顧到《聖經》的連續性和每個故事的完整性，並且盡量包羅那些膾炙人口的情節或經常被引用的典故。然而由於篇幅所限，有時也不得不忍痛捨去一些內容。

　　眾所周知，《聖經》中重複的語句很多，似已形成了它的一個風格。有時還出現整個段落和情節的重複，這同它的作者並非一人有關。流傳下來的《聖經》就是由兩個或更多的版本揉合而成的。至今，對《聖經》作者的考據，仍是研究聖經的學者們的一大課題。比如，前五部分從《創世紀》到《申命記》，到底是否出自摩西一人手筆，一直是學者們爭論不休的問題。這種重複現象造成了我們翻譯中的一些困難。英漢對照這種形式限制較多。一般翻譯可以有較大的伸縮性，完全可省去一些重複的話語，或者把近似的詞句合二、甚至合三為一。而英漢對照則要照顧讀者在閱讀漢語譯文時對照英語的需要，就不便隨意處置。英漢對照更不同於以中文編寫聖經故事，因為編寫實質上是再創作，更加靈活，甚至可以略過許多情節而直取故事梗概。為了既保留原文風格和句式，又盡量省去過多的重複，我們現在的做法是：1）在譯文中把不會造成讀者閱讀困難的一些重複詞句省去，並且不注明任何標誌。2）當故事裏插進了與該故事關係不大的大段其他情節、或者出現了情節相同的整段重複時，我們就把英文大段刪節，由此而引起情節上略有不銜接時，用刪節號（"…"）標明。3）刪節後如上下文出現不銜接處，譯者就在中文部分加上幾句承上啟下的說明，放在括號內，表示並非原文。

在人名同地名的譯法上，為了避免造成不必要的混亂，我們一律採用最早聖經譯文中沿用下來的姓氏和地名譯法，儘管其中有些譯法已明顯過時或不大合適。有些姓名、地名帶有原希伯來語的含義、又同故事情節有密切關係；遇到這種情況，我們除去譯音外，還做了少量的注釋。

幾百年來，《聖經》在世界上，特別是在西方社會的發展中，起了無法估量的巨大作用。它深入人們的生活，影響人們的思想。美國總統林肯早年自修成材，《聖經》就是他的重要讀本之一。而英國十七世紀的文學家班揚，由一個只有初小教育的小爐匠，變成《天路歷程》(The Pilgrim's Progress) 等幾部文學名著的作者，就是靠熟讀《聖經》，從中汲取營養的。聖經的影響是如此之深，以致成為許多人尋求慰藉的精神支柱、待人處世的實踐準則。

英文《聖經》又是一部重要的文學著作，在英美等國的文學藝術史上，它的影響之深遠，也是任何其他作品無法比擬的。許多偉大的詩人、文豪、藝術家以聖經故事和傳說為題材，創造出不少不朽的名作。如眾所熟知的英國十七世紀偉大詩人密爾頓的長詩《失樂園》(Paradise Lost)，《復樂園》(Paradise Regained)，和《力士參孫》(Samson Agonistes)。又如意大利名畫家達‧芬奇的不朽之作《最後的晚餐》。至於在作品和講話中引用《聖經》中的典故，更是在西方作家和政治家中屢見不鮮的現象。

《聖經》的語言和文體在英語形成過程中也佔有一席極重要的位置。今日英語中使用的詞滙，有許多來自《聖經》，如"peacemaker"，"Long-suffering"等字就是首次出現在廷兌勒 (Tindale) 譯的英文聖經中。像"beautiful"這樣一個人人皆知，生活中經常應用的字，也來自《聖經》。至於說《聖經》中的典故變成習語進入英語語滙的例子，更是比比皆是，如 "the Benjamin of the family"，"Noah's Ark"，"the prodigal son"，"a leviathan ship"，"the worship of mammon"，"to cast pearls before swine"，"a howling wilderness" 等等。事實上，《聖經》與莎翁戲劇及一些民間文學已成為西方成語的重要來源。

在某個意義上，我們可以說整個西方文明的形成同《聖經》這本書的影響是分不開的。難怪德國偉大的文學家哥德曾這樣評論過《聖經》，大意是："世界可以按它的步伐飛速前進，人類的科學可以向着最高的階段發展，但却沒有任何東西可以取代《聖經》的地位。"正因為《聖經》在西方及英美社會中如此重要，正因為了解《聖經》可以使我們對西方的文化和意識形態加深認識，我們很高興能借這個機會為廣大讀者熟悉聖經故事和提高英語水平貢獻出一點力量。對我們編譯這本書的不足之處，希望讀者們提出批評指正。

編譯者

一九八六年夏於北京

CONTENTS

i

New Testament 新約

舊約

Old Testament

1   The Creation of the World

Genesis

In the beginning of creation, when God made heaven and earth, the earth was without form and void, with darkness over the face of the abyss, and a mighty wind that swept over the surface of the waters. God said, 'Let there be light', and there was light; and God saw that the light was good, and he separated light from darkness. He called the light day, and the darkness night. So evening came, and morning came, the first day.

God said, 'Let there be a vault between the waters, to separate water from water.' So God made the vault, and separated the water under the vault from the water above it, and so it was; and God called the vault heaven. Evening came, and morning came, a second day.

God said, 'Let the waters under heaven be gathered into one place, so that dry land may appear'; and so it was. God called the dry land earth, and the gathering of the waters he called seas; and God saw that it was good. Then God said, 'Let the earth produce fresh growth, let there be on the earth plants bearing seed, fruit-trees bearing fruit each with seed according to its kind.' So it was; the earth yielded fresh growth, plants bearing seed according to their kind and trees bearing fruit each with seed according to its kind; and God saw that it was good. Evening came, and morning came, a third day.

God said, 'Let there be lights in the vault of heaven to separate day from night, and let them serve as signs both for festi-

一　開天闢地

創世記

太初，上帝始創天地時，大地混沌一片，是個無邊無際的黑暗深淵，強風於水面刮掠。上帝說：“要有光！”立刻就有光。上帝見有光很好，就把光明與黑暗分開，稱光明爲晝，黑暗爲夜。於是黑夜臨，晨光現，是爲第一天。

上帝說：“要有一穹窿將水上下分隔！”於是他就造穹窿，將水分開，有水於穹窿之上，亦有水於穹窿之下。上帝稱穹窿爲天空。黑夜再臨，晨光再現，是爲第二天。

上帝說：“天下之水要滙於一處，使乾涸土地顯露！”於是就出現土地。上帝稱土地爲陸，稱滙集之水爲海。上帝見如此很好。又說：“要大地生機蓬勃，地上要有能結實之樹木，果子要各有其籽實！”於是大地生機蓬勃，出現無數瓜果樹木，籽實纍纍。上帝見如此很好。黑夜又臨，晨光再現，是爲第三天。

上帝說：“天穹中要有光體以區分晝夜，要使光體爲節令與年月季候之標誌，並使於天穹中發出光輝，照亮大地！”於

vals and for seasons and years. Let them also shine in the vault of heaven to give light on earth.' So it was; God made the two great lights, the greater to govern the day and the lesser to govern the night; and with them he made the stars. God put these lights in the vault of heaven to give light on earth, to govern day and night, and to separate light from darkness; and God saw that it was good. Evening came, and morning came, a fourth day.

God said, 'Let the waters teem with countless living creatures, and let birds fly above the earth across the vault of heaven.' God then created the great sea-monsters and all living creatures that move and swarm in the waters, according to their kind, and every kind of bird; and God saw that it was good. So he blessed them and said, 'Be fruitful and increase, fill the waters of the seas; and let the birds increase on land.' Evening came, and morning came, a fifth day.

God said, 'Let the earth bring forth living creatures, according to their kind: cattle, reptiles, and wild animals, all according to their kind.' So it was; God made wild animals, cattle, and all reptiles, each according to its kind; and he saw that it was good. Then God said, 'Let us make man in our image and likeness to rule the fish in the sea, the birds of heaven, the cattle, all wild animals on earth, and all reptiles that crawl upon the earth.' So God created man in his own image; in the image of God he created him; male and female he created them. God blessed them and said to them, 'Be fruitful and increase, fill the earth and subdue it, rule over the fish in the sea, the birds of heaven, and every living thing that moves upon the earth.' God also said, 'I give you all plants that bear seed everywhere on earth, and every tree bearing fruit which yields seed: they shall be yours for food. All green plants I give for food to the wild animals, to all the birds of heaven, and to all reptiles on earth, every living creature.' So it was; and God saw all that he had made, and it was very good. Evening came, and morning came, a sixth day.

Thus heaven and earth were completed with all their

是，上帝造兩個巨大光體，較大之日司晝，較小之月掌夜，並造了星辰。上帝把日月星辰置於天穹之中以照亮大地，司晝夜、分明暗。上帝見如此很好。黑夜臨，晨光現，是爲第四天。

上帝說："水中要有萬種游魚，地上要有無數飛鳥"於是上帝創造出種類繁多的大小魚類及飛鳥。上帝見如此很好。於是賜福與牠們，說："讓海中游魚，天上飛鳥滋生繁衍！"黑夜臨，晨光現，是爲第五天。

上帝說："地上要有爬蟲走獸，大小牲畜，各從其類！"上帝就創造走獸，牲畜和爬行動物，各從其類。上帝見如此很好。他說："要按我形象造人以治理海中游魚、空中飛鳥以及地上各種爬蟲走獸。"於是，上帝按自己形象造出人類，造出男與女。上帝祝福他們說："你們要生育繁衍，散佈及開拓全世界，要做海中魚、空中鳥與地上爬蟲走獸之主宰！"上帝還說："我要使地上到處生長瓜果，結滿籽實，賜與你們爲食。我要把青草綠樹全賜與飛禽走獸、游魚爬蟲、以及一切生物爲食。"話語間一切均成現實。上帝見到所造之一切，他十分滿意。黑夜臨，晨光現，是爲第六日。

天地萬物已造齊。到第六日，上帝造物工作全部完畢。第

mighty throng. On the sixth day God completed all the work he had been doing, and on the seventh day he ceased from all his work. God blessed the seventh day and made it holy, because on that day he ceased from all the work he had set himself to do.

This is the story of the making of heaven and earth when they were created.

七天，他停止工作。上帝賜福於第七天，稱之爲聖日，因那天他要做的一切都已完成，無需工作了。

　　這就是上帝開天闢地的故事。

2   *The Beginnings of History*

Genesis

When the Lord God made earth and heaven, there was neither shrub nor plant growing wild upon the earth, because the Lord God had sent no rain on the earth; nor was there any man to till the ground. A flood used to rise out of the earth and water all the surface of the ground. Then the Lord God formed a man[1] from the dust of the ground and breathed into his nostrils the breath of life. Thus the man became a living creature. Then the Lord God planted a garden in Eden away to the east, and there he put the man whom he had formed. The Lord God made trees spring from the ground, all trees pleasant to look at and good for food; and in the middle of the garden he set the tree of life and the tree of the knowledge of good and evil.

There was a river flowing from Eden to water the garden, and when it left the garden it branched into four streams. The name of the first is Pishon, that is the river which encircles all the land of Havilah, where the gold is. The gold of that land is good; bdellium and cornelians are also to be found there. The name of the second river is Gihon; this is the one which encircles all the land of Cush. The name of the third is Tigris; this is the river which runs east of Asshur. The fourth river is the Euphrates.

The Lord God took the man and put him in the garden of Eden to till it and care for it. He told the man, 'You may eat from every tree in the garden, but not from the tree of the

---

1   Heb. adam.

二 人世之始

創世記

　　上帝造天地時，地上全無野生草叢樹木，因爲天主上帝沒有降雨到大地，亦無人耕耘土地，只靠地上湧出水流灌漑土地表層。後來，天主上帝以泥土造一男人，朝他鼻孔吹一口生氣，他才有了生命。然後天主上帝在東邊之伊甸建造一座花園，他把他造的男人安置在伊甸園中。上帝使地面長出各種樹木，這些樹木不但秀美悅目，而且又有果實可供食用。在花園正中，他種下一株生命之樹和一株能辨善惡的知識之樹。

　　伊甸園中流過一條河，河水可作灌漑之用。這河流出伊甸後分爲四股。第一股名比遜河，它曲折流經哈腓拉全境，此地盛產高成色黃金，還有琥珀及紅瑪瑙。第二股名基訓河，它環繞流經古實全境。第三股名希底結河，亦即流經亞述之東那條河。第四股名伯拉河。

　　天主上帝把他造的男人帶去伊甸園，讓他在園中耕耘管理。他囑咐這人說："你可以隨意採食園中任何樹上之果實，惟獨那能辨善惡之知識樹果子你不能吃。你吃它之時，你就會

9

knowledge of good and evil; for on the day that you eat from it, you will certainly die.' Then the Lord God said, 'It is not good for the man to be alone. I will provide a partner for him.' So God formed out of the ground all the wild animals and all the birds of heaven. He brought them to the man to see what he would call them, and whatever the man called each living creature, that was its name. Thus the man gave names to all cattle, to the birds of heaven, and to every wild animal; but for the man himself no partner had yet been found. And so the Lord God put the man into a trance, and while he slept, he took one of his ribs and closed the flesh over the place. The Lord God then built up the rib, which he had taken out of the man, into a woman. He brought her to the man, and the man said:

'Now this, at last — bone from my bones,
flesh from my flesh! —
this shall be called woman,
for from man was this taken.'

That is why a man leaves his father and mother and is united to his wife, and the two become one flesh. Now they were both naked, the man and his wife, but they had no feeling of shame towards one another.

死去！"天主上帝又說："一人獨居不好，我要爲他找個伴。"於是上帝以泥土塑造出各種飛禽走獸，帶它們到這人的面前，看他如何稱呼它們。那人對每種動物的稱呼就成了這種動物的名稱。這樣，人就給所有的牲畜、飛禽和走獸定了名，但是這男人自己仍然沒有伴侶。於是，天主上帝使他昏睡，在他昏睡時，取他的一條肋骨，然後使傷口癒合。上帝以這人身上取出的肋骨造了一個女人，並領她到這人面前，這人說："如今，終於有了這生靈，骨取自我骨，肉取自我肉，就稱之爲女人。"

　　這就是爲何男人要離開父母，與自己的妻子結合成爲夫婦的緣故。此時，他們兩人，男人和他的妻子都赤身露體，但他們彼此相對，並不難爲情。

3 Man's First Sin

Genesis

The serpent was more crafty than any wild creature that the Lord God had made. He said to the woman, 'Is it true that God has forbidden you to eat from any tree in the garden?' The woman answered the serpent, 'We may eat the fruit of any tree in the garden, except for the tree in the middle of the garden; God has forbidden us either to eat or to touch the fruit of that; if we do, we shall die.' The serpent said, 'Of course you will not die. God knows that as soon as you eat it, your eyes will be opened and you will be like gods knowing both good and evil.' When the woman saw that the fruit of the tree was good to eat, and that it was pleasing to the eye and tempting to contemplate, she took some and ate it. She also gave her husband some and he ate it. Then the eyes of both of them were opened and they discovered that they were naked; so they stitched fig-leaves together and made themselves loincloths.

The man and his wife heard the sound of the Lord God walking in the garden at the time of the evening breeze and hid from the Lord God among the trees of the garden. But the Lord God called to the man and said to him, 'Where are you?' He replied, 'I heard the sound as you were walking in the garden, and I was afraid because I was naked, and I hid myself.' God answered, 'Who told you that you were naked? Have you eaten from the tree which I forbade you?' The man said, 'The woman you gave me for a companion, she gave me fruit from the tree and I ate it.' Then the Lord God said to the woman, 'What is this that you have done?' The woman said,

三　始祖犯戒

創世記

　　蛇比上帝造的其他生物都要狡猾。他對那女人說：“上帝果眞不許你們吃園子裏任何一棵樹上的果子嗎？”女人回答說：“我們可以隨便吃園中樹上的果子，惟獨不能吃園中央那棵樹的。上帝不准我們吃，也不准我們碰它的果子。如果違戒，我們就會死去。”蛇說：“你們不一定會死。上帝知道你們一旦吃了那樹的果子，就會眼睛明亮，同神一樣能明辨善惡了。”女人知道那樹的果子原來可以吃，看上去果子又極悅目誘人，便摘了幾個吃了。她又給她丈夫一些，他也吃了。吃完果子，他們兩人的眼睛頓時明亮起來，這才看到他們自己却是一絲不掛的，於是他們把一些無花果樹葉縫起來，繫在腰間來遮羞。

　　傍晚的微風輕送時，男人和他的妻子聽見天主上帝在園中行走的聲響，他們就在園中樹叢裏躲起來。但是天主上帝叫那男人，說：“你在哪兒呢？”那男人回答：“我聽見你在園中行走的聲音，我怕自己赤身露體，就躲起來了。”上帝問道：“誰告訴你你是赤身露體了？你定是吃了我禁吃的樹上果子了？”男人說：“你給我作伴侶的女人給我那樹的果子，我吃了。”天主上帝於是對那女人說：“你爲何如此？”那女人說：

13

'The serpent tricked me, and I ate.' Then the Lord God said
to the serpent:

> 'Because you have done this you are accursed
> more than all cattle and all wild creatures.
> On your belly you shall crawl, and dust you shall eat
> all the days of your life.
> I will put enmity between you and the woman, between
> your brood and hers.
> They shall strike at your head,
> and you shall strike at their heel.'

To the woman he said:

> 'I will increase your labour and your groaning,
> and in labour you shall bear children.
> You shall be eager for your husband,
> and he shall be your master.'

And to the man he said:

> 'Because you have listened to your wife
> and have eaten from the tree which I forbade you,
> accursed shall be the ground on your account.
> With labour you shall win your food from it
> all the days of your life.
> It will grow thorns and thistles for you,
> none but wild plants for you to eat. You shall gain your
> bread by the sweat of your brow until you return to the
> ground;
> for from it you were taken.
> Dust you are, to dust you shall return.'

The man called his wife Eve because she was the mother of
all who live. The Lord God made tunics of skins for Adam
and his wife and clothed them. He said, 'The man has become
like one of us, knowing good and evil; what if he now reaches
out his hand and takes fruit from the tree of life also, eats it
and lives for ever?' So the Lord God drove him out of the garden of Eden to till the ground from which he had been taken.
He cast him out, and to the east of the garden of Eden he
stationed the cherubim and a sword whirling and flashing to
guard the way to the tree of life.

"蛇誘惑我，我就吃了禁果。"於是，天主上帝對蛇說："你因為誘惑了她，就要比其他牲畜和野獸更倒霉。你要終生以肚皮爬行，啃泥過活。我要使你與那個女人結仇，而且世代為敵。女人都打蛇頭，蛇則咬女人的腳跟。"

他又對女人說："我要增加你的勞累，使你備受懷孕生育之苦楚。你將依附你丈夫，而他則成為你的主宰。"他對那男人說："由於你聽你的妻子的話，偷吃了我禁吃的樹上果實，土地也因你而受累，你要在它上面辛勞一輩子才能勉強糊口。地上因你而長出荊棘和蒺藜，除了野菜，你將沒有其他食物。一直到你入土之日，你都得用汗水來換取飯食。你原來自泥土，你將回到泥土中去。"

男人稱他妻子為夏娃，因為她是人類之母。天主上帝用皮革給亞當和他的妻子做了兩件長上衣，讓他們披上。他說："那人已經和我們神一樣，能辨善惡。如果他再伸手摘取生命樹的果實，吃了它就會得永生，那如何是好？"因此，天主上帝把人趕出了伊甸園，去耕種那片造出他來的土地。上帝把人逐出了伊甸園後，在伊甸園的東邊安置了有翅的天使和一把轉動時火光閃閃的寶劍，來守住通往生命之樹的路。

4   *Cain Killed His Brother*

Genesis

The man lay with his wife Eve, and she conceived and gave birth to Cain. She said, 'With the help of the Lord I have brought a man into being.' Afterwards she had another child, his brother Abel. Abel was a shepherd and Cain a tiller of the soil. The day came when Cain brought some of the produce of the soil as a gift to the Lord; and Abel brought some of the first-born of his flock, the fat portions of them. The Lord received Abel and his gift with favour; but Cain and his gift he did not receive. Cain was very angry and his face fell. Then the Lord said to Cain, 'Why are you so angry and cast down?

If you do well, you are accepted;

if not, sin is a demon crouching at the door.

It shall be eager for you, and you will be mastered by it.'

Cain said to his brother Abel, 'Let us go into the open country.' While they were there, Cain attacked his brother Abel and murdered him. Then the Lord said to Cain, 'Where is your brother Abel?' Cain answered, 'I do not know. Am I my brother's keeper?' The Lord said, 'What have you done? Hark! your brother's blood that has been shed is crying out to me from the ground. Now you are accursed, and banished from the ground which has opened its mouth wide to receive your brother's blood, which you have shed. When you till the ground, it will no longer yield you its wealth. You shall be a vagrant and a wanderer on earth.' Cain said to the Lord, 'My punishment is heavier than I can bear; thou hast driven me today from the ground, and I must hide myself from thy pre-

四 該隱殺弟

創世記

那男人與妻子夏娃同寢，夏娃懷孕，生下該隱。她說："天主助我，我生了一個男丁。"後來，她又生了一個孩子，就是該隱的弟弟亞伯。亞伯是個牧人，該隱則是個耕田人。到了向上帝供奉的日子，該隱拿了些土地的產品獻給天主；亞伯則獻出一些精選的乳羊。天主看中了亞伯和他的供品，而沒看中該隱和他的禮物。該隱很生氣，他的臉沉了下來。天主對該隱說："你為甚麼這樣生氣，臉色也變了呢？如果你做得好，你就會被接受的。反之，罪惡就會像個魔鬼潛伏在你的門前。它在等待時機找你，你會被它控制的。"

該隱對弟弟亞伯說："我們到野外去吧。"當他們到了那裏，該隱就動手把他弟弟殺死。後來，天主問該隱："你的弟弟亞伯在哪裏？"該隱回答說："我不知道。我又不是看守着他的。"天主說："你做了甚麼事？聽着！你弟弟流出的血從地上向我哭訴。你受到控訴，你要被流放，逐離這塊吞噬被你殘殺的兄弟的鮮血的土地。你要耕種，那地也不會再長出佳禾。你會成為流浪漢，到處漂泊。"該隱對天主說："我受不了這個懲罰。今天你把我從這裏趕走，不讓我再出現在你面

sence. I shall be a vagrant and a wanderer on earth, and anyone who meets me can kill me.' The Lord answered him, 'No: if anyone kills Cain, Cain shall be avenged sevenfold.' So the Lord put a mark on Cain, in order that anyone meeting him should not kill him. Then Cain went out from the Lord's presence and settled in the land of Nod to the east of Eden.

前，我將成爲一個流浪漢，到處漂泊，遇見我的人都可能殺死我。"天主回答他說："不，如果有人殺死該隱，他就會遭到七倍的報應。"上帝給該隱做了個標記，這樣遇見他的人就不會殺死他。該隱就離開了天主到伊甸園東邊叫挪得的地方住下來。

5 Noah's Ark

Genesis

(1)

This is the story of Noah. Noah was a righteous man, the one blameless man of his time; he walked with God. He had three sons, Shem, Ham and Japheth. Now God saw that the whole world was corrupt and full of violence. In his sight the world had become corrupted, for all men had lived corrupt lives on earth. God said to Noah, 'The loathsomeness of all mankind has become plain to me, for through them the earth is full of violence. I intend to destroy them, and the earth with them. Make yourself an ark with ribs of cypress; cover it with reeds and coat it inside and out with pitch. I intend to bring the waters of the flood over the earth to destroy every human being under heaven that has the spirit of life; everything on earth shall perish. But with you I will make a covenant, and you shall go into the ark, you and your sons, your wife and your sons' wives with you. And you shall bring living creatures of every kind into the ark to keep them alive with you, two of each kind, a male and a female; two of every kind of bird, beast, and reptile, shall come to you to be kept alive. See that you take and store every kind of food that can be eaten; this shall be food for you and for them.' Exactly as God had commanded him, so Noah did.

And so, to escape the waters of the flood, Noah went into the ark with his sons, his wife, and his sons' wives. And into the ark with Noah went one pair, male and female, of all beasts, clean and unclean, of birds and of everything that

五　挪亞方舟

創世記

（一）

　　下面是挪亞的故事。挪亞是個正直的人，在當時是一個完人。他追隨上帝行事。他有三個兒子：閃、含、和雅弗。上帝看見整個世界腐朽了，到處都是暴力。他認爲世界充斥着罪惡，因爲所有世上的人都過着邪惡的生活。上帝對挪亞說："人類的可憎我再清楚不過了，他們使這世界充滿了仇殺。我有意要毀滅他們，也毀掉同他們一起的這個世界。你要爲自己造一艘方舟，用絲柏木做船架，覆蓋上蘆葦，再在裏外兩面塗上樹脂。我要使洪水泛濫全世界，消滅天下所有活着的人，地上萬物也要消滅光。但我要與你立約。你到時就帶着你的妻子、兒子、兒媳們一起進入方舟。你還要把各種飛禽、走獸、爬蟲，每樣兩隻，雌雄各一帶上，和你一道登舟，在船上餵養好。此外還要帶上各種吃的東西，儲存在船上，作爲你們和動物的食糧。"挪亞遵照上帝的話，一一辦到了。

　　這樣，爲了躲避洪水，挪亞和他的妻、子及兒媳們都上了方舟。和他一起上船的還有那些動物：潔淨的和不潔淨的牲畜，每種都是雌雄一對；所有的鳥類和地上的爬蟲，也是一對

crawls on the ground, two by two, as God had commanded. Towards the end of seven days the waters of the flood came upon the earth. In the year when Noah was six hundred years old, on the seventeenth day of the second month, on that very day, all the springs of the great abyss broke through, the windows of the sky were opened, and rain fell on the earth for forty days and forty nights.... The flood continued upon the earth for forty days, and the waters swelled and lifted up the ark so that it rose high above the ground. More and more the waters increased over the earth until they covered all the high mountains everywhere under heaven. The waters increased and the mountains were covered to a depth of fifteen cubits. Everything died that had the breath of life in its nostrils, everything on dry land. God wiped out every living thing that existed on earth, man and beast, reptile and bird; they were all wiped out over the whole earth, and only Noah and his company in the ark survived.

(2)

After forty days Noah opened the trap-door that he had made in the ark, and released a raven to see whether the water had subsided, but the bird continued flying to and fro until the water on the earth had dried up. Noah waited for seven days, and then he released a dove from the ark to see whether the water on the earth had subsided further. But the dove found no place where she could settle, and so she came back to him in the ark, because there was water over the whole surface of the earth. He waited another seven days and again released the dove from the ark. She came back to him towards evening with a newly plucked olive leaf in her beak. Then Noah knew for certain that the water on the earth had subsided still further. He waited yet another seven days and released the dove, but she never came back. And so it came about that, on the first day of the first month of his six hundred and first year, the water had dried up on the earth, and Noah removed the hatch and looked out of the ark. The surface of the ground was dry.

一對的，按上帝的吩咐那樣都上了船。第七天結束的時候，洪水降臨到大地。那年挪亞是六百歲，二月十七日那天，大深淵的所有泉源一齊噴發起來，天穹洞開，大雨傾盆，不停地下了四十個晝夜。……洪水泛濫了四十天，大水漲起來把方舟托起，高高地升離地面之上。落在地面的水越來越多，淹沒了天下所有的高山。水一直漲到浸沒高山十五腕尺之深。一切有氣息的生物，所有生活在陸地上的東西，全都沒有了。上帝清除了世上的生物，人也好，獸也好，爬蟲也好，飛鳥也好，全部從地面上消滅乾淨，惟獨挪亞和在方舟上和他一起的妻子兒媳、鳥獸爬蟲活了下來。

<h2 align="center">（二）</h2>

四十天後，挪亞打開了他方舟上的天窗，放出一隻烏鴉去看看水退了沒有。但烏鴉飛來飛去，到地面上的水都快乾涸也沒回來。挪亞等了七天，再從舟上放出一隻鴿子去看看地上的水是否再退了些。但因爲地面全部都是水，鴿子沒落腳的地方，就飛回挪亞的方舟那裏。挪亞又等了七天，再次從舟上放出那鴿子去。傍晚時分，鴿子回來了，嘴裏啣着一片剛啄下的橄欖葉。挪亞就知道地面上的水退得差不多了。但他又多等了七天，然後放那鴿子出去。這回牠再也沒有回來了。這樣，在挪亞六百零一歲那年的正月初一，地上的水終於退了，挪亞打開艙口蓋，從方舟上向外探望，地面已經完全乾了。

By the twenty-seventh day of the second month the whole earth was dry. And God said to Noah, 'Come out of the ark, you and your wife, your sons and their wives. Bring out every living creature that is with you, live things of every kind, bird and beast and every reptile that moves on the ground, and let them swarm over the earth and be fruitful and increase there.' So Noah came out with his sons, his wife, and his sons' wives. Every wild animal, all cattle, every bird, and every reptile that moves on the ground, came out of the ark by families. Then Noah built an altar to the Lord. He took ritually clean beasts and birds of every kind, and offered whole-offerings on the altar. When the Lord smelt the soothing odour, he said within himself, 'Never again will I curse the ground because of man, however evil his inclinations may be from his youth upwards. I will never again kill every living creature, as I have just done.

二月二十七日，大地全都乾了。上帝對挪亞說："你和你的妻子，你的兒子兒媳們都從方舟上出來吧。把你帶上方舟去的各種地上生物，鳥獸爬蟲都放出來吧，讓它們滋生繁衍，遍佈全世界吧。"挪亞就同他的妻子、兒子兒媳們從方舟上走出來。各種地上生物：野獸、牲畜、鳥類和爬蟲都是雌雄配對的，也都下了船。接着，挪亞爲天主修了一座祭壇。他選了各種各樣潔淨的鳥獸作爲供品，放在祭壇上奉獻給天主。天主聞到了供品的香味，心裏想道："我再也不會因人類而使大地遭到災禍了。不論人從小就有多少邪念，我都不會像這次那樣殺死一切生靈了。"

6 The Tower of Babel

Genesis

Once upon a time all the world spoke a single language and used the same words. As men journeyed in the east, they came upon a plain in the land of Shinar and settled there. They said to one another, 'Come, let us make bricks and bake them hard'; they used bricks for stone and bitumen for mortar. 'Come,' they said, 'let us build ourselves a city and a tower with its top in the heavens, and make a name for ourselves; or we shall be dispersed all over the earth.' Then the Lord came down to see the city and tower which mortal men had built, and he said, 'Here they are, one people with a single language, and now they have started to do this; henceforward nothing they have a mind to do will be beyond their reach. Come, let us go down there and confuse their speech, so that they will not understand what they say to one another.' So the Lord dispersed them from there all over the earth, and they left off building the city. That is why it is called Babel[1], because the Lord there made a babble of the language of all the world; from that place the Lord scattered men all over the face of the earth.

---

1 That is Babylon.

六　巴別城塔

創世記

從前，世界上說的是同一種語言，用的是同一種文字。當人們向東遷徙來到了示拿地方的一片平原上，就停了下來定居。他們大家商議說：“來罷，我們來燒製一些磚塊。”他們用磚當石頭，瀝青作灰泥。“來吧，”他們說：“我們給自己建造一座城市和造一座頂端入雲的高塔以留名後世。不然，我們就會流散各地，無所依歸了。”不久，天主下來察看世人修建的這座城池和高塔，他說：“他們在這兒是一個使用同一語言的種族。如今他們開始建造城閣，從此他們只要下了決心。就甚麼事都難不倒他們了。來，我們到他們那兒去，弄亂他們的語言。這樣，他們就彼此不能溝通了。”於是，天主把他們分散到世界各地，他們修城築塔的工程也就半途而廢了。這就是為甚麼這座城叫做巴別(1)，因為天主在那裏使世上的語言變成了彼此聽不懂的聲音。上帝從那裏把地上的人都分散到世界的各個角落。

---

(1)Babel就是後來的Babylon（巴比倫）。

7   *Finding Shelter in Egypt*

Genesis

The Lord said to Abram, 'Leave your own country, your kinsmen, and your father's house, and go to a country that I will show you. I will make you into a great nation, I will bless you and make your name so great that it shall be used in blessings:

> Those that bless you I will bless,
> those that curse you, I will execrate.
> All the families on earth
> will pray to be blessed as you are blessed.'

And so Abram set out as the Lord had bidden him. Abram was seventy-five years old when he left Harran. He took his wife Sarai, his nephew Lot, all the property they had collected, and all the dependants they had acquired in Harran, and they started on their journey to Canaan.

There came a famine in the land, so severe that Abram went down to Egypt to live there for a while. When he was approaching Egypt, he said to his wife Sarai, 'I know very well that you are a beautiful woman, and that when the Egyptians see you, they will say, "She is his wife"; then they will kill me but let you live. Tell them that you are my sister, so that all may go well with me because of you and my life may be spared on your account.' When Abram arrived in Egypt, the Egyptians saw that she was indeed very beautiful. Pharaoh's courtiers saw her and praised her to Pharaoh, and she was taken into Pharaoh's household. He treated Abram well because of her, and Abram came to possess sheep and cattle and asses,

七　寄居埃及

創世記

（挪亞有一個後代叫他拉，他有三個兒子：亞伯蘭、拿鶴和哈蘭。亞伯蘭娶妻叫撒萊。撒萊沒有生育。後來他拉帶亞伯蘭、撒萊等去迦南，途中在哈蘭的地方暫住。他拉就是在哈蘭去世的。）

天主對亞伯蘭說："離開你的家鄉，你的親人和你父親的家，到一個我指引你去的地方。我要使你建邦立國；我要賜福於你，使你名聲顯赫，這樣你的名字就成了祝福之詞：我將祝福那些祝福你的人，我也將詛咒那些詛咒你的人。世上家家都將祈求會得到對你那樣的祝福。"

這樣亞伯蘭就按上帝的意旨動身。亞伯蘭離開哈蘭時是七十五歲。他帶着妻子撒萊，姪子羅得及他們在哈蘭積蓄的全部財產和侍從人等，動身去迦南。

後來，迦南發生饑荒，災情十分嚴重，亞伯蘭不得不去埃及暫住。當他們快到埃及時，他對妻子撒萊說："我深知你是個美麗的女人，埃及人見到你就會說：'這是那人的妻子，'他們就會殺死我而留下你。你要告訴他們你是我的妹妹，這樣我就平安了。看你份上他們會饒我一命的。"亞伯蘭到達了埃及，埃及人看到撒萊的確十分美麗。法老的臣子看見她，就把她舉薦給法老，於是她就被帶去收進法老的內宮中。法老為了她對亞伯蘭就很好。亞伯蘭得到賞賜許多羊、牛、驢和男女奴

male and female slaves, she-asses, and camels. But the Lord struck Pharaoh and his household with grave diseases on account of Abram's wife Sarai. Pharaoh summoned Abram and said to him, 'Why have you treated me like this? Why did you not tell me that she is your wife? Why did you say that she was your sister, so that I took her as a wife? Here she is: take her and be gone.' Then Pharaoh gave his men orders, and they sent Abram away with his wife and all that he had.

僕，還有母驢和駱駝。但是因為亞伯蘭妻子撒萊的緣故，天主降疫災于法老一家。法老叫亞伯蘭來對他說：「你為甚麼瞞着我？為甚麼不告訴我她是你的妻子？為甚麼說她是你的妹妹，使我收她為妻？唔，你把她帶走吧。」法老命令他的下人把亞伯蘭連同他的妻子及他所有的財物一起趕走。

8   *Hagar Bore Ishmael*

Genesis

Abram's wife Sarai had borne him no children. Now she had an Egyptian slave-girl whose name was Hagar, and she said to Abram, 'You see that the Lord has not allowed me to bear a child. Take my slave-girl; perhaps I shall found a family through her.' Abram agreed to what his wife said; so Sarai, Abram's wife, brought her slave-girl, Hagar the Egyptian, and gave her to her husband Abram as a wife. When this happened Abram had been in Canaan for ten years. He lay with Hagar and she conceived; and when she knew that she was with child, she despised her mistress. Sarai said to Abram, 'I have been wronged and you must answer for it. It was I who gave my slave-girl into your arms, but since she has known that she is with child, she has despised me. May the Lord see justice done between you and me.' Abram replied to Sarai, 'Your slave-girl is in your hands; deal with her as you will.' So Sarai ill-treated her and she ran away.

The angel of the Lord found her by a spring of water in the wilderness on the way to Shur, and he said, 'Hagar, Sarai's slave-girl, where have you come from and where are you going?' She answered, 'I am running away from Sarai my mistress.' The angel of the Lord said to her, 'Go back to your mistress and submit to her ill-treatment.' The angel also said, 'I will make your descendants too many to be counted.' And the angel of the Lord said to her:

'You are with child and will bear a son.
You shall name him Ishmael,

八　納妾生子

創世記

亞伯蘭的妻子撒萊沒有生育。她有一個埃及女奴，名叫夏甲。撒萊對亞伯蘭說："你看，天主沒讓我生育。收了我的女奴吧，也許我可以利用她養兒育女呢。"亞伯蘭同意妻子的話，於是他妻子撒萊就把她的埃及女奴夏甲帶來給丈夫亞伯蘭做妾。這是亞伯蘭在迦南已住了十年的事。他與夏甲同房，夏甲就懷了孕。夏甲得知自己懷孕後，就瞧不起女主人了。撒萊對亞伯蘭說："我受了欺侮，你得出來說話。是我把這女奴送入你的懷抱，但自從她知道自己有了身孕，她就瞧不起我了。但願天主在你我之間主持公道。"亞伯蘭回答撒萊道："你的女奴由你支配，你可以隨意處置她。"這樣，撒萊就虐待起夏甲來，夏甲就逃跑了。

天主的使臣發現夏甲在去書珥路上的荒野裏一個水泉旁，就說："撒萊的女奴夏甲，你從哪裏來？要到哪裏去？"她回答道："我從女主人撒萊那裏逃出來的。"天主的使臣對她說："回到你的女主人那裏去，忍受她的虐待吧。"又說："我會使你有百子千孫：你已有了身孕，將會生一個兒子。你要給他

because the Lord has heard of your ill-treatment.
He shall be a man like the wild ass,
his hand against every man
and every man's hand against him; and he shall live at
odds with all his kinsmen.'

Hagar bore Abram a son, and he named the child she bore
him Ishmael. Abram was eighty-six years old when Hagar
bore Ishmael.

起個名字叫以實瑪利，因為天主聽說你受到虐待。你這兒子會成為像野驢子那樣的人，他反對所有的人，而所有的人也會反對他。他會與他所有的兄弟不和。"

後來夏甲生了一個兒子，亞伯蘭給她生的這孩子取名為以實瑪利。夏甲生以實瑪利時，亞伯蘭是八十六歲。

9 Abram's Covenant with God

Genesis

When Abram was ninety-nine years old, the Lord appeared to him and said, 'I am God Almighty. Live always in my presence and be perfect, so that I may set my covenant between myself and you and multiply your descendants.' Abram threw himself down on his face, and God spoke with him and said, 'I make this covenant, and I make it with you: you shall be the father of a host of nations. Your name shall no longer be Abram, your name shall be Abraham, for I make you father of a host of nations. I will make you exceedingly fruitful; I will make nations out of you, and kings shall spring from you. I will fulfil my covenant between myself and you and your descendants after you, generation after generation, an everlasting covenant, to be your God, yours and your descendants' after you. As an everlasting possession I will give you and your descendants after you the land in which you now are aliens, all the land of Canaan, and I will be God to your descendants.'

God said to Abraham, 'For your part, you must keep my covenant, you and your descendants after you, generation by generation. This is how you shall keep my covenant between myself and you and your descendants after you; circumcise yourselves, every male among you. Every male among you in every generation shall be circumcised on the eighth day, both those born in your house and any foreigner, not of your blood but bought with your money, thus shall my covenant be marked in your flesh as an everlasting covenant. Every uncir-

九　更名立約

創世記

亞伯蘭九十九歲時，天主在他面前出現說：“我是全能的上帝。你要永遠在我面前生活並做個完美的人，這樣我就可以和你立約，使你的後代繁衍興旺。”亞伯蘭當即俯伏地上，上帝對他說：“我是同你訂立此約：你會成爲萬邦之祖，你不要再叫亞伯蘭了，要改名爲亞伯拉罕，因爲我要使你成爲萬邦之祖，使你多子多孫，要從你這裏衍生出許多國家，你的後代中會出現許多君王。我要執行我和你訂立之約，此約對你和你的後人，世世代代都永遠有效。我是你和你的後代的上帝。我要把你們居此不久的這片土地，即全部迦南的土地賜給你和你的後代，作爲永久的財產。我是你子孫後代的上帝。”

上帝對亞伯拉罕說：“在你那方面，你必須守約。你和你的後代，世世代代也都如此。你和你的後裔履行我同你們所立之約的方法就是：你家族中的每個男人都必須行割禮。你家族中每一代的每一個男丁都必須在出生後的第八天進行割禮，包括生在你家的和那些雖然不屬於你們血統，而是你用錢買來的外姓人。這樣我立的約就在你們肉體上留下印記，成爲永久之

cumcised male shall be cut off from the kin of his father. He has broken my covenant.'

God said to Abraham, 'As for Sarai your wife; you shall call her not Sarai, but Sarah. I will bless her and give you a son by her. I will bless her and she shall be the mother of nations; the kings of many people shall spring from her.' Abraham threw himself down on his face; he laughed and said to himself, 'Can a son be born to a man who is a hundred years old? Can Sarah bear a son when she is ninety?' He said to God, 'If only Ishmael might live under thy special care!' But God replied, 'No. Your wife Sarah shall bear you a son, and you shall call him Isaac. With him I will fulfil my covenant, an everlasting covenant with his descendants after him. I have heard your prayer for Ishmael. I have blessed him and will make him fruitful. I will multiply his descendants; he shall be father of twelve princes, and I will raise a great nation from him. But my covenant I will fulfil with Isaac, whom Sarah will bear to you at this season next year.' When he had finished talking with Abraham, God ascended and left him.

Then Abraham took Ishmael his son, everyone who had been born in his household and everyone bought with money, every male in his household, and he circumcised them that very same day in the flesh of their foreskins as God had told him to do. Abraham was ninety-nine years old when he circumcised the flesh of his foreskin. Ishmael was thirteen years old when he was circumcised in the flesh of his foreskin.

約。任何沒有受割禮的男子都被取消與家族的關係，因爲他違背了我立的約。"

　　上帝對亞伯拉罕說："對你的妻子撒萊，你不要叫她撒萊了，改叫做撒拉。我要賜福給她，讓她爲你生一個兒子。我要賜福給她，讓她成爲萬邦之母，許多民族的君王將出自她的後代。"亞伯拉罕俯伏地上，他笑着自說道："一個一百歲的人還能生子嗎？撒拉已經九十歲了，她還能生孩子嗎？"他對上帝說："只要以實瑪利能在你的特殊關懷下生活已經很好了！"但上帝答道："不，你的妻子撒拉會給你生一個兒子，你要叫他以撒。我將同他及他的後代履行永存的立約。我已聽見你爲以實瑪利的祈禱。我已經祝福了他，使他多子多孫，使他的後代繁衍興旺。他會成爲十二個王子之父，我要使他身後形成一個大邦。但是撒拉明年此時將生下以撒，我是要同以撒履行立約的。"說完這話以後，上帝離開了亞伯拉罕升天而去。當天亞伯拉罕帶了兒子以實瑪利和每一個生在他家的人，每一個用銀子買來的人，總之，他家裏所有的男人，按照上帝的吩咐舉行了割禮。割包皮時，亞伯拉罕是九十九歲，以實瑪利十三歲。

Genesis

(1)

The Lord appeared to Abraham by the terebinths of Mamre. As Abraham was sitting at the opening of his tent in the heat of the day, he looked up and saw three men standing in front of him. He ran from the opening of his tent to meet them and bowed low to the ground. 'Sirs,' he said, 'if I have deserved your favour, do not pass by my humble self without a visit. Let me send for some water so that you may wash your feet and rest under a tree; and let me fetch a little food so that you may refresh yourselves. Afterwards you may continue the journey which has brought you my way.' They said, 'Do by all means as you say.' So Abraham hurried into the tent to Sarah and said, 'Take three measures of flour quickly, knead it and make some cakes.' Then Abraham ran to the cattle, chose a fine tender calf and gave it to a servant, who hurriedly prepared it. He took curds and milk and the calf he had prepared, set it before them, and waited on them himself under the tree while they ate. They asked him where Sarah his wife was, and he said, 'There, in the tent.' The stranger said, 'About this time next year I will be sure to come back to you, and Sarah your wife shall have a son.' Now Sarah was listening at the opening of the tent; and he was close beside it. Both Abraham and Sarah had grown very old, and Sarah was past the age of child-bearing. So Sarah laughed to herself and said, 'I am past bearing children now that I am out of my time, and my husband is old.' The Lord said to Abraham, 'Why did

十　滅所多瑪

創世記

（一）

　　天主在幔利的篤耨香樹旁顯現在亞伯拉罕面前。當時天氣正炎熱，亞伯拉罕坐在帳篷門口，抬頭看見有三個人站在他前面。他就從帳篷門口跑過去接他們，他深鞠一躬說：“先生們，如蒙不棄，就請到敝舍小坐。我會叫人去弄些水來，這樣你們就可以洗洗脚，在樹下歇息歇息。我去取些食物來，你們吃了可以恢復精神。過後你們再繼續你們的行程。”他們說：“那就只好從命了。”亞伯拉罕就趕快回帳篷去對撒拉說：“快量三碗麵粉去做些餅。”然後，亞伯拉罕又跑到牛羣那裏，選了一頭好牛犢交給僕人，讓他很快把牛犢宰了燒好。亞伯拉罕拿着乳酪、牛奶，燒好的小牛肉，放在客人面前，並在樹下侍候他們飲食。他們問他的妻子撒拉在那裏，他說：“在帳篷裏邊。”陌生人說：“明年這個時候，我一定會再到你這裏來，那時你的妻子撒拉會生一個兒子。”撒拉這時正在帳篷門口聽着，而陌生人就坐在離門不遠的地方。亞伯拉罕和撒拉都很老了，撒拉也過了生育年齡，因此她暗笑說：“我已經不會生育的了，已不是當年了，我的丈夫也老了。”天主對亞伯拉罕

Sarah laugh. Is anything impossible for the Lord? In due season I will come back to you, about this time next year, and Sarah shall have a son.'

The men set out and looked down towards Sodom, and Abraham went with them to start them on their way.... So the Lord said, 'There is a great outcry over Sodom and Gomorrah; their sin is very grave. I must go down and see whether their deeds warrant the outcry which has reached me. I am resolved to know the truth.' When the men turned and went towards Sodom, Abraham remained standing before the Lord. Abraham drew near him and said, 'Wilt thou really sweep away good and bad together? Suppose there are fifty good men in the city; wilt thou really sweep it away, and not pardon the place because of the fifty good men? Far be if from thee to do this — to kill good and bad together; for then the good would suffer with the bad. Far be if from thee. Shall not the judge of all the earth do what is just?' The Lord said, 'If I find in the city of Sodom fifty good men, I will pardon the whole place for their sake'... Abraham said, 'I pray thee not to be angry, O Lord, if I speak just once more: suppose ten can be found there?' He said, 'For the sake of the ten I will not destroy it.'

(2)

The two angels came to Sodom in the evening, and Lot was sitting in the gateway of the city. When he saw them he said, 'I pray you, sirs, turn aside to my humble home, spend the night there and wash your feet; you can rise early and continue your journey.' 'No,' they answered, 'we will spend the night in the street.' But Lot was so insistent that they did turn aside and enter his house. He prepared a meal for them, baking unleavened cakes, and they ate them. Before they lay down to sleep, the men of Sodom, both young and old, surrounded the house — everyone without exception. 'Bring them out,' they shouted, 'so that we can have intercourse with them.'

Lot went out into the doorway to them, closed the door

說：「撒拉爲甚麼要笑？對天主來說難道還有不可能的事嗎？到那時節我一定會回來的，明年這時分，撒拉一定會生個兒子的。」

這幾個人動身走了，朝所多瑪城而去。亞伯拉罕送他們上路。……天主說：「所多瑪和蛾摩拉地方罪孽深重，怨聲已傳達我耳中。我必須到那裏去看看他們的所作所爲是否一如傳到我這裏的那樣糟糕。我決定要去了解眞象。」當他們轉身走向所多瑪時，亞伯拉罕仍舊站在天主面前。他靠近天主說：「你眞的打算把善和惡都一起消滅掉嗎？假如城裏有五十個好人，你當眞會把全城消滅掉，不考慮有五十個好人而赦免它嗎？這決不是你的行事方式，你不會把好壞一起消滅掉的，因爲那樣好人就會因壞人而受累。你決不會這樣的。難道主宰世界的你能夠不主持公道嗎？」天主說：「如果我發現所多瑪城裏有五十個好人，我一定會爲了他們而赦免全城的。」……亞伯拉罕說：「請不要生氣，天主啊，我還要說一下：要是在那裏只是有十個好人呢？」上帝說：「爲了這十個人我也不會毀滅那城市。」

（二）

兩位天使晚上到了所多瑪。羅得正坐在城門口。他看見他們說：「我請求你們各位先生到敝舍去過夜吧，洗脚歇息，明日早起再繼續趕路。」他們回答說：「不用了，我們就在街上過夜就可以了。」但羅得堅持要請他們，他們就到他家中去了。羅得爲他們準備飲食，烤硬麵餅給他們吃。在他們正要睡覺時，所多瑪的人們，年輕和年老的全都來了，他們圍着他的房子。「把他們交出來，」他們喊道，「我們要讓他們嘗嘗我們的厲害。」羅得走到門外，先把門帶上，說：「不，朋友們，

behind him and said, 'No, my friends, do not be so wicked. Look, I have two daughters, both virgins; let me bring them out to you, and you can do what you like with them; but do not touch these men, because they have come under the shelter of my roof.' They said, 'Out of our way! This man has come and settled here as an alien, and does he now take it upon himself to judge us? We will treat you worse than them.' They crowded in on the man Lot and pressed close to smash in the door. But the two men inside reached out, pulled Lot in, and closed the door. Then they struck the men in the doorway with blindness, both small and great, so that they could not find the door.

The two men said to Lot, 'Have you anyone else here, sons-in-law, sons, or daughters, or any who belong to you in the city? Get them out of this place, because we are going to destroy it.

As soon as it was dawn, the angels urged Lot to go. When he lingered, they took him by the hand, with his wife and his daughters, and, because the Lord had spared him, led him on until he was outside the city. When they had brought them out, they said, 'Flee for your lives; do not look back and do not stop anywhere in the Plain. Flee to the hills or you will be swept away.' And then the Lord rained down fire and brimstone from the skies on Sodom and Gomorrah. He overthrew those cities and destroyed all the Plain, with everyone living there and everything growing in the ground. But Lot's wife, behind him, looked back, and she turned into a pillar of salt.

別這麼不講理。聽着，我有兩個女兒，都是處女。我把她們領出來交給你們。你們可以對她們任意處置，但不要碰這兩個來人，因爲他們是我家的客人。"這羣人說："滾開！你這人來這裏定居，只不過是個外人。現在居然指責我們？我們對你會比那兩人更不客氣。"他們一擁而上，向羅得衝來，要把門砸破。這時屋裏的兩人馬上出來把羅得拉進門裏，關上門。然後，他們使門外的人不論老少眼睛全都變瞎，看不到門在哪裏。

這兩人對羅得說："你這裏還有其他親人嗎？有女婿、兒子、女兒、或者任何家人嗎？把他們帶走，離開這個地方，因爲我們要毀滅這座城市。這城市惡名昭著，天主派我們來毀滅它。"

天一亮，天使們就催羅得趕快離開。當他捨不得離開時，他們就拉着他的手，把他同妻女一起領到城外，因爲天主赦免了他。到了城外，他們說："逃命吧，不要回頭看，也不要在這平原上停留。逃上山去吧，不然你會被消滅的。"然後，天主把火和硫磺像雨一般灑落在所多瑪和蛾摩拉那裏。他把這兩座城市夷爲平地，摧毀了整個平原。那裏的每一個生靈和地上長的作物都無一倖免。羅得的妻子走在最後，她回頭望了望，就立刻化成一根鹽柱。

11 The Birth of Isaac

Genesis

(1)

The Lord showed favour to Sarah as he had promised, and made good what he had said about her. She conceived and bore a son to Abraham for his old age, at the time which God had appointed. The son whom Sarah bore to him, Abraham named Isaac. When Isaac was eight days old Abraham circumcised him, as God had commanded. Abraham was a hundred years old when his son Isaac was born. Sarah said, 'God has given me good reason to laugh, and everybody who hears will laugh with me.' She said, 'Whoever would have told Abraham that Sarah would suckle children? Yet I have borne him a son for his old age.' The boy grew and was weaned, and on the day of his weaning Abraham gave a feast. Sarah saw the son whom Hagar the Egyptian had borne to Abraham laughing at him, and she said to Abraham, 'Drive out this slave-girl and her son; I will not have this slave-girl's son sharing the inheritance with my son Isaac.' Abraham was vexed at this on his son Ishmael's account, but God said to him, 'Do not be vexed on account of the boy and the slave-girl. Do what Sarah says, because you shall have descendants through Isaac. I will make a great nation of the slave-girl's son too, because he is your own child.'

Abraham rose early in the morning, took some food and a waterskin full of water and gave it to Hagar; he set the child on her shoulder and sent her away, and she went and wandered in the wilderness of Beersheba. When the water in the

十一　百歲得子

創世記

（一）

　　上帝實現了他答允給撒拉的恩惠。撒拉懷了孕，就在上帝擇定的日子，給老年的亞伯拉罕生了一個兒子。亞伯拉罕把兒子起名叫以撒。以撒生下八天，亞伯拉罕按上帝的囑咐，為以撒行了割禮。亞伯拉罕得這兒子時是一百歲。撒拉說：“上帝使我衷心歡笑，每個聽到我笑聲的人都會同我一起歡笑。”她說：“當初誰會告訴亞伯拉罕說撒拉還會哺育嬰兒？但是，我還是在他老年時給他添了個兒子了”。這孩子長大一些後，斷奶了。在斷奶那天，亞伯拉罕擺了筵席。撒拉看見埃及女奴夏甲為亞伯拉罕生的兒子嘲笑他，就對亞伯拉罕說：“趕走那女奴和她的兒子。我不許這女奴的兒子分享我兒以撒的繼承權。”亞伯拉罕為以實瑪利，而對此感到為難。但上帝對他說：“不要為那孩子和女奴而感到為難。按撒拉說的做吧！因為你要靠以撒來繁衍後代。我也要讓女奴的兒子這邊建成一個大國，因為他也是你的親兒子。”

　　亞伯拉罕第二天一早起來，拿了些食物和一皮袋水給夏甲。他讓孩子伏在夏甲肩上送她上路。她走到別是巴荒野裏迷

skin was finished, she thrust the child under a bush, and went and sat down some way off, about two bowshots away, for she said, 'How can I watch the child die?' So she sat some way off, weeping bitterly. God heard the child crying, and the angel of God called from heaven to Hagar, 'What is the matter, Hagar? Do not be afraid: God has heard the child crying where you laid him. Get to your feet, lift the child up and hold him in your arms, because I will make of him a great nation.' Then God opened her eyes and she saw a well full of water; she went to it, filled her waterskin and gave the child a drink. God was with the child, and he grew up and lived in the wilderness of Paran. He became an archer, and his mother found him a wife from Egypt.

(2)

The time came when God put Abraham to the test. 'Abraham', he called, and Abraham replied, 'Here I am,' God said, 'Take your son Isaac, your only son, whom you love, and go to the land of Moriah. There you shall offer him as a sacrifice on one of the hills which I will show you.' So Abraham rose early in the morning and saddled his ass, and he took with him two of his men and his son Isaac; and he split the firewood for the sacrifice, and set out for the place of which God had spoken. On the third day Abraham looked up and saw the place in the distance. He said to his men, 'Stay here with the ass while I and the boy go over there; and when we have worshipped we will come back to you.' So Abraham took the wood for the sacrifice and laid it on his son Isaac's shoulder; he himself carried the fire and the knife, and the two of them went on together. Isaac said to Abraham, 'Father', and he answered, 'What is it, my son?' Isaac said, 'Here are the fire and the wood, but where is the young beast for the sacrifice?' Abraham answered, 'God will provide himself with a young beast for a sacrifice, my son.' And the two of them went on together and came to the place of which God had spoken. There Abraham built an altar and arranged the wood. He bound his son Isaac and laid him on the altar on top

了路。當皮袋中的水喝完後，她把孩子放在小樹叢下，然後坐在稍遠的大約兩箭之遙的地方。她說："我怎麼能當面看着孩子死去呢？"她又再坐遠一點，傷心地哭泣。孩子的哭聲給上帝聽到了，上帝的使臣就從天上對夏甲呼喚道："你怎麼啦，夏甲？別害怕，上帝已聽到你放在那兒的孩子的哭聲。起來吧，去把孩子抱回懷中，我要使他以後也建成一個大國。"於是，上帝使她眼前豁然明亮，她看見前面有一口滿滿的水井。她走過去，把水袋汲滿，又給孩子喝了水。上帝與孩子同在，孩子長大起來，就住在巴蘭這荒野地方。他成爲一個弓箭手，他的母親從埃及爲他娶來一個妻子。

（二）

到了上帝要考驗亞伯拉罕的時候了。他叫他說："亞伯拉罕。"亞伯拉罕應道："我在這裏。"上帝說："帶上你心愛的獨子以撒到摩利亞去。在那裏，在我指定的一座山上，你把他當作祭品奉獻給我。"於是，亞伯拉罕一早起來，給驢備了鞍，帶了兩個家人和兒子以撒，砍了獻牲用的柴火，就出發去上帝指定的地方。第三天，亞伯拉罕眺望見在遠處的目的地。他對從人說："你們帶着驢子留在這裏，我和孩子上那邊去。我們祭祀完畢，就會回到你們這裏來的。"亞伯拉罕拿着祭祀用的木柴，把它放在兒子以撒肩上。他自己帶着火種和刀子，兩人繼續前行。以撒問亞伯拉罕："父親，"亞伯拉罕應道："我兒，你要說什麼？"以撒說："火種和木柴都有了，但是祭祀用的幼牲在那兒？"亞伯拉罕回答道："我兒，上帝已爲自己備好一頭獻牲用的羊羔了。"兩人繼續向前走，到了上帝說的地方。亞伯拉罕在那兒架起祭壇，擺好了柴禾。他捆起兒

of the wood. Then he stretched out his hand and took the knife to kill his son; but the angel of the Lord called to him from heaven, 'Abraham, Abraham.' He answered, 'Here I am.' The angel of the Lord said, 'Do not raise your hand against the boy; do not touch him. Now I know that you are a God-fearing man. You have not withheld from me your son, your only son.' Abraham looked up, and there he saw a ram caught by its horns in a thicket. So he went and took the ram and offered it as a sacrifice instead of his son. Then the angel of the Lord called from heaven a second time to Abraham, 'This is the word of the Lord: By my own self I swear: inasmuch as you have done this and have not withheld your son, your only son, I will bless you abundantly and greatly multiply your descendants until they are as numerous as the stars in the sky and the grains of sand on the sea-shore. Your descendants shall possess the cities of their enemies. All nations on earth shall pray to be blessed as your descendants are blessed, and this because you have obeyed me.'

Abraham went back to his men, and together they returned to Beersheba; and there Abraham remained.

子以撒，把他放在柴火上面的祭壇上。然後他伸手拔刀正要殺他的兒子。但天主的使臣從天上向他喊道："亞伯拉罕，亞伯拉罕。"他回答道："我在這裏。"天主的使臣說："不要動手殺這孩子，不要碰他。現在我知道了你真是虔敬上帝的人。你沒有拒絕把你唯一的兒子獻給我。"亞伯拉罕抬頭一看，他見到一頭公羊，雙角纏在灌木叢中。他就走過去抓住這公羊，把它代替兒子做供品獻給上帝。然後，天主的使臣又從天上向亞伯拉罕喊道："這是天主的旨意：由於你這樣做了，沒有拒絕把唯一的兒子獻給我，我自己立誓要賜洪福於你，使你的後代十分繁榮興旺，多到和天空中的星辰及海灘上的沙粒一樣數不清。你的後人會佔奪他們敵人的城市。世上所有國家都要祈禱像你的後裔那樣得到保祐。這都是因為你聽從了我的話。"

　　亞伯拉罕回到他的隨從那裏，他們一起返回別是巴，並在那裏住下來。

12 The Marriage of Isaac

Genesis

By this time Abraham had become a very old man, and the Lord had blessed him in all that he did. Abraham said to his servant, who had been long in his service and was in charge of all his possessions, 'Put your hand under my thigh: I want you to swear by the Lord, the God of heaven and earth, that you will not take a wife for my son from the women of the Canaanites in whose land I dwell; you must go to my own country and to my own kindred to find a wife for my son Isaac.'.... So the servant put his hand under his master Abraham's thigh and swore an oath in those terms.

The servant took ten camels from his master's herds, and also all kinds of gifts from his master; he set out for Aramnaharaim and arrived at the city where Nahor lived. Towards evening, the time when the women come out to draw water, he made the camels kneel down by the well outside the city. He said, 'O Lord God of my master Abraham, give me good fortune this day; keep faith with my master Abraham. Here I stand by the spring, and the women of the city are coming out to draw water. Let it be like this: I shall say to a girl, "Please lower your jar so that I may drink"; and if she answers, "Drink, and I will water your camels also", that will be the girl whom thou dost intend for thy servant Isaac. In this way I shall know that thou hast kept faith with my master.'

Before he had finished praying silently he saw Rebecca coming out with her water-jug on her shoulder. Abraham's servant hurried to meet her and said, "Give me a sip of water

十二　故里娶妻

創世記

這時亞伯拉罕已經老邁不堪了。天主一直保祐他做的一切事情。亞伯拉罕對一個長期侍隨他的老管家說："把你的手放在我的大腿下，我要你對天主、對天地的上帝發誓，你不要替我兒子從我居住地的迦南人中娶妻。你必須到我的故里、到我親族那裏去給我兒子以撒找個妻子。"……於是那管家就把手放在他主人亞伯拉罕的大腿下面，按照這些條件發了誓。

老管家從他主人的牧羣中挑選了十頭駱駝，還從主人處拿了各式禮品，便出發去阿蘭納哈蘭。他來到了拿鶴住的城市。傍晚，正是婦女出來打水的時候，他讓駱駝跪在城外水井邊。他說："啊，我的主人亞伯拉罕的天主上帝啊，讓我今天交上好運氣，請信守你和我的主人亞伯拉罕的約言。我站在井邊這兒，城裏的女人們都出城來打水了。讓事情像這樣吧：我會對一個姑娘說：'請把你的水罐拿下來，好讓我喝點水！'如果她回答說：'請喝吧，我還給你的駱駝也喝點水。'那她就是你預定要你的僕人以撒迎娶的姑娘。這樣，我就會知道你信守和我的主人的約言了。"

他剛默禱完，就看見利百加肩上扛着水罐走出來。亞伯拉

from your jar. 'Drink, sir', she answered, and at once lowered her jar on to her hand to let him drink. When she had finished giving him a drink, she said, 'Now I will draw water for your camels until they have had enough.' So she quickly empfied her jar into the water-through, hurried again to the well to draw water and watered all the camels. When the camels had finished drinking, the man took a gold nose-ring weighing half a shekel, and two bracelets for her wrists weighing ten shekels, also of gold, and said, 'Tell me, please, whose daughter you are. Is there room in your father's house for us to spend the night?' She answered, 'I am the daughter of Bethuel, the son of Nahor and Milcah; and we have plenty of straw and fodder and also room for you to spend the night.' So the man bowed down and prostrated himself to the Lord. He said, 'Blessed be the Lord the God of my master Abraham, who has not failed to keep faith and truth with my master; for I have been guided by the Lord to the house of my master's kinsman.'

The girl ran to her mother's house and told them what had happened. Now Rebecca had a brother named Laban; and, when he saw the nosering, and also the bracelets on his sister's wrists, and heard his sister Rebecca tell what the man had said to her, he ran out to the man at the spring. When he came to him, he said, 'Come in, sir, whom the Lord has blessed. Why stay outside? I have prepared the house, and there is room for the camels.' So he brought the man into the house, unloaded the camels and provided straw and fodder for them, and water for him and all his men to wash their feet. Food was set before him, but he said, 'I will not eat until I have delivered my message.' Laban said, 'Let us hear it.' He answered, 'I am the servant of Abraham... Now tell me if you will keep faith and truth with my master. If not, say so, and I will turn elsewhere.'

Laban and Bethuel answered, 'This is from the Lord; we can say nothing for or against. Here is Rebecca herself; take her and go. She shall be the wife of your master's son, as the Lord has decreed.' So they let their sister Rebecca and her

罕的老管家趕忙迎上去對她說："求你把罐裏的水給我喝一點。""喝吧，先生。"她回答說，並馬上拿下水罐讓他喝。她給他喝完水後，又說："現在我要弄些水給你的駱駝飲，讓牠們喝個飽。"說着她就一下子把罐裏的水全倒到水槽中，又趕到井邊去打水，並給所有的駱駝都飲了水。當駱駝喝完水後，老家人拿出一個約半舍客勒的金鼻環和兩隻重十舍客勒的金手鐲給那女子，說："請告訴我，你是誰的女兒。你們家有地方讓我們留宿嗎？"她回答："我是拿鶴和密迦的兒子彼土利的女兒。我們家有充足的糧草飼料、也有地方讓你過夜。"老管家向天主彎身下拜說："感謝我的主人亞伯拉罕的上帝，天主你沒有忘記以誠信待我主人，是天主引導我來到我主人的兄弟家裏。"

那女孩跑到她母親住處，告訴他們這件事情。利百加有個哥哥叫拉班，當他看見金鼻環和他妹妹腕上的兩個鐲子，聽到他妹妹利百加告訴他那老管家的要求，他就出門跑到井邊那人那裏對他說："請進來，先生，上帝保祐你。為什麼還在外面站着？我已經給你收拾好房子，也有地方安置駱駝。"接着，他就把老家人帶進屋，卸了駱駝並餵以草料，還備了水給老家人和他的隨從們洗腳。飯食也擺在他面前。老人卻說："我要先轉達一個口信才吃飯。"拉班說："我們在聽着。"老管家回答："我是亞伯拉罕的僕人。（他詳細解釋了為什麼他來到這裏。）現在請告訴我，你們是否願意以誠信待我主人，與他聯姻。如果不願意，也請直說，我就到別處再找。"

拉班和彼土利回答："既然這是上帝的意旨，我們哪能說同意或不同意。利百加在這裏，帶她走吧。她將成為你主人的兒媳，就照天主說的去做吧。"這樣，他們就讓妹子利百加及

nurse go with Abraham's servant and his men.

Isaac meanwhile had moved on as far as Beer-lahai-roi and was living in the Negeb. One evening when he had gone out into the open country to relieve himself, he looked up and saw camels approaching. When Rebecca raised her eyes and saw Isaac, she slipped hastily from her camel, saying to the servant, 'Who is that man walking across the open towards us?' The servant answered, 'It is my master.' So she took her veil and covered herself. The servant related to Isaac all that had happened. Isaac conducted her into the tent and took her as his wife. So she became his wife, and he loved her and was consoled for the death of his mother.

她的乳母隨亞伯拉罕的老家人和隨從們一起去了。

　　以撒此時已搬到老遠的庇耳拉海萊，住在耐格伯。一天黃昏時，他走到野外去舒散身心，抬頭看見有一個駱駝隊向他走來。利百加遠眺看見以撒，就急忙從駱駝上下來，問那老管家：「那邊朝我們走來的男人是誰？」老管家回答：「那就是我家的少爺。」利百加就拿出面紗把臉蒙上。老管家就向以撒講述了全部經過，以撒把利百加領進帳篷，娶她為妻。這樣她就成為他的妻子，他也愛她。自從他母親去世後，以撒到這時才得到一些寬慰。

13   The Twins

Genesis

Isaac appealed to the Lord on behalf of his wife because she was barren; the Lord yielded to his entreaty, and Rebecca conceived. The children pressed hard on each other in her womb. So she went to seek guidance of the Lord. The Lord said to her:

'Two nations in your womb,
two peoples, going their own ways from birth!
One shall be stronger than the other;
the older shall be servant to the younger.'

When her time had come, there were indeed twins in her womb. The first came out red, hairy all over like a hair-cloak, and they named him Esau. Immediately afterwards his brother was born with his hand grasping Esau's heel, and they called him Jacob. Isaac was sixty years old when they were born. The boys grew up; and Esau became skilful in hunting, a man of the open plains, but Jacob led a settled life and stayed among the tents. Isaac favoured Esau because he kept him supplied with venison, but Rebecca favoured Jacob. One day Jacob prepared a broth and when Esau came in from the country, exhausted, he said to Jacob, 'I am exhausted; let me swallow some of that red broth' Jacob said, 'Not till you sell me your rights as the firstborn.' Esau replied, 'I am at death's door; what use is my birthright to me?' Jacob said, 'Not till you swear!'; so he swore an oath and sold his birthright to Jacob...

When Isaac grew old and his eyes became so dim that he

十三　孿生兄弟

創世記

　　以撒因爲妻子不生育而替她祈求上帝。天主答允了他的要求，利百加就有了身孕。兩個胎兒在她的腹內互相擠壓，她就去求天主啟示。天主對她說：“你腹內孕育着兩個國邦，這兩族人從誕生時就會各走各路，一族會比另一族強大，爲兄長的將成爲弟弟的僕從。”

　　到了產期，她果然是生了雙胞胎。先落地的一個渾身發紅而且長滿了毛，像披了件皮衣。他們給他取名以掃。緊跟出生的是他的弟弟，他出來時用手抓着以掃的脚後跟，他們叫他做雅各。他們倆出生時，以撒已六十歲。孩子們長大了，以掃成爲一個熟練的獵人，經常游獵於野外。但雅各却過着定居的生活，以帳篷爲家。以撒較喜歡以掃，因爲以掃經常供給他野味，但利百加却偏愛雅各。有一天雅各煮了扁豆湯，遇上以掃從野外回來，他十分疲勞，就對雅各說：“我累得要死，讓我喝些扁豆湯吧。”雅各說：“你得先賣給我長子權。”以掃回答說：“我都要累死了，長子權對我有甚麼用？”雅各說：“你得先發個誓！”於是，以掃就發了誓，把長子權賣給了雅各。⋯

　　以撒老了，他老眼昏花甚麼也看不見了。他把大兒子以掃

could not see, he called his elder son Esau and said, 'Listen now: I am old and I do not know when I may die. Take your hunting gear, your quiver and your bow, and go out into the country and get me some venison. Then make me a savoury dish of the kind I like, and bring it to me to eat so that I may give you my blessing before I die.' Now Rebecca was listening as Isaac talked to his son Esau. When Esau went off, she said to her son Jacob, 'Listen to me, my son, and do what I tell you. Go to the flock and pick me out two fine young kids, and I will make them into a savoury dish for your father, of the kind he likes. Then take them in to your father, and he will eat them so that he may bless you before he dies.' So Jacob fetched them and brought them to his mother, who made them into a savoury dish of the kind that his father liked. Then Rebecca took her elder son's clothes, Esau's best clothes which she kept by her in the house, and put them on her younger son Jacob. She put the goatskins on his hands and on the smooth nape of his neck; and she handed her son Jacob the savoury dish and the bread she had made. He came to his father and said, 'Father.' He answered, 'Yes, my son; who are you?' Jacob answered his father, 'I am Esau, your elder son. I have done as you told me. Come, sit up and eat some of my venison, so that you may give me your blessing.' Isaac said to his son, 'Come close and let me feel you, my son, to see whether you are really my son Esau.' When Jacob came close to his father, Isaac felt him and said, 'The voice is Jacob's voice, but the hands are the hands of Esau.' Then Jacob brought the vension to him, and he ate it; he brought wine also, and he drank it. Then his father Isaac said to him, 'Come near, my son, and kiss me.' So he came near and kissed him, and when Isaac smelt the smell of his clothes, he blessed him and said:

'Ah! The smell of my son is like the smell of open country blessed by the Lord.
God give you dew from heaven
and the richness of the earth,

叫到面前說："聽着，我老了，不知道那天就會死去。你拿上打獵的用具和弓箭，到野外去給我獵些野味回來，然後弄一個我喜歡的可口的菜給我吃。我就可以在死前賜福與你。"以撒對兒子以掃說這些話，利百加都聽到了。以掃走後，她就對兒子雅各說："聽我說，我的兒，照我的話去做。你到羊羣那裏給我挑兩隻肥羊羔來，我會把它們做成可口的你父親喜愛的菜。然後你把菜端去給你父親，他吃了就可以在死前賜福與你。"於是雅各弄來羊羔，她母親把羊羔做成以撒愛吃的可口的菜，並取來了她收藏的以掃的衣服，讓小兒子雅各穿上。她把山羊皮蓋在雅各的手上和他光滑的脖子上。她把她做的菜和餅交給雅各。雅各來到父親跟前說："父親。"以撒回答道："噯，我的兒，你是哪一個？"雅各回答："我是以掃，你的長子。我已經照你吩咐的做了。來吧，坐起來吃一點我做的野味吧，吃完你好賜福與我。"以撒對兒子說："走近些，讓我摸摸你，我兒，看你是否真的是我兒子以掃。"雅各走近父親，以撒摸了他，說："說話是雅各的聲音，但手却是以掃的手。"雅各把野味捧上，他吃了；雅各又把酒給他父親喝，他也喝了。然後，他父親以撒對他說："上前來吧，我的兒子，親我一下。"雅各上前親了父親。當以撒聞到他衣服上的氣味後，他祝福他說："啊，我兒子身上的氣味是上帝賜福的野外的氣味。願上帝賜你天上的甘露，地上的財富，數不清的寶物

corn and new wine in plenty!
Peoples shall serve you, nations bow down to you.
Be lord over your brothers;
may your mother's sons bow down to you.
A curse upon those who curse you;
a blessing on those who bless you!'

Isaac finished blessing Jacob; and Jacob had scarcely left his father Isaac's presence, when his brother Esau came in from his hunting. He too made a savoury dish and brought it to his father. He said, 'Come, father, and eat some of my venison, so that you may give me your blessing.' His father Isaac said, 'Who are you?' He said, 'I am Esau, your elder son.' Then Isaac became greatly agitated and said, 'Then who was it that hunted and brought me venison? I ate it all before you came in and I blessed him, and the blessing will stand.' When Esau heard what his father said, he gave a loud and bitter cry and said, 'Bless me too, father.' But Isaac said, 'Your brother came treacherously and took away your blessing. What is there left that I can do for you, my son?' Esau asked his father, 'Had you then only one blessing, father? Bless me too, my father.' And Esau cried bitterly. Then his father Isaac answered:

'Your dwelling shall be far from the richness of the earth, far
from the dew of heaven above.
By your sword shall you live,
and you shall serve your brother;
but the time will come when you grow restive
and break off his yoke from your neck.'

Esau bore a grudge against Jacob because of the blessing which his father had given him, and he said to himself, 'The time of mourning for my father will soon be here; then I will kill my brother Jacob.' Whe Rebecca was told what her elder son Esau was saying, she called her younger son Jacob, and she said to him, 'Esau your brother is threatening to kill you. Now, my son, listen to me. Slip away at once to my brother Laban in Harran.

和美酒。各族人民都將服從你，萬國都臣服於你，你會成為你家兄弟之主，你母親的各個孩子都要服從你。誰詛咒你誰就會遭到詛咒，誰祝福你就會得到祝福！」

以撒祝福雅各完畢，雅各剛從父親跟前走開，他的哥哥以掃就打獵歸來了。他也做了個可口的菜捧到父親面前。他說：「父親，請來吃一點我做的野味，然後給我祝福。」他父親以撒說：「你是誰？」他說：「我是以掃，你的長子。」以撒驚異地說：「那末，剛才是誰打獵給我帶來了野味吃呢？你來之前，我已吃過了野味，所以我賜福與他。而且這已生效了。」以掃聽到父親這樣說，傷心地大叫道：「那你也賜福與我吧，父親。」但以撒說：「你弟弟奸詐地來這裏奪去了你的福分。我還有甚麼可以給你的呢，我的兒子？」以掃問父親：「父親，你只能賜福一次嗎？你再賜福給我吧，父親。」以掃傷心地大哭起來。他父親以撒回答說：「你將住到遠離肥沃的土地的地方，那裏也沒有天降的甘露。你將靠刀劍度日，你只好侍服你弟弟，但你總有一天要不服駕馭，掙脫你頸上的束縛的。」

以掃對雅各搶走了父親本來給自己的福分感到很憤恨。他暗自說：「為父親居喪的日子近了，到時我要殺死弟弟雅各。」當利百加知道長子以掃要這樣做，她把小兒子雅各叫來對他說：「你哥哥以掃威脅說要殺死你。你聽我的話，趕快逃走，到哈蘭我哥哥拉班那兒去吧。」

Genesis

(1)

Jacob came to the land of the eastern tribes. There he saw a well in the open country and three flocks of sheep lying beside it, because the flocks were watered from that well. He asked the herdsmen if they knew Laban the grandson of Nahor. They answered, 'Yes, we do.' 'Is he well?' Jacob asked; and they answered 'Yes, he is well, and here is his daughter Rachel coming with the flock.' When Jacob saw Rachel, the daughter of Laban his mother's brother, with Laban's flock, he stepped forward, rolled the stone off the mouth of the well and watered Laban's sheep. He kissed Rachel, and was moved to tears. He told her that he was her father's kinsman and Rebecca's son; so she ran and told her father. When Laban heard the news of his sister's son Jacob, he ran to meet him, embraced him, kissed him warmly and welcomed him to his home. So Jacob stayed with him for a whole month.

Laban said to Jacob, 'Why should you work for me for nothing simply because you are my kinsman? Tell me what your wages ought to be.' Now Laban had two daughters: the elder was called Leah, and the younger Rachel. Leah was dull-eyed, but Rachel was graceful and beautiful. Jacob had fallen in love with Rachel and he said, 'I will work seven years for your younger daughter Rachel.' Laban replied, 'It is better that I should give her to you than to anyone else; stay with me.' So Jacob worked seven years for Rachel, and they

十四　完婚育子

創世記

（一）

　　雅各來到了東方部落的地方。在那兒他看見田野裏有一口井，井旁躺着三羣羊，這些羊是來這口井飲水的。他向牧人打聽是否認識拿鶴的孫子拉班。他們答道："認識。"雅各問："他好嗎？"他們回答："他很好。這不，他的女兒拉結趕着羊羣走過來了麼。"雅各看見他舅舅拉班的女兒拉結趕着拉班的羊羣，就上前一步把井口的石頭推開，給拉班的羊飲水。他親了拉結，激動得流下眼淚。他告訴她，他是她父親的外甥、利百加的兒子。拉結就跑回去報告她父親這個消息。拉班聽到妹妹的兒子雅各到來，就跑出來迎他，擁抱和熱烈親吻他，歡迎他來到自己的家。這樣雅各就和他舅舅一起生活工作了整整一個月。

　　拉班對雅各說："爲甚麼你給我白幹活兒呢？就只爲了你是我的親人嗎？告訴我，你要多少工錢。"拉班有兩個女兒，大的叫利亞，小的叫拉結。利亞目光呆滯，拉結則美貌俊秀。雅各愛上了拉結，就說："我願爲娶你的小女兒拉結而幹七年活兒。"拉班回答說："我把她許配給你比許給別人好。你就和我一起過吧！"這樣，雅各爲了得到拉結而幹七年活兒。因

seemed like a few days because he loved her. Laban gathered all the men of the place together and gave a feast. In the evening he took his daughter Leah and brought her to Jacob, and Jacob slept with her. But when morning came, Jacob saw that it was Leah and said to Laban, 'What have you done to me? Did I not work for Rachel? Why have you deceived me?' Laban answered, 'In our country it is not right to give the younger sister in marriage before the elder. Go through with the seven days' feast for the elder, and the younger shall be given you in return for a further seven years' work.' Jacob agreed.

Then Laban gave Jacob his daughter Rachel as wife; he loved her rather than Leah, and he worked for Laban for a further seven years. When the Lord saw that Leah was not loved, he granted her a child; but Rachel was childless. Leah conceived and bore a son; and she called him Reuben, for she said, 'The Lord has seen my humiliation; now my husband will love me.' Again she conceived and bore a son and said, 'The Lord, hearing that I am not loved, has given me this child also'; and she called him Simeon. She conceived again and bore a son; and she said, 'Now that I have borne him three sons my husband and I will surely be united.' So she called him Levi. Once more she conceived and bore a son; and she said, 'Now I will praise the Lord'; therefore she named him Judah.

(2)

When Rachel found that she bore Jacob no children, she became jealous of her sister and said to Jacob, 'Here is my slave-girl Bilhah. Lie with her, so that she may bear sons to be laid upon my knees, and through her I too may build up a family.' So she gave him her slave-girl Bilhah as a wife, and Jacob

爲他深愛拉結，這七年就像幾天似的過去了。拉班擺了宴席，請齊了當地的人。天入黑後，他却將大女兒利亞帶來給雅各，雅各同她同了房。天亮後，雅各看見原來是利亞，就對拉班說：「你對我幹了好事！我不是爲了拉結才給你幹活的嗎？你爲甚麼騙我？」拉班回答：「在我們這裏，不能讓小女兒先於大女兒結婚。行完這七天娶大女兒的婚宴，我就把小女兒也許配給你，但你得再給我幹七年活兒。」雅各只好同意。

這樣，拉班又把女兒拉結許給雅各爲妻；他愛她勝過利亞。他又給拉班再幹七年活。天主看見利亞不受寵愛，就讓她得了一個孩子，她叫他做流便[1]，她說：「天主看到我受屈辱，這回我丈夫會愛我了。」她又懷孕生了一子。她說：「上帝聽說我仍不受寵愛，又給了我這個孩子。」她叫他西緬[2]。她懷孕又再次生子。她說：「我已給我丈夫生了三個兒子，我丈夫一定會和我好起來的。」她叫這兒子利未[3]。她第四次懷孕生子，她說：「我要讚美天主。」因此，她就叫這孩子做猶大[4]。

（二）

拉結見自己沒給雅各生育，就很嫉妬她的姐姐，她對雅各說：「這是我的女奴辟拉，你和她同房吧，這樣她就可以生兒育女使我不致膝下無兒。通過她我便可以建立一個家族。」她

---

(1) 希伯來語，意思是：看，是個兒子。

(2) 希伯來語，意思是：聽見。

(3) 希伯來語，意思是：結合。

(4) 希伯來語，意思是：讚美。

lay with her. Bilhah conceived and bore Jacob a son. Then Rachel said, 'God has given judgement for me; he has indeed heard me and given me a son', so she named him Dan. Rachel's slave-girl Bilhah again conceived and bore Jacob another son. Rachel said, 'I have played a fine trick on my sister, and it has succeeded'; so she named him Naphtali. When Leah found that she was bearing no more children, she took her slave-girl Zilpah and gave her to Jacob as a wife, and Zilpah bore Jacob a son. Leah said, 'Good fortune has come', and she named him Gad. Zilpah, Leah's slave-girl, bore Jacob another son, and Leah said, 'Happiness has come, for young women will call me happy.' So she named him Asher.

In the time of wheat-harvest Reuben went out and found some mandrakes in the open country and brought them to his mother Leah. Then Rachel asked Leah for some of her son's mandrakes, but Leah said, 'Is it so small a thing to have taken away my husband, that you should take my son's mandrakes as well?' But Rachel said, 'Very well, let him sleep with you tonight in exchange for your son's mandrakes.' So when Jacob came in from the country in the evening, Leah went out to meet him and said, 'You are to sleep with me tonight; I have hired you with my son's mandrakes.' That night he slept with her, and God heard Leah's prayer, and she conceived and bore a fifth son. So she named him Issachar. Leah again conceived and bore a sixth son. She said, 'God has endowed me with a noble dowry. Now my husband will treat me in princely style, because I have borne him six sons.' So she

就把女奴辟拉給丈夫為妾。雅各與她同房，辟拉懷孕給雅各生了一個兒子。於是拉結說："上帝給我做了主，他一定是聽見了我的祈求，就給我一個兒子。"她叫這孩子但(1)。辟拉又懷孕，給雅各生了第二個兒子。拉結說："我對姐姐耍了個妙計，它成功了。"她給孩子起名拿弗他利(2)。當利亞見自己不能再生育時，她把自己的女奴悉帕給雅各為妾，悉帕給雅各生了個兒子。利亞說："好運來了。"她給孩子起名叫迦得(3)。悉帕又給雅各生了一子，利亞說："幸福來了，年輕女人都要說我有福了。"因此，她叫孩子做亞設(4)。

麥收時節來臨，流便往田野裏採集了些風茄(5)並拿給他母親利亞。拉結跟利亞討一些她兒子採來的風茄，但利亞說："你奪走了我丈夫還不夠？你還想要我兒子的風茄？"拉結說："好吧，讓雅各今晚與你同寢來交換你兒子的風茄。"於是，雅各晚上從田裏回來時，利亞就出來迎他說："今晚你同我睡，我用兒子的風茄作交易讓你來的。"那晚雅各和利亞同房，上帝聽到利亞的禱告，讓她懷孕生了第五個兒子。她把孩子叫做以薩迦(6)。後來利亞又懷孕生了第六個兒子。她說："上帝給了我最尊貴的賞賜。現在我丈夫一定會以王室之禮待我了，因為我已給他生了六個兒子。"她給孩子取名叫西布

---

(1) 希伯來語，意思是：他給作了主。

(2) 希伯來語，意思是：詭計。

(3) 希伯來語，意思是：好運氣。

(4) 希伯來語，意思是：幸福。

(5) 植物名，又名曼陀羅，可以入藥，傳說有神力，可刺激性慾。

(6) 希伯來語，意思是：報酬。

named him Zebulun. Later she bore a daughter and named her Dinah. Then God thought of Rachel; he heard her prayer and gave her a child; so she conceived and bore a son and said, 'God has taken away my humiliation.' She named him Joseph, saying, 'May the Lord add another son!'

倫(1)。後來她又生了個女兒，叫她底拿。後來上帝顧念拉結，他聽到她的禱告，給了她一個孩子。這樣她就懷孕生了個兒子。她說："上帝已除掉了我的屈辱。"她叫孩子約瑟(2)，並說："願上帝再給我一個兒子。"

---

(1) 希伯來語，意思是：王子。

(2) 希伯來語，意思是：願他再添加。

15 Taking the Family Home

Genesis

(1)

Jacob learnt that Laban's sons were saying, 'Jacob has taken everything that was our father's, and all his wealth has come from our father's property.' He also noticed that Laban was not so well disposed to him as he had once been. Then the Lord said to Jacob, 'Go back to the land of your fathers and to your kindred. I will be with you'... Jacob at once set his sons and his wives on camels, and drove off all the herds and livestock which he had acquired in Paddan-aram, to go to his father Isaac in Canaan.

Three days later, when Laban heard that Jacob had run away, he took his kinsmen with him, pursued Jacob for seven days and caught up with him in the hill-country of Gilead. But God came to Laban in a dream by night and said to him, 'Be careful to say nothing to Jacob, either good or bad.'

When Laban overtook him, Jacob had pitched his tent in the hill-country of Gilead, and Laban pitched his in the company of his kinsmen in the same hill-country. Laban said to Jacob, 'What have you done? Why did you slip away secretly without telling me? I would have set you on your way with songs and the music of tambourines and harps. You did not even let me kiss my daughters and their children. In this you were at fault. I know that you went away because you were homesick and pining for your father's house, but why did you steal my gods?'

Jacob answered, 'I was afraid; I thought you would take

十五　携眷返鄉

創世記

（一）

　　雅各知道拉班的兒子們議論他：“雅各把我們父親的一切都奪走了，他現在所有的財富都是從我們父親的財產中得來的。”他也看到拉班對他不像以前那樣好了。這時天主對雅各說：“回到你父親的土地上去吧，回到你的親人那裏去，我會與你同在。”……雅各就讓妻妾兒子們上了駱駝，趕着他在巴旦亞蘭獲得的全部牧羣和牲畜，回迦南他父親以撒那裏去。

　　三天後，拉班聽說雅各跑了，就帶着男家人去追雅各，追了七天，在基列山區追上了雅各。但上帝夜裏托夢給拉班，對他說：“你要當心，不要對雅各說這說那，好壞都不要說。”

　　拉班趕上雅各時，他已在基列山區架好帳篷，拉班和他的一些家人也在這地區搭起帳篷。拉班對雅各說：“你都幹了些甚麼事？你爲甚麼不說一聲就偷偷溜走呢？本來我是會以唱歌和奏樂來歡送你上路的。你爲甚麼不讓我同女兒及外孫們吻別？你這樣實在是做錯了。我知道你離開是因爲思念家鄉，但你爲甚麼偷了我的神像？”

　　雅各說：“我怕你奪回你的女兒，至於你的神像，誰拿了

your daughters from me by force. Whoever is found in possession of your gods shall die for it.' Jacob did not know that
Rachel had stolen the gods.

Now she had taken the household gods and put them in the
camel-bag and was sitting on them. Laban went through
everything in the tent and found nothing. Rachel said to her
father, 'Do not take it amiss, sir, that I cannot rise in your presence: the common lot of woman is upon me.' So for all his
search Laban did not find his household gods.

Jacob was angry, and he expostulated with Laban, exclaim-
ing, 'What have I done wrong? What is my offence, that you
have come after me in hot pursuit and gone through all my
possessions? Have you found anything belonging to your
household? You claimed compensation from me for anything
stolen by day or by night. This was the way of it: by day the
heat consumed me and the frost by night, and sleep deserted
me. For twenty years I have been in your household. I worked
for you fourteen years to win your two daughters and six years
for your flocks, and you changed my wages ten times over. If
the God of my father, the God of Abraham and the Fear of
Isaac, had not been with me, you would have sent me away
empty-handed. But God saw my labour and my hard-ships,
and last night he rebuked you.'

Laban answered Jacob, 'The daughters are my daughters,
the children are my children, the flocks are my flocks; all that
you see is mine. But as for my daughters, what can I do today
about them and the children they have borne? Come now, we
will make an agreement, you and I, and let it stand as a witness between us.' And Jacob swore this oath in the name of
the Fear of Isaac his father. He slaughtered an animal for sacrifice, there in the hill-country, and summoned his kinsmen to
the feast. So they ate together and spent the night there.

Laban rose early in the morning, kissed his daughters and
their children, blessed them and went home again.

(2)

Jacob sent messengers on ahead to his brother Esau to the

誰就該死。」雅各不知拉結眞的偸了神像。

拉結是拿了拉班的家神像，她把它藏在駱駝的馱簍裏，然後自己坐在上面。

拉班查遍了所有東西，甚麼也沒找到，拉結對她父親說：「我身上不方便，不能起來迎你，我父你不要介意。」所以拉班找遍了各處都沒搜出他家的神像來。

雅各很生氣，就同拉班吵起來，他喊道：「我做了甚麼錯事？我怎麼冒犯了你，你竟這樣追着我來搜查我的財物？你發現了你家的東西了嗎？你要我賠償白天或黑夜偸走的你的東西。事實上，我白天受日烤，夜裏受霜凍，睡也睡不好。我在你家二十年，替你幹了十四年活兒，才得到你的兩個女兒，幹了六年活才掙得你的一些羊隻。你十次減我的工錢。如果我祖亞伯拉罕的上帝和我父以撒敬畏的神沒有與我同在，你就會讓我空手回老家了。但上帝看到了我的辛勞所以昨夜責備了你。」

拉班回答雅各說：「女兒是我的女兒，孩子們是我的孫兒，羊羣是我的羊羣。你眼前見到的一切都是我的，至於我的女兒們，今天我又會對她們和她們的孩子們怎麼樣呢？來吧，讓你我立一個協定，作爲你我相處的準則吧。」雅各就對父親以撒敬畏的神起誓，他就地在山裏殺牲作祭，又請衆人一起吃飯，晚上就在那裏過夜。

次日拉班一早起來，親吻了兩個女兒和外孫兒，給了他們祝福後就回去了。

（二）

雅各打發人趕在前頭送信給住在埃多瑪西珥地區的哥哥以

district of Seir in the Edomite country. The messengers returned to Jacob and said, 'We met your brother Esau already on the way to meet you with four hundred men.' Jacob, much afraid and distressed, divided the people with him, as well as the sheep, cattle, and camels, into two companies, thinking that , if Esau should come upon one company and destroy it, the other company would survive.

Jacob spent that night there; and as a present for his brother Esau he chose from the herds he had with him two hundred she-goats, twenty he-goats, two hundred ewes and twenty rams, thirty milch-camels with their young, forty cows and ten young bulls, twenty she-asses and ten he-asses. He put each herd separately into the care of a servant and gave these instructions to the first: 'When my brother Esau meets you and asks you to whom you belong and where you are going and who owns these beasts you are driving, you are to say, "They belong to your servant Jacob; he sends them as a present to my lord Esau, and he is behind us."' He gave the same instructions to the second, to the third, and all the drovers. So Jacob's present went on ahead of him, but he himself spent that night at Mahaneh.

During the night Jacob rose, took his two wives, his two slave-girls, and his eleven sons, and crossed the ford of Jabbok. He took them and sent them across the gorge with all that he had. So Jacob was left alone, and a man wrestled with him there till daybreak. When the man saw that he could not throw Jacob, he struck him in the hollow of his thigh, so that Jacob's hip was dislocated as they wrestled. He said to Jacob, 'What is your name?', and he answered, 'Jacob.' The man said, 'Your name shall no longer be Jacob, but Israel, because you strove with God and with men, and prevailed.' Jacob said, 'Tell me, I pray, your name.' He replied, 'Why do you ask my name?', but he gave him his blessing there. Jacob called the place Peniel, 'because', he said, 'I have seen God face to face and my life is spared.' The sun rose as Jacob passed through Penuel, limping because of his hip. This is why

掃。使者回來對雅各說："我們已見到你的哥哥以掃，他正帶着四百人迎着你來。"雅各十分害怕和憂慮，就把他的隨從和牛、羊、駱駝都分成了兩半。他心想，如果以掃碰上其中一半，並且殺掉他們，那另一半還可以幸存。

那晚雅各就在那裏住下。作爲送給哥哥以掃的禮物，他從牧羣中挑了二百頭母山羊，二十頭公山羊，二百頭母綿羊和二十頭公綿羊，三十頭奶崽子的駱駝連同它的幼崽，四十頭母牛和十頭公牛，二十頭母驢同十頭公驢。每羣牲畜讓一個僕人趕着，他對趕頭一羣的人說："當我哥哥以掃遇見你，問你是誰家的，上哪兒去，你趕的牲畜是誰的，你就說：'牠們是你的僕人雅各的，他把牠們作爲禮品送給你以掃老爺，他自己隨後就來。'"他對第二個、第三個和所有趕畜羣的人都這麼吩咐了。這樣，雅各的禮品先走在他的前頭，而他自己却在瑪哈耐歇宿。

到夜裏，雅各就起來把兩個妻子、兩個女奴和十一個兒子都送過了雅博渡口。又使他們和所有財物都過了峽谷。這樣，就剩下雅各一個人。這時，有一個人過來和他摔交，一直到天亮，那人看見無法打敗雅各，就往雅各大腿窩敲了一下，雅各的股關節就脫了臼。那人對雅各說："你叫甚麼名字？"雅各回答："雅各。"那人說："你不要叫雅各了，改名叫以色列，因爲你跟神和人都較量過，並且得勝了。"雅各說："請告訴我你的名字。"那人答道："何必問我名字？"但他賜福與雅各。雅各叫那地方做毘努伊勒 (Peniel)(1)，他說："這是由於我已面對面地見到上帝，而且依然無恙。"太陽出來了，雅各

---

(1) Peniel又可拼作 Penuel，意思是：上帝的臉。

the Israelites to this day do not eat the sinew of the nerve that runs in the hollow of the thigh.

Jacob raised his eyes and saw Esau coming towards him. He then went on, bowing low to the ground seven times as he approached his brother. Esau ran to meet him and embraced him; he threw his arms round him and kissed him, and they wept. When Esau looked up and saw the women and children, he said, 'Who are these with you?' Jacob replied, 'The children whom God has graciously given to your servant.' Esau said, 'What was all that company of yours that I met?' And he answered, 'It was meant to win favour with you, my lord.' Esau answered, 'I have more than enough. Keep what is yours, my brother.' But Jacob said, 'On no account: if I have won your favour, then, I pray, accept this gift from me. So he urged him, and he accepted it.

因為股關節脫臼而一瘸一瘸地走過了毘努伊勒 (Penuel)。這就是為甚麼以色列人至今都不吃獸腿窩的筋肌的緣故。

雅各舉目望見以掃向他走來，他迎向他哥哥時，連續七次拜伏在地上。以掃跑上前擁抱他，張開胳膊摟着他親吻。他們都哭了。以掃抬頭望見那些同來的婦女和孩子，就問：“和你同來的這些人是誰？”雅各說：“是上帝恩賜給你的僕人我的。”以掃說：“我遇見的你那些畜羣又是怎麼一回事？”他回答說：“我的主人，那是我想得到你的恩寵而準備的。”以掃回答：“我已經有足夠的財產了。我的兄弟，你的東西自己留着好了。”但雅各說：“千萬別這樣，如果我可得到你的喜愛，那就請你接受這份禮物吧。”他這樣求以掃，以掃只好接受了。

16 A Trap for Shechem and His Father

Genesis

Dinah, the daughter whom leah had borne to Jacob, went out to visit the women of the country, and Shechem, son of Hamor the Hivite the local prince, saw her; he took her, lay with her and dishonoured her. But he remained true to Jacob's daughter Dinah; he loved the girl and comforted her. So Shechem said to his father Hamor, 'Get me this girl for a wife.' When Jacob heard that Shechem had violated his daughter Dinah, his sons were with the herds in the open country, so he said nothing until they came home. Meanwhile Shechem's father Hamor came out to Jacob to discuss it with him. When Jacob's sons came in from the country and heard, they were grieved and angry, because in lying with Jacob's daughter he had done what the Israelites held to be an outrage, an intolerable thing. Hamor appealed to them in these terms: 'My son Shechem is in love with this girl; I beg you to let him have her as his wife. Let us ally ourselves in marriage; you shall give us your daughters, and you shall take ours in exchange. You must settle among us. The country is open to you; make your home in it, move about freely and acquire land of your own.' And Shechem said to the girl's father and brothers, 'I am eager to win your favour and I will give whatever you ask. Fix the bride-price and the gift as high as you like, and I will give whatever you ask; but you must give me the girl in marriage.'

Jacob's sons gave a dishonest reply to Shechem and his father Hamor, laying a trap for them because Shechem had

十六　巧計復仇

創世記

利亞給雅各生的女兒底拿出門去看望迦南地方的婦女。當地希未人的王公哈抹的兒子示劍見到她，就把她劫回家中奸污了她。不過他的心倒眞是愛雅各這女兒底拿的，他愛這女子，用好話安慰她。示劍對父親哈抹說："你讓我聘這女子爲妻吧。"雅各聽到示劍奸污了他女兒底拿，而他的兒子們還在田野裏照看牧羣未回來，所以他先不說甚麼，等兒子們回來再看怎麼辦。當示劍的父親哈抹出來和雅各家商量這事時。雅各的兒子們從外面回來了，聽說後都很痛心和憤恨，因爲示劍對雅各女兒所幹的是以色列人認爲傷天害理、不能容忍的。哈抹就對他們說："我的兒子示劍愛上這女孩，我求你們把她許配給我兒子爲妻吧。讓我們通過聯姻而結合起來，你們把女兒嫁到我們這邊，你們也可以娶我們的女子作爲交換。你們就在我們這裏定居下來，這個地方全都向你們開放，你們就在這裏安家吧，你們可以自由往來，並得到自己的土地。"示劍對底拿的父兄說："爲了得到你們的好感，你們要甚麼我都給。新娘的聘金禮物要多貴重的都可以，我對你們的一切要求都可以答應，但你們一定要允許我娶這姑娘爲妻。"

雅各的兒子們給了示劍父子一個狡猾的答覆，因爲示劍奸

violated their sister Dinah: 'We cannot do this,' they said; 'we cannot give our sister to a man who is uncircumcised; for we look on that as a disgrace. There is one condition on which we will consent: if you will follow our example and have every male among you circumcised, we will give you our daughters and take yours for ourselves. Then we can live among you, and we shall all become one people. But if you refuse to listen to us and be circumcised, we will take the girl and go away.' Their proposal pleased Hamor and his son Shechem; and the young man, who was held in respect above anyone in his father's house, did not hesitate to do what they had said, because his heart was taken by Jacob's daughter.

So Hamor and Shechem went back to the city gate and addressed their fellow-citizens: 'These men are friendly to us; let them live in our country and move freely in it. The land has room enough for them. Let us marry their daughters and give them ours. But these men will agree to live with us and become one people on this one condition only: every male among us must be circumcised as they have been. Will not their herds, their livestock, and all their chattels then be ours?' All the able-bodied men agreed with Hamor and Shechem, and every single one of them was circumcised, every able-bodied male. Then two days later, while they were still in great pain, Jacob's two sons Simeon and Levi, full brothers to Dinah, armed themselves with swords, boldly entered the city and killed every male. They cut down Hamor and his son Shechem and took Dinah from Shechem's house and went off with her. Then Jacob's other sons came in over the dead bodies and plundered the city, to avenge their sister's dishonour. They seized flocks, cattle, asses, and everything, both inside the city and outside in the open country; they also carried off all their possessions, their dependants, and their women, and plundered everything in the houses.

汚了他們的妹妹底拿，他們就給他設下了一個圈套。他們說：
"我們不能這樣做。我們不能把妹妹許給一個沒有受過割禮的
人，因為我們認為這是一個恥辱。要我們同意得有一個條件：
如果你們隨我們的習俗，對每個男人都施行割禮，我們就把女
兒嫁給你們，也娶你們的女子為妻。然後我們可以在你們這裏
住下來，我們彼此成為一家。但你們如果拒絕我們的條件，不
行割禮，那我們就領妹妹離開這裏。"他們的建議哈抹和他兒
子示劍覺得可以，而示劍在家中又很受尊重，他毫不猶豫地答
應可按他們的建議去做，因為他的心早已為雅各的女兒奪過去
了。

　　於是哈抹和示劍回去在城門口向那城的人說："這些人對
我們是友好的，就讓他們住在我們這裏并可以自由行動。這兒
土地足以容他們住下來。我們可以迎娶他們的姑娘，我們的姑
娘也可以嫁給他們。但這些人同意定居在我們這裏同我們不分
彼此是要有一個條件的：我們每個男子都要像他們那樣舉行割
禮。那樣，他們的羊羣、牲畜和財產將來不就都歸我們了
嗎？"那些成年男子都同意哈抹和示劍的話，他們每個人都行
了割禮，每個健壯男人都無一例外。兩天後，當這些人施割禮
的傷口還十分疼痛的時候，雅各的兒子，底拿的親哥哥西緬和
利未持刀闖入城裏，殺死了所有的男人。他們砍死了哈抹和他
兒子示劍，把底拿從示劍家裏搶回來帶走。接着雅各的其餘幾
個兒子跨過那些屍體進入城內，把那城洗劫一空，來報妹妹受
辱之仇。他們搶走了城裏外的羊羣、牛隻、驢子等，也搶走了
居民的全部財物，搶走了他們的妻女僕從，城裏家家戶戶都被
劫掠一空。

17 Joseph Sold to Egypt

Genesis

When Joseph was a boy of seventeen, he used to accompany his brothers, the sons of Bilhah and Zilpah, his father's wives, when they were in charge of the flock; and he brought their father a bad report of them. Now Israel loved Joseph more than any other of his sons, because he was a child of his old age, and he made him a long, sleeved robe. When his brothers saw that their father loved him more than any of them, they hated him and could not say a kind word to him.

Joseph had a dream, which he told to his father and his brothers. He said, 'Listen: I have had a dream. The sun and moon and eleven stars were bowing down to me.' When he told it to his father and his brothers, his father took him to task: 'What is this dream of yours?' he said. 'Must we come and bow low to the ground before you, I and your mother and your brothers?' His brothers were jealous of him, but his father did not forget.

Joseph's brothers went to mind their father's flocks in Shechem. Israel said to him, 'Go and see if all is well with your brothers and the sheep, and bring me back word....' His brothers saw him in the distance, and before he reached them, they plotted to kill him. They said to each other, 'Here comes that dreamer. Now is our chance; let us kill him and throw him into one of these pits and say that a wild beast has devoured him. Then we shall see what will come of his dreams.' When Reuben heard, he came to his rescue, urging them not to take his life. 'Let us have no bloodshed', he said.

十七　賣往埃及

創世記

約瑟十七歲時，經常和他的異母哥哥們即辟拉和悉帕的兒子們一起牧羊，但他時常在父親面前說他們的壞話。以色列最愛約瑟，因爲約瑟是他老年時得的兒子。他替約瑟做了件有袖的長袍。兄長們看到父親鍾愛約瑟，他們就恨約瑟，都不同他好好說話。

約瑟做了一個夢，他把它講給父親和哥哥們聽。他說："你們聽聽，我做了個夢，在夢中太陽、月亮和十一顆星辰向我下拜。"父兄們聽到他這些話，父親就責備他說："你這是做的甚麼夢？難道我們，我，你的母親以及兄長們，都要在你面前跪拜嗎？"他的哥哥們都忌妒他，他的父親却把這話記在心裏。

約瑟的哥哥們去示劍牧羊，以色列對約瑟說："你去看看你哥哥們和羊羣是否都平安無事並給我回個話。"……約瑟的哥哥們遠遠地看見了約瑟走來，趁他還沒來到就商量要殺死他。他們議論說："瞧，那做夢的來了。這是我們的機會，我們殺死他，把他扔在這兒的亂坑裏，就說是給野獸吃了。看他那些夢如何應驗。"流便聽到這樣說，就要救約瑟，他叫兄弟們不要害他性命。"不要流血，"他說："就把他扔在這荒野

'Throw him into this pit in the wilderness, but do him no bodily harm.' He meant to save him from them so as to restore him to his father. When Joseph came up to his brothers, they stripped him of the long, sleeved robe which he was wearing, took him and threw him into the pit. The pit was empty and had no water in it.

Then they sat down to eat some food and, looking up, they saw an Ishmaelite caravan coming in from Gilead on the way down to Egypt. Judah said to his brothers, 'What shall we gain by killing our brother and concealing his death? Why not sell him to the Ishmaelits?' His brothers agreed with him. Meanwhile some Midianite merchants passed by and drew Joseph up out of the pit. They sold him for twenty pieces of silver to the Ishmaelites, and they brought Joseph to Egypt. When Reuben went back to the pit, Joseph was not there. He rent his clothes and went back to his brothers and said, 'The boy is not there. Where can I go?'

Joseph's brothers took his robe, killed a goat and dipped it in the goat's blood. Then they tore the robe, the long, sleeved robe, brought it to their father and said, 'Look what we have found. Do you recognize it? Is this your son's robe or not?' Jacob did recognize it, and he replied, 'It is my son's robe. A wild beast has devoured him. Joseph has been torn to pieces.' Jacob rent his clothes, put on sackcloth and mourned his son for a long time. Thus Joseph's father wept for him. Meanwhile the Midianites had sold Joseph in Egypt to Potiphar, one of Pharaoh's eunuchs, the captain of the guard....

The Lord was with Joseph and he prospered. Indeed, his Egyptian master put him in charge of his household and entrusted him with all that he had. From the time that he put him in charge of his household and all his property, the Lord blessed the Egyptian's household for Joseph's sake.

Now Joseph was handsome and good-looking, and a time came when his master's wife took notice of him and said, 'Come and lie with me.' But he refused and said to her, 'Think of my master. He does not know as much as I do about his

裏的坑內好了，不必傷他的身體。”其實他想把他從他們手裏救回來交回他父親。當約瑟來到哥哥們跟前時，他們扒掉了他穿着的長袍，抓住他扔進坑裏。坑是空的，裏面沒水。後來他們坐下來吃東西，抬頭看見一個以實瑪利人的商隊從基列來到埃及去。猶大對兄弟們說：“我們殺死我們的弟弟幷隱瞞他死的實情，我們能得到甚麼呢？爲甚麼不把他賣給以實瑪利人呢？”兄弟們都同意他的話。這時，一些米甸商人們從旁走過，約瑟的哥哥們把約瑟從坑裏拉上來，以二十舍客勒銀子把約瑟賣給了以實瑪利人。這樣，約瑟就被帶往埃及去了。流便回到土坑時，約瑟已不在裏面。他憤怒地撕裂了衣服，對兄弟們說：“那孩子沒有了。我該上哪兒去找呢？”

約瑟的哥哥們把約瑟的長袍拿來，殺了一隻羊，把袍子沾上羊血。然後他們又把它撕破，拿回去給他們的父親看，說：“你看我們找到甚麼了？你認得這袍子嗎？它是不是約瑟的長袍？”雅各當然認得它，他答道：“這是我兒子的袍子，野獸把他吃掉了，約瑟被撕成了碎塊了。”雅各傷心地扯破了自己的衣服，圍上蔴布，對兒子哀悼不已。這期間，米甸人把約瑟賣到埃及波提乏家。波提乏是法老的內臣，護衛隊長。

天主與約瑟同在，他又交上好運了。的確這樣，他的埃及主人讓他管理家務，把一切財產都托付給他。從他負責統管主人的家務和財產時起，天主就因約瑟而賜福與他的埃及主人。

現在約瑟已是一個英俊的美少年，有一天，他主人的妻子看上了他，對他說：“來，和我同寢吧。”但他拒絕了，說：“想想我的主人吧，家裏的事他都不如我清楚，他把一切都托

own house, and he has entrusted me with all he has. He has given me authority in this house second only to his own, and has withheld nothing from me except you, because you are his wife. How can I do anything so wicked, and sin against God?' She kept asking Joseph day after day, but he refused to lie with her and be in her company. One day he came into the house as usual to do his work, when none of the men of the household were there indoors. She caught him by his cloak, saying, 'Come and lie with me', but he left the cloak in her hands and ran out of the house. When she saw that he had left his cloak in her hands and had run out of the house, she called out to the men of the household, 'Look at this! My husband has brought in a Hebrew to make a mockery of us. He came in here to lie with me, but I gave a loud scream. When he heard me scream and call out, he left his cloak in my hand and ran off.' She kept his cloak with her until his master came home, and then she repeated her tale. When Joseph's master heard his wife's story of what his slave had done to her, he was furious. He took Joseph and put him in the Round Tower, where the king's prisoners were kept; and there he stayed in the Round Tower. But the Lord was with Joseph and kept faith with him, so that he won the favour of the governor of the Round Tower. He put Joseph in charge of all the prisoners in the tower and of all their work.

付給我了，并讓我在這家中享有僅次於他的權力。他把甚麼都交給了我，只是除了你，因爲你是他的妻子。我怎麼能作這醜事，得罪上帝呢？"她却天天不斷地糾纏約瑟，他則一直不與她同寢，也不和她在一起。有一天，他像平時一樣進屋裏做事，屋裏沒有旁人，她拉住他的外衣，說："來吧，來和我同寢。"約瑟掙脫開跑出了家門，外衣却被她抓在手裏。她看他留下外衣跑了，就叫來所有家人："你們看這個！我丈夫帶來的這個希伯來人玩弄我們。他闖進來要與我同寢。我大聲呼救。他見我叫起來就丟下外衣跑了。"她拿着外衣等主人回來，然後又重複了她編的話。約瑟的主人聽到妻子說他的奴僕如何對她無禮時，大發雷霆。他把約瑟抓來關在國王關囚犯的圓塔樓裏。約瑟就呆在圓塔樓裏。但天主與約瑟同在，他仍舊保祐他。所以約瑟得到了圓塔樓看守長的好感。他讓約瑟負責管理那裏的犯人和他們的工作。

Genesis

It happened later that the king's butler and his baker offended their master the king of Egypt. Pharaoh was angry with these two eunuchs, the chief butler and the chief baker, and he put them in custody in the house of the captain of the guard, in the Round Tower where Joseph was imprisoned. One night, they both had dreams, each needing its own interpretation. They said, 'We have each had a dream and there is no one to interpret it for us.' Joseph said to them, 'Does not interpretation belong to God? Tell me your dreams.' So the chief butler told Joseph his dream: 'In my dream', he said, 'there was a vine in front of me. On the vine there were three branches, and as soon as it budded, it blossomed and its clusters ripened into grapes. Now I had Pharaoh's cup in my hand, and I plucked the grapes, crushed them into Pharaoh's cup and put the cup into Pharaoh's hand.' Joseph said to him, 'This is the interpretation. The three branches are three days: within three days Paraoh will raise you and restore you to your post, and then you will put the cup into Pharaoh's hand as you used to do when you were his butler. But when things go well with you, if you think of me, keep faith with me and bring my case to Pharaoh's notice and help me to get out of this house.'

When the chief baker saw that Joseph had given a favourable interpretation, he said to him, 'I too had a dream, and in my dream there were three baskets of white bread on my head. In the top basket there was every kind of food which the

十八　解夢如神

創世記

後來，恰巧埃及國王的司膳官和麵包師傅冒犯了他們的主子國王。法老對這兩個下屬發了火，叫衛隊長把他們抓起來關在約瑟被監禁的那圓塔樓裏。一夜，兩人都做了夢，他們都想知道自己的夢的寓意……他們對約瑟說："我們每人做了個夢，不知誰能給我們解說一下？"約瑟對他們說："難道上帝也解說不了夢嗎？告訴我你們的夢吧。"於是司膳官對約瑟講了自己的夢，他說："我夢見我面前有一根葡萄籐，籐上有三個枝杈，籐子上有花蕾，很快就開了花，很快又變成串串熟葡萄。當時，我手裏拿着法老的酒杯，我採下葡萄，把汁擠在法老的杯中，幷把杯子遞到法老手裏。"約瑟對他說："你的夢的意思就是：三個枝子就是三天，三天內法老會把你放出監獄，讓你官復原職，那時你就會像從前當司膳官那樣把酒杯遞到他手中。但在你官復原職之後，如果你還想到我，就請關照一下，把我的案子在法老面前說說，幫我釋放出監。"

麵包師傅看到約瑟給那夢做了個吉祥的解釋，便也對約瑟說："我也做了個夢，在夢中，我頭上頂了三籃白麵包。在最上面的籃子裏有爲法老準備的各種食物，許多鳥兒在我頭頂上

baker prepares for Pharaoh, and the birds were eating out of the top basket on my head.' Joseph answered, 'This is the interpretation. The three baskets are three days: within three days Pharaoh will raise you and hang you up on a tree, and the birds of the air will eat your flesh.'

The third day was Pharaoh's birthday and he gave a feast for all his servants. He raised the chief butler and the chief baker in the presence of his court. He restored the chief butler to his post, and the butler put the cup into Pharaoh's hand; but he hanged the chief baker. All went as Joseph had said in interpreting the dreams for them. Even so the chief butler did not remember Joseph, but forgot him.

Nearly two years later Pharaoh had a dream: he was standing by the Nile, and there came up from the river seven cows, sleek and fat, and they grazed on the reeds. After them seven other cows came up from the river, gaunt and lean, and stood on the river-bank beside the first cows. The cows that were gaunt and lean devoured the cows that were sleek and fat. Then Pharaoh woke up. He fell asleep again and had a second dream: he saw seven ears of corn, full and ripe, growing on one stalk. Growing up after them were seven other ears, thin and shrivelled by the east wind. The thin ears swallowed up the ears that were full and ripe. Then Pharaoh woke up and knew that it was a dream. When morning came, Pharaoh was troubled in mind; so he summoned all the magicians and sages of Egypt. He told them his dreams, but there was no one who could interpret them for him. Then Pharaoh's chief butler spoke up and said, 'It is time for me to recall my faults.'

Pharaoh thereupon sent for Joseph. Joseph came in to Pharaoh. Pharaoh said to him 'I have had a dream, and no one can interpret it to me. I have heard it said that you can understand and interpret dreams.' Joseph answered, 'Not I, but God will answer for Pharaoh's welfare.'

Joseph said to Pharaoh, 'The seven good cows are seven years, and the seven good ears of corn are seven years. It is all one dream. The seven lean and gaunt cows that came up after

的籃子裏啄食。」約瑟回答說：「你的夢的意思就是：三個籃子是三天的意思，三天內法老將把你提出監獄，把你吊死在一棵樹上，天上的鳥會飛來吃你的肉。」

第三天是法老的生日，他賜宴給他的羣臣。他從獄中把司膳官和麵包師傅提上庭來，他讓司膳官官復原職，司膳官把酒杯遞到法老手中。但他下令吊死了麵包師傅。一切都按照約瑟的解說那樣出現了。然而，司膳官却竟然記不得約瑟的話了，他竟忘了他。

大約兩年後，法老做了個夢，夢見他站在尼羅河邊，從河裏冒出來七頭母牛，油光水滑的，它們吃着蘆葦，在它們後面又有七頭母牛從河裏冒出來，但是又乾瘦又瘦削，站在河岸上前一批母牛身旁。那乾瘦的牛却把肥壯的牛吃掉了。法老這就醒了。他接着又睡着了，做了第二個夢：他看見一棵麥子上長了七個穗子，顆粒飽滿成熟，在它們後面，又長出了七個穗子，給東風吹得纖瘦乾瘦。那乾枯的穗子吞食了飽滿的穗子。法老醒了過來後，知道這只是一個夢。到了早晨，法老心裏老想着這兩個夢，就召集了埃及所有的術士和哲人。他把夢講給他們聽，但沒有人能給他解說這個夢。這時法老的司膳官說：「這使我記起我的過失來了。」（於是他向法老講述了約瑟如何爲他和麵包師傅解說夢的事。）

法老當即派人去找約瑟來。約瑟來見法老。法老對他說：「我做了個夢，沒有人能解說它。我聽說你懂得解說。」約瑟回答：「不是我，而是上帝，他會爲法老你作解說的。」

約瑟對法老說：「七頭壯牛是指七年，七穗良禾也是指七年，這都是一回事。後來的七頭瘦牛是七年，被東風吹得乾瘦

them are seven years, and the empty ears of corn blighted by the east wind will be seven years of famine. There are to be seven years of great plenty throughout the land. After them will come seven years of famine; all the years of plenty in Egypt will be forgotten and the famine will ruin the country. This is what Pharaoh should do: appoint controllers over the land, and take one fifth of the produce of Egypt during the seven years of plenty. They should collect all this food produced in the good years that are coming and put the corn under Pharaoh's control in store in the cities, and keep it under guard. This food will be a reserve for the country against the seven years of famine which will come upon Egypt. Thus the country will not be devastated by the famine.'

The plan pleased Pharaoh and all his courtiers. Pharaoh said to Joseph, 'Since a god has made all this known to you, there is no one so shrewd and intelligent as you. You shall be in charge of my household, and all my people will depend on your every word. Only my royal throne shall make me greater than you.' Pharaoh named him Zaphenath-paneah, and he gave him as wife Asenath the daughter of Potiphera priest of On. And Joseph's authority extended over the whole of Egypt.

When the seven years of plenty in Egypt came to an end, seven years of famine began, as Joseph had foretold. There was famine in every country, but throughout Egypt there was bread. The whole world came to Egypt to buy corn from Joseph, so severe was the famine everywhere.

的穗子是指七年饑荒。就是說全國會有七個豐收年，接着是七年饑荒。到那時，埃及有過豐收年都會被忘掉了，饑荒將毀滅全國。法老你要做的事就是：在埃及全國派一些官員在豐年時征收五分之一的糧產；他們應該在豐年把這些糧食保存在法老管轄下的城市倉庫裏，派人看管好。這些糧食將作爲國家的儲備供將來七年饑荒之用。這樣國家就不會被饑荒摧垮。"

這個建議使法老和羣臣都非常滿意。法老對約瑟說："既然是神使你通曉夢意，再沒有人會比你更聰敏精明的了。你就來負責管我的家，我的人民都聽你的話。只有我爲王的才居於你之上。"法老賜他名爲撒發那忒巴內亞，並把安城祭司波提非拉的女兒亞西納許配給他爲妻。於是約瑟的權力就遍及全埃及。

埃及七個豐收年過去後，約瑟預言過的七年的饑荒就開始了。許多國家都遭到饑荒的肆虐，唯獨埃及到處都仍然豐衣足食。由於到處災情都很嚴重，全世界都到埃及來向約瑟買糧。

19 *Lost Son Found*

Genesis

When Jacob saw that there was corn in Egypt, he said to his sons,' I have heard that there is corn in Egypt. Go down and buy some so that we may keep ourselves alive and not starve.' So Joseph's brothers, ten of them, went down to buy grain from Egypt, but Jacob did not let Joseph's brother Benjamin go with them, for fear that he might come to harm.

Now Joseph was governor of all Egypt, and it was he who sold the corn to all the people of the land. Joseph's brothers came and bowed to the ground before him'... Although Joseph had recognized his brothers, they did not recognized him. He remembered also the dreams he had had about them; so he said to them, 'You are spies; you have come to spy out the weak points in our defences.' They answered, 'No, sir: your servants have come to buy food. There are twelve of us, all brothers, sons of one man in Canaan. The youngest is still with our father, and one has disappeared.' But Joseph said again to them, 'Do what I say and your lives will be spared; for I am a God-fearing man: if you are honest men, your brother there shall be kept in prison, and the rest of you shall take corn for your hungry households and bring your youngest brother to me, thus your words will be proved true, and you will not die.

First he took Simeon and bound him before their eyes; then he gave orders to fill their bags with grain, to return each man's silver, putting it in his sack, and to give them supplies for the journey. All this was done; and they loaded the corn

十九　買糧認親

創世記

雅各見埃及有糧食，就對兒子們說："我聽說埃及有糧食，到埃及去買些回來，這樣我們就可以活命，不致挨餓。"於是約瑟的弟兄十人一起到埃及去買糧，但雅各沒讓約瑟的弟弟便雅憫去，怕他給人傷害。

約瑟這時正是埃及的當權人物，並由他主管賣糧給所有的人。約瑟的哥哥們來到并向他伏地參拜，約瑟雖然認出了他們，但他們却不認得約瑟。他想起了他做過的有關他們的夢，就對他們說："你們是奸細。你們來是要探聽我們防禦上的虛實。"他們回答道："不，老爺，你的奴僕們是來買糧的。我們一共十二弟兄，都是迦南一人之子。最小的在家和父親一起，還有一個丟失了。"但約瑟却對他們說："那就按我說的去辦才可饒了你們的命。我是個敬畏上帝的人。如果你們是誠實君子，你們的一位兄弟就要先押在監獄裏，其餘人把糧食拿回去給挨餓的家人吃，再把你們的小弟弟帶來給我。這樣你們的話才會使人相信。你們才不會被處死。"他當着他們面讓人捆了起西緬。然後他叫人裝滿他們的糧袋，暗裏又把他們的銀子放回各人的麻袋裏還給他們。並給了他們路上的乾糧。這一

on to their asses and went away.

The famine was still severe in the country. When they had used up the corn they had brought from Egypt, their father said to them, 'Go back and buy a little more corn for us to eat.' But Judah replied, 'The man plainly warned us that we must not go into his presence unless our brother was with us.

Their father Israel said to them, 'If it must be so, then do this: Take your brother with you and go straight back to the man. May God Almighty make him kindly disposed to you, and may he send back the one whom you left behind, and Benjamin too.' So they took the gift and double the amount of silver, and with Benjamin they started at once for Egypt, where they presented themselves to Joseph.

The steward brought them into Joseph's house. When Joseph came into the house, they presented him with the gifts which they had brought, bowing to the ground before him. He asked them how they were and said, 'Is your father well, the old man of whom you spoke? Is he still alive?' Joseph looked and saw his own mother's son, his brother Benjamin, and asked, 'Is this your youngest brother, of whom you told me?', and to Benjamin he said, 'May God be gracious to you, my son!' Joseph was overcome; his feelings for his brother mastered him, and he was near to tears. So he went into the inner room and wept. Then he washed his face and came out; and, holding back his feelings, he ordered the meal to be served.

Joseph gave his steward this order: 'Fill the men's packs with as much food as they can carry and put each man's silver at the top of his pack. And put my goblet, my silver goblet, at the top of the youngest brother's pack with the silver for the corn.' He did as Joseph said. At daybreak the brothers were allowed to take their asses and go on their journey; but before they had gone very far from the city, Joseph said to his steward, 'Go after those men at once, and when you catch up with them, say, "Why have you repaid good with evil? Why have you stolen the silver goblet? It is the one from which my lord drinks, and which he uses for divination. You have done a

切都弄好以後，約瑟的弟兄們把驢子上了馱，就回去了。

　　饑荒仍很嚴重，他們吃完從埃及買來的糧後，他們的父親對他們說：“再去買些糧來吃吧。”但猶大回答說：“那人已清楚地警告我們，除非帶小弟去，否則別再出現在他面前。……”他們的父親以色列對他們說：“事情如果必須如此，那就這樣做吧。帶上你們的弟弟到那個人那裏，願萬能的上帝使他好心對你們，願他放回你們作抵押的那個兄弟，也讓便雅憫回來。”於是，他們帶上了禮品，雙倍的銀子和便雅憫一起，立刻出發去埃及謁見約瑟。

　　管家把他們帶進約瑟的屋裏，當約瑟進屋時，他們俯伏地上把帶來的禮物送給他。約瑟問他們好，並說：“你們說的老人家——你們的父親好嗎？他還活着嗎？”約瑟看見了他的同母弟弟便雅憫。他說：“這就是你們說過的最小的弟弟嗎？”他對便雅憫說：“我的孩子，願上帝賜福於你。”約瑟很激動，手足之情使他一時不知說甚麼好，他幾乎忍不住要哭了。於是他走進屋裏哭起來。然後他洗過臉再出來，按下激動的心情，叫人開飯招待他們。飯後約瑟吩咐他的管家：“盡他們的驢子所能馱的，把他們的袋子裝滿，並把每人的銀子還給他們，放在行李上部，又把我的銀杯放在最小的弟弟的包裹，和他用來買糧的銀子擺在一起。”管家就這麼辦了。天亮時，就打發各兄弟們牽驢子上路，但他們出城不遠，約瑟對管家說：“馬上去追那些人，你趕上他們時就說：‘爲甚麼你們恩將仇報？爲甚麼你們偷了銀杯？那是我主人喝酒用的杯子。他還用它來占卜

wicked thing."' When he caught up with them, he repeated all this to them, but they replied, 'My lord, how can you say such things? No, sir, God forbid that we should do any such thing! If any one of us is found with the goblet, he shall die; and, what is more, my lord, we will all become your slaves.' Each man quickly lowered his pack to the ground and opened it. The steward searched them, beginning with the eldest and finishing with the youngest, and the goblet was found in Benjamin's pack.

At this they rent their clothes; then each man loaded his ass and they returned to the city. Joseph was still in the house when Judah and his brothers came in.

Judah went up to him and said, 'Please listen, my lord. Let me say a word to your lordship, I beg. We have an aged father, and he has a young son born in his old age; this boy's full brother is dead and he alone is left of his mother's children, he alone, and his father loves him he will see that the boy is not with us and will die, and your servants will have brought down our father's grey hairs in sorrow to the grave. Now, my lord, let me remain in place of the boy as your lordship's slave, and let him go with his brothers'.

Joseph could no longer control his feelings in front of his attendants, and he called out, 'Let everyone leave my presence.' So there was nobody present when Joseph made himself known to his brothers, but so loudly did he weep that the Egyptians and Pharaoh's household heard him. Joseph said to his brothers, 'Come closer', and so they came close. He said, 'I am your brother Joseph whom you sold into Egypt. Now do not be distressed or take it amiss that you sold me into slavery here; it was God who sent me ahead of you to save men's lives. Make haste and go back to my father and give him this message from his son Joseph: "God has made me lord of all Egypt. Come down to me; do not delay. I will see that you are not reduced to poverty." Thus they went up from Egypt and came to their father Jacob in Canaan. There they gave him the news that Joseph was still alive and that he was ruler of all

的，你們幹的這醜事。'"管家追上衆兄弟時，就這樣說了。但他們回答："老爺，你怎能這麼說呢？不，上帝哪能讓我們幹這種事情！如果我們中間有人偷了這銀杯，他就該死罪。而且我們都願做你的奴僕。"他們每人都把包卸下來打開，管家從老大開始搜查一直到最小一個，杯子在便雅憫的袋子裏找出來了。

事情變成這樣，各兄弟都急得扯破了衣裳，只好把東西裝回驢子上回到城裏去。猶大和他的弟兄們進入約瑟屋裏時，約瑟還在屋裏。

猶大走到他面前說："請老爺明察，求你允許我說句話。我們有個年邁的父親，他老年時得了這個兒子，這個孩子的同母哥哥已經死了，他現在是他母親唯一膝下的孩子，所以父親疼愛他。他看到兒子沒回來，就會死的，這無異是你的奴僕們讓白髮老父憂傷而死。老爺，讓我替這孩子做你的奴僕，讓他和兄弟們回去吧。"

約瑟再也無法在他的隨從面前控制自己的感情了，他喊道："你們都給我走開！"這樣，當約瑟同兄弟們相認時，沒有一個外人在場，但他哭得那麼厲害，埃及人和法老家人都聽見了。約瑟對他的弟兄們說："你們走近一些。"他們就走攏過來。他說："我就是你們賣到埃及的兄弟約瑟。現在，也不用因爲你們曾把我賣到這裏作奴僕而不安，是上帝把我先送到這裏來去救世人的。趕快回到父親那裏，把他兒子約瑟的口信帶給他：'上帝使我成了埃及之主，到我這兒來吧，不要躭擱了。我不會使你們窮困的。"於是他們就從埃及回到迦南父親雅各的身邊。他們把約瑟還活着，並且做了埃及的宰相的好消

Egypt. He was stunned and could not believe it.

So Israel set out with all that he had and came to Beersheba where he offered sacrifices to the God of his father Isaac. God said to Israel in a vision by night, 'Jacob, Jacob', and he answered, 'I am here.' God said, 'I am God, the God of your father. Do not be afraid to go down to Egypt, for there I will make you a great nation. I will go down with you to Egypt, and I myself will bring you back again without fail; and Joseph shall close your eyes.' So Jacob set out from Beersheba. Israel's sons conveyed their father Jacob, their dependants and their wives in the wagons which Pharaoh had sent to carry them. They took the herds and the stock which they had acquired in Canaan and came to Egypt.

息告訴了雅各。他大吃一驚，不敢相信這是眞的。

這樣，以色列帶上了他的一切財產，出發到了別是巴，在那裏他向父親以撒的上帝獻牲。夜裏上帝顯靈對以色列說：“雅各，雅各。”他回答道：“我在這兒。”上帝說：“我是上帝，你父親的主。不要害怕去埃及，我會使你在那裏成爲一個大族。我會同你一起去埃及，我也一定會親自把你帶回故土，約瑟也會給你送終的。”於是雅各再從別是巴啓程。以色列的兒子們讓父親雅各、他們的家裏人、他們的妻子乘上法老派來接他們的車上了路，他們也帶上了在迦南的牲畜羣到了埃及。

20 The Birth of Moses

Exodus

In course of time Joseph died, he and all his brothers and that whole generation. Now the Israelites were fruitful and prolific; they increased in numbers and became very powerful, so that the country was overrun by them. Then a new king ascended the throne of Egypt, one who knew nothing of Joseph. He said to his people, 'These Israelites have become too many and too strong for us. We must take precautions to see that they do not increase any further; or we shall find that, if war breaks out, they will join the enemy and fight against us, and they will become masters of the country.' So they were made to work in gangs with officers set over them, to break their spirit with heavy labour. But the more harshly they were treated, the more their numbers increased beyond all bounds, until the Egyptians came to loathe the sight of them.

Then the king of Egypt spoke to the Hebrew midwives, whose names were Shiphrah and Puah. 'When you are attending the Hebrew women in child-birth', he told them, 'watch as the child is delivered and if it is a boy, kill him; if it is a girl, let her live.' But they were God-fearing women. They did not do what the king of Egypt had told them to do, but let the boys live. Pharaoh then ordered all his people to throw every new-born Hebrew boy into the Nile, but to let the girls live.

A descendant of Levi married a Levite woman who conceived and bore a son. When she saw what a fine child he was, she hid him for three months, but she could conceal him no

二十　摩西出世

出埃及記

約瑟和他的兄弟及那一代人都死了。到這時以色列人人丁興旺、日益強盛、而且遍佈埃及各地。後來，一個不識約瑟的埃及新王登基，對他的人民說："以色列人太多太强盛了，我們要採取一些措施去防止他們繼續繁衍。不然，一旦戰爭爆發，他們就會聯合我們的敵人和我們作對，他們將成爲埃及的主人。"於是以色列人被編成一隊隊，在官員的監督下做苦工，用勞役來壓垮他們。……但是他們越受苦，人口却越興旺，數目無止境地增加，直到埃及人看見他們就覺得討厭。

於是，埃及王就對希伯來接生婆施弗拉和普阿說："你們給希伯來女人接生的時候，要注意生下的孩子，男的就殺掉，女的就讓它活下來。"可是這兩個女人是敬畏上帝的，她們沒有照埃及王的話去做，而讓男孩子也活下來了。法老又命令他的子民見到剛出生的希伯來男嬰就都扔到尼羅河裏，女嬰則留下。

一個利未人娶了個本族女子。女子懷孕生了個兒子。她看孩子很漂亮，藏了他三個月。再也藏不住時，她便給他弄來個

longer. So she got a rush basket for him, made it watertight with clay and tar, laid him in it, and put it among the reeds by the bank of the Nile. The child's sister took her stand at a distance to see what would happen to him. Pharaoh's daughter came down to bathe in the river, while her ladies-in-waiting walked along the bank. She noticed the basket among the reeds and sent her slave-girl for it. She took it from her and when she opened it, she saw the child. It was crying, and she was filled with pity for it. 'Why,' she said, 'it is a little Hebrew boy.' Thereupon the sister said to Pharaoh's daughter, 'Shall I go and fetch one of the Hebrew women as a wet-nurse to suckle the child for you?' Pharaoh's daughter told her to go; so the girl went and called the bady's mother. Then Pharaoh's daughter said to her, 'Here is the child, suckle him for me, and I will pay you for it myself.' So the woman took the child and suckled him. When the child was old enough, she brought him to Pharaoh's daughter, who adopted him and called him Moses, 'because', she said, 'I drew him out of the water.'

燈芯草籃子，塗上黏土和瀝青防止滲水，把孩子放進去，再把籃子放在尼羅河畔的蘆葦叢中。孩子的姐姐遠遠地站着看看會發生甚麼情況。這時法老的女兒下河沐浴，使女們則在岸上聽使喚。公主發現葦叢中有一個籃子，就叫婢女取了來。她接過籃子，打開來看裏面那孩子。孩子在哭，她動了憐憫之心。

"呀，"她說，"原來是個希伯來男娃娃。"那孩子的姐姐就對法老的女兒說："要不要我去找一個希伯來女人來爲你奶這個孩子？"法老的女兒就叫她去找，女孩便去找來了孩子的母親。法老的女兒對她說："就是這個孩子，你替我奶着，我會酬勞你的。"女人便把孩子帶去奶着，孩子大了，她把他帶去交給法老的女兒。法老的女兒收他爲養子，給他起名叫摩西(1)。"因爲，"她說，"他是我從水中得來的。"

----

(1) 希伯來文Mosheh意爲：得子。

21   God Appeared to Moses

Exodus

One day when Moses was grown up, he went out to his own kinsmen and saw them at their heavy labour. He saw an Egyptian strike one of his fellow-Hebrews. He looked this way and that, and, seeing there was no one about, he struck the Egyptian down and hid his body in the sand. When he went out next day, two Hebrews were fighting together. He asked the man who was in the wrong, 'Why are you striking him?' 'Who set you up as an officer and judge over us?' the man replied. 'Do you mean to murder me as you murdered the Egyptian?' Moses was alarmed. 'The thing must have become known', he said to himself. When Pharaoh heard of it, he tried to put Moses to death, but Moses made good his escape and settled in the land of Midian.

Now the priest of Midian had seven daughters. One day as Moses sat by a well, they came to draw water and filled the troughs to water their father's sheep. Some shepherds came and drove them away; but Moses got up, took the girls' part and watered their sheep himself. When the girls came back to their father Reuel, he asked, 'How is it that you are back so quickly today?' 'An Egyptian rescued us from the shepherds', they answered; 'and he even drew the water for us and watered the sheep.' 'But where is he then?' he said to his daughters. 'Why did you leave him behind? Go and invite him to eat with us.' So it came about that Moses agreed to live with the man, and he gave Moses his daughter Zipporah in marriage. She bore him a son, and Moses called him Gershom.

二十一　受命於天

出埃及記

摩西長大了。一天，他來到他的同胞那裏，看見他們做苦工。他見到一個埃及人打一個希伯來兄弟。他看看周圍沒有人，便把這個埃及人打死，屍體藏在沙土裏。第二天他外出時，見兩個希伯來人在打架，他便問那個理虧的人：“你爲甚麼要打他？”那人答道：“誰封你做官來給我們作裁判的？難道你要像謀殺那埃及人一樣殺掉我嗎？”摩西大吃一驚，心想：“這事一定泄露了。”當法老得知此事，便要處死摩西。可是摩西早已逃之夭夭，在米甸那地方住下來。

米甸的祭司有七個女兒。一天，摩西正坐在井邊，她們來打水去灌滿水槽給她們父親的羊喝。這時有一些牧人過來要趕她們走。摩西就起來幫她們說話，並親自替她們給羊飲水。女孩子們回到父親流珥那裏，他便問：“今天你們怎麼這麼快就回來了？”“有一個埃及人幫我們免得受牧羊人的欺負，”她們回答道，“他還替我們打水並幫我們給羊飲水。”“那他現在在哪兒呢？”他對女兒們說，“你們爲什麼不招呼他留下？快去請他來和我們一起吃飯吧。”這樣摩西就留下和流珥一起生活，而流珥則把他的女兒西坡拉許配給摩西。她給摩西生了個兒子，摩西給他起名叫革舜。

Years passed, and the king of Egypt died, but the Israelites still groaned in slavery.

Moses was minding the flock of his father-in-law Jethro, priest of Midian. He led the flock along the side of the wilderness and came to Horeb, the mountain of God. There the angel of the Lord appeared to him in the flame of a burning bush. Moses noticed that, although the bush was on fire, it was not being burnt up; so he said to himself, 'I must go across to see this wonderful sight. Why does not the bush burn away?' When the Lord saw that Moses had turned aside to look, he called to him out of the bush, 'Moses, Moses.' And Moses answered, 'Yes, I am here.' God said, 'Come no nearer; take off your sandals; the place where you are standing is holy ground.' Then he said, 'I am the God of your forefathers, the God of Abraham, the God of Isaac, the God of Jacob.' Moses covered his face, for he was afraid to gaze on God.

The Lord said, 'I have indeed seen the misery of my people in Egypt. I have heard their outcry against their slave-masters. I have taken heed of their sufferings, and have come down to rescue them from the power of Egypt, and to bring them up out of that country into a fine, broad land; it is a land flowing with milk and honey. Come now; I will send you to Pharaoh and you shall bring my people Israel out of Egypt.'

Moses answered, 'But they will never believe me or listen to me; they will say, "The Lord did not appear to you."'The Lord said, 'What have you there in your hand?' 'A staff', Moses answered. The Lord said, 'Throw it on the ground.' Moses threw it down and it turned into a snake. He ran away from it, but the Lord said, 'Put your hand out and seize it by the tail.' He did so and gripped it firmly, and it turned back into a staff in his hand. 'This is to convince the people that the Lord the God of their forefathers has appeared to you.' Then the Lord said, 'Put your hand inside the fold of your cloak.' He did so, and when he drew it out the skin was diseased, white as snow. The Lord said, 'Put it back again', and he did

許多年過去，埃及王死了，可是以色列人仍在奴役中呻吟。

（一天），摩西在放牧他岳父、米甸祭司葉忒羅[1]的羊羣，他沿着荒野來到阿烈山旁，那是上帝的山。上帝的使臣在荊叢的火熖裏顯現。摩西看到荊叢雖然給火燒，却並沒有焚毀，他自忖道：“我要過去看看這奇怪的現象，荊叢爲何不會被燒掉？”上帝見他在那兒察看，便從荊叢中向他叫喚：“摩西、摩西。”摩西答道：“是，我在這裏。”上帝說：“不要再走近了，你把鞋脫掉，你現在站的地方是聖地。”他又說：“我是你祖先的上帝，亞伯拉罕的上帝，以撒的上帝，雅各的上帝。”摩西蒙上臉，他怕看見上帝。

上帝說：“我很清楚知道我的人民在埃及受苦難，他們對監工的怨聲我也聽到了。我已注意到他們的苦難，並且下來救他們脫離埃及人的統治，領他們離開這個國家，去到一片美好寬廣的土地，那是流着奶與蜜的好地方。來，我派你到法老那裏，你去把我的以色列民帶出埃及。”

摩西回答說：“可是他們不會相信我，也不會聽我的。他們會說：‘上帝沒有向你顯靈。’”上帝說：“你手裏拿的甚麼？”“手杖。”摩西答道。上帝說：“把它扔到地上。”摩西把它丟到地上，它便變作一條蛇。他嚇得退開幾步，上帝說：“伸出手來抓住它的尾巴吧。”他照樣做了，緊緊的攮着，這蛇就在他手裏變回一根手杖。“這就可以讓人民相信，他們祖先的天主上帝曾經向你顯靈了。”上帝又說：“把手放在你外衣的衣襟裏。”他照辦了。當他把手拿出來時，上面像患了皮膚病，像雪一樣白。上帝說：“把手放回去。”他照辦了。這回，

---

(1)　叶忒羅是摩西岳父，他的另一個名字叫流珥 (Reuel)。

so. When he drew it out this time it was as healthy as the rest of his body. 'Now,' said the Lord, 'if they do not believe you and do not accept the evidence of the first sign, they may accept the evidence of the second. But if they are not convinced even by these two signs, and will not accept what you say, then fetch some water from the Nile and pour it out on the dry ground, and the water you take from the Nile will turn to blood on the ground.'

But Moses said, 'O Lord, I have never been a man of ready speech, never in my life, not even now that thou hast spoken to me; I am slow and hesitant of speech.' At this the Lord grew angry with Moses and said, 'Have you not a brother, Aaron the Levite? He, I know, will do all the speaking. You shall speak to him and put the words in his mouth; I will help both of you to speak and tell you both what to do. He will do all the speaking to the people for you, he will be the mouthpiece, and you will be the god he speaks for. But take this staff, for with it you are to work the signs.'

At length Moses went back to Jethro his father-in-law and said, 'Let me return to my kinsfolk in Egypt and see if they are still alive.' Jethro told him to go and wished him well.

當他把手拿出來時，它已和身上其他部位完全一樣正常。"那麼，"上帝說，"如果他們不相信你，不相信第一個神迹，他們將會相信這第二個神迹。如果這兩個神迹都不足以使他們信服，仍然不信你的話，那你就從尼羅河裏取些水潑在地上。這些河裏取來的水會在地上變成血。"可摩西對上帝說："主啊，我素來不善辭令，即使你現在對我講了這些話，我還是訥訥說不出口的。"上帝聽了不禁有點生氣："你不是有個哥哥利未人亞倫嗎？我知道他會代你說話的。你把要說的話都告訴他，我自然會教你們怎樣說，教你們如何行事。你哥哥將替你向人民說話，成爲你的喉舌，你將是向他授意的神。拿上手杖吧，帶着它你好行神迹。"

終於，摩西回到他岳父葉忐羅那裏，對他說："讓我回到我在埃及的同胞那裏去吧，看他們是否還在。"葉忐羅答允了，並祝他一路平安。

Exodus

Moses and Aaron went and assembled all the elders of Israel. Aaron told them everything that the Lord had said to Moses; he performed the signs before the people, and they were convinced. They heard that the Lord had shown his concern for the Israelites and seen their misery; and they bowed themselves to the ground in worship.

After this, Moses and Aaron came to Pharaoh and said, 'It has happened that the God of the Hebrews met us. So let us go three days' journey into the wilderness to offer sacrifice to the Lord our God, or else he will attack us with pestilence or sword.' But the king of Egypt said, 'Moses and Aaron, what do you mean by distracting the people from their work? Back to your labours! Your people already outnumber the native Egyptians; yet you would have them stop working!'

That very day Pharaoh ordered the people's overseers and their foremen not to supply the people with the straw used in making bricks, as they had done hitherto. 'Let them go and collect their own straw, but see that they produce the same tally of bricks as before. On no account reduce it. They are a lazy people, and that is why they are clamouring to go and offer sacrifice to their god.' So the people scattered all over Egypt to gather stubble for straw, while the overseers kept urging them on, bidding them complete, day after day, the same quantity as when straw was supplied. Then the Israelite foremen were flogged because they were held responsible by Pharaoh's overseers. So the foremen came and appealed to

二十二　降災埃及

……摩西和亞倫去召集來以色列的衆長老。亞倫把天主對摩西講的話都告訴了他們，摩西又向他們顯了神迹，使他們信服。他們聽說主顧憐以色列人，體察他們的痛苦，便伏地下拜。

這之後，摩西和亞倫來到法老面前說："希伯來人的上帝曾經見過我們。請讓我們走三天的路程，到曠野裏去向我主上帝供奉祭品，否則，他將以瘟疫或刀劍攻擊我們。"但埃及王說："摩西、亞倫，你們爲甚麼蠱惑人心使他們曠工呢？回去幹活吧！你們的人數已比埃及人多了，可你們還想讓他們不幹活！"

當天，法老吩咐督工和工頭，改變一貫的做法，不供給以色列人做磚用的草："讓他們自己去找草，但做磚的數目不能比以前少，一點都不能少。他們都是懶人，所以才吵嚷要去祭祀他們的神。"於是希伯來人到埃及各處去撿麥稭當草用。而督工仍舊催促他們每日要完成和有草供應時一樣的磚數。法老的督工責打以色列的工頭，要他們切實負起責任。於是工頭們

Pharaoh. But Pharaoh replied, 'You are lazy. That is why you talk about going to offer sacrifice to the Lord. Now go; get on with your work. You will be given no straw, but you must produce the tally of bricks.' As they came out from Pharaoh's presence they found Moses and Aaron waiting to meet them, and said, 'May this bring the Lord's judgement down upon you: you have made us stink in the nostrils of Pharaoh and his subjects; you have put a sword in their hands to kill us.'

Moses went back to the Lord, and said, 'Why, O Lord, hast thou brought misfortune on this people? The Lord answered, 'Pharaoh will let the Israelites go out of his country; but I will make him stubborn. Then will I show sign after sign and portent after portent in the land of Egypt. I will bring my people, the Israelites, out of Egypt in their tribal hosts.'

When Moses and Aaron came to Pharaoh, they did as the Lord had told them. Aaron threw down his staff in front of Pharaoh and his courtiers, and it turned into a serpent. At this, Pharaoh summoned the wise men and the sorcerers, and the Egyptian magicians too did the same thing by their spells. Every man threw his staff down, and each staff turned into a serpent; but Aaron's staff swallowed up theirs. Pharaoh, however, was obstinate; as the Lord had foretold, he would not listen to Moses and Aaron.

Then the Lord said to Moses, 'Pharaoh is obdurate: he has refused to set the people free. Go to him in the morning on his way out to the river. Stand and wait on the bank of the Nile to meet him, and take with you the staff that turned into a snake. Say this to him: "With this rod that I have in my hand, I shall now strike the water in the Nile and it will be changed into blood. The fish will die and the river will stink, and the Egyptians will be unable to drink water from the Nile."'

So Moses and Aaron did as the Lord had commanded. He lifted up his staff and struck the water of the Nile in the sight of Pharaoh and his courtiers, and all the water was changed into blood. But the Egyptian magicians did the same thing by their spells; and still Pharaoh remained obstinate, as the Lord

就去找法老求情。但法老說："你們懶，所以要說去祭祀上帝。去幹活吧，不會給你們草，但還要做那麼多的磚。"他們從法老那裏出來，見摩西和亞倫正等着見他們，就說："這事讓上帝給你們裁處吧。你們使法老和他的臣民都討厭我們，等於把殺我們的刀交到他們手裏。"

摩西回到天主的面前，說："主啊，你為甚麼使這些人民遭受責難呢？"天主對摩西說："法老將讓以色列人離開他的國家。而我將使他愚頑不化。然後我將不斷地在埃及顯現神迹。我會把我的以色列人民一部族一部族地全帶出埃及。"

摩西和亞倫就來到法老面前，按天主的話去做。亞倫把手杖丟在法老和他的朝臣面前，手杖變成了一條毒蛇。法老就召來了智者與術士，這些埃及的術士用咒語也做到了同樣的事：他們都丟下自己的手杖，每根手杖都變成了一條毒蛇。但亞倫的杖却吞掉了術士們的手杖。可是法老很固執，就像天主預言的那樣，仍然不聽摩西和亞倫的話。

於是天主對摩西說："法老頑固不化，他拒絕放走那些人民。早晨，你在他去河邊的路上去見他。你站在尼羅河的岸邊等他來。並且帶上變過蛇的那根手杖。你對他說："我現在用手杖擊打尼羅河裏的水，尼羅河的水就會變成血。魚都會死掉，水也要發臭，埃及人將無法飲用尼羅河的水了。"摩西和亞倫就按天主的指示做。他在法老和他的朝臣面前舉起手杖擊打尼羅河的水，水全部變成血。可是埃及的術士也用咒語做了同樣的事。就像天主所預言的那樣。法老仍然頑固地不聽摩西

had foretold, and did not listen to Moses and Aaron.

The Lord then told Moses to go into Pharaoh's presence and say to him, 'These are the words of the Lord: "Let my people go in order to worship me. If you refuse to let them go, I will plague the whole of your territory with frogs. So Aaron stretched out his hand over the waters of Egypt, and the frogs came up and covered all the land. The magicians did the same thing by their spells: they too brought up frogs upon the land of Egypt. Then Pharaoh summoned Moses and Aaron. 'Pray to the Lord', he said, 'to take the frogs away from me and my people, and I will let the people go to sacrifice to the Lord.' Moses and Aaron left Pharaoh's presence, and Moses appealed to the Lord to remove the frogs which he had brought on Pharaoh. The Lord did as Moses had asked, and in house and courtyard and in the open the frogs all perished. But when Pharaoh found that he was given relief he became obdurate; as the Lord had foretold, he did not listen to Moses and Aaron.

The Lord then told Moses to say to Aaron, 'Stretch out your staff and strike the dust on the ground, and it will turn into maggots throughout the land of Egypt', and they obeyed. All the dust turned into maggots throughout the land of Egypt. But Pharaoh remained obstinate.

和亞倫的話。……

天主又讓摩西來到法老面前對他說："天主這樣說：讓我的人民去參拜我，如果你不讓他們去，我將使你的國土遭受蛙害"。

亞倫伸手到尼羅河上方，青蛙便從河裏爬上來，滿地都是。術士也用咒語做出同樣的事，把青蛙也帶到埃及的土地上。法老召摩西和亞倫來說："求天主把青蛙從我和我的人民身邊趕走吧，我將讓人民去祭祀主。"

摩西和亞倫便離開法老。摩西去請求天主把他召到法老這裏來的青蛙弄走。天主依了摩西的請求，屋裏、院裏和外面地上的青蛙都死掉了。…但法老看見災害已消除就又固執起來，就像天主預言那樣，又不聽摩西和亞倫的話了。

天主便讓摩西對亞倫說："伸出你的杖擊打地上的塵土，使塵土變作蛆虫遍佈埃及的土地。"他們照做了。所有的塵土都變作蛆虫，遍佈埃及各地。可是法老依然像先前一樣頑固。

（後來上帝又降了蠅災、疫病、畜瘟、雹災和蝗災。後來，又使黑暗遍佈埃及。最後，他殺了埃及所有頭胎的生靈，才使法老回心轉意。）

23 The Passover

Exodus

Moses summoned all the elders of Israel and said to them, 'Go at once and get sheep for your families and slaughter the Passover. Then take a bunch of marjoram, dip it in the blood in the basin and smear some blood from the basin on the lintel and the two door-posts. Nobody may go out through the door of his house till morning. The Lord will go through Egypt and strike it, but when he sees the blood on the lintel and the two door-posts, he will pass over that door and will not let the destroyer enter your houses to strike you. You shall keep this as a rule for you and your children for all time. When you enter the land which the Lord will give you as he promised, you shall observe this rite. Then, when your children ask you, "What is the meaning of this rite?" you shall say, "It is the Lord's Passover, for he passed over the houses of the Israelites in Egypt when he struck the Egyptians but spared our house."' The people bowed down and prostrated themselves.

The Israelites went and did all that the Lord had commanded Moses and Aaron; and by midnight the Lord had struck down every first-born in Egypt, from the first-born of Pharaoh on his throne to the first-born of the captive in the dungeon, and the first-born of cattle. Before night was over Pharaoh rose, he and all his courtiers and all the Egyptians, and a great cry of anguish went up, because not a house in Egypt was without its dead. Pharaoh summoned Moses and Aaron while it was still night and said, 'Up with you! Be off, and leave my people, you and your Israelites. Go and worship

二十三　逾越聖節

出埃及記

摩西召集以色列的衆長老，對他們說："快回自己家中取羊羔，把羊羔宰了作逾越節之用：要拿一把牛膝草蘸上盆裏的血塗在門楣和兩邊門框上。天不亮人不要走出門外。天主將到埃及各地去打擊埃及人，他看見門楣和門框上的血，就會越過這門，不讓殺戮者進你們的屋子殺害你們。你們和你們的子孫都要時刻恪守這一誡律，到了天主賜給你們他所應諾的那塊土地上，你們也要遵守這個儀式。當你們的子孫問你們：'這種儀式是什麼意思？'你們就說：'這是天主的逾越節。以色列人在埃及時，他越過了以色列人的房屋去殺埃及人，放過了我們的住宅。'"長老們聽了都拜倒在地上。

以色列人按天主令摩西和亞倫說的一一照辦；到了夜半的時候，天主殺了埃及家家戶戶的頭一個孩子，上至在位法老的太子，下至土牢裏俘虜中的長子以及頭胎幼畜。天還不亮，法老、他的朝臣和所有的埃及人都起來了，他們都痛哭失聲。因爲，家家戶戶埃及人都有人死去。法老連夜召摩西和亞倫來，說："起來，你們和你們以色列人都走吧，離開我的人民。按

the Lord, as you ask; take your sheep and cattle, and go; and ask God's blessing on me also.' The Egyptians urged on the people and hurried them out of the country, 'or else', they said, 'we shall all be dead.' The people picked up their dough before it was leavened, wrapped their kneading-troughs in their cloaks, and slung them on their shoulders. Meanwhile the Israelites had done as Moses had told them, asking the Egyptians for jewellery of silver and gold and for clothing. As the Lord had made the Egyptians well-disposed towards them, they let them have what they asked; in this way they plundered the Egyptians.

Then Moses said to the people, 'Remember this day, the day on which you have come out of Egypt, the land of slavery, because the Lord by the strength of his hand has brought you out.

你們所要求那樣去祭祀天主吧；帶着你們的牛羊走吧，求上帝也保祐我。"埃及人催促以色列人趕快離開這片國土。"不然，"他們說，"我們就都沒命了。"以色列人拿着還未發酵的麵，把和面盆裹在斗篷中，背在肩上。同時，以色列人還按摩西吩咐他們那樣向埃及人索取珠寶、金銀和衣物。由於上帝要埃及人善待他們，埃及人便讓他們拿走想要的東西。這樣，他們就把埃及人的財富掠奪一空。……

後來，摩西對他的人民說："記住這一天，這天你們走出了受役的埃及這地方，因爲是天主用他萬能的手把你們帶領出來的。"

24   Two of God's Miracles

Exodus

(1)

When the king of Egypt was told that the Israelites had slipped away, he and his courtiers changed their minds completely. So Pharaoh put horses to his chariot, and took his troops with him. He took six hundred picked chariots and all the other chariots of Egypt, with a commander in each, pursued them and overtook them encamped beside the sea by Pihahiroth to the east of Baal-zephon. Pharaoh was almost upon them when the Israelites looked up and saw the Egyptians close behind. In their terror they clamoured to the Lord for help and said to Moses, 'Were there no graves in Egypt, that you should have brought us here to die in the wilderness? We would rather be slaves to the Egyptians than die here in the wilderness.' 'Have no fear,' Moses answered; 'The Lord will fight for you; so hold your peace.'

The angel of God, who had kept in front of the Israelites, moved away to the rear. The pillar of cloud moved from the front and took its place behind them and so came between the Egyptians and the Israelites. And the cloud brought on darkness and early nightfall, so that contact was lost throughout the night.

二十四　神迹兩則

出埃及記

（一）

　　當埃及王聽說以色列人都跑掉了，他同他的朝臣又都後悔起來。於是法老備了馬拉戰車，率領軍隊去追趕。他帶領了六百輛特選戰車及埃及其他的戰車，每輛都由一指揮官率領去追趕以色列人。在巴力洗分以東靠近比哈希錄的海邊上，趕上了在那兒安營的以色列人。以色列人舉目望見埃及人在他們後面追來，馬上就到，感到十分懼怕，他們向天主呼救，並對摩西說："難道埃及沒有葬身之地，你把我們帶到這野地來送死麼？我們寧可在埃及為奴，也不願在這荒野地死去。""別怕，"摩西說，"天主一定會為你們而戰的，大家要保持鎮靜。"

　　一直在以色列人前面引路的上帝的使臣，這時轉到隊伍的後面。雲柱(1)也從前方移到以色列人身後，介乎以色列人與埃及人之間。雲遮住了光綫，使黑暗提早降臨，這樣埃及人整夜都無法接近以色列人。

----

(1)　雲柱(Pillar of Cloud)是上帝給以色列人出埃及時白天引路用的，一
　　直在隊伍前面。

Then Moses stretched out his hand over the sea, and the Lord drove the sea away all night with a strong east wind and turned the sea-bed into dry land. The waters were torn apart, and the Israelites went through the sea on the dry ground, while the waters made a wall for them to right and to left. The Egyptians went in pursuit of them far into the sea, all Pharaoh's horse, his chariots, and his cavalry. In the morning watch the Lord looked down on the Egyptian army through the pillar of fire and cloud, and he threw them into a panic. He clogged their chariot wheels and made them lumber along heavily, so that the Egyptians said, 'It is the Lord fighting for Israel against Egypt; let us flee.' Then the Lord said to Moses, 'Stretch out your hand over the sea, and let the water flow back over the Egyptians, their chariots and their cavalry.' So Moses stretched out his hand over the sea, and at daybreak the water returned to its accustomed place; The water flowed back and covered all Pharaoh's army, the chariots and the cavalry, which had pressed the pursuit into the sea. Not one man was left alive. Meanwhile the Israelites had passed along the dry ground through the sea, with the water making a wall for them to right and to left. When Isreal saw the great power which the Lord had put forth against Egypt, all the people feared the Lord, and they put their faith in him and in Moses his servant.

(2)

Moses led Israel from the red sea out into the wilderness of Shur. For three days they travelled through the wilderness without finding water. They came to Marah, but could not drink the Marah water because it was bitter; The people complained to Moses and asked, 'What are we to drink?' Moses cried to the Lord, and the Lord showed him a log which he threw into the water, and then the water became sweet.

They came to Elim, where there were twelve springs and seventy palm-trees, and there they encamped beside the water.

The whole community of the Israelites set out from Elim

然後摩西向海面上伸出手，天主的神力使整夜刮起強勁的東風把海水吹開，使大海中出現一塊乾地。海水向兩旁分開，以色列人就從海中露出的乾地穿行過去，海水在他們的左右像兩堵高牆。埃及人緊緊尾隨以色列人，法老的全部馬匹、戰車和騎兵也都追入海裏。到了晨更時分，耶和華透過雲火柱裏看那埃及的軍隊，他使埃及人陷於慌亂，使他們的戰車車輪脫落，難於前行。埃及人都說：“天主為以色列人打埃及人，我們快逃命吧！”這時，天主對摩西說：“你向海水伸出手，讓水流回來淹沒埃及人和他們的戰車、騎兵。”摩西就向大海伸出手，天亮時，海水都流回原處；海水淹沒了法老派來緊追到海裏的軍隊、戰車和騎兵。沒有一個人活下來。而這時以色列人都已從海水形成的左右兩堵牆之間的海底乾地上穿過了那大海。當以色列人目睹了天主在消滅埃及人時所顯出的巨大威力，所有人都敬畏天主，對他和他的僕人摩西都信服了。

(二)

摩西帶領以色列人從紅海走到書珥的曠野。在曠野裏走了三天都找不到水。到了瑪拉，那兒的水苦也不能喝；大家都向摩西抱怨道：“我們喝甚麼呢？”摩西向天主呼求，天主使他看到一株樹，他把這樹木扔在水中，水就變甜了。

（後來）他們來到以琳，那裏有十二股泉水，七十棵棕櫚。以色列人就在泉水旁安下營寨。

這些以色列人從以琳去到了以琳和西乃中間一個叫汛的曠

and came into the wilderness of Sin, which lies between Elim and Sinai. The Israelites complained to Moses and Aaron in the wilderness and said, 'If only we had died at the Lord's hand in Egypt, where we sat round the fleshpots and had plenty of bread to eat! But you have brought us out into this wilderness to let this whole assembly starve to death.' The Lord said to Moses, 'I will rain down bread from heaven for you. Each day the people shall go out and gather a day's supply. But on the sixth day, when they prepare what they bring in, it shall be twice as much as they have gathered on other days.'

That evening a flock a quails flew in and settled all over the camp, and in the morning a fall of dew lay all around it. When the dew was gone, there in the wilderness, fine flakes appeared, fine as hoar-frost on the ground. Moses said to them, 'That is the bread which the Lord has given you to eat. This is the command the Lord has given: 'Each of you is to gather as much as he can eat: let every man take an omer a head for every person in his tent. No one may keep any of it till morning.' Some, however, did not listen to Moses; they kept part of it till morning, and it became full of maggots and stank. On the sixth day they gathered twice as much food, two omers each. All the chiefs of the community came and told Moses. 'This', he answered, 'is what the Lord has said: "Tomorrow is a day of sacred rest, a sabbath holy to the Lord." So bake what you want to bake now, and boil what you want to boil; put aside what remains over and keep it safe till morning.' So they put it aside till morning as Moses had commanded, and it did not stink, nor did maggots appear in it.

Israel called the food manna; it was white, like coriander seed, and it tasted like a wafer made with honey.

野裏。他們在荒野中向摩西和亞倫抱怨道：“要是我們在埃及時，已死在天主手裏就好了。在那兒我們還可以坐在肉鍋旁，有足夠的食物吃。可你們却把我們領到這樣的荒野裏，讓我們大夥兒餓死。”天主就對摩西說：“我會從天降食物給你們。你們可以每天出去得到一天的口糧。但是到第六天，他們做飯時會見到食物比前幾天拿回來的多了一倍。”

那天晚上，一羣鵪鶉飛來，落在營房上。次晨營地四圍下滿露水。當露水蒸發後，荒野裏地上出現了像白霜一樣的小薄片。摩西對以色列人說：“那就是天主給你們送來的食物。上帝命令說：‘你們每人只能拿自己需要的數量，每個男人可以替他帳篷裏的人每人取一俄梅珥食物。任何人都不要把食物留到第二天早晨。’”有些人却不聽摩西的話，把食物留到第二天早晨，結果全都生了蛆變臭。到第六日，他們得到了雙倍食物，每人兩俄梅珥。衆領頭人都來報告摩西，他回答說：“這是天主的旨意：‘明日是神聖的休息之日，是天主的聖安息日。’你們現在可以把要烤的烤好，要煮的煮熟，然後把剩下的食物放在一邊，保存好到明天早晨。”他們就照摩西的吩咐把食物留到第二天早上，吃的東西一點也不臭，也沒長蛆虫。

以色列人叫這食物做嗎哪，它是白色的，像芫荽子，吃起來味道似攙了蜜的薄餅。

25 The Ten Commandments

Exodus

In the third month after Israel had left Egypt, they came to the wilderness of Sinai, where they encamped, pitching their tents opposite the mountain. Moses went up the mountain of God, and the Lord called to him from the mountain and said, 'Speak thus to the house of Jacob, and tell this to the sons of Israrl: You have seen with your own eyes what I did to Egypt, and how I have carried you on eagles' wings and brought you here to me. If only you will now listen to me and keep my covenant, then out of all peoples you shall become my special possession. There are the words you shall speak to the Israelites.'

Moses came and summoned the elders of the people and set before them all these commands which the Lord had laid upon him. The people all answered together, 'Whatever the Lord has said we will do.' Moses brought this answer back to the Lord. The Lord said to Moses, 'I am now coming to you in a thick cloud, so that I may speak to you in the hearing of the people, and their faith in you may never fail. Go to the people and hallow them today and tomorrow and make them wash their clothes. They must be ready by the third day, because on the third day the Lord will descend upon Mount Sinai in the sight of all the people. You must put barriers round the mountain and say, "Take care not to go up the mountain or even to touch the edge of it." Any man who touches the mountain must be put to death. But when the ram's horn sounds, they may go up the mountain.'

二十五　主論十誡

　　以色列人出埃及後第三個月，他們來到了西乃的曠野。在那兒他們安下營寨，帳篷對着山。摩西登上了天主的山，天主從山上向他召喚，對他說：“你要這樣對雅各的後代和以色列的子孫講：你們都親眼見到我對埃及所做的事，看見我如何讓你們乘上鷹的翅膀把你們帶到這裏我的面前。只要你們聽從我的話，遵守對我的誓約，那末在萬民中你們將成爲我最愛的子民。這就是你要去對他們說的話。”

　　摩西回來召集了各族長老，把天主囑他說的話講給他們聽。這些人都同聲回答：“天主怎麼說我們就怎麼辦。”摩西把他們的話帶回給天主，天主對摩西說：“我將在密雲中降臨到你們那裏，這樣我同你說話時，人們就可以聽到，他們對你就永信不疑了。回到你的人民那兒，叫他們今天和明天先把衣服洗乾淨，第三天前都要準備好，因爲第三天天主要在衆人眼前降到西乃山上。你要在山的四周設置界限，並告訴大家：‘當心不要上山去，也不要靠近山邊。’任何闖進山的人必須處死。但到羊角吹响時，他們就可以上山來了。”

Moses brought the people out from the camp to meet God, and they took their stand at the foot of the mountain. Mount Sinai was all smoking because the Lord had come down upon it in fire; the smoke went up like the smoke of a kiln; all the people were terrified, and the sound of the trumpet grew ever louder. Whenever Moses spoke, God answered him in a peal of thunder.

God spoke, and these were his words:

I am the Lord your God who brought you out of Egypt, out of the land of slavery.

You shall have no other god to set against me.

You shall not make a carved image for yourself nor the likeness of anything in the heavens above, or on the earth below, or in the waters under the earth.

You shall not bow down to them or worship them; for I, the Lord your God, am a jealous god. I punish the children for the sins of the fathers to the third and fourth generations of those who hate me. But I keep faith with thousands, with those who love me and keep my commandments.

You shall not make wrong use of the name of the Lord your God: the Lord will not leave unpunished the man who misuses his name.

Remember to keep the sabbath day holy. You have six days to labour and do all your work. But the seventh day is a sabbath of the Lord your God; that day you shall not do any work, you, your son or your daughter, your slave or your slave-girl, your cattle or the alien within your gates; for in six days the Lord made heaven and earth, the sea, and all that is in them, and on the seventh day he rested. Therefore the Lord blessed the sabbath day and declared it holy.

Honour your father and your mother, that you may live long in the land which the Lord your God is giving you.

Yor shall not commit murder.

You shall not commit adultery.

摩西把人們帶出營寨去見天主，他們在山腳下站好。西乃山煙霧繚繞，因為天主在火中降臨到山上，煙霧上升，像燒窰一樣；人們都害怕起來，號角聲也異常响亮。摩西說話時，天主用雷鳴般的聲音回答。

天主說話了，下面就是他的十誡：

我是你們的上帝天主，是我把你們帶出埃及，帶出那奴役你們的地方。

你們不可信別的神來反對我。

你們不可擅自雕刻偶像，也不可崇奉天上、地上或水下的任何東西。

你們不可向它們下拜，因為我，你們的上帝天主是個不容別的神的上帝。恨我的人，我必向他問罪，直到三、四代子孫。但對那些愛我、守我誡命的人，我一定信守諾言直至萬世。

你們不得濫用你們的上帝天主的名字，對那些妄用他的名義的人，天主必定拿他問罪。

記住要奉行聖安息日。你們用六天去幹活，做好你們的工作，但第七天是你們上帝天主的安息日，這天你們不要工作。你和你們的兒女，你們的婢僕、你們的牲畜或寄居於你們家中的外人都不要工作，因為天主在六天裏造就了天地和海洋，以及天地間的萬物，第七天他就休息了。因此天主賜福安息日，宣佈它為聖日。

你們要尊父敬母，這樣你們才會在天主上帝賜予的土地上長久生活下去。

你們不可殺人。

你們不可通姦。

You shall not steal.

You shall not give false evidence against your neighbour.

You shall not covet your neighbour's house; you shall not covet your neighbour's wife, his slave, his slave-girl, his ox, his ass, or anything that belongs to him.

When all the people saw how it thundered and the lightning flashed, when they heard the trumpet sound and saw the mountain smoking, they trembled and stood at a distance. 'Speak to us yourself,' they said to Moses, 'and we will listen; but if God speaks to us we shall die.' So the people stood at a distance, while Moses approached the dark cloud where God was.

你們不得偷盜。

你們不得作假見證陷害鄰人。

你們不許貪圖別人的房屋、或貪圖別人的妻子、奴婢、牛、驢或他擁有的東西。

當眾人都看到了雷擊電閃，聽到了號角的聲音，並看到山上的煙霧時，他們都渾身發抖，站得遠遠的。他們對摩西說：“由你同我們講吧，我們都會聽從的。如果由上帝對我們說話，我們就會死去的。”於是人們都站得遠遠的，摩西則站到靠近上帝所在的有烏雲的地方。

Joshua

After the death of Moses the servant of the Lord, the Lord said to Joshua son of Nun, his assistant, 'My servant Moses is dead; now it is for you to cross the Jordan, you and this whole people of Israel, to the land which I am giving them. Be strong, be resolute; it is you who are to put this people in possession of the land which I swore to give to their fathers.'

Joshua son of Nun sent two spies out from Shittim secretly with orders to reconnoitre the country. The two men came to Jericho and went to the house of a prostitute named Rahab, and spent the night there. It was reported to the king of Jericho that some Israelites had arrived that night to explore the country. So the king sent to Rahab and said, 'Bring out the men who have come to you and are now in your house; they are here to explore the whole country.' The woman replies, 'Yes, the men did come to me, but I did not know where they came from; and when it was time to shut the gate at nightfall, they had gone. I do not know where they were going, but if you hurry after them, you will catch them up.' In fact, she had taken them up on to the roof and concealed them among the stalks of flax which she had laid out there in rows. The messengers went in pursuit of them down the road to the fords of the Jordan, and the gate was closed as soon as they had gone out. The men had not yet settled down, when Rahab came up to them on the roof and said to them, 'I know that the Lord has given this land to you. Swear to me now by the Lord that you will keep faith with my family, as I have kept faith

二十六　取耶利哥

約書亞紀

　　天主的僕人摩西去世後，天主對摩西的助手、嫩的兒子約書亞說：“我的僕人摩西死了，現在由你帶領以色列的全體人民渡約旦河，到我賜予他們的地方去。你應當剛強、堅定，你的責任就是把這些人民引到我向他們列祖立誓要給他們的那塊土地上去。”

　　嫩的兒子約書亞從什亭暗地派出了兩名探子去窺探那地方的情況。兩人來到耶利哥，在一個名叫喇合的妓女家中過夜。有人就報告給耶利哥的國王，說夜裏來了以色列人窺探虛實。於是國王派人去找喇合說：“把到你這兒來的人交出來，他們現在還在你家中，他們是來剌探我們的情況的。”這女人回答說：“是的，他們是來過我這裏，但我不知道他們的來歷。而且在天要入黑城門沒關前他們就走了。我也不知他們到什麼地方去。但如果你們趕快去追，你們還能追上的。”實際上，她已把他們弄到房頂上，藏在堆放在那兒的成排的蔴稭捆裏。來人趕忙沿路向約旦河的渡口追去。他們剛一出城，城門就關了。兩個以色列人還沒有安心下來，喇合上屋頂對他們說：“我知道天主已把這塊土地給了你們。現在既然我恩待了你們，那你們得以天主的名義向我發誓將來也要恩待我全家。”

with you.' The men replied, 'Our lives for yours, so long as you do not betray our business. When the Lord gives us the country, we will deal honestly and faithfully by you.' She then let them down through an opening by a rope; for the house where she lived was on an angle of the wall. 'Take to the hills,' she said, 'or the pursuers will come upon you. Hide yourselves there for three days until they come back, and then go on your way.' 'When we enter the land,' they said, 'you must fasten this strand of scarlet cord in the opening through which you have lowered us, and get everybody together here in the house, your father and mother, your brothers and all your family. If anybody goes out of doors into the street, his blood shall be on his own head; we shall be quit of the oath.' The men made their way into the hills and stayed there three days until the pursuers returned. The two men then turned and came down from the hills, crossed the river and returned to Joshua son of Nun. They told him all that had happened to them.

Joshua rose early in the morning, and he and all the Israelites set out from Shittim and came to the Jordan, where they encamped before crossing the river. At the end of three days the officers passed through the camp, and gave this order to the people: 'When you see the Ark of the Covenant of the Lord your God being carried forward by the levitical priests, then you too shall leave your positions and set out.'

So the people set out from their tents to cross the Jordan, with the priests in front of them carrying the Ark of the Covenant. Now the Jordan is in full flood in all its reaches throughout the time of harvest. When the priests reached the Jordan and dipped their feet in the water at the edge, the water coming down from upstream was brought to a standstill; it piled up like a bank for a long way back, as far as Adam, a town near Zarethan. The waters coming down to the Sea of the Arabah, the Dead Sea, were completely cut off, and the people crossed over opposite Jericho.

Jericho was bolted and barred against the Israelites; no one

這兩人回答說：“只要你不告發我們的事，我們用自己的性命擔保，當天主把這國家交給我們時，我們一定會好好待你一家。”於是她把他們用的繩子從房子上一個豁口縋下城外去，因她住的房子在城牆角上。“往山裏跑吧，”她說，“不然追趕的人會碰上你們。在山裏躲三天，直到他們回城後，你們才可以走。”“當我們攻進來時，”這兩人說，“你必須把這條紅繩紮在你縋我們下來的豁口上，把你的父母兄弟姐妹全家人都聚集到你這兒。如果他們有人擅自跑到外面街上去，那他就自招被殺了，我們是不受這許諾約束的。”兩人逃到山裏躲了三天，直到追捕者返回耶利哥。這兩人便回頭下山，渡河回到嫩的兒子約書亞那裏。他們向他報告了看到的情況。

約書亞第二天早上很早起來。他帶上了全體以色列人從什亭向納旦進發。在約旦河邊他們停下來安營準備渡河。三天過去了，那些頭人到了帳篷傳令：“當你們看見你們的天主上帝的約櫃由利未人祭司抬着向前走時，你們就開拔出發，跟着前行。”

於是人們離開帳篷出發，渡約旦河，前面走的是抬着約櫃的祭司。約旦河流域在這收穫時節一直漲水。當祭司們到達河邊，脚一踏進岸邊河水，從上游下來的流水立即停住，水在原地堆成堤岸形狀，一直延到撒拉但附近的亞當城。那向亞拉巴海即死海流出去的水則被完全切斷。這樣人們就可以走過去，到達對岸的耶利哥。

爲了防以色列人，耶利哥城門關得緊緊的，沒有人出，也

went out, no one came in. So Joshua son of Nun summoned the priests and gave them their orders: 'Take up the Ark of the Covenant; let seven priests with seven trumpets of ram's horn go in front of the Ark of the Lord.' Then he said to the army, 'March on and make the circuit of the city, and let the men drafted from the two and a half tribes go in front of the Ark of the Lord.' Thus he caused the Ark of the Lord to go round the city, making the circuit of it once, and then they went back to the camp and spent the night there. They marched round the city once on the second day and returned to the camp; this they did for six days. But on the seventh day they rose at dawn and marched seven times round the city in the same way; that was the only day on which they marched round seven times. The seventh time the priests blew the trumpets and Joshua said to the army, 'Shout! The Lord has given you the city. The city shall be under solemn ban: everything in it belongs to the Lord. No one is to be spared except the prostitute Rahab and everyone who is with her in the house, because she hid the men whom we sent. You must take none of it for yourselves; this would put the Israelite camp itself under the ban and bring trouble on it.' So they blew the trumpets, and when the army heard the trumpet sound, they raised a great shout, and down fell the walls. The army advanced on the city, every man straight ahead, and took it. Under the ban they destroyed everything in the city; they put everyone to the sword, men and women, young and old, and also cattle, sheep, and asses.

But the two men who had been sent out as spies were told by Joshua to go into the porstitute's house and bring out her and all who belonged to her, as they had sworn to do.

沒有人入。於是，嫩的兒子約書亞召來了祭司，命令他們：
"抬上主的約櫃，叫七個祭司吹着七支羊角號，走在天主的約
櫃前面。"然後他對軍隊發命令："向前進，把城市包圍起來，
並讓那些從兩個半部族選拔出來的兵走在約櫃前面。"這樣他
讓天主的約櫃繞城一周，然後他們就回到營地，在那兒過夜。
第二天他們又繞城走了一圈後回到營地。這樣連續做了六天。
但到第七日，他們黎明一早起來，跟以前一樣繞城走了七圈，
這是他們唯一的繞城走七次的一天。在第七次祭司吹响喇叭
時，約書亞就對軍隊說："喊吧！天主把城給你們了，這城已
處於神聖禁令之下：城中的一切都屬於天主的。全城的人都要
殺掉，但妓女喇合以及在她屋裏所有的人除外，因爲她掩護過
我們派去的人。你們不得自取任何財物，這樣做將置以色列全
營於上帝懲罰之下，並給它帶來災禍。"

於是，他們吹响了號角，當軍隊聽見號角聲時就齊聲大
喊，城牆應聲坍塌下來。軍隊進入城內，人人奮力前衝占領了
這座城。按禁令他們摧毀了城中的一切，殺死城裏的每一個
人，男女老幼，牛羊和驢馬無一倖免。

約書亞吩咐兩個派去做探子的人到那妓女家，把她和她家
人帶了出來，實現了他們的許諾。

27 Victory at Ai

Joshua

Joshua sent men from Jericho with orders to go up to Ai, near Beth-aven, east of Bethel, and see how the land lay. They returned to Joshua and reported that there was no need for the whole army to move. And so about three thousand men went up, but they turned tail before the men of Ai, who killed some thirty-six of them; they chased them all the way from the gate to the Quarries and killed them on the pass. At this the courage of the people melted and flowed away like water. Joshua and the elders of Israel rent their clothes and flung themselves face downwards to the ground; they lay before the Ark of the Lord till evening and threw dust on their heads. Joshua said, 'Alas, O Lord God, why didst thou bring this people across the Jordan only to hand us over to the Amorites to be destroyed?'

The Lord said to Joshua, 'Stand up; why lie prostrate on your face? Israel has sinned: they have broken the covenant which I laid upon them, by taking forbidden things for themselves. In the morning come forward tribe by tribe, and the tribe which the Lord chooses shall come forward clan by clan; the clan which the Lord chooses shall come forward family by family; and the family which the Lord chooses shall come forward man by man. The man who is chosen as the harbourer of forbidden things shall be burnt, he and all that is his, because he has broken the covenant of the Lord and committed outrage in Israel.' Early in the morning Joshua rose...., Achan son of Carmi, of the tribe of Judah, was chosen. Then Joshua

二十七　艾城之役

約書亞記

　　約書亞派人從耶利哥去伯特利東部靠近伯亞文的艾城，去窺探那裏地形。去的人回來報告約書亞說，用不着出動大軍。這樣，就派了大約三千人去，但他們在艾城人面前却敗退回來，三十六人被殺，艾城人一路追殺，從城門追到可利斯，把他們殺死在路上。見此情景，以色列人的勇氣像水一樣全都消退了。約書亞和以色列的長老們憤怒地撕裂了衣服，他們俯伏在天主的約櫃前的地上一直到晚上，並往自己的頭上撒灰土。約書亞說："天哪，天主上帝，你把人民帶過約旦河，難道就是要讓我們給亞摩利人殺戮嗎？"

　　天主對約書亞說："起來吧，你爲什麼這樣俯伏在地呢？以色列人犯了罪，他們違背了我給他們立的約言，把不該拿的東西據爲己有。明天早上，你們要按着部落一個個走出來，天主挑出的部落要按氏族一個個走出來；天主挑出的氏族要按家庭一個個走出來；天主挑出的家庭則按一個個人走出來。那被挑出來的人就是偷取禁物的人，他和他的一切都要被燒毀。因爲他違背了天主立的約，在以色列人中違法亂紀。"第二天一早，約書亞起來，（按天主所說的，）找出那人就是猶大部落

said to Achan, 'My son, give honour to the Lord the God of Israel and make your confession to him: tell me what you have done, hide nothing from me.' Achan answered Joshua, 'I confess, I have sinned against the Lord the God of Israel. This is what I did: among the booty I caught sight of a fine mantle from Shinar, two hundred shekels of silver, and a bar of gold weighing fifty shekels. I coveted them and I took them. You will find them hidden in the ground inside my tent, with the silver under-nearth.' Then Joshua took Achan with the silver, the mantle, and the bar of gold, together with his sons and daughters, his oxen, his asses, and his sheep, his tent, and everything he had, and he and all Israel brought them up to the Vale of Achor. Then all the Israelites stoned him to death. So the Lord's anger was abated.

The Lord said to Joshua, 'Do not be fearful or dismayed; take the whole army and attack Ai. I deliver the king of Ai into your hands, him and his people, his city and his country.

Early in the morning Joshua rose, mustered the army and marched against Ai, he himself and the elders of Israel at its head. When the king of Ai saw them, he and the citizens rose with all speed that morning and marched out to do battle against Israel; he did not know that there was an ambush set for him to the west of the city. Joshua and all the Israelites made as if they were routed by them and fled towards the wilderness, and all the people in the city were called out in pursuit.

Then the Lord said to Joshua, 'Point towards Ai with the dagger you are holding, for I will deliver the city into your hands.' So Joshua pointed with his dagger towards Ai. At his signal, the men in ambush rose quickly from their places and, entering the city at a run, took it and promptly set fire to it. The men of Ai looked back and saw the smoke from the city already going up to the sky; they were powerless to make their escape in any direction, and the Israelites who had feigned flight towards the wilderness turned on their pursuers. Those who had come out to meet the Israelites were

的迦米之子亞干。於是約書亞對亞干說："我的孩子，以色列人的天主上帝在上，你向他坦白罪行吧：告訴我你都幹了些什麼事了？別再隱瞞了。"亞干回答約書亞："我坦白，我做了得罪以色列的天主上帝的事。那就是：在戰利品中我看上一件很好的示拿袍子，兩百舍客勒銀子，和一塊重五十舍客勒的金子，我貪心就拿起來。你們在我的帳篷裏地下可以找到它們，銀子藏在最底下。"約書亞和以色列人就把亞干，連同那些銀子、衣服、金條、以及他的兒女、牛、驢、羊、他的帳篷和一切財物都帶到亞割谷裏。然後，以色列人用亂石把他打死。這樣上帝的怒氣才平息了。

上帝對約書亞說："你不必害怕和沮喪，你要率領全體人馬去進攻艾城。我會把艾城的王君、他的百姓、他的城池和國土都送到你手中。"

第二天清晨，約書亞起來，集合起人馬，向艾城進軍，他自己同以色列的長老們行在隊伍前面。艾城的國王見他們來了，他和他的人民一早迅速起來出城迎戰以色列人；他不知道在城西邊已有埋伏。約書亞和以色列人裝做被擊潰，落荒而逃，城裏的人都被召喚出來去追擊。

上帝這時對約書亞說："把你手中的短劍指向艾城罷，我就要把它交到你手中了。"於是約書亞用他的短劍指向艾城。見到這個信號，他的伏兵迅速從藏身處躍起，跑步攻入城中，並放火燒城。艾城人回頭一看，見城裏黑煙衝天而起；他們已無力往哪裏逃跑了。而假裝落荒逃走的以色列人這時就回過頭來向追他們的艾城人殺來。那些出城來迎戰以色列的艾城人現

now hemmed in with Israelites on both sides of them, and the Israelites cut them down until there was not a single survivor, nor had any escaped. The king of Ai was taken alive and brought to Joshua. The number who were killed that day, men and women, was twelve thousand, the whole population of Ai. Joshua hanged the king of Ai on a tree and left him there till sunset.

在腹背受敵，以色列人把他們殺得沒有一個可以幸存或逃掉的。艾城王被活捉，押到約書亞面前。

那天被殺死的男女數達一萬二千人，全部艾城人都殺絕了。約書亞把艾城國王吊死在一棵樹上，並曝屍直到日落。

28   The Stratagem of the Gibeonites

Joshua

When the inhabitants of Gibeon heard how Joshua had dealt with Jericho and Ai, they adopted a ruse of their own. They went and disguised themselves, with old sacking for their asses, old wine-skins split and mended, old and patched sandals for their feet, old clothing to wear, and by way of provisions nothing but dry and mouldy bread. They came to Joshua in the camp at Gilgal and said to him and the Israelites, 'We have come from a distant country to ask you now to grant us a treaty.' The Israelites said to the Hivites, 'But maybe you live in our neighbourhood: if so, how can we grant you a treaty?' They said to Joshua, 'We are your slaves.' Joshua asked them who they were and where they came from. 'Sir,' they replied, 'our country is very far away, and we have come because of the renown of the Lord your God. We have heard of his fame, of all that he did to Egypt, and to the two Amorite kings east of the Jordan. Our elders and all the people of our country told us to take provisions for the journey and come to meet you, and say, "We are your slaves; please grant us a treaty." Look at our bread; it was hot from the oven when we packed it at home on the day we came away. Now it is dry and mouldy. Look at the wine-skins; they were new when we filled them, and now they are all split; look at our clothes and our sandals, worn out by the long journey.' The chief men of the community accepted some of their provisions and did not at first seek guidance from the Lord. So Joshua received them peaceably and granted them a treaty,

二十八　妙計求和

約書亞記

　　當基遍的居民聽到約書亞如何對付耶利哥和艾城時，他們就想出一個詭計。他們化裝去見約書亞：驢子駄着的是舊麻袋，羊皮酒囊是補過的，他們自己則脚穿補釘鞋，衣衫襤褸，至於口糧，就只帶着發霉的麵包乾。他們來到吉甲營見約書亞，對他和以色列人說：“我們遠道而來，想請求你們與我們簽定協約。”以色列人對這些希未人說：“也許你們就住在我們附近，如果是這樣，我們怎麼能同你們簽約呢？”希未人對約書亞說：“我們是你的奴僕。”約書亞問他們是什麼人，從哪兒來。他們說：“先生，我們的國家離這裏很遠，我們來這裏是因爲久聞你們天主上帝的盛名。我們聽到了他的威名，他對埃及和約旦河東兩個亞摩利王所行的事。我們的長老們和全國人民讓我們帶上口糧上路來見你們，對你們說：‘我們是你們的奴隸，請與我們簽定協約。’看看我們的麵包吧，我們離家那天才出爐的，現在已經發乾變霉；看看我們的羊皮酒囊吧，我們裝酒時還是新的，現在都破裂了；再看看我們的衣服和鞋子吧，因爲長途跋涉全都穿破了。”以色列人的頭領們聽了這些話，就收取了他們一些糧食，也沒有先問一下天主的意旨。這樣約書亞以禮對待他們，與他們簽了協約，保證饒他們

promising to spare their lives, and the chiefs pledged their faith to them on oath.

Within three days of granting them the treaty, the Israelites learnt that they were in fact neighbours and lived near by. So the Israelites set out and on the third day they reached their cities; these were Gibeon, Kephirah, Beeroth, and Kiriath-jearim. The Israelites did not slaughter them, because of the oath which the chief men of the community had sworn to them by the Lord the God of Israel, but the people were all indignant with their chiefs. Joshua summoned the Gibeonites and said, 'Why did you play this trick on us? You told us that you live a long way off, when you are near neighbours. There is a curse upon you for this: for all time you shall provide us with slaves, to chop wood and draw water for the house of my God.'

的性命。那些頭領們也發誓要善待他們。

立約後不到三天，以色列人發現希未人事實上只是近隣，就住在附近。於是以色列人就出發，第三天到達希未人的城市，就是基遍、基非拉、比錄、基列耶琳。因為族中頭領已向希未人指以色列的天主上帝為誓，所以沒有殺戮他們，但以色列人民卻對頭領們的做法都很惱火。約書亞召基遍人來對他們說：“為什麼你們對我們要這個花招兒？你們說你們住得很遠，實際上你們卻是我們的近隣。為此你們要受到天罰：你們要永遠當我們的奴隸，為我們上帝的聖殿砍柴打水。”

29   *Victory Over The Five Kings*

Joshua

When Adoni-zedek king of Jerusalem heard that Joshua had captured Ai and destroyed it, and that the inhabitants of Gibeon had made their peace with Israel and were living among them, he was greatly alarmed; for Gibeon was a large place, like a royal city: it was larger than Ai, and its men were all good fighters. So Adoni-zedek king of Jerusalem sent to Hoham king of Hebron, Piram king of Jarmuth, Japhia king of Lachish, and Debir king of Eglon, and said, 'Come up and help me, and we will attack the Gibeonites, because they have made their peace with Joshua and the Israelites.' So the five Amorite kings, joined forces and advanced to take up their positions for the attack on Gibeon. But the men of Gibeon sent this message to Joshua in the camp at Gilgal: 'We are your slaves, do not abandon us, come quickly to our relief. All the Amorite kings in the hill-country have joined forces against us; come and help us.' So Joshua went up from Gilgal with all his forces and all his fighting men. The Lord said to Joshua, 'Do not be afraid of them; I have delivered them into your hands, and not a man will be able to stand against you.' Joshua came upon them suddenly, after marching all night from Gilgal. The Lord threw them into confusion before the Israelites, and Joshua defeated them utterly in Gibeon. As they were fleeing from Israel down the pass, the Lord hurled great hailstones at them out of the sky all the way to Azekah: more died from the hailstones than the Israelites slew by the sword.

二十九　五王覆滅

約書亞記

　　耶路撒冷王亞多尼洗德聽到約書亞攻佔了艾城，並毀滅了它，而且基遍人已同以色列人媾和，在以色列人中間生活；這使他感到十分不安。因爲基遍是個大地方，像座王城，它比艾城大，而且它的人民都英勇善戰。於是，耶路撒冷的亞多尼洗德國王就派人去見希伯侖王何咸、耶末王毘蘭、拉吉王雅非亞和伊磯倫王底壁，對他們說："請都來帮我吧，我們一起去進攻基遍人，因爲他們跟約書亞和以色列人締了和約。"於是，五位亞摩利王聯合起他們的軍隊，擺開陣勢去攻打基遍。但基遍人通知吉甲營中的約書亞，說："我們是你們的奴隸，不要拋棄我們，快給我們援手。山地裏的亞摩利王已聯合起來向我們進攻，快來帮我們罷。"約書亞就從吉甲帶他的軍隊兵勇前去營救。上帝對約書亞說："你不必怕他們；我已把他們交到你的手中，沒有任何人能抵擋你的。"約書亞的人連夜從吉甲急行軍，突然降臨到敵人面前。天主使亞摩利人在以色列人面前陷於一片混亂。約書亞在基遍把他們徹底擊潰。亞摩利的軍隊從以色列人陣前向坡路逃跑時，天主從天降下大粒冰雹，在逃往亞西加的路上，他們被冰雹打死的人比死於以色列人刀下的還要多。

On that day when the Lord delivered the Amorites into the hands of Israel, Joshua spoke with the Lord, and he said in the presence of Israel:

Stand still, O Sun, in Gibeon;
stand , Moon, in the Vale of Aijalon.

So the sun stood still and the moon halted until a nation had taken vengeance on its enemies, as indeed is written in the Book of Jashar. The sun stayed in mid heaven and made no haste to set for almost a whole day. Never before or since has there been such a day as this day on which the Lord listened to the voice of a man; for the Lord fought for Israel. So Joshua and all the Israelites returned to the camp at Gilgal.

The five kings fled and hid themselves in a cave at Makkedah, and Joshua was told that they had been found hidden in this cave. Joshua replied, 'Roll some great stones to the mouth of the cave and post men there to keep watch over the kings. But you must not stay; keep up the pursuit, attack your enemies from the rear and do not let them reach their cities; the Lord your God has delivered them into your hands.' When Joshua and the Israelites had finished the work of slaughter and all had been put to the sword — except a few survivors who escaped and entered the fortified cities — the whole army rejoined Joshua at Makkedah in peace; not a man of the Israelites suffered so much as a scratch on his tongue. Then Joshua said, 'Open the mouth of the cave, and bring me out those five kings.' They did so; they brought the five kings out of the cave, the kings of Jerusalem, Hebron, Jarmuth, Lachish, and Eglon. When they had brought them to Joshua, he summoned all the Israelites and said to the commanders of the troops who had served with him, 'Come forward and put your feet on the necks of these kings.' So they came forward and put their feet on their necks. Joshua said to them, 'Do not be fearful or dismayed; be strong and resolute; for the Lord will do this to every enemy you fight against.' And he struck down the kings and slew them; then he hung their bodies on five trees, where they remained hanging till evening. At sunset, on Joshua's orders they took them down from the trees

就在天主把亞摩利人交到以色列人手中的那一天，約書亞向天主禱告，他當着以色列人說："太陽啊，你停在基遍吧；月亮啊，你止在亞雅命谷吧。"於是，太陽就眞的不動，月亮就眞的靜止，直到這個國家對敵人報復完爲止。就像雅煞珥書上寫的那樣，太陽在天空當中停住，遲遲不西下，有一整天之久。這是空前絕後的一個日子，在這天，天主聽了一個人的禱告，天主爲以色列而戰。這之後，約書亞和以色列人都回到了吉甲營地。

五位國王逃跑到瑪基大藏在一個山洞裏。約書亞聽說他們藏身在那山洞裏，就說："推一些大石頭堵住洞口，派人去看守住他們。但你們也不停留，要繼續追擊，從後攻擊敵人，不要讓他們回到城裏。你們的天主上帝，已把他們交在你們手裏。"當約書亞和以色列人結束他們的屠殺時，除了有幾個人僥倖逃回設了防的城裏外，一切都給以色列人殺個乾淨了。然後以色列的人馬安然回到瑪基大和約書亞滙合。沒有一個以色列人受到什麼損傷。約書亞下令："打開那洞口，把那五個國王帶到我這裏來。"人們照辦了，把五位國王——耶路撒冷王、希伯侖王、耶末王、拉吉王和伊磯倫王——押出洞來。他們被帶到約書亞面前時，他召集全體以色列人，對爲他効勞的軍隊頭領們說："上前用腳踏在這些君王的脖子上。"他們就走出來把腳踩在他們脖子上。約書亞說："不要害怕和沮喪，要剛強堅定，因爲天主對你們攻打的每個敵人都會這樣做。"隨後，他把五個國王擊倒殺死，然後他把他們的屍體掛在五棵樹上，一直吊到入黑。日落後，約書亞命令把屍體從樹上放下

and threw them into the cave in which they had hidden; they piled great stones against its mouth, and there the stones are to this day.

來扔進他們躲藏過的山洞裏。在洞口再堆上大石頭，那些石頭一直保留到現在。

Judges

There was a man from Zorah of the tribe of Dan whose name was Manoah and whose wife was barren and childless. The angel of the Lord appeared to her and said, 'you will conceive and give birth to a son, and no razor shall touch his head, for the boy is to be a Nazirite consecrated to God from the day of his birth. He will strike the first blow to deliver Israel from the power of the Philistines.' The woman gave birth to a son and named him Samson....

Samson went down to Timnath, and there he saw a woman, one of the Philistines. When he came back, he told his father and mother that he had seen a Philistine woman in Timnath and asked them to get her for him as his wife. His father and mother did not know that the Lord was at work in this, seeking an opportunity against the Philistines, who at that time were masters of Israel.

Samson went down to Timnath and, when he reached the vineyards there, a young lion came at him growling. The spirit of the Lord suddenly seized him and, having no weapon in his hand, he tore the lion in pieces as if it were a kid. After a time he went down again to take her to wife; he turned aside to look at the carcass of the lion, and he saw a swarm of bees in it, and honey. He scraped the honey into his hands and went on, eating as he went.

His father went down to see the woman, and Samson gave a feast there as the custom of young men was. When the people saw him, they brought thirty young men to be his

三十　力士參孫

士師記

　　從瑣拉來的但族人有個名叫瑪挪亞的。他的妻子不育，沒
有孩子。天主的使臣向她顯靈說："你會懷孕生下一子，但是
千萬不要給他剃頭，因爲這孩子一生下來就是獻身給上帝的拿
細耳人，他將開始爲把以色列人從非利士人統治中解救出來而
鬥爭。"

　　這女人後來生下一個男孩，取名參孫。參孫（長大後）去
亭拿，在那兒見到一個女子，一個非利士人。他回來後就告訴
了父母，說他在亭拿看見一個非利士女子，他要父母討她回來
做他妻子。他父母不知這是上帝的旨意，是想找這個機會去反
對當時奴役以色列人的非利士人。

　　參孫去亭拿，當他走到葡萄園時，一頭小獅子吼叫着向他
撲來。天主的神靈突然降到參孫身上，他手無寸鐵就把獅子撕
成碎片，好像它只是隻羊羔一樣。過了一段時間，他又到亭拿
去，要娶那女子爲妻，途中他轉入道旁去看看那獅子的屍體，
他發現一窩蜜蜂和一些蜜在那上面。他把蜜收集起來，用手捧
着一邊走一邊吃。……

　　（後來），他父親去看那女子，參孫還按當時年輕人的習
俗擺了宴席。當地人見了參孫，就派了三十個年輕人給他作

escort. Samson said to them, 'Let me ask you a riddle. If you can guess it during the seven days of the feast, I will give you thirty lengths of linen and thirty changes of clothing; but if you cannot guess the answer, then you shall give me thirty lengths of linen and thirty changes of clothing.' So he said to them:

> Out of the eater came something to eat;
>
> out of the strong came something sweet.

At the end of three days they had failed to guess the riddle. On the fourth day they said to Samson's wife, 'Coax your husband and make him tell you the riddle, or we shall burn you and your father's house.' So Samson's wife wept over him and said, 'You do not love me, you only hate me. You have asked my kinsfolk a riddle and you have not told it to me.' He said to her, 'I have not told it even to my father and mother; and am I to tell you?' But she wept over him every day, and on the seventh day, because she pestered him, he told her, and she told the riddle to her kinsfolk. So that same day the men of the city said to Samson before he entered the bridal chamber:

> What is sweeter than honey?
>
> What is stronger than a lion?

and he replied, 'If you had not ploughed with my heifer, you would not have found out my riddle.' Then the spirit of the Lord suddenly seized him. He went down to Ashkelon and there he killed thirty men, took their belts and gave their clothes to the men who had answered his riddle; but he was very angry and went off to his father's house. And Samson's wife was given in marriage to the friend who had been his groomsman.

After a while, during the time of wheat harvest, Samson went to visit his wife, taking a kid as a present for her. He said, 'I am going to my wife in our bridal chamber', but her father would not let him in. He said, 'I was sure that you hated her, so I gave her in marriage to your groomsman. Her young sister is better than she — take her instead.' But Samson said, 'This time I will settle my score with the Philistines; I will do

陪。參孫對他們說："我來出一個謎語，如果你們有人能在這七天擺宴席時間內猜對了，我就給他三十件襯衣和三十件外衣。但如果你們猜不出來，那就要給我三十件襯衣和三十件外衣。於是他就對他們說那謎語："從食者處得到可食物，從强者處得到甜食物。"三天過去了，那些人誰也猜不中答案。第四天，他們對參孫的妻子說："哄哄你丈夫，讓他告訴你謎底，否則我們就把你和你父親的房子燒了。……"參孫的妻子就向參孫哭泣說："你不愛我，你只是討厭我。你給我的親戚們出了一個謎語，但你沒給我謎底。"參孫說："我連父母都沒說，難道就告訴你嗎？"爲此她每天對他哭哭啼啼，到了第七天，因爲她糾纏不休，參孫就對她說了，她就把謎底告訴了那些親戚。因此，當天，那些城裏人在參孫要進新娘房間時對他說："有什麼比蜜還甜的呢？有什麼能比獅子更强壯的呢？"參孫說："如果你們不是利用了我的女人，你們就不可能找到謎底。"這時，天主之靈突然攫住他，他就到亞實基倫去，殺死了三十個非利士人，拿了他們的腰帶，把他們的衣裳給了那些答出謎底的人。他怒氣冲冲地走了，他回到了父親家裏。而他的妻子已被改嫁給了做他男儐相的那個朋友。

過了一段時間，到了收割時節，參孫去看他的妻子，帶了一頭羊羔送給她作爲禮物。他說："我要進新房去找我的妻子。"她父親却不讓他進去。他說："我以爲你恨她，所以我已把她許配給你的男儐相了。她的妹妹比她好，你就討她妹妹爲妻吧。"但參孫說："這次我是要來同非利士人算賬的。我

them some real harm.' So he went and caught three hundred jackals and got some torches; he tied the jackals tail to tail and fastened a torch between each pair of tails. He then set the torches alight and turned the jackals loose in the standing corn of the Philistines. He burnt up standing corn and stooks as well, vineyards and olive groves. The Philistines said, 'Who has done this?' They were told that it was Samson, because the Timnite, his father-in-law, had taken his wife and given her to his groomsman. So the Philistines came and burnt her and her father. Samson said, 'If you do things like this, I swear I will be revenged upon you before I have done.' He smote them hip and thigh with great slaughter; and after that he went down to live in a cave in the Rock of Etam.

The Philistines came up and pitched camp in Judah, and overran Lehi. The men of Judah said, 'Why have you attacked us?' They answered, 'We have come to take Samson prisoner and serve him as he served us.' So three thousand men from Judah went down to the cave in the Rock of Etam. They said to Samson, 'We have come down to bind you and hand you over to the Philistines.' So they bound him with two new ropes and brought him up from the cave in the Rock. He came to Lehi, and when they met him, the Philistines shouted in triumph; but the spirit of the Lord suddenly seized him, the ropes on his arms became like burnt tow and his bonds melted away. He found the jawbone of an ass, all raw, and picked it up and slew a thousand men.

Samson was judge over Israel for twenty years in the days of the Philistines.

要給他們點厲害看看。」他去捉了三百隻豺狗並拿了一些火把。他把每兩隻豺狗尾巴捆在一起，中間拴上一個火把。他點着了火把，把豺狗驅趕到非利士人的禾草堆裏。這樣就把一堆堆的禾捆莊稼，把葡萄園和橄欖樹都燒個精光。非利士人說：「這是誰幹的事？」他們聽說是參孫幹的，說因爲參孫不滿他的岳父（一個亭那人）把他的妻子許給了他的儐相。於是非利士人就把參孫的妻子和她父親燒死。參孫說：「你們這樣行事，我發誓一定要向你們報復。」他就動手殺戮那些人，砍得折腿斷腰的。完事之後他就離開那地方住到以坦一個岩洞裏。

非利士人來到猶大紮下營寨，並且擴展到利希。猶大的人說：「你們爲什麼侵犯我們？」他們回答說：「我們是來抓捕參孫的，要以其人之道還治其身。」於是三千猶大人去以坦岩洞。他們對參孫說：「我們來把你捆了交給非利士人。」他們就用兩根新繩子把他捆上，把他從岩洞裏帶出來。他到了利希，當非利士人看見參孫不禁勝利地大聲歡呼，但天主的神靈突然又降到參孫身上，捆着他臂膀的繩子變得像燒焦了的蔴一樣，散落下來，他看到有一片驢子的下巴骨，十分尖利，就拾起它來砍殺了成千個非利士人。……

在非利士人當權的時期，參孫做過以色列的士師二十年。

Judges

Samson fell in love with a woman named Delilah, who lived in the valley of Sorek. The lords of the Philistines went up country to see her and said, 'Coax him and find out what gives him his great strength, and how we can master him, bind him and so hold him captive; then we will each give you eleven hundred pieces of silver.' So Delilah said to Samson, 'Tell me what gives you your great strength, and how you can be bound and held captive.' Samson replied, 'If they bind me with seven fresh bowstrings not yet dry, then I shall become as weak as any other man.' So the lords of the Philistines brought her seven fresh bowstrings not yet dry, and she bound him with them. She had men already hidden in the inner room, and she cried, 'The Philistines are upon you, Samson!' But he snapped the bowstrings as a strand of tow snaps when it feels the fire, and his strength was not tamed. Delilah said to Samson, 'I see you have made a fool of me and told me lies. Tell me this time how you can be bound.' He said to her, 'If you bind me tightly with new ropes that have never been used, then I shall become as weak as any other man.' So Delilah took new ropes and bound him with them. Then she cried, 'The Philistines are upon you, Samson!', while the men waited hidden in the inner room. He snapped the ropes off his arms like pack-thread. Delilah said to him, 'You are still making a fool of me and have told me lies. Tell me: how can you be bound?' He said, 'Take the seven loose locks of my hair and weave them into the warp, and then drive them tight with

三十一　參孫復仇

士師記

　　（後來，）參孫愛上了一個住在梭烈谷叫大利拉的女子。非利士的幾個首領就到梭烈谷去見那女人，說："求求你哄哄他，問他的神力是從何而來的，我們怎樣才能制服他，捆住他，使他成爲我們的階下囚；事成之後，我們每人會給你一千一百舍客勒銀子。"於是大利拉對參孫說："告訴我什麼給你那麼大的力氣，怎樣才能把你捆住制服。"參孫答道："如果他們用七根未乾的新繩索把我捆上，我就會變得同常人一樣無力。"非利士的首領們就給她拿來了七根還未乾的新繩索，她用這繩把參孫捆起來。她事先又把非利士人藏在裏屋，這時她喊道："參孫，非利士人來抓你了！"但參孫一下子就掙斷了繩子，就像掙斷一束燒過的蔴綫一樣，他的力氣一點都沒減退。大利拉對參孫說："原來你耍弄我，對我說假話。這次你得告訴我怎樣才能捆住你。"他對她說："如果你用沒用過的新繩子把我捆緊，我就會變得和常人一樣無力。"大利拉就拿了新繩子把參孫捆上。然後他大叫："參孫，非利士人來抓你了！"當時裏屋也有非利士人潛伏着。參孫掙斷了繩索，就像扯斷包東西的繩子一樣。大利拉對他說："你還在耍弄我，又對我說假話。告訴我：怎樣才能把你捆住？"他說："把我頭上七綹頭髮，用緯綫編織起來，然後用織布機的橛子把它們拴

the beater; and I shall become as weak as any other man.' So she lulled him to sleep, and drove his hair tight with the beater, and cried, 'The Philistines are upon you, Samson!' He woke from sleep and pulled away the warp and the loom with it. She said to him, 'How can you say you love me when you do not confide in me? This is the third time you have made a fool of me and have not told me what gives you your great strength.' She so pestered him with these words day after day, pressing him hard and wearying him to death, that he told her his secret. 'No razor has touched my head,' he said, 'because I am a Nazirite, consecrated to God from the day of my birth. If my head were shaved, then my strength would leave me, and I should become as weak as any other man.' Delilah saw that he had told her his secret; so she sent to the lords of the Philistines and said, 'Come up at once, he has told me his secret.' So the lords of the Philistines came up and brought the money with them. She lulled him to sleep on her knees, summoned a man and he shaved the seven locks of his hair for her. She began to take him captive and his strength left him. Then she cried, 'The Philistines are upon you, Samson!' He woke from his sleep and said, 'I will go out as usual and shake myself'; he did not know that the Lord had left him. The Philistines seized him, gouged out his eyes and brought him down to Gaza. There they bound him with fetters of bronze, and he was set to grinding corn in the prison. But his hair, after it had been shaved, began to grow again.

The lords of the Philistines assembled together to offer a great sacrifice to their god Dagon and to rejoice before him. They said, 'Our god has delivered Samson our enemy into our hands.' When they grew merry, they said, 'Call Samson, and let him fight to make sport for us.' So they summoned Samson from prison and he made sport before them all. They stood him between the pillars, and Samson said to the boy who held his hand, 'Put me where I can feel the pillars which support the temple, so that I may lean against them.' The temple was full of men and women, and all the lords of the Philistines

緊，我就會變得和常人一樣無力。"於是她就把參孫哄得睡着了，照他說的把他的頭髮拴緊然後大喊："參孫，非利士人來抓你了！"他醒過來，把拴住的頭髮連同織布機一下扯脫開。大利拉對參孫說："你根本不相信我。這怎麼能說你愛我呢？這是你第三次耍弄我，不告訴我是什麼東西使你有神力的了。"她日夜用這種的話去糾纏他，催逼他，使他煩得要死，逼得他講出他的秘密。他說："我的頭從來沒有用剃刀剃過，因爲我自出娘胎就是獻身給上帝的拿細耳人。如果我的頭髮被剃掉，力氣也就沒了，我就同常人一樣無力。"大利拉一看他已說出了秘密，就派人告訴非利士首領們："趕快來吧，他已告訴我他的秘密了。"於是，非利士人的首領馬上來，並帶上答應給她的錢。大利拉使參孫枕着她的膝蓋睡着了，便找來一個人，把參孫頭上的七綹頭髮剃掉。這樣她抓他時，他就沒有力氣了。她大叫："參孫，非利士人來抓你了！"他醒過來，說："我要像平常那樣到外面伸展一下。"他不知道天主已離開了他，非利士人抓住他，摳掉他的雙眼，把他押到迦薩。在那兒他們用銅鐐銬鎖住他，讓他在監獄裏磨麵。但他的頭髮在剃過之後，又開始長出來了。

非利士的首領們聚在一起來對他們的神大袞舉行祭祀大禮，並在神前飲酒作樂。他們說："我們的神把敵人參孫交到了我們手中。"他們玩樂得十分高興，就說："把參孫叫來，讓他給我們戲弄耍樂。"他們就從獄中把參孫提來，在衆人面前戲弄他。他們讓他站在兩根柱子中間，參孫對引着他的手的男孩說："把我領到能摸到這廟宇的支柱旁邊，這樣我好靠着它們。"這時廟裏滿都是非利士男女，他們的首領也全部在那

were there, and there were about three thousand men and women on the roof watching Samson as he fought. Samson called on the Lord and said, 'Remember me, O Lord God, remember me: give me strength only this once, O God, and let me at one stroke be avenged on the Philistines for my two eyes.' He put his arms round the two central pillars which supported the temple, his right arm round one and his left round the other, and braced himself and said, 'Let me die with the Philistines.' Then Samson leaned forward with all his might, and the temple fell on the lords and on all the people who were in it. So the dead whom he killed at his death were more than those he had killed in his life. His brothers and all his father's family came down, carried him up to the grave of his father Manoah between Zorah and Eshtaol and buried him there.

裏，還有大約三千男女在房上高處看參孫被戲弄。參孫向天主呼喚，他說："天主上帝啊，求你眷顧我吧，請再給我一次力量。上帝啊，讓我以一擊來報復非利士人剜眼之仇。"他用雙臂各抱住一根居中支撐廟宇的柱子，左臂一根，右臂一根，振起精神說："我要和非利士人同歸於盡。"參孫傾全力向前一躬身，整座廟就塌了下來，壓在那些首領和廟裏的人的頭上，這樣，他死時殺掉的人比他生前殺掉的還要多。他的兄弟們和親族來到迦薩，把他的屍體抬回他父親在瑣拉和以實陶之間的瑪挪亞墓地裏埋葬。

Ruth

Long ago, there was a famine in the land, and a man from Bethlehem in Judah went to live in the Moabite country with his wife and his two sons. The man's name was Elimelech, his wife's name was Naomi, and the names of his two sons Mahlon and Chilion.

Elimelech Naomi's husband died, so that she was left with her two sons. These sons married Moabite women, one of whom was called Orpah and the other Ruth. They had lived there about ten years, when both Mahlon and Chilion died, so that the woman was bereaved of her two sons as well as of her husband. Thereupon she set out with her two daughters-in-law to return home. Then Naomi said to her two daughters-in-law, 'Go back, both of you, to your mothers' homes. May the Lord grant each of you security in the home of a new husband.' They said to her, 'We will return with you to your own people.' But Naomi said, 'Go back, my daughters. Why should you go with me? Am I likely to bear any more sons to be husbands for you? Go back, my daughters, go.' Then Orpah kissed her mother-in-law and returned to her people, but Ruth clung to her.

Now Naomi had a Kinsman on her husband's side, a well-to-do man of the family to Elimelech; his name was Boaz. Ruth the Moabitess said to Naomi, 'May I go out to the cornfields and glean behind anyone who will grant me that favour?' 'Yes, go, my daughter', she replied. So Ruth went gleaning in that strip of the fields which belonged to Boaz of

三十二　路得再醮

路得記

　　許久以前，猶大境內發生一次饑荒。有一個伯利恒地方的人帶着妻子和兩個兒子，搬到摩押去居住。這個人的名字叫以利米勒，他妻子叫拿俄米，兩個兒子叫瑪倫和基連。

　　拿俄米的丈夫以利米勒死了，就剩下她同兩個兒子。兩個兒子都娶了摩押女子，一個叫俄珥巴，一個叫路得。他們在那地方住了十年，當瑪倫和基連都相繼死去後，拿俄米既無丈夫又沒有兒子。因此她和兩個媳婦返故里。拿俄米對她們說："你們兩人都回到你們娘家去吧。願上帝賜給你們新的夫婿和一個安定的家。"兩個媳婦對她說："我們要同你一起回你的鄉里那兒去。"但拿俄米說："你們回去吧。你們幹什麼要跟我走呢？我還會再生兒子做你們的丈夫嗎？回去吧，你們走吧。"大媳婦俄珥巴親吻了婆婆，返回她娘家那兒去了，但路得却不離開她。

　　拿俄米丈夫有個親戚，是以利米勒家族的一個有錢人，他的名字叫波阿斯。路得這個摩押人對拿俄米說："如果得到許可，我可以到莊稼地裏跟在別人後面拾麥子嗎？""可以，去吧，我的女兒。"拿俄米回答。於是路得來到一塊屬於以利米

Elimelech's family, and there was Boaz coming out from Bethlehem. He asked his servant in charge of the reapers, 'Whose girl is this?' 'She is a Moabite girl', the servant answered, 'who has just come back with Naomi from the Moabite country. Boaz said to Ruth, 'Listen to me, my daughter: do not go and glean in any other field, and do not look any further, but keep close to my girls. She fell prostrate before him and said, 'Why are you so kind as to take notice of me when I am only a foreigner?' Boaz answered, 'They have told me all that you have done for your mother-in-law since your husband's death, how you left your father and mother and the land of your birth, and came to a people you did not know before. The Lord reward your deed; may the Lord the God of Israel, under whose wings you have come to take refuge, give you all that you deserve.'

Boaz gave the men orders. 'She', he said, 'may glean even among the sheaves; do not scold her. Or you may even pull out some corn from the bundles and leave it for her to glean, without reproving her.'

So Ruth gleaned in the field till evening, and when she beat out what she had gleaned, it came to about a bushel of barley. Her mother-in-law asked her, 'Where did you glean today?' She told her mother-in-law whom she had been working with. 'Blessings on him from the Lord', said Naomi. 'The Lord has kept faith with the living and the dead. For this man is related to us and is our next-of-kin.'

One day Ruth's mother-in-law Naomi said to her, 'My daughter, I want to see you happily settled. Now there is our kinsman Boaz; you were with his girls. Tonight he is winnowing barley at his threshing-floor. Wash and anoint yourself, put on your cloak and go down to the threshing-floor, but do not make yourself known to the man until he has finished eating and drinking. But when he lies down, take note of the place where he lies. Then go in, turn back the covering at his feet and lie down. He will tell you what to do.' 'I will do whatever you tell me', Ruth answered.

About midnight something disturbed the man as he slept;

勒家族波阿斯的地裏拾麥穗，剛好波阿斯從伯利恒城出來。他問負責收割的僕人："那是誰家的女子？"僕人說："她是個摩押女子，同拿俄米一道剛從摩押來的。"波阿斯就問路得："聽我說，女子，你不用去別的地裏拾穗了，也不要去遠處了；就同我的使女們在一起幹吧。"她俯伏向他叩拜說："你爲什麼對我這樣仁慈，特別關照我？我只不過是個外邦人。"波阿斯回答說："他們對我說了你自丈夫去世後爲婆婆做的好事，你離開了父母和生養你的土地，來到這個你過去不了解的人們當中，天主對你做的事要給予獎賞，願以色列的上帝，你來尋求庇護的主賜給你應得的一切。"波阿斯命令僕人們說："她可以在麥捆中拾麥子，你們不但不要罵她甚至可以從麥捆中抽出些麥子讓她去拾，也不要去責難她。"

這樣，路得在地裏一直拾到天黑，當她把拾的穗子打出來後，一共有一蒲式耳大麥。她婆婆問她："你今天在什麼地方拾麥子？"路得就把她跟誰一起幹活的情形告訴了婆婆。"願天帝保祐他，"拿俄米說，"天主恩待了生者和死者，這人是我們的親戚，是一個至親。"

一天，路得的婆婆拿俄米對她說："我的女兒，我願見到你有個安身之處。現在有我們這個親戚波阿斯，你這幾天同他的使女在一起，今夜他在場上簸大麥。你沐浴之後塗上油，換好衣服到打穀場去，但不要給人注意到，直到他吃飽喝醉躺下睡覺時，看好他睡在哪裏，然後你就進去，掀起他蓋着腳部的被子躺下。他就會教你怎麼做的。"路得說："我一定照你的吩咐去做。"

大約半夜時分，什麼東西把（波阿斯）弄醒了，他翻身一

he turned over and, lo and behold, there was a woman lying at his feet. 'Who are you?'he asked. 'I am your servant, Ruth', she replied. 'Now spread your skirt over your servant, because you are my next-of-kin.' He said, 'The Lord has blessed you, my dauthter. I will do whatever you ask; for, as the whole neighbourhood knows, you are a capable woman. Are you sure that I am the next-of-kin? There is a kinsman even closer than I. Spend the night here and then in the morning, if he is willing to act as your next-of-kin, well and good; but if he is not willing, I will do so.' So she lay at his feet till morning.

Now Boaz had gone up to the city gate, and was sitting there; and, after a time, the next-of-kin of whom he had spoken passed by. 'Here,' he cried, calling him by name, 'come and sit down.' He came and sat down. Then Boaz stopped ten elders of the town, and asked them to sit there, and they did so. Then he said to the next-of-kin, 'You will remember the strip of field that belonged to our brother Elimelech. Naomi has returned from the Moabite country and is selling it. I promised to open the matter with you, to ask you to acquire it in the presence of those who sit here, in the presence of the elders of my people.' He answered, 'I will act as next-of-kin.' Then Boaz said, 'On the day when you acquire the field from Naomi, you also acquire Ruth the Moabitess, the dead man's wife, so as to perpetuate the name of the dead man with his patrimony.' Thereupon the next-of-kin said, 'I cannot act myself, for I should risk losing my own patrimony. You must therefore do my duty as next-of-kin. I cannot act.'

Then Boaz declared to the elders and all the people, 'You are witnesses today that I have acquired from Naomi all that belonged to Elimelech and all that belonged to Mahlon and Chilion; and, further, that I have myself acquired Ruth the Moabitess, wife of Mahlon, to be my wife, to perpetuate the name of the deceased with his patrimony.

So Boaz took Ruth and made her his wife. When they came together, the Lord caused her to conceive and she bore Boaz a son.... He was the father of Jesse, the father of David.

看，脚邊躺着個女人。"你是誰？"他問。"我是你的僕人路得。"她回答，"張開你的衣襟蔭蔽你的僕人吧，因爲你是我的至親。"他說："上帝保祐你，我的女兒，我會答允你的要求，因爲這裏人都知道你是個能幹的女子。你認爲我是你最近的親屬嗎？其實你還有一個比我更近的親屬。今晚就在這裏過吧，如果明天早上他願意履行作你的至親的義務，那就由他吧。但如果他不願意，那我就會這樣做。"她就在他脚下躺到早晨。

早上波阿斯去城門口並坐在那裏等待。過了一會，他提到的那個親屬走來了。"喂，"他叫他的名字，"過來坐下。"那人過來坐下了。波阿斯叫住了路過的十位城裏長者，請他們也坐下來。他們坐下以後，波阿斯對那人說："你還記得我們的兄弟以利米勒的那塊地吧。拿俄米已從摩押回來並要賣掉它。我想跟你說清楚，請你當着坐在這兒的長者們把它買下。"那人說："我願意履行作爲至親的義務。"波阿斯便說："你買下拿俄米的地時，你也就得到了摩押女子路得，她是拿俄米的寡媳。這樣就可以讓死者在他的遺產上留名。"這麼一說，那人連忙道："我可不幹這事了，因爲那樣我就要冒失去自己的產業的危險，因此，你替我行至親的義務吧。我不幹了。"

波阿斯就對長老們和所有在場的人說："你們是今日的見證人。我要從拿俄米那裏買下全部屬於以利米勒、瑪倫和基連的東西，而且我也要娶瑪倫遺妻摩押女子路得爲妻，並讓死者的名字得以在他的產業上永存。"

這樣波阿斯就娶了路得爲妻。他們婚後，上帝讓路得懷了孕，給波阿斯生了一個兒子。（名叫俄備得）他就是耶西的父親，而耶西是大衞的父親。

33   The Birth of Samuel

1 Samuel

There was a man from Ramathaim, a Zuphite from the hill-country of Ephraim, named Elkanah son of Jeroham, and he had two wives named Hannah and Peninnah. Peninnah had children, but Hannah was childless. This man used to go up from his own town every year to worship and to offer sacrifice to the Lord of Hosts in Shiloh. There Eli's two sons, Hophni and Phinehas, were priests of the Lord. On the day when Elkanah sacrificed, he gave several shares of the meat to his wife Peninnah with all her sons and daughters; but, although he loved Hannah, he gave her only one share, because the Lord had not granted her children. Further, Hannah's rival used to torment her and humiliate her because she had no children. Year after year this happened when they went up to the house of the Lord; her rival used to torment her. Once when she was in tears and would not eat, her husband Elkanah said to her, 'Hannah, why are you crying and eating nothing? Why are you so miserable? Am I not more to you than ten sons?' After they had finished eating and drinking at the sacrifice at Shiloh, Hannah rose in deep distress, and stood before the Lord and prayed to him, weeping bitterly. Meanwhile Eli the priest was sitting on his seat beside the door of the temple of the Lord. For a long time she went on praying before the Lord, while Eli watched her lips. Hannah was praying silently; but, although her voice could not be heard, her lips were moving and Eli took her for a drunken woman. He said to her, 'Enough of this drunken behaviour!

三十三　撒母耳生

　　以法蓮山地拉瑪瑣非有一個人名叫以利加拿，是耶羅罕的兒子，他有兩個妻子，哈拿和毗尼拿。毗尼拿有子女，哈拿却沒有。以利加拿每年都從自己住的城市到示羅去拜祭萬軍之主。那兒有以利的兩個兒子：何弗尼和非尼哈，都是天主的祭司。每逢獻祭之日以利加拿就給妻子毗尼拿和她的子女好幾份祭肉；他雖然愛哈拿，却只給她一份，因爲上帝沒有給她孩子。而哈拿的對頭毗尼拿也欺負她，羞辱她不能生育。年年他們去天主聖殿時都是如此，她的對頭人總是譏笑她。有一次，她哭着不吃東西，她丈夫以利加拿對她說：“哈拿，你爲什麼啼啼哭哭，不吃東西呢？你爲什麼這麼傷心？難道我對你來講不比十個兒子還好嗎？”他們在示羅吃喝完了，哈拿滿懷悲傷地站起來在天主面前祈禱，傷心地哭泣。這時祭司以利正坐在聖殿門旁的座位上。哈拿在天主面前長時間地祈禱，以利注視着她的嘴唇。哈拿在輕聲禱告，雖然聽不見聲音但她的嘴唇在動，以利就把她當作是個喝醉的女人。他對她說：“你要醉到

Go away till the wine has worn off.' 'No, sir,' she answered, 'I am a sober person, I have drunk no wine or strong drink, and I have been pouring out my heart before the Lord.' 'Go in peace,' said Eli, and may the God of Israel answer the prayer you have made to him.'

Next morning they were up early and, after prostrating themselves before the Lord, returned to their own home at Ramah. Elkanah had intercourse with his wife Hannah, and the Lord remembered her. She conceived, and in due time bore a son, whom she named Samuel.

Elkanah, with his whole household, went up to make the annual sacrifice to the Lord and to redeem his vow. Hannah did not go with them, but said to her husband, 'When the child is weaned I will come up with him to enter the presence of the Lord, and he shall stay there always.' So the woman stayed and nursed her son until she had weaned him; and when she had weaned him, she took him up with her. She took also a bull three years old, an ephah of meal, and a flagon of wine, and she brought him, child as he was, into the house of the Lord at Shiloh. They slaughtered the bull, and brought the boy to Eli. Hannah said to him, 'Sir, as sure as you live, I am the woman who stood near you here praying to the Lord. It was this boy that I prayed for and the Lord has given me what I asked. What I asked I have received; and now I lend him to the Lord; for his whole life he is lent to the Lord.'

幾時呢？快走開，等酒醒了再來。""不，先生，"她回答說，"我是個不喝酒的人，我什麼酒也沒喝，我是在對天主傾訴我心中的愁苦呢。"以利說："安心回去吧，願以色列的上帝應允你對他的祈求。"

第二天一早他們就起身了，在天主面前伏拜之後，回到了在拉瑪的家中。以利加拿同妻子哈拿同房，上帝眷顧她。她懷孕了，足月後生下一個兒子，取名爲撒母耳。

以利加拿和全家去向天主作年祭和還願。哈拿沒有去，但她對丈夫說："到這孩子斷奶時，我就帶他去朝見天主，他要長留在那裏。"於是她留下來照看兒子直到他斷了奶。斷奶後，她帶上兒子，還有一頭養了三年的小牛犢，一伊法食物和一大壺酒，這樣她帶着孩子到了示羅的天主殿堂。宰了牛犢，把男孩領到以利面前。哈拿對他說："先生，我是那個曾經站在你身邊向天主禱告的女人。我當時祈求的就是這個男孩，天主果然給了我我要求的東西。我要求的已得到了，現在我把他歸還天主，他一輩子都要歸屬天主的。"

34 The Death of Eli

1 Samuel

(1)

Then Elkanah went to Ramah with his household, but the boy remained behind in the service of the Lord under Eli the priest.

Now Eli's sons were scoundrels and had no regard for the Lord.... In those days the word of the Lord was seldom heard, and no vision was granted. But one night Eli, whose eyes were dim and his sight failing, was lying down in his usual place, while Samuel slept in the temple of the Lord where the Ark of God was. Before the lamp of God had gone out, the Lord called him, and Samuel answered, 'Here I am', and ran to Eli saying, 'You called me: here I am.' 'No, I did not call you,' said Eli; 'lie down again.' So he went and lay down. The Lord called Samuel again, and he got up and went to Eli. 'Here I am,' he said; 'surely you called me.' 'I did not call, my son,' he answered; 'lie down again.' Now Samuel had not yet come to know the Lord, and the word of the Lord had not been disclosed to him. When the Lord called him for the third time, he again went to Eli. Then Eli understood that it was the Lord calling the child; he told Samuel to go and lie down and said, 'If he calls again, say, "Speak, Lord; thy servant hears thee."' So Samuel went and lay down in his place.

The Lord came and stood there, and called, 'Samuel, Samuel' as before. Samuel answered, 'Speak; thy servant hears thee.' The Lord said, 'Soon I shall do something in Israel which will ring in the ears of all who hear it. When that

三十四 以利之死

撒母耳記上

（一）

以利加拿和他的家人回到了拉瑪，但那孩子撒母耳却留在祭司以利那裏侍奉天主。

以利的兩個兒子是無賴，他們不尊敬天主。在那時天主的話也很少聽到，更不用說親眼見到他了。但是一天夜裏，以利躺在他平時睡覺的地方，眼睛昏花看不清東西，而撒母耳則睡在放上帝約櫃的聖殿內。上帝的燈還沒有熄滅時，天主呼喚他，撒母耳應道："我在這兒。"他跑向以利說："是你叫我吧，我在這裏。""沒有，我沒叫你，"以利說："去睡吧。"他就回去躺下。天主又呼喚撒母耳，他起身到以利那裏，說："我在這裏，你是叫我了。""我的兒，我沒叫你，"他答道，"再去睡吧。"撒母耳那時還沒認識天主，也沒親自得過天主的指點。當天主第三次喚他時，他又跑去找以利，這時，以利才明白是天主喚那孩子。他就叫撒母耳回去躺下，說："如果他再呼喚你，你就說：'天主，請說吧，你的僕人在聽着呢。'"撒母耳就回去躺下。

天主來了，他站在那兒和前幾次那樣呼喚道："撒母耳，撒母耳。"撒母耳答道："請說吧，你的僕人在聽着呢。"天主說："不久我將在以色列做一件事，這事會在所有聽到的人

day comes I will make good every word I have spoken against Eli and his family from beginning to end.

Samuel lay down till morning and then opened the doors of the house of the Lord, but he was afraid to tell Eli about the vision. Eli called Samuel: 'Samuel, my son', he said; and he answered, 'Here I am.' Eli asked, 'What did the Lord say to you? Do not hide it from me. God forgive you if you hide one word of all that he said to you.' Then Samuel told him everything and hid nothing. Eli said, 'The Lord must do what is good in his eyes.'

As Samuel grew up, the Lord was with him, and none of his words went unfulfilled. From Dan to Beersheba, all Israel recognized that Samuel was confirmed as a prophet of the Lord.

(2)

So Samuel's word had authority throughout Israel. And the time came when the Philistines mustered for battle against Israel, and the Israelites went out to meet them. The Israelites encamped at Eben-ezer and the Philistines at Aphek. The Philistines drew up their lines facing the Israelites, and when they joined battle the Israelites were routed by the Philistines, who killed about four thousand men on the field. When the army got back to the camp, the elders of Israel asked, 'Why did the Lord let us be routed today by the Philistines? Let us fetch the Ark of the Covenant of the Lord from Shiloh to go with us and deliver us from the power of our enemies.' So the people sent to Shiloh and fetched the Ark of the Covenant of the Lord of Hosts, Eli's two sons, Hophni and Phinehas, were there with the Ark. When the Ark came into the camp all the Israelites greeted it with a great shout, and the earth rang with the shouting. The Philistines heard the noise and asked, 'What is this great shouting in the camp of the Hebrews?' When they knew that the Ark of the Lord had come into the camp, they were afraid and cried, 'A god has come into the camp. We are lost! Who can deliver us from the power of these mighty gods? These are the very gods who broke the

耳中迴响。當那天來到時，我就要兌現我早就說過的話：要懲罰以利和他一家人的。"

撒母耳躺下直到天亮，然後打開聖殿的門，但他不敢把耶和華的啟示告訴以利。以利叫撒母耳："撒母耳，我的孩子，"他說。撒母耳答道："我在這兒。"以利問："耶和華對你說什麼了？別瞞着我。要是你對我隱瞞了他說的話，哪怕一個字，願上帝饒恕你吧。"撒母耳只好告訴他天主的話，一點也不隱瞞。以利說："天主一定要做他認爲是好的事情。"

撒母耳長大後，天主與他同在，而他的每句話都得到應驗。因此從但到別是巴，所有以色列人都認爲撒母耳是透露天主旨意的人。

（二）

撒母耳的話在全以色列都具有權威性。不久非利士人集結力量來攻打以色列，以色列人出而迎戰。以色列人紮營在以便以謝，而非利士人則下寨在亞弗。非利士人對以色列人擺開陣勢，雙方交戰時，以色列人被非利士人擊潰了，大約四千人陣亡。當敗軍回營後，以色列的長老們問："爲什麼今天天主讓我們給非利士人打得慘敗？我們把天主的約櫃從示羅抬到這裏來吧，這樣我們才能從敵人手中解救出來。"於是就派人去示羅，取來了萬軍之主的約櫃。以利的兩個兒子何弗尼和非尼哈和約櫃一起來。當約櫃抬進營地時，以色列人都歡呼着迎接它，呼聲響遍大地。非利士人聽到這聲音就問："希伯來人營中大叫大喊什麼？"當他們得知是天主的約櫃運到營地來時，他們害怕得喊道："神來了，我們完了！有誰能從這些萬能的神手中把我們解救出來呢？就是這些神曾經毀了埃及人，把他

Egyptians and crushed them in the wilderness. Courage, Philistines, and act like men, or you will become slaves to the Hebrews as they were yours.' The Philistines then gave battle, and the Israelites were defeated and fled to their homes. It was a great defeat, and thirty thousand Israelite foot-soldiers perished. The Ark of God was taken, and Eli's two sons, Hophni and Phinehas, were killed.

A Benjamite ran from the battlefield and reached Shiloh on the same day, his clothes rent and dust on his head. When he arrived Eli was sitting on a seat by the road to Mizpah, for he was deeply troubled about the Ark of God. The man entered the city with his news, and all the people cried out in horror. Eli asked, 'What is the news, my son?' The runner answered, 'The Israelites have fled from the Philistines; utter panic has struck the army; your two sons, Hophni and Phinehas, are killed, and the Ark of God is taken.' At the mention of the Ark of God, Eli fell backwards from his seat by the gate and broke his neck, for he was old and heavy. So he died; he had been judge over Israel for forty years.

們消滅在荒野裏。非利士人，拿出勇氣來，要作大丈夫，否則你們就要淪爲希伯來人的奴僕，就像他們曾經是你們的奴僕那樣。"非利士人接着就奮起戰鬥，以色列人被打敗了，逃回家去，這是一次慘敗，三萬以色列步兵被消滅了，約櫃被奪走，以利的兩個兒子何弗尼和非尼哈也被殺死。

當日一個便雅憫人從戰場上逃跑到示羅，他的衣裳也扯爛了，滿頭塵土。他到達時，以利正坐在通向米斯巴的路旁，因爲他十分担心上帝的約櫃。這人帶着這壞消息進城去，所有居民都嚇得大哭起來。以利問道："我的孩子，有什麼消息嗎？"那跑回來的人回答說："以色列人給非利士人打得亡命逃跑了，整個軍隊都驚恐萬狀。你的兩個兒子何弗尼、非尼哈都被殺死了，約櫃也被搶走了。"說到約櫃這兒，以利從他在門旁的座上仰後摔了下來，因爲他年紀老邁，身體又沉重，把脖子摔斷，就這樣死了。他在以色列任士師共四十年。

1 Samuel

After the Philistines had captured the Ark of God, they brought it from Eben-ezer to Ashdod; and there they carried it into the temple of Dagon and set it beside Dagon himself. When the people of Ashdod rose next morning, there was Dagon fallen face downwards before the Ark of the Lord; so they took him and put him back in his place. Next morning when they rose, Dagon had again fallen face downwards before the Ark of the Lord, with his head and his two hands lying broken off beside his platform; only Dagon's body remained on it.

Then the Lord laid a heavy hand upon the people of Ashdod; he threw them into distress and plagued them with tumours, and their territory swarmed with rats. There was death and destruction all through the city. When the men of Ashdod saw this they said, 'The Ark of the God of Israel shall not stay here, for he has laid a heavy hand upon us and upon Dagon our god.' So they sent and called all the Philistine princes together to ask what should be done with the Ark. They said, 'Let the Ark of the God of Israel be taken across to Gath.' They took it there, and after its arrival the hand of the Lord caused great havoc in the city; he plagued everybody, high and low alike, with the tumours which broke out. Then they sent the Ark of God on to Ekron. When the Ark reached Ekron, the people cried, 'They have brought the Ark of the God of Israel over to us, to kill us and our families.'

When the Ark of the Lord had been in their territory for

三十五　奪櫃招懲

撒母耳記上

　　非利士人奪走了約櫃後，他們把它從以便以謝抬到亞實
突，在那兒他們把它抬進大袞神廟裏，放在大袞神身邊。第二
天早上，亞實突百姓起來後，發現大袞神臉朝下倒在天主約櫃
之前。他們把他扶起，放回原處。次日早上，他們起來，又發
現大袞神臉朝下倒在天主約櫃之前，它的頭和雙手都摔斷了，
落在像座的旁邊，只有它的身體還在像座上立着。

　　這之後，天主重重地懲罰亞實突人，他使他們陷入苦難
中，使他們患上腫瘤病，境內老鼠橫行。整個城市充滿了死亡
和毀滅。亞實突人看見這情形就說："以色列神的約櫃不能放
在這裏，因為天主如此重懲了我們和我們的大袞神。"於是他
們請來所有非利士頭領，商議該對約櫃怎麼辦才好。他們說：
"把以色列神的約櫃抬過迦特去吧。"他們把它抬到那裏，約
櫃到達後，天主之手使這個城市引起浩劫。他使每個人，不論
貴賤，都患上腫瘤病。後來他們把約櫃送到以革倫。約櫃到了
以革倫，百姓就喊道："他們把以色列神的約櫃抬到這裏來殺
害我們和我們的家族了。"

　　當天主的約櫃在非利士人境內放了七個月之後，非利士人

seven months, the Philistines summoned the priests and soothsayers and asked, 'What shall we do with the Ark of the Lord? Tell us how we ought to send it back to its own place.' They answered, 'If you send the Ark of the God of Israel back, do not let it go without a gift, but send it back with a gift for him by way of indemnity; then you will be healed and restored to favour.

召集了祭司和占卜者，說：“我們該怎麼處理這天主的約櫃呢？告訴我們應怎樣把它送回原處。”他們回答說：“如果要把以色列神的約櫃送回去，不能讓它沒有禮物而歸。千萬要同時送件禮品給天主賠罪。那樣你們就會身體康復，得到寬恕。”

（後來非利士人就照這話辦了，把以色列神的約櫃還給以色列人，並送了禮物作爲賠罪。）

1 Samuel

There was a man from the district of Benjamin, whose name was Kish. He was a man of substance, and had a son named Saul, a young man in his prime; there was no better man among the Israelites than he. He was a head taller than any of his fellows.

One day some asses belonging to Saul's father Kish had strayed, so he said to his son Saul, 'Take one of the servants with you, and go and look for the asses.' They crossed the hill-country of Ephraim and went through the district of Shalisha but did not find them. When they had entered the district of Zuph, Saul said to the servant with him, 'Come, we ought to turn back, or my father will stop thinking about the asses and begin to worry about us.' The servant answered, 'There is a man of God in the city here, who has a great reputation, because everything he says comes true. Suppose we go there; he may tell us something about this errand of ours.' Saul said, 'If we do go, what shall we offer him? There is no food left in our packs and we have no present for the man of God, nothing at all.' The servant answered him again, 'Wait! I have here a quarter-shekel of silver. I can give that to the man, to tell us what we should do.' Saul said, 'Good! let us go to him.' So they went to the city where the man of God was.

三十六　掃羅登基

撒母耳記上

（以利死後，撒母耳成了以色列人的領袖。但撒母耳步以利的後塵：他的兒子們貪贓枉法，不行他的道。撒母耳迫於長老們的壓力，答應為他們立一個王。）

便雅憫地區有個人叫基士……他是個有產業的富人。他有個兒子叫掃羅，年富力強，整個以色列沒有一個人比他強的。他是一個比同伴們高出一頭的人。

一天，掃羅父親基士的幾頭驢子散失了。他就對兒子掃羅說："帶上個僕人去把驢子找回來。"他們越過了以法蓮山地，又穿過沙利沙地區，但仍舊沒有找到驢子。當他們進入蘇弗地區時，掃羅對僕人說："喂，我們該回去了，否則我父親會顧不上想驢子，反而要為我們擔心了。"那僕人回答說："這城裏有個神人，他很有名氣，因為他說的每樁事都能兌現。要是我們上那兒去，他會指點我們怎麼去辦好這樁差事。"掃羅說："如果我們真要去，那我們送點什麼給他呢？我們馱包中已經沒剩下食物了，沒有禮物可送給這位神人，什麼也沒有。"僕人却回答說："等等，我這兒有個四分之一舍客勒的銀子。我可以把它給那人，讓他告訴我們該怎麼辦。"掃羅說："好！我們就去找他。"於是他們就出發到那神人的城市去。

Now the day before Saul came, the Lord had disclosed his intention to Samuel in these words: 'At this same time tomorrow I will send you a man from the land of Benjamin. Anoint him prince over my people Israel, and then he shall deliver my people from the Philistines. I have seen the sufferings of my people and their cry has reached my ears.' The moment Saul appeared the Lord said to Samuel, 'Here is the man of whom I spoke to you. This man shall rule my people.' Saul came up to Samuel in the gateway and said, 'Would you tell me where the seer lives?' Samuel replied, 'I am the seer. Go on ahead of me to the hill-shrine and you shall eat with me today; in the morning I will set you on your way, after telling you what you have on your mind. Trouble yourself no more about the asses lost three days ago, for they have been found. But what is it that all Israel is wanting? It is you and your ancestral house.' 'But I am a Benjamite,' said Saul, 'from the smallest of the tribes of Israel, and my family is the least important of all the families of the tribe of Benjamin. Why do you say this to me?' Samuel then brought Saul and his servant into the dining-hall and gave them a place at the head of the company, which numbered about thirty. Then he said to the cook, 'Bring the portion that I gave you and told you to put on one side.' So the cook took up the whole haunch and leg and put it before Saul; and Samuel said, 'Here is the portion of meat kept for you. Eat it: it has been reserved for you at this feast to which I have invited the people.' So Saul dined with Samuel that day, and he stayed there that night. At down when Saul rose, he and Samuel went out together into the street. As they came to the end of the town, Samuel said to Saul, 'Stay here a moment, and I will tell you the word of God.'

Samuel took a flask of oil and poured it over Saul's head, and he kissed him and said, 'The Lord anoints you prince over his people Israel; you shall rule the people of the Lord and deliver them from the enemies round about them. You shall go down to Gilgal ahead of me, and I will come to you to sacrifice whole-offerings and shared-offerings. Wait seven days until I join you; then I will tell you what to do.'

在掃羅來到的前一天，天主把他的意圖透露給撒母耳：
“明天這時辰我會給你帶來一個便雅憫人。要按天意選他來治
理我的以色列人民。他會把以色列人從非利士人手裏拯救出
來。我已經看到了我的人民所受的苦難，他們的怨聲已傳到我
耳中。”掃羅出現時，耶和華就對撒母耳說：“這就是我對你
說過的那個人。這人將治理我的人民。”掃羅走到城門撒母耳
跟前說：“請問你知道先知住在哪裏嗎？”撒母耳回答：“我
就是那個先知。你先到山上的神祠那裏去，你今天要同我共
餐。明天一早我會告訴你該怎樣辦你想辦的事，然後送你上
路。不用為三天前丟失的驢子煩惱了，驢子已經找到了。整個
以色列所需的是什麼呢？是你和你們家族。”掃羅說：“但是
我是一個便雅憫人，是以色列最小的部族，我的家族又是便雅
憫部族裏最不重要的。你為什麼給我講這些呢？”撒母耳把掃
羅和他的僕人帶到飯廳，讓他們坐在席首，共同進餐的約有三
十人。然後，撒母耳對廚子說：“把那份我交給你並叫你收在
一邊的那份肉拿上來。”廚子取來了一整個後臀和腿，放在掃
羅面前；撒母耳說：“這塊肉是留給你的，吃吧。這是特別留
着給你在我邀請眾人參加的這個宴席上吃的。”那天掃羅，就
和撒母耳一齊用餐，並在那兒留宿。天亮後掃羅起身同撒母耳
一起上街。當他們走到城根下時，撒母耳對掃羅說：“在這裏
呆一會兒，我要把上帝的話告訴你。”

　　撒母耳拿了瓶膏油倒在掃羅頭上，親吻他說：“天主選定
你替他治理以色列人民的人，你將治理天主的人民，並把他們
從周圍敵人手中拯救出來。你要在我之前先去吉甲，我會隨後
去那裏和你去獻燔祭和平安祭。等七天我就會到那裏找你，那
時我會告訴你該做什麼。”

Meanwhile Samuel summoned the Israelites to the Lord at Mizpah and said to the people, 'This is the word of the Lord the God of Israel: I brought Israel up from Egypt; I delivered you from the Egyptians and from all the kingdoms that oppressed you; but today you have rejected your God who saved you from all your misery and distress; you have said, "No, set up a king over us." Now therefore take up your positions before the Lord tribe by tribe and clan by clan.' Samuel then presented all the tribes of Israel, and Benjamin was picked by lot. Then he presented the tribe of Benjamin, family by family, and the family of Matri was picked. Then he presented the family of Matri, man by man, and Saul son of Kish was picked; but when they looked for him he could not be found. They went on to ask the Lord, 'Will the man be coming back?' The Lord answered, 'There he is , hiding among the baggage.' So someone ran and fetched him out, and as he took his stand among the people, he was a head taller than anyone else. Samuel said to the people, 'Look at the man whom the Lord has chosen; there is no one like him in this whole nation.' They all acclaimed him, shouting, 'Long live the king!'

這期間撒母耳召集了以色列人來米斯巴到天主那裏，他對眾人說：“這是以色列的天主上帝說的話：我把以色列人從埃及引領出來，把你們從埃及人和所有壓迫你們的國家手中解救出來；但今天你們厭棄了把你們從苦難中救出來的上帝，你們說過：‘不，給我們立一個王吧。’因此，現在你們就按部族一個個在天主面前站好。”撒母耳於是讓以色列各部族一一出來抽籤，便雅憫族抽中了。然後讓便雅憫部族裏一家家地抽籤，瑪特利家族抽中了，接着瑪特利家裏的男丁一個個抽籤，基士的兒子掃羅抽中了。但當他們找他時，他却不在。他們去問天主：“這人會回來嗎？”上帝回答：“他就在那裏，藏在行李堆中。”有人就去把他接來，當他置身站在人羣中時，他比其他人都高出一頭。撒母耳對人們說：“看看天主選中的這個人吧，在我們整個國家中沒有人可以與他相比。”人民都歡呼擁戴他，他們高呼：“國王萬歲！”

1 Samuel

About a month later Nahash the Ammonite attacked and besieged Jabesh-gilead. The men of Jabesh said to Nahash, 'Come to terms with us and we will be your subjects.' Nahash answered them, 'On one condition only will I come to terms with you: that I gouge out your right eyes and bring disgrace on Israel.' The elders of Jabesh-gilead then said, 'Give us seven days' respite to send messengers throughout Israel and then, if no one relieves us, we will surrender to you.' When the messengers came to Gibeah, where Saul lived, and delivered their message, all the people broke into lamentation. Saul was just coming from the field driving in the oxen, and asked why the people were lamenting; and they repeated what the men of Jabesh had said. When Saul heard this, the spirit of God suddenly seized him. In his anger he took a pair of oxen and cut them in pieces, and sent messengers with the pieces, all through Israel to proclaim that the same would be done to the oxen of any man who did not follow Saul and Samuel into battle. The fear of the Lord fell upon the people and they came out, to a man. Saul mustered them in Bezek; there were three hundred thousand men from Israel and thirty thousand from Judah. He said to the men who brought the message, 'Tell the men of Jabesh-gilead, "Victory will be yours tomorrow by the time the sun is hot." The men of Jabesh heard what the messengers reported and took heart; and they said to Nahash, 'Tomorrow we will surrender to you, and then you may deal with us as you think fit.' Next day Saul

三十七　首戰告捷

撒母耳記上

大約一個月以後，亞捫人的王拿轄圍攻雅比基列。雅比的人對拿轄說："你與我們立約，我們就做你的順民。"拿轄回答說：要我與你們立約，有一個條件，那就是我要剜出你們的右眼，以此羞辱以色列。"雅比基列的長老對他說："那你給我們七天期限，讓我們送信給以色列各處，如果沒有人來援救我們，我們就向你投降。"送信的人到了掃羅住的基比亞報告這事，那裏的人聽了都痛哭起來。這時掃羅正趕着牛從地裏回來。他問為什麼大家都在痛哭，他們就把雅比來人說的話告訴他。掃羅聽到此事，上帝的精靈突然降到他身上，他怒氣冲冲地抓住一對公牛，把牠們砍成許多小塊，讓人把肉塊拿到以色列各處，宣佈凡是不跟隨掃羅和撒母耳去作戰的人，他們的牛都會遭到這樣對待。對天主的敬畏使人們全都出來參戰了。掃羅把人都結集在比色，共有以色列來的三十萬人和猶大來的三萬人。他對那些送信的人說："告訴雅比基列人：'明早太陽最熱之際，就是你們勝利之時！'"雅比人聽到送信人傳達的話就勇氣大增，他們對拿轄說："明天我們就歸順你，到時你

drew up his men in three columns; they forced their way right into the enemy camp during the morning watch and massacred the Ammonites while the day grew hot, after which the survivors scattered until no two men were left together.

Then the people said to Samuel, 'Who said that Saul should not reign over us? Hand the men over to us to be put to death.' But Saul said, 'No man shall be put to death on a day when the Lord has won such a victory in Israel.' Samuel said to the people, 'Let us now go to Gilgal and there renew our allegiance to the kingdom.' So they all went to Gilgal and invested Saul there as king in the presence of the Lord, sacrificing shared-offerings before the Lord; and Saul and all the Israelites celebrated the occasion with great joy.

可以任意處置我們。"第二天掃羅把他的人馬分爲三個縱隊，在晨更時分，長驅直進攻入敵營，到正午時殺戮了無數亞捫人。那些幸存的都四散逃跑，各自東西了。

於是人們對撒母耳說："誰說掃羅不該治理我們？把這些人交出來給我們處死。"但掃羅說："在天主給以色列取得如此巨大勝利的喜慶日子裏，不要處死任何人。"撒母耳對人們說："我們去吉甲重新宣佈效忠王國吧。"於是他們就去吉甲，在天主面前立掃羅爲王，並向天主獻平安祭。掃羅同所有以色列人以狂歡來慶祝勝利。

When Saul had made his throne secure in Israel, he fought
against his enemies on every side, the Moabites, the Ammonites, the Edomites, the king of Zobah, and the Philistines;
and wherever he turned he was successful. He displayed his
strength by defeating the Amalekites and freeing Israel from
hostile raids.

There was bitter warfare with the Philistines throughout
Saul's lifetime; any strong man and any brave man that he
found he took into his own service.

Samuel said to Saul, 'The Lord sent me to anoint you king
over his people Israel. Now listen to the voice of the Lord.
This is the very word of the Lord of Hosts: "I am resolved to
punish the Amalekites for what they did to Israel, how they
attacked them on their way up from Egypt." Go now and fall
upon the Amalekites and destroy them, and put their property under ban. Spare no one; put them all to death, men and
women, children and babes in arms, herds and flocks, camels
and asses.' Thereupon Saul called out the levy and mustered
them in Telaim. There were two hundred thousand footsol-
diers and another ten thousand from Judah. He came to the
Amalekite city and halted for a time in the gorge. Meanwhile
he sent word to the Kenites to leave the Amalekites and come
down, 'or', he said, 'I shall destroy you as well as them; but
you were friendly to Israel when they came up from Egypt.'
So the Kenites left the Amalekites. Then Saul cut the Amalekites to pieces, all the way from Havilah to Shur on the bor-

三十八　悔立掃羅

撒母耳記上

　　掃羅在以色列鞏固了王權後，他南征北戰去攻打他的敵人，如摩押人、亞捫人、以東人和瑣巴國王，還有非利士人。他所向披靡。由於打敗了亞瑪力人，把以色列從敵人的侵襲中解救出來，他顯示出自己的威力。

　　掃羅的一生都在不斷地同非利士人苦戰，他把能找到的每個強壯、英勇的男子都用到征戰中去。

　　（有一次），撒母耳對掃羅說：“天主派我立你爲他的以色列人民之王。現在你聽天主的聲音吧，這就是萬軍之主的原來旨意：‘我決定因亞瑪力人施於以色列人的惡行而懲處他們，他們在以色列人出埃及的途中攻擊過以色列人。’你馬上就去進攻亞瑪力人，把他們摧毀，他們的財產全部查禁。不要留下一個人，把他們全部殺掉，男女老幼直至懷抱嬰兒無一例外，牛隻羊羣，駱駝驢子也要消滅乾淨。”於是掃羅立刻把人馬召集到提拉因，共有步兵二十萬另外加上猶大來的一萬人。他來到亞瑪力城，在峽谷中停了一段時間。這期間他派人告訴基尼人，要他們離開亞瑪力人下到谷裏來。他說：“因爲在以色列人出埃及途中你們曾對他們好，所以我手下留情，否則，我就連你們也一同消滅掉。”於是基尼人就離開了亞瑪力人。而掃羅就沿着哈腓拉到書珥的埃及邊境綫把亞瑪力人殺個片甲

ders of Egypt. Agag the king of the Amalekites he took alive, but he destroyed all the people, putting them to the sword. Saul and his army spared Agag and the best of the sheep and cattle, the fat beasts and the lambs and everything worth keeping; they were unwilling to destroy them, but anything that was useless and of no value they destroyed.

Then the word of the Lord came to Samuel: 'I repent of having made Saul king, for he has turned his back on me and has not obeyed my commands.' Samuel was angry; all night he cried aloud to the Lord. Early next morning he went to meet Saul, but was told that he had gone to Carmel; Saul had set up a monument for himself there, and had then turned and gone down to Gilgal. There Samuel found him, and Saul greeted him with the words, 'The Lord's blessing upon you! I have obeyed the Lord's commands.' But Samuel said, 'What then is this bleating of sheep in my ears? Why do I hear the lowing of cattle?' Saul answered, 'The people have taken them from the Amalekites. These are what they spared, the best of the sheep and cattle, to sacrifice to the Lord your God. The rest we completely destroyed.' Samuel said to Saul, 'Let be, and I will tell you what the Lord said to me last night.' 'Tell me', said Saul. So Samuel went on, 'Time was when you thought little of yourself, but now you are head of the tribes of Israel, and the Lord has anointed you king over Israel. The Lord sent you with strict instructions to destroy that wicked nation, the Amalekites; you were to fight against them until you had wiped them out. Why then did you not obey the Lord? Why did you pounce upon the spoil and do what was wrong in the eyes of the Lord?'

Saul said to Samuel, 'I have sinned. I have ignored the Lord's command and your orders: I was afraid of the people and deferred to them. But now forgive my sin, I implore you, and come back with me, and I will make my submission before the Lord.' Samuel answered, 'I will not come back with you; you have rejected the word of the Lord and there-fore the Lord has rejected you as king over Israel.' He turned

不留。他活捉了亞瑪力王亞甲，但亞瑪力人就無一幸免，都被砍死了。掃羅和他的軍隊饒了亞甲，也沒殺掉最好的牛羊和肥美的家畜、羔羊，也沒毀掉一切值得保存的東西，他們不願毀掉它們。但他們對無用和無價值的東西就全都毀掉。

事後，天主對撒母耳說話：“我後悔選了掃羅爲王，因爲他已背叛了我，不聽我的命令。”撒母耳聽了很生氣，他整夜向天主苦求恕罪。第二天一早，他去見掃羅，但聽說掃羅已去了迦密；掃羅在那裏爲自己豎了一座碑後，又轉往吉甲去了。在吉甲撒母耳才找到了他，掃羅迎接他說：“願天主保祐你！我遵從了天主之命。”但撒母耳說：“那末，爲什麼我聽到羊叫聲呢？爲什麼我又聽到牛哞呢？”掃羅回答：“那是人們從亞瑪力人手中奪來的牛羊，都是他們沒殺掉的最好牛羊，是用來供奉你的天主的。其餘的全都毀掉了。”撒母耳對掃羅說：“別說了，我要把昨天晚上天主對我說的話告訴你。”掃羅說：“告訴我吧。”撒母耳就說：“過去有一段時間，你總認爲自己出生小族，但現在你是以色列各部族的首領了。天主已封你爲以色列國王。天主嚴格命令你要摧毀那有罪的民族亞捫人。你應該對他們格殺勿論直到全部消滅他們。爲什麼你不服從天主的話？爲什麼你擄掠財物，做了天主認爲是不對的事？”

掃羅對撒母耳說：“我犯了罪，我不顧天主的旨意和你的命令。我害怕人民，聽從了他們。但請饒恕我的罪過，我懇求你和我一起回去，我要向天主認罪。”撒母耳說：“我不跟你一道回去。你違背了天主的旨意，因此天主也撤消你的以色列

to go, but Saul caught the edge of his cloak and it tore. And Samuel said to him, 'The Lord has torn the kingdom of Israel from your hand today and will give it to another, a better man than you.

Saul went to his own home at Gibeah, and Samuel went to Ramah; and he never saw Saul again to his dying day, but he mourned for him, because the Lord had repented of having made him king over Israel.

國王的地位。"說完轉身要走，但掃羅拉住了他的袍角，把袍也扯破了。撒母耳對他說："天主今天已把以色列王國從你手中奪回去，他要把它給另一個人，一個比你好的人。"

掃羅回到他自己在基比亞的家中，撒母耳回到拉瑪，他直到死那天也再沒見掃羅，但他為掃羅悲嘆，因為天主後悔立他為以色列王。

1 Samuel

The Lord said to Samuel, 'How long will you mourn for Saul because I have rejected him as king over Israel? Fill your horn with oil and take it with you; I am sending you to Jesse of Bethlehem; for I have chosen myself a king among his sons.' Samuel did as the Lord had told him, and went to Bethlehem.

He himself hallowed Jesse and his sons and invited them to the sacrifice also. Then Samuel asked, 'Are these all?' Jesse answered, 'There is still the youngest, but he is looking after the sheep.' Samuel said to Jesse, 'Send and fetch him; we will not sit down until he comes.' So he sent and fetched him. He was handsome, with ruddy cheeks and bright eyes. The Lord said, 'Rise and anoint him: this is the man.' Samuel took the horn of oil and anointed him in the presence of his brothers. Then the spirit of the Lord came upon David and was with him from that day onwards.

The Philistines collected their forces for war and massed at Socoh in Judah; Saul and the Israelites also massed, and camped in the Vale of Elah. They drew up their lines facing the Philistines. A champion came out from the Philistine camp, a man named Goliath, from Gath; he was over nine feet in height. He had a bronze helmet on his head, and he wore platearmour of bronze, weighing five thousand shekels. On his legs were bronze greaves, and one of his weapons was a dagger of bronze. The shaft of his spear was like a weaver's beam, and its head, which was of iron, weighed six hundred

三十九　牧童克敵

撒母耳記上

　　天主對撒母耳說：“你還要因我廢掉了掃羅的以色列王位而為他悲嘆多久呢？把你的羊角裝滿膏油，帶在身邊。我要派你到伯利恒人耶西那裏去，我已在他的孩子中選了一個為國王。”撒母耳按天主吩咐的去做，到伯利恒去。

　　（到了伯利恒城，）他使耶西和他的兒子潔了身，並請他們一起去獻祭。之後，撒母耳問：“你的兒子全都在這裏嗎？”耶西答道：“還有最小的一個，他在放羊呢。”撒母耳對耶西說：“派人去把他接來，他不來我們就不坐下。”這樣，耶西就派人去把他叫回來。他長得很英俊，兩頰緋紅，雙目炯炯有神。天主說：“起來給他塗油吧，就是這個人了。”撒母耳拿起盛油的羊角，在他的兄弟面前給他額上塗了油。於是天主之精靈就降到大衞身上，從此與他同在。

　　非利士人徵集兵力準備作戰，他們聚集在猶大的梭哥。掃羅和以色列人也結集兵力，他們安營在以拉谷，排開陣勢和非利士人對峙。非利士營裏出來一個戰將，叫歌利亞，是迦特人。他身高九英尺多，頭戴銅戰盔，身穿重達五千舍客勒的銅鎧甲。他腿上戴着銅護膝，武器中有一把銅短劍，而矛槍杆子有織布機軸那麼粗，槍尖是鐵的，重達六百舍客勒。這個人站

shekels; The champion stood and shouted to the ranks of Israel. I am the Philistine champion; choose your man to meet me. If he can kill me in fair fight, we will become your slaves; but if I prove too strong for him and kill him, you shall be our slaves and serve us. When Saul and the Israelites heard what the Philistine said, they were shaken and dismayed.

Morning and evening for forty days the Philistine came forward and took up his position. Then one day Jesse said to his son David, 'Take your brothers an ephah of this parched grain and these ten loaves of bread, and run with them to the camp. See if your brothers are well and bring back some token from them.'

Early next morning David left someone in charge of the sheep, set out on his errand and went as Jesse had told him. He reached the lines just as the army was going out to take up position and was raising the war-cry. Goliath, came out from the Philistine ranks and issued his challenge in the same words as before; David turned to his neighbours and said, 'What is to be done for the man who kills this Philistine and wipes out our disgrace? And who is he, an uncircumcised Philistine, to defy the army of the living God?'

What David had said was overheard and reported to Saul, who sent for him. David said to Saul, 'Sir, I am my father's shepherd; when a lion or bear comes and carries off a sheep from the flock, I go after it and attack it and rescue the victim from its jaws. Lions I have killed and bears, and this uncircumcised Philistine will fare no better than they.' 'Go then,' said Saul; 'and the Lord will be with you.' He put his own tunic on David, placed a bronze helmet on his head and gave him a coat of mail to wear; he then fastened his sword on David over his tunic. But David hesitated, because he had not tried them. So he took them off. Then he picked up his stick, chose five smooth stones from the brook and put them in a shepherd's bag which served as his pouch. He walked out to meet the Philistine with his sling in his hand.

The Philistine came on towards David, with his shield-

在陣前對以色列士兵大喊：「我是非利士戰將，找個人來和我交手吧。如果在公平的交戰中他把我殺死，我們就甘願做你們的奴僕。但如果我比他強，殺了他，那你們就得做我們的奴隸，供我們差使。」掃羅和以色列人聽見這非利士人的話都嚇得發抖，十分害怕。

這樣每天早晚，整整四十天歌利亞都到陣前來罵戰。有一天，耶西對兒子大衛說：「給你幾個哥哥拿上一伊法烤麥和十個大麵包，快到他們的營地去。看看你哥哥們好不好，給我捎個回話來。」

第二天一早，大衛讓別人替他看羊，自己就出發去完成耶西派給他的差事。他到達前綫時正是大軍出發列陣吶喊的時候。歌利亞從非利士人隊伍中走出陣前，像以前那樣對他們罵戰，大衛問他身邊的人說：「如果有人能殺死這個非利士人，除掉以色列的恥辱，會得到什麼獎賞？這個沒行割禮的非利士人是誰？他竟敢對抗永生的上帝的軍隊？」

大衛說的話有人報告給掃羅，掃羅叫人找大衛去見他。大衛對掃羅說：「我替我父親牧羊，當獅子或熊來羊羣抓羊吃時，我就去追逐它，打它，把羊從虎口中救出來。我殺死過獅子和熊，這個沒行割禮的非利士人不會比它們強多少。」「那就去吧！」掃羅說：「願天主保祐你。」他把他的戰袍給大衛穿上，又給他帶上銅盔，戰袍外面又加上鎧甲，然後把他的劍給大衛佩在戰袍上。但大衛不要，因為他從沒有這樣武裝過自己。他脫掉了這套戰衣，拾起自己的棍子，從小溪裏挑了五塊光滑的石頭放在他當口袋用的牧羊袋裏。他就拿着投石彈弓走出去迎戰那非利士人。

那非利士人迎大衛走過來，前面是攜盾的士兵，他上下打

bearer marching ahead; and he looked David up and down and had nothing but contempt for this handsome lad with his ruddy cheeks and bright eyes. He said to David, 'Am I a dog that you come out against me with sticks?' And he swore at him in the name of his god. 'Come on,' he said, 'and I will give your flesh to the birds and the beasts.' David answered, 'The Lord will put you into my power this day; I will kill you and cut your head off and leave your carcass and the carcasses of the Philistines to the birds and the wild beasts; all the world shall know that there is a God in Israel.'

When the Philistine began moving towards him again, David ran quickly to engage him. He put his hand into his bag, took out a stone, slung it, and struck the Philistine on the forehead. The stone sank into his forehead, he fell flat on his face on the ground. Then he ran to the Philistine, dispatched him and cut off his head. The Philistines, when they saw that their hero was dead, turned and ran. The men of Israel and Judah at once raised the war-cry and hotly pursued them all the way to Gath and even to the gates of Ekron.

At the home-coming of the army when David returned from the slaughter of the Philistines, the women as they made merry sang to one another:

Saul made havoc among thousands
but David among tens of thousands.

Saul was furious, and the words rankled. From that day forward Saul kept a jealous eye on David.

量一下大衞，對這臉頰緋紅，目光炯炯的俊小子顯出一副輕蔑的神情。他對大衞說：「你把我當作是狗嗎？你拿着棍子來迎戰我？」他向自己的神起誓，指罵大衞：「來吧，我要拿你的肉餵鳥獸。」大衞說：「今天天主把你交到我手裏，我要殺死你，砍下你的頭，把你和其他非利士人的屍體扔去餵鳥獸，讓全世界都會知道以色列有上帝庇佑。」

當那非利士人要走近他時，大衞迅速地迎向他。他探手入口袋，掏出一塊石頭，彈射進歌利亞的前額裏，他就向前扑倒在地上。大衞跑向歌利亞迅速地割下他的頭顱。那些非利士士兵看到他們的英雄已經死去，轉身就逃命。以色列人和猶大人立即一擁而前，吶喊起來，窮追敵人直至迦特，甚至追到以革倫城下。

在大衞和非利士人廝殺完凱旋返回家園時，婦女們編了曲子對唱取樂：「掃羅殺死幾千，大衞殺死幾萬。」掃羅聽了很生氣，這話使他耿耿於懷。從此他對大衞心存妒忌。

40 *David Became a Fugitive*

1 Samuel

Saul spoke to Jonathan his son and all his household about killing David. But Jonathan was devoted to David and told him that his father Saul was looking for an opportunity to kill him.

An evil spirit from the Lord came upon Saul as he was sitting in the house with his spear in his hand; and David was playing the harp. Saul tried to pin David to the wall with the spear, but he avoided the king's thrust so that Saul drove the spear into the wall. David escaped and got safely away. That night Saul sent servants to keep watch on David's house, intending to kill him in the morning, but David's wife Michal warned him to get away that night, She let David down through a window and he slipped away and escaped.

Then David made his escape from Naioth in Ramah and came to Jonathan. He asked, 'What is my offence? What does your father think I have done wrong, that he seeks my life?' Jonathan answered him, 'God forbid! There is no thought of putting you to death.' David answered, 'It is new moon tomorrow, and I ought to dine with the king. Let me go and lie hidden in the fields until the third evening. If your father happens to miss me, if he flies into a rage, you will know that he is set on doing me wrong.'

So David hid in the fields. The new moon came, the dinner was prepared, and the king sat down to eat. Jonathan too was present, but David's place was empty. That day Saul said nothing. But on the second day, the day after the new moon,

四十　大衛逃亡

撒母耳記上

　　掃羅對兒子約拿丹和家人說要殺死大衛。但約拿丹喜歡大衛，他告訴大衛他父親要找機會殺他。

　　上帝以魔靈降在掃羅身上，他正坐在家中，手持長矛，大衛則在彈豎琴。掃羅企圖用長矛擲大衛，把他刺穿紮在牆上，但大衛躲開了掃羅的突襲，結果那矛只穿了牆壁。大衛逃掉躲了起來，當晚掃羅又派人去守着大衛的房外，打算翌晨殺死他，但大衛的妻子米甲催他連夜趕快逃走。她從一扇窗戶上把大衛縋下去，大衛就悄悄逃掉了。

　　後來，大衛又從拉瑪的拿約逃去找約拿丹。他問，"我犯了什麼錯？我幹了什麼錯事使你父親認為非要我的命不可？"約拿丹回答他："但願沒有這樣的事！沒有人要殺死你。"大衛回答："明天是初一，我該同王共餐。我想藏在田野裏三個晚上。如果你父親發現我不在，……大發脾氣，你就知道他是決心要殺我的。"

　　於是大衛就藏在田野裏。新月升起，宴席擺好了，國王坐下來吃飯。約拿丹也在場，但大衛的座位是空着的。那天掃羅也沒說甚麼。但是第二天，初二那天，大衛的座位還是空着，

David's place was still empty, and Saul said to his son Jonathan, 'Why has not the son of Jesse come to the feast, either yesterday or today?' Jonathan answered Saul. 'David asked my leave and said, "Our family is holding a sacrifice in the town and my brother himself has ordered me to be there. Now, if you have any regard for me, let me slip away to see my brothers." That is why he has not come to dine with the king.' Saul was angry with Jonathan, 'As long as Jesse's son remains alive on earth, neither you nor your crown will be safe. Send at once and fetch him; he deserves to die.' Jonathan answered his father, 'Deserves to die! Why? What has he done?' At that, Saul picked up his spear and threatened to kill him; and he knew that his father was bent on David's death. Jonathan left the table in a rage.

Next morning, Jonathan went out into the fields to meet David at the appointed time. David got up from behind the mound and bowed humbly three times. Then they kissed one another and shed tears together. Jonathan said to David, 'Go in safety; we have pledged each other in the name of the Lord who is witness for ever between you and me and between your descendants and mine.'

David made his escape and went from there to the cave of Adullam. When his brothers and all his family heard that he was there, they joined him. Men in any kind of distress or in debt or with a grievance gathered round him, about four hundred in number, and he became the chief.

When Saul returned from the pursuit of the Philistines, he learnt that David was in the wilderness of En-gedi. So he took three thousand men picked from the whole of Israel and went in search of David and his men to the east of the Rocks of the Wild Goats. There beside the road were some sheepfolds, and near by was a cave, at the far end of which David and his men were sitting concealed. Saul came to the cave and went in to relieve himself. His men said to David, 'The day has come: the Lord has put your enemy into your hands, as he promised he would, and you may do what you please with him.' David

掃羅就對兒子約拿丹說：“爲什麼耶西的兒子昨天和今天都不來吃飯？”約拿丹回答掃羅：“大衞向我請假說：‘我家人要在城裏獻祭，我哥哥囑咐我回去。如果你照顧我，那就讓我悄悄去見我的哥哥們。’這就是他沒來同王共餐的原因。”掃羅對約拿丹大發脾氣說：“只要耶西的兒子還活在世上，你也好，你將來的王位也好，都不會安全的。趕快派人抓他來，他該被處死。”約拿丹說：“該被處死！爲什麼？他幹了什麼啦？”聽到這話，掃羅拿起長矛威脅要殺他，約拿丹明白他父親是橫下心要殺大衞。他就怒氣冲冲地離開飯桌走了。

第二天早上，按約好的時間約拿丹到地裏去見大衞，大衞從土坡後面站起來，向他恭順地三鞠躬。然後他們倆互相親吻，一齊淌起眼淚來。約拿丹對大衞說：“你可以安全地走了。我們曾彼此以天主的名義發過誓，天主是你同我及你我後代之間的永遠見証人。”

大衞從那兒逃到了亞杜蘭山洞。他的哥哥們同家人聽到他在那裏就去找他。各種各樣不幸的、受寃屈的和欠債的人都去投奔他，有大約四百人左右，他就成爲他們的首領。

掃羅追趕非利士人回來，聽說大衞在隱基底的曠野裏。掃羅就從全以色列挑了三千人去追捕大衞和他的手下，他們一直追到野羊岩東面。在那兒沿路旁有一些羊圈，不遠處還有個山洞，而大衞和他的隨從就在洞的深處藏着。掃羅來到了山洞，就進去解手。大衞手下的人對大衞說：“這一天可來了，天主像他曾經答應過的那樣，把你的敵人送到你手中，你現在可以

said to his men, 'God forbid that I should harm my master, the Lord's anointed, or lift a finger against him. He himself got up stealthily and cut off a piece of Saul's cloak; Saul rose, left the cave and went on his way; whereupon David also came out of the cave and called after Saul, 'My lord the king!' When Saul looked round, David prostrated himself in obeisance and said to him, 'Why do you listen when they say that David is out to do you harm? Today you can see for yourself that the Lord put you into my power in the cave; I had a mind to kill you, but no, I spared your life. Look, my dear lord, look at this piece of your cloak in my hand. I cut it off, but I did not kill you. I will never lift my hand against you.'

When David had finished speaking, Saul said, 'Is that you, David my son?', and he wept. Then he said, 'The right is on your side, not mine;... so may the Lord reward you well for what you have done for me today! I know now for certain that you will become king, and that the kingdom of Israel will flourish under your rule. Swear to me by the Lord then that you will not exterminate my descendants and blot out my name from my father's house.' David swore an oath to Saul; and Saul went back to his home, while David and his men went up to their fastness.

隨意處置掃羅了。"大衛對他手下的人說："上帝不許我傷害我主人，他是天主封的王，動個指頭傷他也不行的。"他悄悄走過去割下掃羅衣服的一角。掃羅解手完起來出山洞繼續前行，大衛隨着也走出洞來，在掃羅後呼喚他："我主，我王！"掃羅回頭看，大衛拜倒在地向王表示尊敬。他對掃羅說："你為什麼聽信別人說大衛想害你呢？今天你可以自己看到，在洞裏天主把你交到我手中，我本想殺了你，但沒有這麼做。我沒有殺你。看吧，親愛的王，看看我手上你的一角衣襟吧。我割下了它，却沒有傷你。我永遠不會提起手來反對你的。"

大衛說完後，掃羅說："原來是你，大衛，我的孩子？"他哭了起來。然後他說："正義在你的一邊，我是沒理的，願上帝為你今天對我行善而讓你得善報。我現在確信你將成為一國之君，以色列王國會在你的治理下繁榮興盛。你在天主前對我起誓吧：你不會滅絕我的後代，不會把我的名字從我的家族中抹掉。"大衛向掃羅發了誓，掃羅就回家去了。大衛則同他的人馬返回營寨。

41 David and Abigail

1 Samuel

There was a man at Carmel in Maon, who had great influence and owned three thousand sheep and a thousand goats; and he was shearing his flocks in Carmel. His name was Nabal and his wife's name Abigail; she was a beautiful and intelligent woman, but her husband, a Calebite, was surly and mean. David heard in the wilderness that Nabal was shearing his flocks, and sent ten of his men, saying to them, 'Go up to Carmel, find Nabal and give him my greetings. You are to say, "All good wishes for the year ahead! Prosperity to yourself, your household, and all that is yours! I hear that you are shearing. Your shepherds have been with us lately and we did not molest them; nothing of theirs was missing all the time they were in Carmel. Receive my men kindly, for this is an auspicious day with us, and give what you can to David your son and your servant."' David's servants came and delivered this message to Nabal in David's name. When they paused, Nabal answered, 'Who is David? Who is this son of Jesse? In these days every slave who breaks away from his master sets himself up as a chief. Am I to take my food and my wine and the meat I have provided for my shearers and give it to men who come from I know not where?' David's men turned and made their way back to him and told him all this. He said to his men, 'Buckle on your swords, all of you.' So they buckled on their swords and followed David, four hundred of them, while two hundred stayed behind with the baggage.

One of the young men said to Abigail, Nabal's wife, 'David

四十一　娶亞比該

撒母耳記上

　　在瑪雲的迦密有一個勢力很大的人，他擁有三千頭綿羊，一千頭山羊，他通常是在迦密剪羊毛。他的名字叫拿八，他的妻子叫亞比該，她是一個美麗而聰明的女人，但她的丈夫，那個迦勒族人却是個又粗暴又小氣的人。大衞在曠野裏聽說拿八在剪羊毛，就派了十個人去那裏。大衞對他們說："到迦密找拿八，代我向他問好。你們就說：'願你今年萬事如意，你和你全家及你的一切東西都興旺繁榮！我聽說你在剪羊毛，你的牧羊人近來一直都跟我們在一起，我們沒有欺侮他們，他們在迦密時也沒丟失過任何東西。請善待我的來人，因爲對我們來說這是個吉祥的日子。求你隨便賞賜點東西給你的兒子和僕人大衞吧。'"大衞的僕人到了那裏向拿八轉告了大衞的話。他們說完，拿八就說："誰是大衞？這個耶西的兒子是誰？現在的世道是每個逃離主人的奴僕都自稱是頭領。難道我該把給剪羊毛工人的食物和酒肉轉送給這些不知從什麼地方來的人嗎？"大衞派的人只好折回，告訴大衞事情的經過。大衞對他們說："你們每個人都帶上刀劍。"他們就拿了刀劍跟着大衞，一共四百人，還有兩百人留下照看行李雜物。

　　有個青年對拿八的妻子亞比該說："大衞派了使者從曠野

219

sent messengers from the wilderness to ask our master politely for a present, and he flew out at them. The men have been very good to us and have not molested us, nor did we miss anything all the time we were going about with them in the open country. They were as good as a wall round us, night and day, while we were minding the flocks. Think carefully what you had better do, for it is certain ruin for our master and his whole family; he is such a good-for-nothing that it is no good talking to him.' So Abigail hastily collected two hundred loaves and two skins of wine, five sheep ready dressed, five measures of parched grain, a hundred bunches of raisins, and two hundred cakes of dried figs, and loaded them on asses, but told her husband nothing about it. Then she said to her servants, 'Go on ahead, I will follow you.' As she made her way on her ass, hidden by the hill, there were David and his men coming down towards her, and she met them.

When Abigail saw David she dismounted in haste and prostrated herself before him, bowing low to the ground at his feet, and said, 'Let me take the blame, my lord, but allow me, your humble servant, to speak out and let my lord give me a hearing. How can you take any notice of this good-for-nothing? He is just what his name Nabal means: "Churl" is his name, and churlish his behaviour. Here is the present which I, your humble servant, have brought; give it to the young men under your command. When the Lord has made good all his promises to you, and has made you ruler of Israel, you will remember me, your servant.' David said to Abigail, 'Blessed is the Lord the God of Israel who has sent you today to meet me. A blessing on your good sense, a blessing on you because you have saved me today from the guilt of bloodshed and from giving way to my anger.' Then David took from her what she had brought him and said, 'Go home in peace, I have listened to you and I grant your request.'

On her return she found Nabal holding a banquet in his house, a banquet fit for a king. He grew merry and became very drunk, so drunk that his wife said nothing to him, trivial

裏來，很有禮貌地向我們主人討個禮，他却激怒了他們。這些人一直對我們很好，和他們在野外相處時，他們從不欺侮我們，我們也從來沒有丟失過東西。他們就像圍牆一樣，日夜保護着我們看管羊羣。你該想想怎麼辦才好，因爲這肯定會對我們主人拿八和他一家不利。他是個無用的人，和他說也沒用。"於是亞比該急忙準備了兩百個大麵包和兩皮袋酒，五隻收拾好的羊，五細亞烘麥，一百串葡萄乾，兩百個乾無花果餅，把他們都馱在驢上，但她並沒有對丈夫說此事。然後她對僕人說："你們先走，我隨後就到。"當她騎着驢子在山間小路上走時，大衞和他的人正下山朝她來走，她和他們相遇了。

亞比該一見大衞就趕忙從驢子上下來，拜倒在地，俯伏在他脚前說："讓我來承担罪過吧，我主，讓你卑下的婢僕我說幾句話，請我主聽我說。你不必理會拿八這樣一個不成器的人，他就像他的名字拿八那樣，意思就是"愚頑"，他爲人就是愚頑。這裏是你的卑賤的婢僕我帶來送給你的禮品，把它送給你手下的年輕人吧。當天主兌現給你的諾言，使你成爲以色列的君主時，求你記得我，你的婢僕。"大衞對亞比該說："感謝以色列的天主上帝讓你今天來見我，感謝你和你的好意，因爲你使我今天不致於進行一場殺戮，不致於聽任我意氣行事。"大衞就收下了她帶來的東西，說："安心地回家吧，我聽從你，接受你的要求。"

亞比該到家後發現拿八正在家裏擺酒席，像國王那樣的排場。他心情愉快，喝得酩酊大醉，以致他妻子甚麼也沒法跟他

or serious, till daybreak. In the morning, when the wine had worn off, she told him everything, and he had a seizure and lay there like a stone. Ten days later the Lord struck him again and he died. When David heard that Nabal was dead he said, 'Blessed be the Lord, who has himself punished Nabal for his insult, and has kept me his servant from doing wrong. The Lord has made Nabal's wrongdoing recoil on his own head.' David then sent to make proposals that Abigail should become his wife. And his servants came to Abigail at Carmel and said to her, 'David has sent us to fetch you to be his wife.' She rose and prostrated herself with her face to the ground, and said, 'I am his slave to command, I would wash the feet of my lord's servants.' So Abigail made her preparations with all speed and, with her five maids in attendance, accompanied by David's messengers, rode away on an ass; and she became David's wife.

說，這樣直到天亮。早上，酒勁過去後，她才對他說了那事，他突然中風不醒人事，躺在那兒像塊石頭。十天後，天主再給他一擊，他就死去了。大衛聽到拿八的死訊，說："讚美天主，他親手懲罰了拿八侮辱人的罪過，又沒有讓他的僕人我去做錯事。天主已讓拿八惡有惡報。"大衛於是派人向亞比該求婚。他的僕人到了迦密見到亞比該說："大衛派我們來接你去做他妻子。"她起身俯伏地上叩拜，說："我是她的奴婢，聽他的吩咐。我願爲我主的僕人洗腳。"於是，亞比該很快收拾停當，帶上五個隨身侍婢，在大衛的使者陪伴下，騎驢子出發。她就做了大衛的妻子。

42   The Death of Saul

1,2 Samuel

The Philistines fought a battle against Israel, and the men of Israel were routed, leaving their dead on Mount Gilboa. The Philistines hotly pursued Saul and his sons and killed the three sons, Jonathan, Abinadab and Malchishua. The battle went hard for Saul, for some archers came upon him and he was wounded in the belly by the archers. So he said to his armour-bearer, 'Draw your sword and run me through, so that these uncircumcised brutes may not come and taunt me and make sport of me.' But the armour-bearer refused, he dared not; whereupon Saul took his own sword and fell on it. When the armour-bearer saw that Saul was dead, he too fell on his sword and died with him.

Next day, when the Philistines came to strip the slain, they found Saul and his three sons lying dead on Mount Gilboa. They cut off his head and stripped him of his weapons; then they sent messengers through the length and breadth of their land to take the good news to idols and people alike. They nailed his body on the wall of Beth-shan. When the inhabitants of Jabeshgilead heard what the Philistines had done to Saul, the bravest of them journeyed together all night long and recovered the bodies of Saul and his sons from the wall of Beth-shan.

David made this lament over Saul and Jonathan his son; and he ordered that this dirge over them should be taught to the people of Judah. It was written down and may be found in the Book of Jashar:

四十二 掃羅之死

撒母耳記上，下

　　非利士人對以色列人開戰，以色列人被擊敗，屍體棄遍基利波山上。非利士人緊追掃羅和他的幾個兒子，把他的三個兒子：約拿丹、亞比拿達和麥基舒亞都殺死了。掃羅這仗打得很艱苦，敵人的弓箭手追上他，他中箭腹部受傷。他就對他的侍衛說："拔出你的劍刺死我吧，不要讓這些沒行過割禮的畜生來奚落耻笑我。"但他的侍衛不肯這樣做，也沒勇氣這樣做。掃羅就拔出劍來臥劍自殺了。侍衛見掃羅死了，自己也撲在劍上以身殉主。

　　第二天非利士人來搜掠屍物，發現掃羅和他三個兒子的陳屍在基利波山上。他們割下他的首級，取下他的武器，又派人到非利士人全境各處去向人民和他們崇拜的偶像報喜。他們把掃羅的屍體釘在伯珊的城牆上。雅比基列的居民聽到非利士人那樣對掃羅，他們當中的一些勇士就連夜趕路到伯珊，把掃羅和他幾個兒子的屍體從城牆上奪回來。

　　大衞哀悼掃羅和掃羅的兒子約拿丹；他命令把他為死者作的哀歌教給猶大人民唱。這就是在雅煞珥書上可以找到的那首哀歌：

O prince of Israel, laid low in death!
How are the men of war fallen!

Tell it not in Gath,
proclaim it not in the streets of
    Ashkelon,
    lest the Philistine women rejoice,
    lest the daughters of the uncircumcised exult.

Hills of Gilboa, let no dew or rain fall on you,
no showers on the uplands!
For there the shields of the warriors lie tarnished,
and the shield of Saul, no longer bright with oil.
The bow of Jonathan never held back
from the breast of the foeman, from the blood of the slain;
the sword of Saul never returned empty to the scabbard.

Delightful and dearly loved were Saul and Jonathan;
in life, in death, they were not parted.
They were swifter than eagles, stronger than lions.

Weep for Saul, O daughters of Israel!
who clothed you in scarlet and rich embroideries,
who spangled your dress with jewels of gold.

How are the men of war fallen, fallen on the field!
    O Jonathan, laid low in death!
I grieve for you, Jonathan my brother;
    dear and delightful you were to me;

啊，以色列之王，你已倒臥沙場！
無數戰士都已陣亡！
不要在迦特流傳，
也不要在亞實基倫街上宣揚，
否則非利士的女人就高興，
否則異教徒的女兒更歡狂。

基利波的山岳，願你雨露稀罕，
高原萬物枯乾。
只因英雄的盾甲散棄山上，
掃羅的鎧甲已暗淡無光，
約拿丹之弓從不在強敵和鮮血前退卻，
掃羅之劍也從不未沾血歸鞘。

掃羅和約拿丹，父子情深，
生不分，死也不離。
他們猛如飛鷹，強勝獅子。

痛哭吧，以色列的女兒，爲掃羅痛哭吧！
是他讓你們穿上繡花紅裳，
是他使你們配上鑽石金裝。

無數戰士都已陣亡！
啊，約拿丹，你已倒臥沙場！
我爲你悲傷，約拿丹，我的兄弟。
你對我曾是那麼可愛可親，

your love for me was wonderful, surpassing the love of women.

Fallen, fallen are the men of war;
    and their armour left on the field.

你的愛對我是至高無上，
遠比兒女私情更强。

一個個英勇的戰士倒下去了，
他們的盔甲遍佈沙場。

2 Samuel

After this David inquired of the Lord, 'Shall I go up into one of the cities of Judah?' The Lord answered, 'To Hebron.' So David went to Hebron with his two wives. The men of Judah came, and there they anointed David king over the house of Judah.

Meanwhile Saul's commander-in-chief, Abner son of Ner, had taken Saul's son Ishbosheth, brought him across the Jordan to Mahanaim, and made him king over Gilead, the Asherites, Jezreel, Ephraim, and Benjamin, and all Israel. Ishbosheth was forty years old when he became king over Israel, and he reigned two years. The tribe of Judah, however, followed David. David's rule over Judah in Hebron lasted seven years and a half.

As the war between the houses of Saul and David went on, Abner made his position gradually stronger in the house of Saul. Now Saul had had a concubine named Rizpah daughter of Aiah. Ishbosheth asked Abner, 'Why have you slept with my father's concubine?' Abner was very angry at this and exclaimed, '...But now, so help me God, I will do all I can to bring about what the Lord swore to do for David: I will set to work to bring down the house of Saul and to put David on the throne over Israel and Judah from Dan to Beersheba.' Ishbosheth could not say another word; he was too much afraid of Abner.

Abner now approached the elders of Israel and said, 'For some time past you have wanted David for your king; now is

四十三　大衞稱王

撒母耳記下

掃羅死後大衞問天主："我是否應該上猶大的一個城邦去？"天主回答："去希伯侖吧。"於是大衞帶了兩個妻子去了希伯侖。猶大的人民到希伯侖來封大衞爲猶大王。

在這同時掃羅的總司令尼珥的兒子押尼珥把掃羅之子伊施波設帶過約旦河到瑪哈念，並立他爲王，去治理基列、亞書利、耶斯列、以法蓮和便雅憫以及以色列全境。伊施波設做以色列王時四十歲。他治理了兩年。猶大的部族就隨了大衞。大衞在希伯侖治理猶大七年半。

當掃羅和大衞兩家彼此長期爭鬥時，押尼珥在掃羅家的勢力逐漸強大。掃羅有個妾叫利斯巴，是愛亞的女兒。伊施波設問押尼珥："你爲什麼與我父親的妾睡覺呢？"押尼珥大怒，就喊道："好吧，願上帝幫我，我現在要盡我所能，做天主要爲大衞做的事情：竭力讓掃羅家族完蛋，把大衞扶上王位，讓他統治從但到別是巴的以色列和猶大兩國。"伊施波設無法再說，他是很怕押尼珥的。

押尼珥去見以色列長老們說："你們很久以來就想要大衞

the time to act.' Abner spoke also to the Benjamites and then went on to report to David at Hebron all that the Israelites and the Benjamites had agreed. When Abner was admitted to David's presence, there were twenty men with him and David gave a feast for them all.

David's men and Joab returned from a raid bringing a great deal of plunder with them, and by this time Abner, after his dismissal, was no longer with David in Hebron. When he left David's presence, Joab sent messengers after Abner and they brought him back from the Pool of Sirah. In revenge for his brother Asahel, he stabbed him in the belly, and he died. When David heard the news he said, 'I and my realm are for ever innocent in the sight of the Lord of the blood of Abner son of Ner. May it recoil upon the head of Joab and upon all his family!'

Joab and Abishai his brother slew Abner because he had killed their brother Asahel in battle at Gibeon.

When Saul's son Ishbosheth heard that Abner had been killed in Hebron, his courage failed him and all Israel was dismayed. Now Ishbosheth had two officers, who were captains of raiding parties, and whose names were Baanah and Rechab; they were Benjamites, the sons of Rimmon of Beeroth. They came to the house of Ishbosheth in the heat of the day and went in, while he was taking his midday rest. Rechab and his brother Baanah crept in, found their way to the room where he was asleep on the bed, and struck him dead. They cut off his head and took it with them. They brought Ishbosheth's head to David at Hebron. David answered Rechab and his brother Baanah, with an oath: 'As the Lord lives, who has rescued me from all my troubles! I seized the man who brought me word that Saul was dead and thought it good news; I killed him in Ziklag, and that was how I rewarded him for his news. How much more when ruffians have killed an innocent man on his bed in his own house? Am I not to take vengeance on you now for the blood you have shed, and rid the earth of you?' David gave the word, and the

做國王，現在是實現它的時刻了。"

押尼珥也同便雅憫人這樣說了。然後他上希伯侖去要找大衛告訴他以色列人和便雅憫人都同意讓他做王。押尼珥帶了二十人去見大衛，大衛設宴招待他們。

大衛的部下和約押去襲擊敵人，滿載掠得的財物而歸。這時押尼珥已告辭回去，不在希伯侖大衛那裏。約押背着大衛打發人去追押尼珥，把他從西拉湖帶回來。爲了給他兄弟亞撒黑報仇，他用刀刺穿了押尼珥肚子，他死了。大衛聽到這消息，他說："我和我的王國在天主面前是無罪的，我們沒沾尼珥之子押尼珥的血，讓這罪過落在約押和他家族的頭上吧！"

約押和他的兄弟亞比篩之所以殺押尼珥，是因爲押尼珥在基遍戰鬥中殺死了他們的兄弟亞撒黑。

當掃羅之子伊施波設聽說押尼珥在希伯侖身被殺死時，他的勇氣全消了，整個以色列都驚慌失措。伊施波設有兩名軍官，是征討隊隊長，名叫巴拿和利甲，是便雅憫人，比錄人臨門的兒子。他們中午正當炎熱時到伊施波設的家中，入屋時伊施波設在午睡。利甲和他兄弟巴拿悄悄進入伊施波設睡覺的房間，把他殺死了。他們割下他的首級帶到希伯侖大衛面前，大衛對利甲和他兄弟巴拿發誓說："永生的天主救我脫離苦難。在洗革拉時，我曾把拿掃羅的死訊當作好消息向我報告的人抓起來殺掉。這就是我報答他帶來這種消息的方法。而這次是你們兩個暴徒竟將一個無辜的人殺死在他自己家中的床上，我能不爲你們的血腥罪行向你們討還血債，從世上把你們除掉

young men killed them; they cut off their hands and feet and hung them up beside the pool in Hebron, but the head of Ishbosheth they took and buried in Abner's tomb at Hebron.

Now all the tribes of Israel came to David at Hebron. David came to the throne at the age of thirty and reigned for forty years.

嗎？"於是大衛下令年輕衛士殺了兄弟兩人，把他們的手、腳砍掉掛在希伯崙池邊。而伊施波設的首級則被送回去埋在希伯崙押尼珥的墓裏。

　　就這樣，以色列的所有部族都歸順了希伯崙的大衛，大衛登基時三十歲，他統治了四十年。

2 Samuel

At the turn of the year, when kings take the field, David
sent Joab out with his other officers and all the Israelite
forces, and they ravaged Ammon and laid siege to Rabbah,
while David remained in Jerusalem. One evening David got
up from his couch and, as he walked about on the roof of the
palace, he saw from there a woman bathing, and she was very
beautiful. He sent to inquire who she was, and the answer
came, 'It must be Bathsheba daughter of Eliam and wife of
Uriah the Hittite.' So he sent messengers to fetch her, and
when she came to him, he had intercourse with her, though
she was still being purified after her period, and then she went
home. She conceived, and sent word to David that she was
pregnant. David ordered Joab to send Uriah the Hittite to
him. So Joab sent him to David, and when he arrived, David
asked him for news of Joab and the troops and how the cam-
paign was going; and then said to him, 'Go down to your
house and wash your feet after your journey.' As he left the
palace, a present from the king followed him. But Uriah did
not return to his house; he lay down by the palace gate with
the king's slaves. David heard that Uriah had not gone home,
and said to him, 'You have had a long journey, why did you
not go home?' Uriah answered David, 'Israel and Judah are
under canvas, and so is the Ark, and my lord Joab and your
majesty's officers are camping in the open; how can I go home
to eat and drink and to sleep with my wife?' David then said
to Uriah, 'Stay here another day, and tomorrow I will let you
go.' The next day David invited him to eat and drink with him

四十四　殺人奪妻

撒母耳記下

又一年到了，在列王出戰的時候，大衞派了約押率領以色列所有官兵出戰。他們打敗了亞捫人，圍攻拉巴城，而大衞却留在耶路撒冷。一個晚上大衞從臥榻起來到宮殿的平頂上散步，他從上面看見遠處有一個婦人在沐浴，容貌很美。他派人去打聽她是誰，回報說："這婦人準是以連的女兒，赫人烏利亞之妻拔示巴。"他就派人去把她接來。接來了之後，大衞就與她同房，恰巧那時她月經剛淨，事後她回了家。她懷了孕，就捎個訊給大衞。大衞命約押把赫人烏利亞叫回來。約押就把烏利亞召來見大衞。烏利亞來到後，大衞只問他約押和軍隊的情況以及戰事的進展，最後對他說："回家去吧，旅途勞累，洗洗脚休息休息。"烏利亞離開宮殿時，國王還派人隨送去一份禮品。但烏利亞沒回家，他同王的奴僕一起臥在宮門口。大衞聽說烏利亞沒回去，就對他說："你長途跋涉，還不回家休息？"烏利亞回答大衞："以色列和猶大士兵都住在帳篷裏，約櫃也在帳篷裏。我主約押和陛下的將領都紮營宿於野外，我怎麼能回家吃喝，與妻子同寢呢？"大衞就對烏利亞說："再留一天吧，明日我讓你回前方。"第二天大衞又邀他一同進

and made him drunk. But in the evening Uriah went out to lie down in his blanket among the king's slaves and did not go home.

The following morning David wrote a letter to Joab and sent Uriah with it. He wrote in the letter, 'Put Uriah opposite the enemy where the fighting is fiercest and then fall back, and leave him to meet his death.' Joab had been watching the city, and he stationed Uriah at a point where he knew they would put up a stout fight. The men of the city sallied out and engaged Joab, and some of David's guards fell; Uriah the Hittite was also killed. Joab sent David a dispatch with all the news of the battle and gave the messenger these instructions: 'When you have finished your report to the king, if he is angry and asks, "Why did you go so near the city during the fight? You must have known there would be shooting from the wall." — if he asks this, then tell him, "Your servant Uriah the Hittite also is dead."'

So the messenger set out and, when he came to David, he made his report as Joab had instructed. David said to the man, 'Give Joab this message: "Do not let this distress you — there is no knowing where the sword will strike; press home your attack on the city, and you will take it and raze it to the ground"; and tell him to take heart.'

When Uriah's wife heard that her husband was dead, she mourned for him; and when the period of mourning was over, David sent for her and brought her into his house. She became his wife and bore him a son. But what David had done was wrong in the eyes of the Lord.

The Lord sent Nathan the prophet to David, he said to him, 'There were once two men in the same city, one rich and the other poor. The rich man had large flocks and herds, but the poor man had nothing of his own except one little ewe lamb. One day a traveller came to the rich man's house, and he, too mean to take something from his own flocks and herds to serve to his guest, took the poor man's lamb and served up that.' David was very angry, and burst out, 'As the Lord lives, the man who did this deserves to die!' Then Nathan said to

餐，並且把他灌醉。但到晚上烏利亞還是裹着毯子睡在王的奴僕那裏，沒有回家。

第二天早上，大衞寫了封信給約押，交給烏利亞帶去。他在信裏寫道：「把烏利亞派到與敵人激戰最厲害的地方，然後你們先撤退，讓他被殺死。」約押一直在圍攻着那座城池，他就把烏利亞派到一個他知道戰鬥會最激烈的地方。城裏的敵人出擊和約押的人廝殺，大衞的一些士兵倒下了，赫人烏利亞也被殺死。約押給大衞送了個報告戰況的急信，他指示信使這麼說：「當你向王報告完畢後，如果他生氣地問你：『爲什麼你們打仗時要那麼靠近城下？你明知城上會射箭下來的。』那你就告訴他：『你的奴僕赫人烏利亞也被殺死了。』」

信使就出發了，當他見到大衞，照約押吩咐的話向大衞報告。大衞對他說：「給約押帶個信，告訴他：『不要爲此難過——誰也難料刀劍向哪兒砍，加緊攻城吧，你們會攻佔它的，要把它夷爲平地。』叫他提起勇氣來。」

當烏利亞的妻子聽到丈夫的死訊，就爲他哀哭。哀悼的日子過去後，大衞就派人把她接進了王宮。她做了他的妻子，給他生了一個兒子。但大衞的所爲被天主視爲大惡。

天主派了先知拿單去見大衞，他對大衞說：「從前，一個城市裏有兩個人，一個富有，另一個貧窮。富人有大羣的牛羊，但窮人除了一隻小母羊外再沒有別的東西。一天，一個旅人來到富人家。這富人小氣，不願從自己的牛羊羣裏拿出一隻去款待客人，就殺了窮人的羊羔給客人吃。」大衞聽了，生氣地大喊：「永生的天主在上，做這事的人該當死罪！」拿單就對大

David, 'You are the man. This is the word of the Lord the God of Israel to you: "I anointed you king over Israel, I rescued you from the power of Saul, I gave you your master's daughter and his wives to be your own, and, had this not been enough, I would have added other favours as great. Why then have you flouted the word of the Lord by doing what is wrong in my eyes? You have struck down Uriah the Hittite with the sword; the man himself you murdered by the sword of the Ammonites, and you have stolen his wife. Now, your family shall never again have rest from the sword." This is the word of the Lord: "I will bring trouble upon you from within your own family; I will take your wives and give them to another man before your eyes."' David said to Nathan, 'I have sinned against the Lord.' Nathan answered him, 'The Lord has laid on another the consequences of your sin: you shall not die, but, because in this you have shown your contempt for the Lord, the boy that will be born to you shall die.'

When Nathan had gone home, the Lord struck the boy whom Uriah's wife had borne to David, and he was very ill. David prayed to God for the child; he fasted and went in and spent the night fasting, lying on the ground. On the seventh day the boy died, and David's servants were afraid to tell him. But David saw his servants whispering among themselves and guessed that the boy was dead. Then David rose from the ground, washed and anointed himself, and put on fresh clothes; he entered the house of the Lord and prostrated himself there. Then he went home, asked for food to be brought, and when it was ready, he ate it. He said, 'While the boy was still alive I fasted and wept, thinking, "It may be that the Lord will be gracious to me, and the boy may live." But now that he is dead, why should I fast? Can I bring him back again? I shall go to him; he will not come back to me.' David consoled Bathsheba his wife; he went to her and had intercourse with her, and she gave birth to a son and called him Solomon. And because the Lord loved him, he sent word through Nathan the prophet that for the Lord's sake he should be given the name Jedidiah.

衞說：“你就是那個人。這是天主以色列的上帝對你說的話：‘我立你爲全以色列之王，我把你從掃羅的手裏救出來，我把你主人的女兒配給你，他的妻妾都成了你的了。如果這些還不夠，我還會再給你其他的大恩大惠。你爲什麼要做我認爲大惡的事來違抗我的意旨呢？是你殺了赫人烏利亞，借亞捫人的刀殺死他，奪了他的妻子。因此你的家族從此將永受刀劍之災。’這是天主的話：‘我要在你家中降災：我要當着你把你的妻妾交給另一個人。’”大衞對拿單說：“我對天主犯了罪。”拿單答道：“天主對你的罪行還作出了另一個懲罰：你不會死，但你這件事是蔑視天主，那你降生的兒子將會死去。”

拿單回家去了，天主降禍於烏利亞妻子給大衞生的兒子，使他病得很厲害。大衞爲孩子向上帝祈禱，他禁了食，進宮裏整夜不吃不喝，躺在地上。到了第七天，孩子死了。大衞的僕人害怕告訴他。但大衞看見僕人們彼此耳語，就猜到孩子死了。於是他從地上起來，沐浴，抹膏，並換了衣裳。他進聖殿向天主伏拜，然後回家，讓僕人開飯。飯來就吃了。他說：“孩子活着時，我不吃不喝，整日哭泣，我想：‘天主也許會寬待我，讓孩子活下去。’現在孩子已死，我爲什麼還要禁食呢？我能使他死而復生嗎？我會去他那兒，他却回不來了。”大衞安慰妻子拔示巴，他與她同寢，她又生了個兒子，起名所羅門。因爲天主愛這孩子，他讓先知拿單轉告大衞：爲了天主，他應起名叫耶底底亞(1)。

_____

(1) 意思是：天主所愛的人。

45   *The Rape of Tamar*

2 Samuel

Now David's son Absalom had a beautiful sister named Tamar, and Amnon, another of David's sons, fell in love with her. Amnon was so distressed that he fell sick with love for his half-sister; for he thought it an impossible thing to approach her since she was a virgin. But he had a friend named Jonadab, son of David's brother Shimeah, who was a very shrewd man. He said to Amnon, 'Why are you so low-spirited morning after morning, my lord? Will you not tell me?' So Amnon told him that he was in love with Tamar, his brother Absalom's sister. Jonadab said to him, 'Take to your bed and pretend to be ill. When your father comes to visit you, say to him, "Please let my sister Tamar come and give me my food. Let her prepare it in front of me, so that I may watch her and then take it from her own hands."' So David sent a message to Tamar in the palace. Tamar came to her brother and found him lying down; she took some dough and kneaded it, made the cakes in front of him and baked them. Then she took the pan and turned them out before him. But Amnon refused to eat and ordered everyone out of the room. When they had all left, he said to Tamar, 'Bring the food over to the recess so that I may eat from your own hands.' Tamar took the cakes she had made and brought them to Amnon in the recess. But when she offered them to him, he caught hold of her and said, 'Come to bed with me, sister.' But she answered, 'No, brother, do not dishonour me, we do not do such things in Israel; do not behave like a beast. Why not speak to the king

四十五　他瑪被姦

撒母耳記下

　　大衛之子押沙龍有個美貌的妹妹叫他瑪。大衛的另一個兒子暗嫩愛上她。暗嫩對他的同父異母妹妹相思成疾，因爲他覺得和還是處女的他瑪親近是不可能的。他有個朋友，名叫約拿達，是大衛兄弟示米亞的兒子，他是個精於世故的人。他對暗嫩說："你爲什麼每天的情緒都如此低落？您不能告訴我嗎？"暗嫩就說出他愛他兄弟押沙龍的妹妹這回事。約拿達就對他說："你躺在床上裝成生病的樣子。你父親來看你時就對他說：'讓我妹子他瑪來給我做吃的，她在我面前做這樣我就可以看着她弄，讓她親手遞給我吃。'"（暗嫩就照他的話做去求大衛。）大衛就打發人去宮中叫他瑪。他瑪來到她哥哥的屋裏，見他躺在床上。她拿了些麵團，在他面前揉好烘成餅。然後她端起鍋把餅倒出來放在他面前。但暗嫩不吃，先把人都打發出房間。待他們都出去了，就對他瑪說："把餅拿前來，你親手給我吃吧。"他瑪把她做的餅拿到暗嫩的跟前。當她把餅遞給他時，他抓住她說："來與我同寢，妹妹。"她說："不，哥哥，不要污辱我，在以色列不能容許有這種事，不要做那禽

for me? He will not refuse you leave to marry me.' He would not listen, but overpowered her, dishonoured her and raped her.

Then Amnon was filled with utter hatred for her; his hatred was stronger than the love he had felt, and he said to her, 'Get up and go.' She answered, 'No. It is wicked to send me away. This is harder to bear than all you have done to me.' He would not listen to her, but summoned the boy who attended him and said, 'Get rid of this woman, put her out and bolt the door after her.' She had on a long, sleeved robe, the usual dress of unmarried princesses; and the boy turned her out and bolted the door. Tamar threw ashes over her head, rent the long, sleeved robe that she was wearing, put her hands on her head and went away, sobbing as she went. Her brother Absalom asked her, 'Has your brother Amnon been with you? Keep this to yourself, he is your brother; do not take it to heart.' So Tamar remained in her brother Absalom's house, desolate. When King David heard the whole story he was very angry; but he would not hurt Amnon because he was his eldest son and he loved him. Absalom did not speak a single word to Amnon, friendly or unfriendly; he hated him for having dishonoured his sister Tamar.

Two years later Absalom invited all the king's sons to his sheep-shearing at Baal-hazor, near Ephron. He approached the king and said, 'Sir, I am shearing; will your majesty and your servants come?' The king answered, 'No, my son, we must not all come and be a burden to you.' Absalom pressed him, but David was still unwilling to go and dismissed him with his blessing. But Absalom said, 'If you cannot, may my brother Amnon come with us?' 'Why should he go with you?' the king asked; but Absalom pressed him again, so he let Amnon and all the other princes go with him.

Then Absalom prepared a feast fit for a king. He gave his servants these order: 'Bide your time, and when Amnon is merry with wine I shall say to you, "Strike." Then kill Amnon. You have nothing to fear, these are my orders; be

獸所爲。你爲什麼不對王說要娶我？他不會拒絕你娶我的。"
他却不聽，強行姦污了她。

　　事後，暗嫩却對她變得滿懷恨意，而且這恨意又遠遠超過
了他原來對她的愛。他對她說："快起來出去。"她答道：
"不，你趕我走是多麼卑劣，這比你對我幹的事更難容忍。"
他不聽她的，就叫來個侍從說："把這女人趕出門外，把門插
上。"她當時身上穿着一件未婚公主們常穿的長袍。那侍從把
她逐出門外，把門插上。他瑪就把灰撒在頭上，扯破身上的衣
服，雙手抱在頭上，哭泣着走回去。她哥哥押沙龍問她："是
你哥哥暗嫩同你親近了嗎？別張揚出去。他是你哥哥，且不要
記在心上。"他瑪就留在押沙龍家中，和外界隔絕。當大衞王
聽到這事，他非常生氣。但他沒有責罵暗嫩，因爲他是他的長
子，他寵愛他。押沙龍對暗嫩却不動聲色，若無其事，他心裏
恨暗嫩，因爲他污辱了他的妹妹他瑪。

　　兩年後，押沙龍邀請大衞所有的兒子去觀看他在以法蓮附
近巴力夏瑣剪羊毛。他竭見國王說："我王，我在剪羊毛，陛
下和你的僕從來嗎？"王答道："不，我兒，我們不能都去，
那會給你造成負擔。"押沙龍再三懇求，大衞還是不想去，他
給他祝福並要他回去。但押沙龍說："你不來，那我哥哥暗嫩
來吧？"王問："爲什麼要他同你去呢？"押沙龍再三請求，
大衞就讓暗嫩和其他王子一同去了。

　　押沙龍備下了款待國王那樣豐盛的宴席，他吩咐僕人們
說："注意時機，當暗嫩喝得有點醉時，我就會說：'動手。'

bold and resolute.' Absalom's servants did as he had told them, whereupon all the king's sons mounted their mules in haste and set off for home.

你們就把暗嫩殺了。你們不要怕，這是我的命令。大膽堅決地幹吧！"押沙龍的僕人就照他說的去做，把暗嫩殺了。其他的王子見了就都趕快騎上騾子四散回家去了。

46 Absalom's Rebellion

2 Samuel

After this, Absalom provided himself with a chariot and horses and an escort of fifty men. He made it a practice to rise early and stand beside the road which runs through the city gate. He would hail every man who had a case to bring before the king for judgement and would say to him, 'I can see that you have a very good case, but you will get no hearing from the king. If only I were appointed judge in the land, it would be my business to see that everyone who brought a suit or a claim got justice from me.' Absalom stole the affections of the Israelites.

At the end of four years, Absalom said to the king, 'May I have leave now to go to Hebron to fulfil a vow there that I made to the Lord? The king answered, 'Certainly you may go'; so he set off for Hebron at once. Absalom sent runners through all the tribes of Israel with this message: 'As soon as you hear the sound of the trumpet, then say, "Absalom is king in Hebron."' Absalom also sent to summon Ahithophel the Gilonite, David's counsellor, from Giloh his city. The conspiracy gathered strength, and Absalom's supporters increased in number.

When news reached David that the men of Israel had transferred their allegiance to Absalom, he said to those who were with him in Jerusalem, 'We must get away at once; or there will be no escape from Absalom for any of us.

When the king departed, all his household followed him except ten concubines, whom he left in charge of the palace.

四十六　押沙龍叛

撒母耳記下

（押沙龍殺暗嫩後逃往基述，在那裏住了三年。大衛思念他，遣約押把他接回耶路撒冷。）後來，押沙龍弄來一輛車和馬匹，配上五十個衛士。他每日早起站在城門的通道旁向每個入城找國王告狀的人拉關係，並說："我認爲你是有道理的，只不過國王不聽你的申訴。如果我當這國家的士司，我就會讓每個告狀的人都得到我公正的裁決。"押沙龍就這樣竊取了以色列人的愛戴。

四年過去了，押沙龍對國王說："我可以去希伯侖還我對天主許過的願嗎？"國王回答："你當然可以去。"他就立即出發去希伯侖。押沙龍派人跑遍了以色列的各個部族去傳話："你們一聽到號聲就說：'押沙龍是希伯侖王。'"押沙龍又派人去把大衛的謀士，基羅人亞希多弗從他住的基羅城找來。反叛的力量聚集起來了，支持押沙龍的人越來越多。

這消息傳到大衛處，說以色列人的人心都轉向押沙龍時，大衛對他那些在耶路撒冷的手下說："我們得馬上離開，不然我們誰也逃不出押沙龍的手心了。"

國王和他的家人一起離開時，十個嬪妃沒有走，他留下她們去看管王宮。

By now Absalom and all his Israelites had reached Jerusalem, and Ahithophel with him. When Hushai the Archite, David's friend, met Absalom he said to him, 'Long live the king! Long live the King!' But Absalom retorted, 'Is this your loyalty to your friend? Why did you not go with him?' Hushai answered Absalom, 'Because I mean to attach myself to the man chosen by the Lord, by this people, and by all the men of Israel.' Then Absalom said to Ahithophel, 'Give us your advice: how shall we act?' Ahithophel answered, 'Have intercourse with your father's concubines whom he left in charge of the palace. Then all Israel will come to hear that you have given great cause of offence to your father, and this will confirm the resolution of your followers.' So they set up a tent for Absalom on the roof and he lay with his father's concubines in the sight of all Israel.

Ahithophel said to Absalom, 'Let me pick twelve thousand men, and I will pursue David tonight. I shall overtake him when he is tired and dispirited. Absalom and all the elders of Israel approved of Ahithophel's advice; but Absalom said, 'Summon Hushai the Archite and let us hear what he too has to say.'

Hushai came, and said to Absalom, 'For once the counsel that Ahithophel has given is not good. You know', he went on, 'that your father and the men with him are hardened warriors. Now he will be lying hidden in a pit or in some such place. My advice is this. Wait until the whole of Israel, from Dan to Beersheba, is gathered about you, countless as grains of sand on the ses-shore, and then you shall march with them in person.' Absalom and all the men of Israel said, 'Hushai the Archite gives us better advice than Ahithophel.' It was the Lord's purpose to frustrate Ahithophel's good advice and so bring disaster upon Absalom.

Hushai told Zadok and Abiathar the priests all the advice that Ahithophel had given to Absalom and the elders of Israel, and also his own. 'Now send quickly to David,' he said, 'and warn him not to spend the night at the Fords of the Wil-

押沙龍同他的以色列衛士此時已到達耶路撒冷，亞希多弗也和他一道。大衛的朋友亞基人戶篩迎着押沙龍說："我王萬歲！我王萬歲！"但押沙龍不以爲然地說："你這是忠於朋友之道嗎？爲什麼你不與大衛同走？"戶篩回答押沙龍："因爲我要歸順天主選中的人，歸順人民和全部以色列人選中的人。"押沙龍就對亞希多弗說："給我們出個主意吧，我們該怎麼做？"亞希多弗說："同你父親的嬪妃同寢吧，他留下她們來看管王宮的。這樣全以色列都會知道你已大大開罪了你的父親，這就使追隨你的人更決心跟你了。"於是他們在宮殿平台上爲押沙龍搭起一個篷所，讓以色列人都知道他同父親的妃子同寢。

亞希多弗對押沙龍說："給我一萬二千人，我要連夜去追大衛，乘他又乏又累時突襲他。"押沙龍同以色列的長老們都贊同亞希多弗的主意。押沙龍說："叫亞基人戶篩來，我們也聽聽他有什麼意見。"

戶篩來了，他對押沙龍說："這一次亞希多弗的主意可不好，你知道，你父親和他的人都是久經沙場的勇士。他現在一定會在一個什麼穴洞裏藏起來。我的意見是等整個以色列，即從但到別是巴像海邊沙粒那麼多的人都歸順於你時，你再親自率領他們去進軍。"押沙龍和長老們說："亞基人戶篩的主意比亞希多弗的要好。"其實這是天主的旨意：以此來阻撓亞希多弗的好計，這一來押沙龍就遭殃了。

戶篩把亞希多弗給押沙龍和以色列長老獻的計謀和他自己出的主意都告訴祭司撒督和亞比亞他。他說："趕快去找大衛，警告他不要在曠野渡口的地方過夜，要立刻渡河，不然王

derness but to cross the river at once, before a blow can be struck at the king and his followers.'

David mustered the people who were with him. Then he divided the army in three, one division under the command of Joab, one under Joab's brother Abishai son of Zeruiah, and the third under Ittai the Gittite. The king gave orders to Joab, Abishai, and Ittai: 'Deal gently with the young man Absalom for my sake.'

The army took the field against the Israelites and the battle was fought in the forest of Ephron.

Now some of David's men caught sight of Absalom. He was riding a mule and, as it passed beneath a great oak, his head was caught in its boughs; he found himself in mid air and the mule went on from under him. One of the men who saw it went and told Joab, 'I saw Absalom hanging from an oak.' While the man was telling him, Joab broke in, 'You saw him? Why did you not strike him to the ground then and there?' The man answered, 'We all heard the king giving orders to you and Abishai and Ittai that whoever finds himself near the young man Absalom must take great care of him.' Joab said, 'I will make a start and show you.' So he picked up three stout sticks and drove them against Absalom's chest while he was held fast in the tree and still alive. Then ten young men who were Joab's armour-bearers closed in on Absalom, struck at him, and killed him. The Israelites all fled to their homes....

The king was deeply moved and went up to the roof-chamber over the gate and wept, crying out as he went, 'O, my son! Absalom my son, my son Absalom! If only I had died instead of you.'

和他的人馬就會全軍覆沒的。"

（聽到了這個消息），大衛把同他一起的人集結起來，然後把隊伍分成三部分，一隊由約押率領，一隊由約押兄弟洗魯雅之子亞比篩率領，第三隊由迦特人以太率領。大衛王吩咐三個頭領："看我面上，寬待年輕不懂事的押沙龍吧。"

國王的軍隊開上戰場和以色列人在以法蓮的樹林裏打起來。

大衛手下一些人發現了押沙龍，他騎着一匹騾子穿過一棵大橡樹下時，頭部被枝椏纏着，人被懸空吊起來，騾子則從他身下跑掉了。看見這情形的一個士兵去報告約押："我看見押沙龍吊在一棵橡樹上。"約押打斷他的話說："你看見他了？為什麼不當場把他打翻在地？"那人回答說："我們都聽見過國王命令你、亞比篩和以太：無論誰對年輕的押沙龍都要好好對待的。"約押說："我要開個頭給你們看看。"於是他拾起三根結實的棍子向吊在樹上活生生的押沙龍的胸部捅去，接着約押手下的十名青壯士兵上前把押沙龍亂刀殺死。以色列人便都四散逃回家去。

（國王聽到押沙龍的死訊）他心裏十分悲痛。他走上城樓邊哭邊喊道："啊，我兒啊，押沙龍，我的兒，我的兒，押沙龍！但願我能替你死去。"

1 Kings

King David was now a very old man and, though they wrapped clothes round him, he could not keep warm. So his household said to him, 'Let us find a young virgin for your majesty, to attend you and take care of you; and let her lie in your bosom, sir, and make you warm.' So they searched all over Israel for a beautiful maiden and found Abishag, a Shunammite, and brought her to the king. She was a very beautiful girl, and she took care of the king and waited on him, but he had no intercourse with her.

Now Adonijah, whose mother was Haggith, was boasting that he was to be king; and he had already provided himself with chariots and horsemen and fifty outrunners. Never in his life had his father corrected him or asked why he behaved as he did. He was a very handsome man, too, and was next in age to Absalom. He talked with Joab son of Zeruiah and with Abiathar the priest, and they gave him their strong support; but Zadok the priest, Benaiah son of Jehoiada, Nathan the prophet, Shimei, Rei, and David's bodyguard of heroes, did not take his side. Adonijah then held a sacrifice of sheep, oxen, and buffaloes. But he did not invite Nathan the prophet, Benaiah and the bodyguard, or Solomon his brother.

Then Nathan said to Bathsheba, the mother of Solomon, 'Have you not heard that Adonijah son of Haggith has become king, all unknown to our lord David? Now come, let me advise you what to do for your own safety and for the

四十七　宮庭傾軋

列王記上

　　大衛到了年紀很老時，雖然衣被裹身，還是覺得不暖和。他的僕從就對他說：“我們去給陛下找一個年輕的處女來侍候你，讓她躺在你懷裏，來暖我主你的身子。”他們走遍以色列去找個美貌的姑娘，終於找來了書念地方的一個少女亞比煞。她是一個十分美貌的少女，她照料國王，侍候他，但他沒同她同寢。

　　（大衛的一個妻子）哈及的兒子亞多尼雅吹噓說自己就要做國王，並且自己已備下了車輛和騎兵，還有五十名差役。他父親從未批評過他，也沒過問他的所作所為。亞多尼雅也是一個英俊的青年，年齡稍比押沙龍小一點。他同洗魯雅之子約押和祭司亞比亞他很投契，他們都很支持他。但祭司撒督、耶何耶大的兒子比拿雅，先知拿單、示每、利以和大衛的警衛都不站在他一邊。於是亞多尼雅舉行了一個獻牛、羊、水牛的祭祀儀式，但他沒有邀請先知拿單，比拿雅和大衛的衛士，也沒請他的兄弟所羅門。

　　先知拿單對所羅門的母親拔示巴說：“你沒聽說嗎？哈及的兒子亞多尼雅在我們國王大衛不知情下自稱國王了。來吧，我來給你出主意去保住你自己並使你的兒子所羅門平安無事。

safety of your son Solomon. Go in and see King David and say to him, "Did not your majesty swear to me, your servant, that my son Solomon should succeed you as king; that it was he who should sit on your throne? Why then has Adonijah become king?" Then while you are still speaking there with the king, I will follow you in and tell the whole story.'...

They came into the king's presence and he gave them these orders: 'Take the officers of the household with you; mount my son Solomon on the king's mule and escort him down to Gihon. There Zadok the priest and Nathan the prophet shall anoint him king over Israel. Sound the trumper and shout "Long live King Solomon!"'...

Adonijah and his guests had finished their banquet when the noise reached their ears. Joab, hearing the sound of the trumpet, exclaimed, 'What is all this uproar in the city? What has happened?' While he was still speaking, Jonathan son of Abiathar the priest arrived. 'Come in', said Adonijah. 'You are an honourable man and bring good news.' 'Far otherwise,' Jonathan replied; 'our lord King David has made Solomon king, and Zadok the priest and Nathan the prophet have anointed him king at Gihon, and they have now escorted him home rejoicing, and the city is in an uproar.' Then Adonijah's guests all rose in panic and scattered. Adonijah himself, in fear of Solomon, sprang up and went to the altar and caught hold of its horns. Then a message was sent to Solomon: 'Adonijah has said, "Let King Solomon first swear to me that he will not put his servant to the sword."' Solomon said, 'If he proves himself a man of worth, not a hair of his head shall fall to the ground; but if he is found to be troublesome, he shall die.' Then King Solomon sent and had him brought down from the altar; he came in and prostrated himself before the king, and Solomon ordered him home.

你去見大衛王，就說：'陛下不是對我起過誓，我的兒子所羅門應繼承王位的嗎？不是說過該讓他登上王位的嗎？那爲什麼現在亞多尼雅成國王了呢？'你說這話時，我就會隨着進去，告訴國王這事前後的經過。"（他們就這樣做了，大衛聽到他們的報告，感到事不宜遲，就命令把祭司，先知等人叫到面前。）

他們來到王面前，國王吩咐道："帶上家將，讓我兒子所羅門騎上國王的騾子，護送他去基訓。在那裏，祭司撒督和先知拿單，給他塗油，封他爲全以色列國王。你們要吹起號角，高呼'所羅門王萬歲！'"（撒督等人按旨辦了。民眾歡呼所羅門王萬歲。）

這時亞多尼雅和他的客人們的宴席剛完，喧鬧之聲傳到他們耳中。約押聽到號角聲，叫起來："城裏喧聲震天是什麼一回事？"他說這話時，祭司亞比亞他的兒子約拿單來到了。亞多尼雅說："請進來，你是位貴客，必帶來好消息。""剛巧相反，"約拿單說："我王大衛已封所羅門爲王了，祭司撒督和先知拿單已在基訓給他塗油，他們現在正護送他回家，一路歡天喜地，歡聲震動了全城。"亞多尼雅的客人聽了都急忙起身、驚慌四散。亞多尼雅自己因爲懼怕所羅門王，跳起身跑到聖壇那裏，抓住了聖壇的角(1)。並請人送訊給所羅門，說"亞多尼雅說：'讓所羅門王先向我起誓。他不會殺死他的僕人我。'"所羅門王說："如果他證實自己是個有品德的人，他頭上一根頭髮也不會掉下，但如果他圖謀不軌，他就必死無疑。"於是所羅門王派人把亞多尼雅從聖壇上叫下來，他謁見所羅門，俯伏叩拜在國王面前。所羅門就讓他回家去了。

_____

(1) 表示要贖罪之意。

When the time of David's death drew near, he gave this last charge to his son Solomon: 'I am going the way of all the earth. Be strong and show yourself a man. Fulfil your duty to the Lord your God; conform to his ways, observe his statutes and his commandments, his judgements and his solemn precepts, as they are written in the law of Moses, so that you may prosper in whatever you do and whichever way you turn. You know how Joab son of Zeruiah treated me and what he did to two commanders-in-chief in Israel, Abner son of Ner and Amasa son of Jether. He killed them both. Do as your wisdom prompts you, and do not let his grey hairs go down to the grave in peace. Show constant friendship to the family of Barzillai of Gilead; they befriended me when I was a fugitive from your brother Absalom.'

So David rested with his forefathers and was buried in the city of David, having reigned over Israel for forty years, seven in Hebron and thirty-three in Jerusalem; and Solomon succeeded his father David as king and was firmly established on the throne.

Then Adonijah son of Haggith came to Bathsheba, the mother of Solomon. 'Do you come as a friend?' she asked. 'As a friend,' he answered; 'I have something to say to you.' 'Tell me', she said. 'You know', he went on, 'that the throne was mine and that all Israel was looking to me to be king; but I was passed over and the throne has gone to my brother; it was his by the Lord's will. And now I have one request to make of you; do not refuse me.' 'What is it?' she said. He

四十八　消除異己

列王記上

　　大衞臨終時對兒子所羅門囑咐："我要走世人皆走之路了。你要做個堅強的大丈夫，完成你對天主的職責，按上帝的吩咐去做，遵守寫在摩西戒律中的那些法規，這樣你就不論做什麼，不論去何處都會順利亨通的。你知道洗魯雅的兒子約押如何對待我以及他如何對待以色列的兩個元帥：尼珥的兒子押尼珥和益帖的兒子亞瑪撒的了。他殺了他們兩人。你要見機行事，不要讓他安然終老。對基列人巴西萊的一家要永遠恩待，當我逃避你哥哥押沙龍之禍時，他們善待過我。"

　　大衞就這樣同他的列祖一起葬在大衞城，他治理以色列共四十年：統治希伯侖七年，而在耶路撒冷三十三年。所羅門繼他而登基爲王，他建立了鞏固的王權。

　　哈及之子亞多尼雅去見所羅門的母親拔示巴。"你是以朋友身分來的嗎？"她問。"是朋友，"他回答，"我要對你說件事。"她說："你說吧。"他說，"你知道，王位本是我的，全以色列都期望我做國王，可是我的却被給了別人，王位落在我弟弟手裏。那是天主之意。現在我求你一件事。請不要拒絕

259

answered, 'Will you ask King Solomon (he will never refuse you) to give me Abishag the Shunammite in marriage?' 'Very well,' said Bathsheba, 'I will speak for you to the king.' So Bathsheba went in to King Solomon to speak for Adonijah. The king rose to meet her and kissed her, and seated himself on his throne. A throne was set for the king's mother and she sat at his right hand. Then she said, 'I have one small request to make of you; do not refuse me.' 'What is it, mother?' he replied; 'I will not refuse you.' 'It is this, that Abishag the Shunammite should be given to your brother Adonijah in marriage.' At that Solomon answered his mother, 'Why do you ask for Abishag the Shunammite as wife for Adonijah? you might as well ask for the throne, for he is my elder brother and has both Abiathar the priest and Joab son of Zeruiah on his side.' Then King Solomon swore by the Lord: 'So help me God, Adonijah shall pay for this with his life.' Thereupon King Solomon gave Benaiah son of Jehoiada his orders, and he struck him down and he died.

Abiathar the priest was told by the king to go off to Anathoth to his own estate. 'You deserve to die,' he said, 'but in spite of this day's work I shall not put you to death, for you carried the Ark of the Lord God before my father David, and you shared in all the hardships that he endured.' So Solomon dismissed Abiathar from his office as priest of the Lord, and so fulfilled the sentence that the Lord had pronounced against the house of Eli in Shiloh.

News of all this reached Joab, and he fled to the Tent of the Lord and caught hold of the horns of the altar; for he had sided with Adonijah, though not with Absalom. When King Solomon learnt that Joab had fled to the Tent of the Lord and that he was by the altar, he sent Benaiah son of Jehoiada with orders to strike him down. Benaiah came to the Tent of the Lord and ordered Joab in the king's name to come away; but he said, 'No; I will die here.' Benaiah reported Joab's answer to the king, and the king said, 'Let him have his way; strike him down and bury him, and so rid me and my father's house of the guilt for the blood that he wantonly shed.

我。"她問："什麼事？"他回答："你同所羅門王求一下（他絕不會拒絕你），把書念女子亞比煞賜我爲妻行不行？"拔示巴說："好吧，我會替你向國王請求。"於是拔示巴就進宮去見所羅門王，爲亞多尼雅說情。王起身親吻迎她，自己坐在王位上，請王母就坐在自己右邊的寶座上。她就說："我對你有個小小的請求，不要拒絕我。"他答道："母親，是什麼事呢？我不會拒絕你的。""是這樣，書念女子亞比煞應該配給你哥哥亞多尼雅爲妻。"聽到這話，所羅門回答他母親道："你怎麼爲亞多尼雅請求娶書念女子亞比煞？你還不如直接要王位好了，因爲他是我哥哥，又有祭司亞比亞他同洗魯雅之子約押輔助。"於是所羅門王以天主的名義起誓："上帝助我，亞多尼雅要爲此而付出性命。"隨後，所羅門王就下令耶何耶大之子比雅，讓他將亞多尼雅處死了。

祭司亞比亞他被國王命令返回家鄉亞拿突去。王說："你本該死，儘管你行事不好，我也不殺你，因爲你在我父大衞面前抬過天主上帝的約櫃，並與我父共過患難。"所羅門撤掉亞比亞他的天主祭司的職位，這樣就實現了天主懲罰示羅的以利一家的話。

這些消息傳到約押耳裏，他逃到天主的帳幕裏，抓住聖壇的角。因爲他雖然沒支持押沙龍，却支持過亞多尼雅。所羅門王聽說了約押逃往天主的帳幕，在聖壇那裏，就派耶何耶大之子比拿雅去殺他。比拿雅來到天主的帳幕，用國王的名義命令約押出來，但他說："不，我就死在這兒。"比拿雅把約押的話報告了國王，王說："按他所願吧，殺了他，埋了，這樣就使我和我父親的家族都擺脫由於約押任意殘殺而欠的血債。……"

49   Solomon's Wisdom

1 Kings

Now King Solomon went to Gibeon to offer a sacrifice, for that was the chief hill-shrine, and he used to offer a thousand whole-offerings on its altar. There that night the Lord God appeared to him in a dream and said, 'What shall I give you? Tell me.' And Solomon answered, 'Thou didst show great and constant, love to thy servant David my father, and thou hast maintained this great and constant love towards him and hast now given him a son to succeed him on the throne. Now, O Lord my God, thou hast made thy servant king in place of my father David, though I am a mere child, unskilled in leadership. Give thy servant, therefore, a heart with skill to listen, so that he may govern thy people justly and distinguish good from evil.' The Lord was well pleased that Solomon had asked for this, and he said to him, 'Because you have asked for this, and not for long life for yourself, or for wealth, or for the lives of your enemies, I grant your request; I give you a heart so wise and so understanding that there has been none like you before your time nor will be after you. I give you furthermore those things for which you did not ask, such wealth and honour as no king of your time can match. And if you conform to my ways and observe my ordinances and commandments, as your father David did, I will give you long life.' Then he awoke, and knew it was a dream.

Then there came into the king's presence two women who were prostitutes and stood before him. The first said, 'My lord, this woman and I share the same house, and I gave birth

四十九　智斷疑案

列王記上

　　所羅門王到基遍去獻祭，因爲國內主要的山地神殿就建在那裏，他每次都要在祭台上獻上一千隻祭牲。在基遍，那夜天主就托夢給他，說：“要我賜你什麼呢？告訴我吧。”所羅門答道：“你確實一直非常恩待你的僕人我父大衞，你一直很眷顧他，如今又給他一個可繼承王位的兒子。天主上帝啊，雖然我還是個少年，也不善於領導，你却讓你的僕人我繼承了父親大衞的王位。因此，請賜給你的僕人兼聽的智慧吧，這樣他才可以公正地治理人民，分辨善惡。”天主聽了所羅門要求的是這，他很高興，他說：“因爲你要求的是這而不是自己的長壽、財富或取你敵人的性命，我答應你的要求。我要賜你智慧，讓你比任何你的前人和後人都聰明，通達事理。我還要給你你沒要求的財富和榮譽，使現世的王君沒有一個能和你相比。如果你像你父親那樣，遵照我的指示行事，恪守我的訓令和戒律，我就賜你長壽。”所羅門醒來，知道是自己做的一個夢。

　　一日，有兩個妓女來見所羅門王，她們站在他面前。第一個說：“主上，這個女人和我同住在一所房子裏，我生孩子時

to a child when she was there with me. On the third day after my baby was born she too gave birth to a child. We were quite alone; no one else was with us in the house; only the two of us were there. During the night this women's child died because she overlaid it, and she got up in the middle of the night, took my baby from my side while I, your servant, was asleep, and laid it in her bosom, putting her dead child in mine. When I got up in the morning to feed my baby, I found him dead; but when I looked at him closely, I found that it was not the child that I had borne.' The other woman broke in, 'No; the living child is mine; yours is the dead one', while the first retorted, 'No; the dead child is yours; mine is the living one.' So they went on arguing in the king's presence. The king thought to himself, 'One of them says, "This is my child, the living one; yours is the dead one", The other says, "No, it is your child that is dead and mine that is alive."' Then he said, 'Fetch me a sword.' They brought in a sword and the king gave the order: 'Cut the living child in two and give half to one and half to the other.' At this the woman who was the mother of the living child, moved with love for her child, said to the king, 'Oh! sir, let her have the baby; whatever you do, do not kill it.' The other said, 'Let neither of us have it; cut it in two.' Thereupon the king gave judgement: 'Give the living baby to the first woman; do not kill it. She is its mother.' When Israel heard the judgement which the king had given, they all stood in awe of him; for they saw that he had the wisdom of God within him to administer justice.

她也和我在一起。生孩子後第三天她也生了個孩子。我們都沒跟別人住，單立門戶，一屋裏只有我們兩人。那夜裏這女人的孩子被她在睡中壓死了，她就半夜起來，乘你的奴婢我睡着時，把我身邊的孩子抱去摟在她懷裏，却把她的死孩子放在我懷中。早上我起身餵奶，發覺孩子死了；但我仔細一看，發現那不是我的親生孩子。"另一個女人打斷她的話說："不對，活着的孩子是我的，死的才是你的。"第一個女人反駁說："不，死孩是你的，活孩是我的。"她們就這樣在國王面前爭吵不休。國王心裏想："她們一個說：'活的是我的孩子；死的是你的。'另一個說：'不，死的是你的，活的是我的。'"於是他下令："給我拿把劍來。"下人拿了把劍來，國王就命令："把這活娃娃切成兩半，一半給這女人，另一半給那女人。"聽到這話，那孩子的生母因為愛自己的骨肉，就對王說："啊，主上，讓她得到孩子吧，無論如何，都別殺這孩子。"另一個女人却說："殺就殺吧，我們倆誰也別想要。"這時國王就下了判斷了："把活着的孩子給第一個女人，不必殺孩子了。她才是孩子的母親。"當以色列人民聽到國王這樣判決時，他們對他都肅然起敬，他們看到他具有天主賜予的智慧，真正能夠主持公道。

1 Kings

God gave Solomon depth of wisdom and insight, and understanding as wide as the sand on the sea-shore, so that Solomon's wisdom surpassed that of all the men of the east and of all Egypt. His fame spread among all the surrounding nations. He uttered three thousand proverbs, and his songs numbered a thousand and five. He discoursed of trees, from the cedar of Lebanon down to the marjoram that grows out of the wall, of beasts and birds, or reptiles and fishes. Men of all races came to listen to the wisdom of Solomon, and from all the kings of the earth who had heard of his wisdom he received gifts.

When Hiram king of tyre heard that Solomon had been anointed king in his father's place, he sent envoys to him, because he had always been a friend of David. Solomon sent this answer to Hiram: 'You know that my father David could not build a house in honour of the name of the Lord his God, because he was surrounded by armed nations until the Lord made them subject to him. But now on every side the Lord my God has given me peace; there is no one to oppose me. So I propose to build a house in honour of the name of the Lord my God. If therefore you will now give orders that cedars be felled and brought from Lebanon, my men will work with yours, and I will pay you for your men whatever sum you fix; for, as you know, we have none so skilled at felling timber as your Sidonians.'

When Hiram received Solomon's message, he was greatly

五十　興建聖殿

列王記上

上帝賜予所羅門極大的智慧和洞悉事物、通達事理的能力，他的才智有如海邊沙粒那樣無窮盡，遠遠超過了埃及和東方的君王。他的名聲傳遍他周圍各國。他作了箴言三千句，詩歌一千零五首。他講草木可以從黎巴嫩的雪松講到牆頭上的牛膝草，也可以縱談飛禽走獸、爬虫魚鱉。各地各種族的人都慕名來聽他的啟迪，世界上許多仰慕他的君王都給他送上禮品。

當推羅王希蘭聽到所羅門受塗油和登基繼父執政後，他派了使者來朝見，因為他一直是大衛的朋友。所羅門回話給希蘭說：“你知道我父親大衛一直無法為他的天主上帝建立一座聖殿，因為當時他四周受敵，後來天主才讓他們歸順了他。如今上帝使我四鄰和睦，沒有人反對我。我因此提議要為天主上帝建一座殿堂。如果你下旨砍一些雪松木，從黎巴嫩運來，我的人將同你的匠人一起工作。我會按你要的價付工錢給你的匠人，如你所知，我們的人不像你們西頓人那樣善於伐木。”

希蘭收到所羅門的信十分高興。於是希蘭不斷供給所羅門

pleased. So Hiram kept Solomon supplied with all the cedar and pine that he wanted, and Solomon supplied Hiram with twenty thousand kor of wheat as food for his household and twenty kor of oil of pounded olives. King Solomon raised a forced levy from the whole of Israel amounting to thirty thousand men. He sent them to Lebanon in monthly relays of ten thousand, so that the men spent one month in Lebanon and two at home.

The house which King Solomon built for the Lord was sixty cubits long by twenty cubits broad, and its height was thirty cubits. The vestibule in front of the sanctuary was twenty cubits long, spanning the whole breadth of the house, while it projected ten cubits in front of the house. Then he built a terrace against its wall round both the sanctuary and the inner shrine. In the building of the house, only blocks of undressed stone direct from the quarry were used; no hammer or axe or any iron tool whatever was heard in the house while it was being built.

He lined the inner walls of the house with cedar boards, the floor he laid with boards of pine. In the innermost part of the house he partitioned off a space of twenty cubits with cedar boards from floor to rafters and made of it an inner shrine, to be the Most Holy Place. The cedar inside the house was carved with open flowers and gourds; all was cedar, no stone was left visible.

He prepared an inner shrine in the furthest recesses of the house to receive the Ark of the Covenant of the Lord. This inner shrine was twenty cubits square and it stood twenty cubits high; he overlaid it with red gold and made an altar of cedar. And Solomon overlaid the inside of the house with red gold and drew a Veil with golden chains across in front of the inner shrine. It had taken seven years to build.

Solomon had been engaged on his building for thirteen years by the time he had finished it. He built the house of Forest of Lebanon. He made also the colonnade with a cornice above.

需要的雪松等木料，而所羅門則給希蘭兩萬侯爾麥子做他家的糧食，還有兩萬侯爾橄欖油。所羅門王從以色列全境徵集了一支三萬人的隊伍，輪流地每月派一萬人去黎巴嫩，這些人去黎巴嫩幹一個月，回來幹兩個月。

所羅門王爲天主造的大殿長六十腕尺，寬二十腕尺，高三十腕尺。聖殿前的門廊長二十腕尺，與殿寬一樣，突出殿前十腕尺。他又靠牆環繞內、外殿修了柱廊。建築時只用從採石場運來的原石料，整個修建過程中，都聽不到錘敲斧砍聲。

所羅門用雪松木鑲屋子的內牆，用松木鋪地板。在房子最裏面他用雪松木從地板到房頂隔出一塊二十腕尺的地方作內殿，這是最神聖的地方。屋內的雪松木鑲板上都刻有瓜果和盛開的花朵，室內只見雪松木，完全見不到石頭。

他在殿的最裏面設內殿來安放天主的約櫃。這內殿二十腕尺見方，二十腕尺高，全都貼上赤金，又造了一個雪松木的祭壇。所羅門把整個殿堂內面都貼上赤金，在內殿前以一個用金鏈編成的帷幕遮住。建這殿歷時七年。

所羅門建自己的宮室整整用了十三年才完工。他建了黎巴嫩林宮。他又建了一個上有花簷的柱廊。

He built the Hall of Judgement, the hall containing the throne where he was to give judgement; this was panelled in cedar from floor to rafters.

His own house where he was to reside, in a court set back from the colonnade, and the house he made for Pharaoh's daughter whom he had married, were constructed like the hall.

When all the work which King Solomon did for the house of the Lord was completed, he brought in the sacred treasures of his father David, the silver, the gold, and the vessels, and deposited them in the storehouses of the house of the Lord.

Then Solomon summoned the elders of Israel, all the heads of the tribes who were chiefs of families in Israel, to assemble in Jerusalem, in order to bring up the Ark of the Covenant of the Lord from the City of David.... King Solomon and the whole congregation of Israel, assembled with him before the Ark, sacrificed sheep and oxen in numbers past counting or reckoning. Then the priests brought in the Ark of the Covenant of the Lord to its place, the inner shrine of the house, the Most Holy Place, beneath the wings of the cherubim.

Then the priests came out of the Holy Place, since the cloud was filling the house of the Lord, and they could not continue to minister because of it, for the glory of the Lord filled his house. And Solomon said:

O   Lord who hast set the sun in heaven,
   but hast chosen to dwell in thick darkness,
here have I built thee a lofty house,
   a habitation for thee to occupy for ever.

他修了審判廳。廳上設有寶座可給他作判案之用。這廳堂從地面到屋頂都鑲了雪松木。

他自己住的房子在柱廊後的院內。他爲他娶的埃及法老之女修建的住宅所用的材料和做法都和審判廳差不多。

當所羅門王爲天主建的殿堂工程峻工後，他把父親大衞的聖物財寶、金銀器皿等都存放在殿堂的儲藏室內。

然後他召集以色列的長老們和各部族的頭人到耶路撒冷來，商議把天主上帝的約櫃從大衞城搬來。（祭司和利未人把約櫃和祭品抬來後，）所羅門王同以色列所有的人民，在約櫃前獻上數不盡的羊和牛。然後由祭司把約櫃抬進內殿至聖所裏，即有翅天使像的翅膀下放好。

祭司從內殿至聖所出來，因爲神殿上充滿了雲靄，他們只好中斷了祭祀儀式，天主的光榮充滿了神殿。這時所羅門說：「啊，創造天上太陽的主啊，你自己却選住在幽暗之處；我在這裏爲你建了一座宏偉的殿堂，一個供你永遠安居的地方。」

1 Kings

The Queen of Sheba heard of Solomon's fame and came to test him with hard questions. She arrived in Jerusalem with a very large retinue, camels laden with spices, gold in great quantity, and precious stones. When she came to Solomon, she told him everything she had in her mind, and Solomon answered all her questions; not one of them was too abstruse for the king to answer. When the queen of Sheba saw all the wisdom of Solomon, the house which he had built, the food on his table, the courtiers sitting round him, and his attendants standing behind in their livery, his cupbearers, and the whole-offerings which he used to offer in the house of the Lord, there was no more spirit left in her. Then she said to the king, 'The report which I heard in my own country about you and your wisdom was true, but I did not believe it until I came and saw for myself. Happy are your wives, happy these courtiers of yours who wait on you every day and hear your wisdom! Blessed be the Lord your God who has delighted in you and has set you on the throne of Israel; because he loves Israel for ever, he has made you their king to maintain law and justice.' Then she gave the king a hundred and twenty talents of gold, spices in great abundance, and precious stones.

And King Solomon gave the queen of Sheba all she desired, whatever she asked, in addition to all that he gave her of his royal bounty. So she departed and returned with her retinue to her own land.

五十一　示巴女王

列王記上

　　示巴女王聽說所羅門賢明，就親自前來用難題考他。她帶了一大隊隨從，用駱駝馱上大批香料和金銀珠寶來到耶路撒冷。會見所羅門時她把她要問的話全都提出來了，所羅門王對答如流，沒有一個問題能難倒他。示巴女王看到了所羅門的智慧，也看到了他建築的宮殿和他桌上的珍饈，還看到了坐在他周圍的朝臣、站在身後穿着制服的侍從、他的上酒侍臣以及他通常給聖殿奉獻的祭牲，她心悅誠服了。她對國王說："我在國內聽到對你和你的智慧的種種稱讚都是真的，我原先不信，現在來了，並親眼看到了。你的妻室和朝臣每天侍隨你，聽你的教誨，他們真是幸福。感謝愛你並讓你登上以色列王位的天主上帝，因為他永遠愛以色列，他讓你當國王來維護法紀和公正。"於是她贈給國王一百二十他連得金子和大批香料和珠寶。……

　　而所羅門王也回贈了示巴女王，除了饋贈的一份厚禮之外，還給了她想要的一切東西。她便告辭和她的隨從返回自己的國家去。

52   The Division of the Two Kingdoms

1 Kings

Jeroboam son of Nebat, one of Solomon's courtiers, an Ephrathite from Zeredah, rebelled against the king. And this is the story of his rebellion. Solomon had built the Millo and closed the breach in the wall of the city of his father David. Now this Jeroboam was a man of great energy; and Solomon, seeing how the young man worked, had put him in charge of all the labour-gangs in the tribal district of Joseph. On one occasion Jeroboam had left Jerusalem, and the prophet Ahijah from Shiloh met him on the road. The prophet was wrapped in a new cloak, and the two of them were alone in the open country. Then Ahijah took hold of the new cloak he was wearing, tore it into twelve pieces and said to Jeroboam, 'Take ten pieces, for this is the word of the Lord the God of Israel: "I am going to tear the kingdom from the hand of Solomon and give you ten tribes. But one tribe will remain his, for the sake of my servant David and for the sake of Jerusalem. I have done this because Solomon has forsaken me; he has prostrated himself before Ashtoreth goddess of the Sidonians, Kemosh god of Moab, and Milcom god of the Ammonites, and has not conformed to my ways. I will appoint you to rule over all that you can desire, and to be king over Israel.

After this Solomon sought to kill Jeroboam, but he fled to King Shishak in Egypt and remained there till Solomon's death.

The reign of King Solomon in Jerusalem over the whole of Israel lasted forty years. Then he rested with his forefathers and was buried in the city of David his father, and he was suc-

五十二　王國兩分

列王記上

　　所羅門的一位臣子、以法蓮支派洗利達人尼八的兒子耶羅波安起來反對國王。他反叛的原因是這樣的：所羅門建造了米羅宮，修補了他父親大衛城的城牆缺口。這耶羅波安是個精力充沛的人，所羅門見這年輕人幹得不錯，就把他派去做管約瑟族工人的監工。有一次耶羅波安離開了耶路撒冷，示羅人先知亞希雅在途中遇見他。亞希雅穿着一件新大衣，這時曠野裏只有他們兩人，亞希雅拿着自己身上的新衣裳，把它扯成十二塊，對耶羅波安說："你拿十塊去，這是以色列的天主上帝的眞言：'我要把王國從所羅門手裏奪回來，現在分給你們十個部族。但爲了我的僕人大衛和耶路撒冷，有一個部族還留在他手中。我這樣做是由於所羅門背棄了我，轉而崇拜西頓人的女神亞斯他錄、摩押神基抹和亞捫人的神米勒公，他沒照我的旨意行事。我將讓你去治理所有你想要統治的地方，成爲全以色列之王。'"

　　因此，所羅門伺機要殺耶羅波安，但他逃往埃及王示撒那裏，在那兒一直住到所羅門去世。所羅門王在耶路撒冷統治了以色列四十年。他死後和列祖一樣在他父親大衛的城裏，由

ceeded by his son Rehoboam.

Rehoboam went to Shechem, for all Israel had gone there to make him king. When Jeroboam son of Nebat, who was still in Egypt, heard of it, he remained there. They now recalled him, and he and all the assembly of Israel came to Rehoboam and said, 'Your father laid a cruel yoke upon us; but if you will now lighten the cruel slavery he imposed on us and the heavy yoke he laid on us, we will serve you.' 'Give me three days,' he said, 'and come back again.' So the people went away. King Rehoboam then consulted the elders who had been in attendance on his father Solomon while he lived: 'What answer do you advise me to give to this people?' And they said, 'If today you are willing to serve this people, show yourself their servant now and speak kindly to them and they will be your servants ever after.' But he rejected the advice which the elders gave him. He next consulted those who had grown up with him, the young men in attendance, and asked them, 'What answer do you advise me to give to this people's request that I should lighten the yoke which my father laid on them?' The young men replied, 'Tell them: "My little finger is thicker than my father's loins. My father laid a heavy yoke on you; I will make it heavier. My father used the whip on you; but I will use the lash."' Jeroboam and the people all came back to Rehoboam on the third day, as the king had ordered. And the king gave them a harsh answer.

When all Israel saw that the king would not listen to them, they went to their homes, and Rehoboam ruled over those Israelites who lived in the cities of Judah.

Then King Rehoboam sent out Adoram, the commander of the forced levies, but the Israelites stoned him to death; thereupon King Rehoboam mounted his chariot in haste and fled to Jerusalem. From that day to this, the whole of Israel has been in rebellion against the house of David.

When the men of Israel heard that Jeroboam had returned, they sent and called him to the assembly and made him king over the whole of Israel. The tribe of Judah alone followed the house of David.

兒子羅波安繼承王位。

羅波安到示劍去，因為所有的以色列人要到那裏去擁他為王。在埃及的尼八之子耶羅波安聽到這消息，他留在埃及沒有來。後來他被召回，他同他的以色列人來見羅波安說："你父親給我們加上了嚴厲的約束，如果你現在減輕他對我們那種奴役和放鬆對我們的約束，我們就歸順你。""給我三天時間，"羅波安說，"到時你們再來吧。"於是耶羅波安他們就離去了。羅波安王就找侍從他父親的元老們來商議："你們給我出個主意該怎麼答覆他們？"元老們說："如果現在你願意為這些以色列人服務，那就讓他們看到你是他們的公僕，以好言對他們，他們以後就會永遠歸順你。"但他不聽這些元老的勸告。他去找那些同他一起長大的年輕侍從商量，問他們："對這些要我減輕我父親加給他們的束縛的人，你們有什麼意見？"這些年輕人回答："告訴他們：'我的小拇指比我父親的腰還粗，我要使我父親給你們的負擔，更重一些。我父親用鞭繩打你們，我却要用皮鞭抽你們。'"當耶羅波安和他的人第三天如約回來見羅波安王時。羅波安就給了他們一個惡狠狠的答覆。

以色列人看到國王無視他們的要求，他們就返回家鄉，由羅波安管治着猶大城的以色列人。

羅波安王派遣監管苦役的亞多蘭去以色列人那裏，却被以色列人用石頭打死了。羅波安王見勢不對就登車逃往耶路撒冷，從那時起到此時，整個以色列都是反叛大衛家族的。

以色列人聽到耶羅波安回來了，他們派人請他到人民面前，擁戴他為整個以色列的國王。只有猶大部族還由大衛家族治理。

53   Elijah's Work

1 Kings

Ahab son of Omri became king of Israel in the thirty-eighth year of Asa king of Judah, and he reigned over Israel in Samaria for twenty-two years. He did more that was wrong in the eyes of the Lord than all his predecessors.

Elijah the Tishbite, of Tishbe in Gilead, said to Ahab, 'I swear by the life of the Lord the God of Israel, whose servant I am, that there shall be neither dew nor rain these coming years unless I give the word.' Then the word of the Lord came to him: 'Leave this place and turn eastwards; and go into hiding in the ravine of Kerith east of the Jordan. You shall drink from the stream, and I have commanded the ravens to feed you there.' He did as the Lord had told him: After a while the stream dried up, for there had been no rain in the land. Then the word of the Lord came to him: 'Go now to Zarephath, a village of Sidon, and stay there; I have commanded a widow there to feed you.' So he went off to Zarephath. When he reached the entrance to the village, he saw a widow gathering sticks, and he called to her and said, 'Please bring me a little water in a pitcher to drink.' As she went to fetch it, he called after her, 'Bring me, please, a piece of bread as well.' But she said, 'As the Lord your God lives, I have no food to sustain me except a handful of flour in a jar and a little oil in a flask. Here I am, gathering two or three sticks to go and cook something for my son and myself before we die.' 'Never fear,' said Elijah; 'go and do as you say; but first make me a small cake from what you have and bring it out to me; and after that

五十三 起死回生

列王記上

（以色列在猶大分治後，經歷了不少動亂和朝代更換。後來暗利建立了以色列第四代王朝，長達五十年之久。）

暗利之子亞哈在猶大王亞撒三十八年時登基爲以色列王，在撒瑪利亞統治以色列達二十二年。他做了許多天主認爲是有罪的事，罪孽比他的前人更甚。

在基列居住的提斯比人以利亞對亞哈說："我是以色列的天主上帝的僕人，我指着永生的天主起誓，除非有我的眞言，否則未來幾年中，將不降露水也不會下雨。"後來天主對他說："離開這兒向東去，到約旦之東基立的溪谷深處隱居。你可以取泉水飲，我則令鴉雀每日給你送食物。"他就照上帝的話做了。過了一個時期，因爲老不下雨，泉水枯竭了。上帝就又給他指點："你到西頓的一個村子叫撒勒法那裏去，就住在那裏。我已吩咐那裏的一個寡婦照顧你。"以利亞就動身去撒勒法。在村口他看見一個寡婦拾柴，就喚她說："請用水罐打點水給我喝。"她就去打水。他從她背後叫道："還請你帶塊麵包給我。"但她說："我對永生的天主上帝發誓，除了罐子裏的一把麵粉和瓶裏的一點油之外，我都沒有別的東西可以維持生活了。我在這裏找些柴禾棍去給我們娘兒倆做點吃的，免得餓死。""別怕，"以利亞說："你就按你說的去做，但先

make something for your son and yourself. For this is the word of the Lord the God of Israel: "The jar of flour shall not give out nor the flask of oil fail, until the Lord sends rain on the land."' She went and did as Elijah had said, and there was food for him and for her and her family for a long time.

Afterwards the son of this woman, the mistress of the house, fell ill and grew worse and worse, until at last his breathing ceased. Then she said to Elijah, 'What made you interfere, you man of God? You came here to bring my sins to light and kill my son!' 'Give me your son', he said. He took the boy from her arms and carried him up to the roof-chamber where his lodging was, and laid him on his own bed. Then he called out to the Lord, 'O Lord my God, is this thy care for the widow with whom I lodge, that thou hast been so cruel to her son?' Then he breathed deeply upon the child three times and called on the Lord, 'O Lord my God, let the breath of life, I pray, return to the body of this child.' The Lord listened to Elijah's cry, and the breath of life returned to the child's body, and he revived; Elijah lifted him up and took him down from the roof into the house, gave him to his mother and said, 'Look, your son is alive.' Then she said to Elijah, 'Now I know for certain that you are a man of God and that the word of the Lord on your lips is truth.'

用你的麵粉給我做一小塊餅，之後再給你們娘兒倆做吃的，因爲以色列天主上帝說了：'麵罐裏的麵粉不會吃完，油瓶裏的油也用不完，一直可以支持到上帝降雨給這片土地之時。'"她就去照以利亞的話做了，果然吃的東西夠以利亞和她娘兒倆吃很長的時間。

後來，這女人的兒子生病了，而且越來越嚴重，終於斷了氣。她就對以利亞說："神人，你爲什麼要干擾我的生活呢？你來到我這裏，讓我的罪過顯露出來，使我兒子死掉！""你把兒子給我吧。"以利亞說。他從她懷裏接過孩子，抱到他住的樓頂小房裏去。他把孩子放在自己床上，然後向天主呼告："我的主啊，你是這樣對待我留宿這家的寡婦嗎？你對她的兒子太殘酷了。"然後他對孩子作了三下深呼吸，並向天主央告："我的主啊，我求你讓這孩子恢復氣息。"天主聽到以利亞的呼告，就讓孩子恢復了氣息，他活過來了。以利亞抱起他，從頂樓把他抱下來交還給他母親，說："看，你兒子活過來了。"她就對以利亞說："我現在真相信你是個神人了，天主借你的口說的話都是真的。"

1 Kings

Naboth of Jezreel had a vineyard near the palace of Ahab king of Samaria. One day Ahab made a proposal to Naboth: 'Your vineyard is close to my palace; let me have it for a garden; I will give you a better vineyard in exchange for it or, if you prefer, its value in silver.' But Naboth answered, 'The Lord forbid that I should let you have land which has always been in my family.' So Ahab went home sullen and angry. He lay down on his bed, covered his face and refused to eat. His wife Jezebel came in to him and said, 'What makes you so sullen and why do you refuse to eat?' 'Are you or are you not king in Israel?' said Jezebel. 'Come, eat and take heart; I will make you a gift of the vineyard of Naboth of Jezreel.' So she wrote a letter in Ahab's name, sealed it with his seal and sent it to the elders and notables of Naboth's city. She wrote: 'Proclaim a fast and give Naboth the seat of honour among the people. And see that two scoundrels are seated opposite him to charge him with cursing God and the king, then take him out and stone him to death.' So the elders and notables of Naboth's city, carried out the instructions Jezebel had sent them in her letter; and sent word to Jezebel that Naboth had been stoned to death.

As soon as Jezebel heard that Naboth had been stoned and was dead, she said to Ahab, 'Get up and take possession of the vineyard which Naboth refused to sell you, for he is no longer alive.' When Ahab heard that Naboth was dead, he got up and went to the vineyard to take possession. Then the

五十四　殺人奪園

列王記上

　　耶斯列人拿伯在撒瑪利亞王亞哈的宮殿附近有個葡萄園。一日，亞哈對拿伯建議說：“你的葡萄園離我宮殿很近，把它讓給我做花園吧。我拿一個更好的葡萄園跟你換，要是你願意，我也可付銀子來買。”但拿伯回答：“天主不容我把祖傳的產業讓給你。”亞哈回到家中很不高興。他躺在床上蒙着臉不吃飯。他的妻子耶洗別進來對他說：“你為什麼這麼不高興？為什麼不吃飯？”（他對她說了此事。）耶洗別說：“你不是以色列的國王嗎？來吧，吃飯吧，也別喪氣。我會把這耶斯列人拿伯的葡萄園作為禮物送給你的。”於是她以亞哈的名義寫了封信，蓋上他的印封好，送去給拿伯那城市的長老和要人。信中她寫道：“你們先齋戒，然後讓拿伯坐在人羣中的高位上。再找兩個無賴坐在他對面，告他褻瀆上帝和國王，然後把他拉出去用亂石打死。”於是拿伯城中的長老和要人就照着耶洗別信上的指示做了；然後找人報告耶洗別，說拿伯已被石頭打死了。

　　耶洗別一聽到拿伯已被亂石打死，就對亞哈說：“起來，你現在擁有拿伯不肯賣給你的葡萄園了，他已經沒命了。”亞哈聽說拿伯死了，他就起來去接收葡萄園。天主就對提斯比人

word of the Lord came to Elijah the Tishbite: 'Go down at once to Ahab king of Israel, who is in Samaria; you will find him in Naboth's vineyard. Say to him, "This is the word of the Lord: Where dogs licked the blood of Naboth, there dogs shall lick your blood."' And the Lord went on to say of Jezebel, 'Jezebel shall be eaten by dogs by the rampart of Jezreel. Of the house of Ahab, those who die in the city shall be food for the dogs, and those who die in the country shall be food for the birds.' When Ahab heard this, he rent his clothes, put on sackcloth and fasted; he lay down in his sackcloth and went about muttering to himself. Then the word of the Lord came to Elijah the Tishbite: 'Have you seen how Ahab has humbled himself before me? Because he has thus humbled himself, I will not bring disaster upon his house in his own lifetime, but in his son's.'

以利亞說：“你立刻去撒瑪利亞見以色列王亞哈，你會在拿伯的葡萄園裏見到他。你對他說：“這是天主的旨意：‘狗隻舔食拿伯的血，也就會舔你的血。’”

上帝又接着說到耶洗別：“狗隻要在耶斯列的城堡外吃耶洗別的肉。凡是亞哈家的人在城裏死的屍體就成為狗食，在城外死的屍體就成為鳥食。”亞哈聽到這話就把衣服撕破，身穿喪服，並且齋戒表示懺悔。他睡覺時也穿着喪服，走來走去，喃喃自語。於是天主對提斯比人以利亞說：“你看見亞哈在我面前這樣低聲下氣了嗎？因為他這樣做，我就暫且不在他活着時降禍於他的家人，但到他兒子那一代我一定要懲罰他們的。”

2 Kings

(1)

The time came when the Lord would take Elijah up to heaven in a whirlwind. Elijah and Elisha left Gilgal.

Fifty of the prophets followed them, and stood watching from a distance as the two of them stopped by the Jordan. Elijah took his cloak, rolled it up and struck the water with it. The water divided to right and left, and they both crossed over on dry ground. While they were crossing. Elijah said to Elisha, 'Tell me what I can do for you before I am taken from you.' Elisha said, 'Let me inherit a double share of your spirit.' 'You have asked a hard thing', said Elijah. 'If you see me taken from you, may your wish be granted.' They went on, talking as they went, and suddenly there appeared chariots of fire and horses of fire, which separated them one from the other, and Elijah was carried up in the whirlwind to heaven. When Elisha saw it, he cried, 'My father, my father, the chariots and the horsemen of Israel!', and he saw him no more.

(2)

The people of the city said to Elisha, 'You can see how pleasantly our city is situated, but the water is polluted and the country is troubled with miscarriages.' He said, 'Fetch me a new bowl and put some salt in it.' When they had fetched it, he went out to the spring and, throwing the salt into it, he said, 'This is the word of the Lord: "I purifty this water. It shall cause no more death or miscarriage."' The water has

五十五　屢顯神迹

列王記下

（一）

到了天主要以利亞乘旋風歸天的日子，以利亞和（他的門徒）以利沙離開吉甲。

五十名先知跟在他們身後，當師徒二人停在約旦河邊時，這些人站在遠處瞧着。以利亞脫下外衣，把它捲起來去擊水，水就分成左右兩半，他們倆就從乾河底走過去。在過河途中，以利亞對以利沙說：“告訴我，在我離去之前我能爲你做些什麼呢？”以利沙說：“讓我能得到雙倍降於你身上的靈。”以利亞說：“這可是一件難事。你如果能看着我怎樣被接上天去，你的願望也許就能實現的。”他們繼續前行，邊走邊說，突然出現了一些火馬和一些火戰車把他們師徒分隔開了。以利亞就被旋風接上天去了。以利沙看見了，就大喊：“我父啊，以色列的戰車和戰馬啊！”說着他已再看不見以利亞了。

（二）

（以利亞身上的神靈降到以利沙身上後）耶利哥城的百姓對以利沙說：“這城位置很好，但水受到污染，女人總是小產。”他說：“給我拿一隻新碗來，裏面放上一些鹽。”他們把碗和鹽拿來了，他走到水源那裏把鹽倒進水中，說：“天主說了：‘我把這水淨化，它再不會造成夭折或小產了。’”那水

remained pure till this day, in fulfilment of Elisha's word.

(3)

A man came from Baal-shalisha, bringing the man of God some of the new season's bread, twenty barley loaves, and fresh ripe ears of corn. Elisha said, 'Give this to the people to eat.' But his disciple protested, 'I cannot set this before a hundred men.' Still he repeated, 'Give it to the people to eat; for this is the word of the Lord: "They will eat and there will be some left over."' So he set it before them, and they ate and left some over, as the Lord had said.

(4)

Naaman, commander of the king of Aram's army, was a great man highly esteemed by his master, because by his means the Lord had given victory to Aram; but he was a leper. On one of their raids the Aramaeans brought back as a captive from the land of Israel a little girl, who became a servant to Naaman's wife. She said to her mistress, 'If only my master could meet the prophet who lives in Samaria, he would get rid of the disease for him.' Naaman went in and reported to his master word for word what the girl from the land of Israel had said. 'Very well, you may go,' said the king of Aram. So Naaman came with his horses and chariots and stood at the entrance to Elisha's house. Elisha sent out a messenger to say to him, 'If you will go and wash seven times in the Jordan, your flesh will be restored and you will be clean'.... So he went down and dipped himself in the Jordan seven times as the man of God had told him, and his flesh was retored as a little child's, and he was clean.

Then he and his retinue went back to the man of God and stood before him; and he said, 'Now I know that there is no god anywhere on earth except in Israel. Will you accept a token of gratitude from your servant?' But he refused.

Naaman had gone only a short distance on his way. When Gehazi, the servant of Elisha the man of God, said to himself, 'What? Has my master let this Aramaean, Naaman, go scot-free, and not accepted what he brought? As the Lord lives, I

直到今天都是潔淨的，以利沙的話完全應驗了。

（三）

　　有一個人從巴利沙利沙來，給神人以利沙帶來一些新收的麵做的麵包，二十個大麥麵包和一些新鮮的麥穗。以利沙說：「把這給人們吃吧。」但他的信徒不同意：「我沒法把這點麵包分給一百個人。」以利沙堅持說：「把它分給人們吃，這是天主的旨意：‘他們吃了還會有剩餘的。’」信徒把餅分給人們，他們吃了真的還有剩餘，和天主說的一點不差。

（四）

　　亞蘭軍隊的統帥乃縵是亞蘭王的寵臣，因為天主通過他使亞蘭獲得了勝利，但他是個麻瘋病人。一次他們襲擊以色列時，亞蘭人擄回了一個小女孩，她成了乃縵妻子的奴婢。這小女孩對女主人說：「如果我男主人能去見撒瑪利亞的先知，他的病就會治好的。」乃縵就向國王報告那以色列女孩的話。亞蘭王說：「好吧，你可以去。」（神人以利沙聽說乃縵找他，就讓人叫他來。）乃縵坐着馬車來找以利沙，站在他家入門的地方。以利沙派一個人出來對他說：「到約旦河去洗七次澡，你身上的麻瘋就會消失，你的身體就會回復光潔了。」乃縵就下到約旦河裏去泡了七次，按神人吩咐的去做了。他身上的皮肉果然平復了，像孩子的那麼光潔。

　　他和他的隨從就回到神人以利沙面前，說：「我現在知道了，這世上只有以色列有上帝。你能接受你僕人的一點禮物表示謝意嗎？」但以利沙不要。

　　乃縵在回家路上行走不遠，以利沙的僕人基哈西想道：「怎麼？我主人讓這亞蘭人乃縵不花一文就走掉了，也不收他

will run after him and get something from him.' So Gehazi hurried after Naaman.... Elisha said, 'Is it not true that you have the money? You may buy gardens with it, and olive-trees and vineyards, sheep and oxen, slaves and slave-girls; but the disease of Naaman will fasten on you and on your descendants for ever.' Gehazi left his presence, his skin diseased, white as snow.

一點東西？我指上帝發誓，我要追他要點東西回來。"基哈西就去追乃縵（他向乃縵要了兩他連得銀子和兩套衣裳回來，但這事被以利沙知道了。）以利沙說："你不是有錢了嗎？你可以用它買園子，買橄欖樹和葡萄園，買牛羊，買男女奴婢了；但乃縵的病却就永遠落在你和你的後代身上。"基哈西剛離開以利沙，皮膚馬上染上痲瘋病，像雪那樣發白。

56   *Jehu Overthrew the Dynasty of Omri*

2 Kings

Elisha the prophet summoned one of the company of prophets and said to him, 'Hitch up your cloak, take this flask of oil with you and go to Ramoth-gilead. When you arrive, you will find Jehu son of Jehoshaphat, go in and call him aside from his fellow-officers, and lead him through to an inner room. Then take the flask and pour the oil on his head and say, "This is the word of the Lord: I anoint you king over Israel"; then open the door and flee for your life.' So the young prophet went to Ramoth-gilead.... When Jehu rejoined the king's officers, they said to him, 'Is all well? What did this crazy fellow want with you?' 'I will tell you exactly what he said: "This is the word of the Lord: I anoint you king over Israel."' They snatched up their cloaks and spread them under him on the stones of the steps, and sounded the trumpet and shouted, 'Jehu is king.'

Then Jehu son of Jehoshaphat, laid his plans against Jehoram, while Jehoram and the Israelites were defending Ramoth-gilead against Hazael king of Aram.King Jehoram had returned to Jezreel to recover from the wounds inflicted on him by the Aramaeans. Jehu said to them, 'If you are on my side, see that no one escapes from the city to tell the news in Jezreel.' he mounted his chariot and drove to Jezreel, for Jehoram was laid up there, and Ahaziah king of Judah had gone down to visit him.

五十六　王朝⁽¹⁾末日

列王記下

先知以利沙叫來一個門徒說："繫上腰帶，拿這瓶膏油去基列的拉末。你到那裏就會見到約沙法的兒子耶戶，進屋後先把他從其他官員中叫到一邊，再帶他進入裏間。然後拿這瓶膏油塗在他額上，說：'這是天主的旨意：我給你塗油，封你爲以色列王。'說完就開門快回來。"於是這年輕使徒就去基列的拉末（按以利沙的話辦了）。當耶戶回到國王的官員中時，他們問他："沒什麼事吧？這古怪的人見你有什麼事？"耶戶說："我把他的話一字不差地告訴你們吧：這是天主的旨意：我給你塗油，封你爲以色列王。'"衆人就把他們的外衣鋪在石階上給耶戶作墊座，吹響號角，然後高呼："耶戶我王。"

約沙法的兒子耶戶定好計劃進攻約蘭。此時，約蘭和以色列的人正在保衞基列的拉末，對抗亞蘭王哈薛。約蘭王回到耶斯列醫治與亞蘭交戰時受的傷。耶戶對衆軍官說："如果你們支持我，就別讓一個人從城裏逃回耶斯列去報信。"他登上戰車直驅耶斯列，因爲約蘭受傷在那兒養傷，而猶大王亞哈謝也去了那裏看望約蘭。

---

(1)　這裏指的是暗利(Omri)的以色列王朝。

The watchman standing on the watch-tower in Jezreel saw Jehu and his troop approaching and called out, 'I see a troop of men.' Then Jehoram said, 'Fetch a horseman and send to find out if they come peaceably.' The horseman went to meet him and said, 'The king asks, "Is it peace?"' Jehu said, 'Peace? What is peace to you? Fall in behind me.' Thereupon the watchman reported, 'The messenger has met them but he is not coming back.' 'Harness my chariot', said Jehoram. They harnessed it, and Jehoram king of Israel and Ahaziah king of Judah went out each in his own chariot to meet Jehu, and met him by the plot of Naboth of Jezreel. When Jehoram saw Jehu, he said, 'Is it peace, Jehu?' But he replied, 'Do you call it peace while your mother Jezebel keeps up her obscene idol-worship and monstrous sorceries?' Jehoram wheeled about and fled, crying out to Ahaziah, 'Treachery, Ahaziah!' Jehu seized his bow and shot Jehoram between the shoulders; the arrow pierced his heart and he sank down in his chariot. Then Jehu said to Bidkar, his lieutenant, 'Pick him up and throw him into the plot of land belonging to Naboth of Jezreel, and thus fulfil the word of the Lord.'

Jehu came to Jezreel. Now Jezebel had heard what had happened; she had painted her eyes and dressed her hair, and she stood looking down from a window. As Jehu entered the gate, she said, 'Is it peace, you Zimri, you murderer of your master?' He looked up at the window and said, 'Who is on my side, who?' Two or three eunuchs looked out, and he said, 'Throw her down.' They threw her down, and some of her blood splashed on to the wall and the horses, which trampled her underfoot. Then he went in and ate and drank. 'See to this accursed woman', he said, 'and bury her; for she is a king's daughter.' But when they went to bury her they found nothing of her but the skull, the feet, and the palms of the hands; and they went back and told him. Jehu said, 'It is the word of the Lord which his servant Elijah the Tishbite spoke, when he said, "In the plot of ground at Jezreel the dogs shall devour the flesh of Jezebel.

耶斯列瞭望樓上的哨兵看見耶戶和他的人馬來到，就喊：“我見到一支軍隊來了。”約蘭說：“找個人騎馬出城去看看他們是否為親善而來。”使者去見耶戶說：“王上問：‘你們為親善而來嗎？’”耶戶說：“什麼親善不親善，與你又何干？跟在我後面吧。”這時瞭望哨又報告：“使者見到了他們了，可他沒回來。”“給我備戰車，”約蘭說。他們備好車，以色列王約蘭和猶大王亞哈謝各乘一輛戰車去見耶戶，他們在耶斯列拿伯的地裏見耶戶。約蘭問耶戶：“你是親善而來的嗎，耶戶？”但他回答：“怎能與你親善呢？你的母親耶洗別老是搞些淫行邪術。”約蘭調過車就要逃，他對亞哈謝大喊：“有人造反啦，亞哈謝！”耶戶拿起弓一箭射中了約蘭的兩肩間的心窩，他仆倒在車裏。耶戶對副官畢甲說：“把他的屍體扔在耶斯列人拿伯的地裏，這樣就應驗了天主的話。”

耶戶來到耶斯列。耶洗別已聽到此事。她梳粧打扮一下，站在窗口往下看。耶戶進宮門時，她說：“殺主人的心利⑴，你是來者不善吧？”耶戶抬頭看那窗戶說：“有誰支持我嗎，有沒有？”兩三個太監從窗口往外看他，他就說：“把她扔下來。”太監就把她從窗戶扔下來，她的血濺在牆上和馬的身上，她的屍體被馬踐踏。這之後耶戶進去吃食喝酒，他說：“把這該死的女人埋了，她到底是個國王的女兒。”可是隨從們去埋她時却找不到她的屍體了，只拾回個頭骨、雙腳和手掌。他們回來向耶戶報告，耶戶說：“這是天主的旨意，他借他的僕人提斯比人以利亞的嘴說過：‘在耶斯列的地裏，野狗要吃耶洗別的肉。’”

⑴ 心利(Zimri)出現在《列王記上》第十六章，他殺害了以色列王以拉(Elah)篡了王權。這裏是比喻耶戶是弑君之人。

Now seventy sons of Ahab were left in Samaria. Jehu therefore sent a letter to Samaria, to the elders, the rulers of the city. They were panic-stricken.... Therefore the comptroller of the household and the governor of the city, with the elders and the tutors, sent this message to Jehu: 'We are your servants. Whatever you tell us we will do; but we will not make anyone king. Do as you think fit.' Then he wrote them a second letter: 'If you are on my side and will obey my orders, then bring the heads of your master's sons to me at Jezreel by this time tomorrow.' Now the royal princes, seventy in all, were with the nobles of the city who were bringing them up. When the letter reached them, they took the royal princes and killed all seventy; they put their heads in baskets and sent them to Jehu in Jezreel.

Then he set out for Samaria, and on the way there, when he had reached a shepherds' shelter, he came upon the kinsmen of Ahaziah king of Judah. 'Take them alive', he said. So they took them alive; then they slew them and flung them into the pit that was there, forty-two of them; they did not leave a single survivor.

亞哈有七十個兒子在撒瑪利亞。耶戶就派人送了一封信到那裏，給城裏的長老和首領們，（說他們可以立其中一個兒子為王。但）他們十分恐慌。於是家宰、邑宰和長老們，孩子的監護等人聯名寫信給耶戶："我們是你的僕人，你要我們怎麼做就怎麼做，我們並無意立什麼人為王，你認為該怎樣就怎樣吧！"耶戶又寫信給他們："如果你們歸順我，聽我的命令，就把你們主人的兒子們的首級在明天此時給我送到耶斯列來。"當時七十個王子都跟城裏撫養他們的貴族同住。信到後，他們就把全部七十個王子一個不留都殺死了，把頭都放在筐裏送到耶斯列給耶戶。

耶戶起程去撒瑪利亞，路上他在牧羊人的風雨棚裏碰上猶大王亞哈謝的兄弟們，他命令："把他們捉起來。"士兵們把那些人抓起來然後都殺死了，扔進一個坑裏。一共四十二個，沒有一個可以活命。

（耶戶到了撒瑪利亞，把亞哈家剩在那裏的人全部處死。這樣就實現了天主對以利亞預示的話。）

57 Athaliah

2 Kings

As soom as Athaliah mother of Ahaziah saw that her son was dead, she set out to destroy all the royal line. But Jehosheba daughter of King Joram, sister of Ahaziah, took Ahaziah's son Joash and stole him away from among the princes who were being murdered; she put him and his nurse in a bedchamber where he was hidden from Athaliah and was not put to death. He remained concealed with her in the house of the Lord for six years, while Athaliah ruled the country. In the seventh year Jehoiada sent for the captains of units of a hundred, both of the Carites and of the guards, and he brought them into the house of the Lord; he made an agreement with them and put them on their oath in the house of the Lord, and showed them the king's son, and gave them the following orders: 'One third of you who are on duty on the sabbath are to be on guard in the palace; the rest of you are to be on special duty in the house of the Lord, you shall be on guard round the King, and anyone who comes near the ranks is to be put to death; you must be with the king wherever he goes.'

The captains carried out the orders of Jehoiada the priest to the letter. Then he brought out the king's son, put the crown on his head, handed him the warrant and anointed him king. The people clapped their hands and shouted, 'Long live the king.' When Athaliah heard the noise made by the guards and

五十七　亞他利雅[1]

列王記下

　　亞哈謝的母親亞他利雅見兒子已死，她就起來剿滅王室後裔，但約蘭[2]王的女兒，亞哈謝的妹子約示巴把亞哈謝的兒子約阿施從那些正在被剿除的王子中偷了出來，把他同乳母藏在一間臥室裏，他在那裏躲過了亞他利雅的屠殺。他和王的女兒一起在天主聖殿裏藏了六年。這期間，亞他利雅統治着國家。到第七年耶何耶大打發人叫迦利人的和衞隊的百夫隊長來，他把他們帶到天主聖殿，同他們講好，要他們在殿裏起誓，然後將亞哈謝的兒子帶出來給他們看，對他們下令說：“安息日值班的人三分一守住宮殿；其餘人在天主聖殿執行特別任務，就是守在國王的周圍，任何人擅自來到你們身邊都要處死，不論國王上哪兒，你們都要緊跟着他。”

　　衞隊長們一絲不苟地執行了祭司耶何耶大的命令。然後他帶王子出來，把王冠帶在他頭上，授權與他，給他塗油封王。人們鼓掌歡呼：“國王萬歲！”亞他利雅聽到了衞隊和人們的

---

(1)　亞他利雅(Athaliah)是猶大王約蘭(Jehoram)的妻子，亞哈(Ahab)和耶洗別(Jezebel)的女兒。她篡權後統治猶大六年。

(2)　約蘭有兩個拼法，一個是 Jehoram，另一個是 Joram。

the people, she came into the house of the Lord where the people were and found the king standing, as was the custom, on the dais, amidst outbursts of song and fanfares of trumpets in his honour, and all the populace rejoicing and blowing trumpets. Then Athaliah rent her clothes and cried, 'Treason! Treason!' Jehoiada the priest gave orders to the captains in command of the troops: 'Bring her outside the precincts and put to the sword anyone in attendance on her'; for the priest said, 'She shall not be put to death in the house of the Lord.' So they laid hands on her and took her out by the entry for horses to the royal palace, and there she was put to death.

喊聲，就來到擠滿人的天主聖殿，她看見約阿施正按照禮儀站在台上，人民歡呼，樂聲四起慶祝約阿施登基。亞他利雅就撕破衣服怒喊："反了！反了！"祭司耶何耶大命令衛隊長們："把她拉到外面，先把她的隨從都處死。"因為祭司說不要在聖殿裏處死她，他們就把她抓住，帶到馬匹進出王宮的入口外面殺死了。（約阿施登基時，年方七歲。）

In the twelfth year of Ahaz king of Judah, Hoshea son of Elah became king over Israel in Samaria and reigned nine years. He did what was wrong in the eyes of the Lord, but not as the previous kings of Israel had done. Shalmaneser king of Assyria made war upon him and Hoshea became tributary to him. But when the king of Assyria discovered that Hoshea was being disloyal to him, sending messengers to the king of Egypt at So, and withholding the tribute which he had been paying year by year, the king of Assyria arrested him and put him in prison. Then he invaded the whole country and, reaching Samaria, besieged it for three years. In the ninth year of Hoshea he captured Samaria and deported its people to Assyria and settled them in Halah and on the Habor, the river of Gozan, and in the cities of Media.

All this happened to the Israelites because they had sinned against the Lord their God who brought them up from Egypt, they paid homage to other gods and uttered blasphemies against the Lord their God....

The Lord banished the Israelites from his presence, as he had threatened through his servants the prophets, and they were carried into exile from their own land to Assyria; and there they are to this day.

Then the king of Assyria brought people from Babylon, Cuthah, Avva, Hamath, and Sepharvaim, and settled them in the cities of Samaria in place of the Israelites; so they occupied Samaria and lived in its cities.

五十八 以色列亡

列王記下

　　猶大王亞哈斯十二年，以拉之子何細亞在撒瑪利亞登基，作以色列王九年。他做了天主認為是錯的事，只是他的錯不同於他的先人。亞述王撒縵以色對以色列開戰，何細亞就成了他的附庸。但亞述王發現何細亞並不忠於他：暗地派人去梭那裏和埃及王拉關係，不肯向亞述交每年應納的貢品。亞述王就把他抓起下了囚。然後他興兵入侵全國，直抵撒瑪利亞，並將該城圍困三年。到何細亞第九年時攻佔了撒瑪利亞，把它的居民都趕到亞述，讓他們住在哈臘、歌散的哈博河邊及瑪代人的城邑裏。

　　以色列人遭此劫難是因為他們對帶他們出埃及的天主犯了罪，他們崇敬了別的神，又說了褻瀆天主上帝的話。天主就像通過先知們曾預言的那樣，把以色列人從他面前趕走。以色列人被趕出自己的國土，流落到亞述，在那裏一直住到今日。

　　亞述王從巴比倫、古他、亞瓦、哈馬和西法瓦音遷來人民，代替以色列人住在撒瑪利亞，這樣他們就佔領了撒瑪利亞，定居在它的城邑中。

2 Kings

Josiah was eight years old when he came to the throne, and he reigned in Jerusalem for thirty-one years; his mother was Jedidah daughter of Adaiah of Bozkath. He did what was right in the eyes of the Lord; he followed closely in the footsteps of his forefather David, swerving neither right nor left.

In the eighteenth year of his reign Josiah sent Shaphan son of Azaliah, the adjutant-general, to the house of the Lord. 'Go to the high priest Hilkiah,' he said, 'and tell him to melt down the silver that has been brought into the house of the Lord, which those on duty at the entrance have received from the people, and to hand it over to the foremen in the house of the Lord, to pay the workmen who are carrying out repairs in it.' The high priest Hilkiah told Shaphan the adjutant-general that he had discovered the book of the law in the house of the Lord, and he gave it to him, and Shaphan read it. Then Shaphan came to report to the king. When the king heard what was in the book of the law, he rent his clothes, and ordered the priest Hilkiah, Shaphan the adjutant-general, and Asaiah the king's attendant, to go and seek guidance of the Lord for himself, for the people, and for all Judah, about what was written in this book that had been discovered. 'Great is the wrath of the Lord', he said, 'that has been kindled against us, because our forefathers did not obey the commands in this book and do all that is laid upon us.'

Then the king sent and called all the elders of Judah and

五十九　猶大衰敗

列王記下

　　約西亞⑴登基（爲猶大王）時年僅八歲，他在耶路撒冷爲王三十一年，他母親是波斯加人亞大雅之女，叫耶底大。約西亞行品端正，爲天主所贊許，他緊跟先王大衞的足跡，絕不左搖右擺。

　　約西亞執政第十八年，他派亞薩利的兒子，副官長沙番去聖殿，他說："你去見大祭司希勒家，叫他把朝拜者獻給天主聖殿的銀子化了，讓領工去付修聖殿工人的工錢。"大祭司希勒家見了副官長沙番，說他在聖殿裏發現了律法書，並把書交給沙番。沙番看了後就向國王報告此事。國王看到律法書的內容，就痛心地撕裂衣服，讓大祭司希勒家、副官長沙番和國王侍從亞撒雅代他和全猶大人民去求天主指點按書中所說的他們該怎麼辦。"上帝對我們十分不滿，"他說，"因爲我們的先人沒有做這本書規定要我們去做的事情。"

　　國王叫人把猶大和以色列全體長老叫到聖殿來，他自己把

⑴　約西亞(Josiah)是猶大王國末期的一個重要的國王，八歲時繼他父親亞們(Amon)爲王。

Jerusalem together, and went up to the house of the Lord; he took with him the men of Judah and the inhabitants of Jerusalem, the priests and the prophets, the whole population, high and low. There he read out to them all the book of the covenant discovered in the house of the Lord; and then, standing on the dais, the king made a covenant before the Lord to obey him and keep his commandments, his testimonies, and his statutes, with all his heart and soul, and so fulfil the terms of the covenant written in this book. And all the people pledged themselves to the covenant.

Yet the Lord did not abate his fierce anger; it still burned against Judah because of all the provocation which Manasseh had given him. 'Judah also I will banish from my presence', he declared, 'as I banished Israel; and I will cast off this city of Jerusalem which once I chose, and the house where I promised that my Name should be.'

It was in his reign that Pharaoh Necho king of Egypt set out for the river Euphrates to help the king of Assyria. King Josiah went to meet him; and when they met at Megiddo, Pharaoh Necho slew him. His attendants conveyed his body in a chariot from Megiddo to Jerusalem and buried him in his own burial place. Then the people of the land took Josiah's son Jehoahaz and anointed him king in place of his father.

Jehoahaz was twenty-three years old when he came to the throne, and he reigned in Jerusalem for three months. Pharaoh Necho removed him from the throne in Jerusalem, and imposed on the land a fine of a hundred talents of silver and one talent of gold. Pharaoh Necho made Josiah's son Eliakim king in place of his father and changed his name to Jehoiakim. He took Jehoahaz and brought him to Egypt, where he died. Jehoiakim paid the silver and gold to Pharaoh, taxing the country to meet Pharaoh's demands.

Jehoiakim was twenty-five years old when he came to the throne, and he reigned in Jerusalem for eleven years. During his reign Nebuchadnezzar king of Babylon took the field, and Jehoiakim became his vassal; but three years later he broke

猶大人和耶路撒冷的居民，祭司和先知，全體人民不分貴賤都找了來。他把聖殿中找到的約書整個給大家唸了。然後他站在講壇上，在耶和華面前立約，要盡心盡意地順從天主，遵守他的誠命、法度和律例以完成書中寫的約言。在場所有的人也都保證遵守約言。

然而上帝對猶大的盛怒仍未消除，他還爲（猶大前王）瑪拿西(1)做的壞事氣惱。他說：“我也要把猶大從我面前趕走，就像我趕走以色列人一樣。我要把我自己選中的耶路撒冷和以我名字稱呼的聖殿都拋棄掉。”

在約西亞統治時期埃及王法老尼哥去到伯拉河帮亞述王。約西亞王出而迎戰，雙方在米吉多遭遇，法老尼哥殺死了約西亞。他的隨從把屍體從米吉多用車運回耶路撒冷，埋在他自己的墓地裏。之後，人們擁戴約西亞之子約哈斯爲王。

約哈斯登基時二十三歲，他治理耶路撒冷三個月。埃及王法老尼哥把他趕下耶路撒冷的王位，並向猶大強徵了一百他連得銀子，一他連得金子。又立約西亞之子以利亞敬爲王，並把他名字改爲約雅敬。他把約哈斯帶到埃及，約哈斯後來就死在那裏。約雅敬向法老繳納金銀，向全國徵稅來應付法老的需求。

約雅敬登基時二十五歲，他在耶路撒冷爲王十一年。……

在他掌政期間，巴比倫王尼布甲尼撒出兵猶大，約雅敬淪爲他的臣僕，但三年後約雅敬同他決裂，起來造反。天主發動

---

(1) 瑪拿西(Manasseh)是猶大王希西家(Hezekiah)的兒子。他登基後崇敬異教神，殺害反對者，做了許多惡事。約西亞(Josiah)是他孫子。

with him and revolted. The Lord launched against him raiding-parties of Chaldaeans, Aramaeans, Moabites, and Ammonites, letting them range through Judah. He rested with his forefathers, and was succeeded by his son Jehoiachin.

Jehoiachin was eighteen years old when he came to the throne. He did what was wrong in the eyes of the Lord, as his father had done. At that time the troops of Nebuchadnezzar king of Babylon advanced on Jerusalem and besieged the city. Jehoiachin king of Judah, his mother, his courtiers, his officers, and his eunuchs, all surrendered to the king of Babylon. The king of Babylon, now in the eighth year of his reign, took him prisoner; and , as the Lord had foretold, he carried off all the treasures of the house of the Lord and of the royal palace and broke up all the vessels of gold which Solomon king of Israel had made for the temple of the Lord. He carried the people of Jerusalem into exile, the officers and the fighting men, ten thousand in number, together with all the craftsmen and smiths; only the weakest class of people were left. He deported Jehoiachin to Babylon; he also took into exile from Jerusalem to Babylon the king's mother and his wives, his eunuchs and the foremost men of the land. He made Mattaniah, uncle of Jehoiachin, king in his place and changed his name to Zedekiah.

In the ninth year of his reign, in the tenth month, on the tenth day of the month, Nebuchadnezzar king of Babylon advanced with all his army against Jerusalem, the siege lasted till the eleventh year of King Zedekiah. In the fourth month of that year, on the ninth day of the month, when famine was severe in the city and there was no food for the common people, the city was thrown open. When Zedekiah king of Judah saw this, he and all his armed escort left the city and fled by night through the gate called Between the Two Walls, near the king's garden. But the Chaldaean army pursued the king and overtook him in the lowlands of Jericho; and all his company was dispersed. The king was seized and brought before the king of Babylon at Riblah, where he pleaded his

迦勒底、亞蘭、摩押和亞捫人聯軍襲擊約雅敬，踐踏猶大全境。（後來）約雅敬去世，他的兒子約雅斤繼位。約雅斤登基時十八歲。他同他的父親一樣做了天主認為是錯的事。在那時，巴比倫王尼布甲尼撒的軍隊推進到耶路撒冷，把城團團圍上。猶大王約雅斤，他母親、朝臣、武官和太監都投降了巴比倫王。巴比倫王當時是登基後第八年，他囚禁了約雅斤，就像天主預言那樣，把天主聖殿和王宮的財寶洗劫一空，把以色列王所羅門為神殿造的金器全給毀壞了。他把耶路撒冷上萬官兵擄去，連同手藝人和匠人也弄走，只把貧民留下了。他把約雅斤帶到巴比倫，同時帶走的還有國王的母親、妃嬪、太監和國家的首腦人物。他讓約雅斤的叔叔瑪探雅為國王，並讓他改名為西底家。（西底家後來又起來反對巴比倫王。）

當西底家為王的第九年，十月十日，巴比倫王尼布甲尼撒率大軍來攻耶路撒冷，並圍困該城直到西底家十一年四月九日。這時城裏大鬧饑荒，百姓沒吃的，城就被攻破了。猶大王西底家見勢不妙，就同他的衞隊連夜經國王花園不遠處叫做"兩牆間"的門逃出城。但加勒底人在後窮追並在耶利哥平原上趕上他。他的人馬四散奔逃。國王被俘並帶到在利比拉的

case before him. Zedekiah's sons were slain before his eyes; then his eyes were put out, and he was brought to Babylon in fetters of bronze.

In the fifth month, on the seventh day of the month, in the nineteenth year of Nebuchadnezzar king of Babylon, Nebuzaradan, captain of the king's bodyguard, came to Jerusalem and set fire to the house of the Lord and the royal palace; all the houses in the city, including the mansion of Gedaliah, were burnt down.

Nebuchadnezzar king of Babylon appointed Gedaliah son of Ahikam, son of Shaphan, governor over the few people whom he had left in Judah.

In the thirty-seventh year of the exile of Jehoiachin king of Judah, on the twenty-seventh day of the twelfth month, Evil-merodach king of Babylon in the year of his accession showed favour to Jehoiachin king of Judah. He brought him out of prison, treated him kindly and gave him a seat at table above the kings with him in Babylon. So Jehoiachin discarded his prison clothes and lived as a pensioner of the king for the rest of his life.

巴比倫王面前受審。他的兒子們當着他面被殺戮。然後他們剜了他的雙眼，用銅鍊鎖上，把他帶到巴比倫。

巴比倫王尼布甲尼撒十九年五月初七，國王衛隊長尼布撒拉旦來到耶路撒冷，放火燒了天主聖殿和王宮以及城裏全部房屋，各大戶(1)的宅子也都被夷爲平地。

巴比倫王尼布甲尼撒指定沙番的孫子，亞希甘之子基大利作他們的總督，統治仍在猶大的人數不多的人民。

猶大王約雅斤被俘的三十七年後，巴比倫王以未米羅達登基。那年十二月二十七日，他施恩於約雅斤，讓他出獄，並且善待他，使他佔有高於巴比倫其他各王的一席位。約雅斤脫掉囚衣，靠巴比倫王的供養度其餘生。

_____

(1) Gedaliah 意思是：a great man。

Esther

The events here related happened in the days of Ahasuerus, the Ahasuerus who ruled from India to Ethiopia, a hundred and twenty-seven provinces. At this time he sat on his royal throne in Susa the capital city. In the third year of his reign he gave a banquet for all his officers and his courtiers.

On the seventh day, when he was merry with wine, the king ordered the seven eunuchs who were in attendance on the king's person, to bring Queen Vashti before him wearing her royal crown, in order to display her beauty to the people and the officers; for she was indeed a beautiful woman. But Queen Vashti refused to come in answer to the royal command conveyed by the eunuchs. This greatly incensed the king, and he grew hot with anger.

Then the king conferred with his wise men, 'What does the law require to be done with Queen Vashti for disobeying the command of King Ahasuerus brought to her by the eunuchs?' Then Memucan made answer before the king and the princes: 'If it please your majesty, let a royal decree go out from you that Vashti shall not again appear before King Ahasuerus; and let the king give her place as queen to another woman who is more worthy of it than she.' Memucan's advice pleased the king and the princes, and the king did as he had proposed.

Now there was in Susa the capital city a Jew named Mordecai, a Benjamite. He had a foster-child Hadassah, that is Esther, his uncle's daughter, who had neither father nor mother. She was a beautiful and charming girl. When the

六十　入宮爲后

以斯帖記

　　故事發生在亞哈隨魯(1)時期，亞哈隨魯當時統治從印度到埃塞俄比亞的一百二十七個省份。他在首都書珊城登基。在登基後第三年，他設盛宴招待所有官員朝臣。盛宴到了第七日，國王乘酒興吩咐侍候他的七名太監去請王后瓦實提戴上王冠前來見客，使臣民們一仰她的國色天姿，因爲她確實美麗非凡。但王后瓦實提拒絕了太監所傳的王命。這可惹惱了國王，他怒不可遏。

　　於是國王就咨詢他的賢人們，"瓦實提王后不聽太監傳達我的旨意，依法該怎麼處置她呢？"賢人米母干對國王和衆人說："如果陛下願意，請下一道聖旨：瓦實提再也不許在亞哈隨魯王面前出現，國王可把她的后位給另一個比她更相稱的女子。"米母干的意見使王和衆人都很高興，王就按他的建議辦了。

　　在首都書珊有個猶太人叫末底改的，是便雅憫人。他有個養女哈大沙，原是他叔叔的女兒，父母已不在。她又叫以斯

---

(1)　亞哈隨魯(Ahasuerus)：波斯王，於紀元前486登基。

king's order and his edict were published, and many girls were brought to Susa the capital city. Esther too was taken to the king's palace.

The full period of preparation prescribed for the women was twelve months, six months with oil and myrrh and six months with perfumes and cosmetics. When the period was complete, each girl's turn came to go to King Ahasuerus.

When the turn came for Esther to go to the king, and Esther charmed all who saw her. The king loved her more than any of his other women and treated her with greater favour and kindness than the rest of the virgins. He put a royal crown on her head and made her queen in place of Vashti.

Mordecai was in attendance at court. One day when Mordecai was in attendance at court, Bigthan and Teresh, two of the king's eunuchs, keepers of the threshold, who were disaffected, were plotting to lay hands on King Ahasuerus. This became known to Mordecai, who told Queen Esther; and she told the king, mentioning Mordecai by name. The affair was investigated and the report confirmed; the two men were hanged on the gallows.

After this, King Ahasuerus promoted Haman son of Hammedatha the Agagite, advancing him and giving him precedence above all his fellow-officers. So the king's attendants at court all bowed down to Haman and did obeisance, for so the king had commanded; but Mordecai did not bow down to him. When Haman saw that Mordecai was not bowing down to him or doing obeisance, he was infuriated. He looked for a way to destroy all the Jews throughout the whole kingdom.

When Mordecai learnt all that had been done, he rent his clothes, put on sackcloth and ashes, and went through the city crying loudly and bitterly. He came within sight of the palace gate, because no one clothed with sackcloth was allowed to pass through the gate. Then Esther summoned Hathach, one of the king's eunuchs who had been appointed to wait upon her, and ordered him to find out from Mordecai what the trouble was and what it meant. And Mordecai told him all

帖，是個美麗絕倫的女子。當國王的命令和諭旨傳下，許多姑娘被選入書珊京城，以斯帖也被送到宮裏。

這些女子照規定要潔淨身體十二個月，六個月用沒藥和膏油，六個月用香水和化粧品。期滿後，她們就依次送去給國王亞哈隨魯。

到以斯帖進宮見國王的時候了。她的美色使所有見到她的人都傾倒。國王愛她勝過其他妃嬪，對她也比對其他女子好。他給戴上后冠，讓她代替了瓦實提王后的位置。

末底改在宮中作侍從。有一天末底改正在宮中值班，兩個太監守門人辟探和提列因爲對國王不滿，陰謀暗算亞哈隨魯王。末底改得知此事，就報告了以斯帖王后，王后告訴了國王，並提到末底改的功勞。後來這事調查屬實，兩個太監就被吊死了。……

這以後，亞哈隨魯王提拔了亞甲族哈米大的兒子哈曼。使他位高於他所有同事之上。這樣王的臣僕都向哈曼跪拜，表示順從，因爲這是王的旨意。但是末底改拒絕對他叩拜。哈曼見末底改不向他低頭，心裏十分惱火。他就設法想要去消滅全國的猶太人。

（他游說國王在一月十三日殺猶太人，掠奪他們的財物。）當末底改聽說哈曼要這樣幹，他憤怒地撕裂了衣服，穿上了蔴衣，把灰土撒在頭上，走遍全城痛哭哀號。他只能走到靠近宮門的地方，因爲穿蔴衣的人是不許入宮的。於是，以斯帖叫國王派來侍候她的太監哈他革，令他去問末底改出了什麼

that had happened to him. Hathach went and told Esther what Mordecai had said, and she sent him back with this message: 'All the king's courtiers and the people of the provinces are aware that if any person, man or woman, enters the king's presence in the inner court unbidden, there is one law only: that person shall be put to death, unless the king stretches out to him the golden sceptre; then and then only shall he live. It is now thirty days since I myself was called to go to the king.' But when they told Mordecai what Esther had said, he bade them go back to her and say, 'Do not imagine that you alone of all the Jews will escape because you are in the royal palace. If you remain silent at such a time as this, relief and deliverance for the Jews will appear from another quarter, but you and your father's family will perish. Esther gave them this answer to take back to Mordecai: 'Go and assemble all the Jews to be found in Susa and fast for me; take neither food nor drink for three days, and I and my maids will fast as you do. After that I will go to the king, although it is against the law; and if I perish, I perish.'

事，他想幹什麼。末底改把一切都說了。哈他革回宮把末底改的話稟報了王后，王后又打發他去說：「王的朝臣和各省的人民都知道，不論男女，沒有王召見就擅入國王內院禁宮的人，按法律就要被處死，除非國王向他伸出金仗，只有這樣他才能免於死。我已有三十天沒被召見了。」隨從把這話告訴末底改，末底改請他們對以斯帖回話說：「別以為你身在宮中就同其他猶太人不同而可以幸存。如果你這個時候不作聲，猶太人可能從別的方面得到解救，到時你和你父親的家族都會遭殃的。」以斯帖就讓他們給末底改回話說：「去把書珊所有的猶太人召集起來，為我禁食；三天不吃不喝，我同我的侍女也如此。然後即使違法我也要去見國王，如果我被處死，那我就死吧。」

Esther

On the third day Esther put on her royal robes and stood in the inner court of the king's palace. When the king caught sight of Queen Esther standing in the court, she won his favour and he stretched out to her the golden sceptre which he was holding. Then the king said to her, 'What is it, Queen Esther?' 'If it please your majesty,' said Esther, 'will you come today, sire, and Haman with you, to a banquet which I have made ready for you?' The king gave orders that Haman should be fetched quickly, so that Esther's wish might be fulfilled; and the king and Haman went to the banquet which she had prepared. Over the wine the king said to Esther, 'Whatever you ask of me shall be given to you. Whatever you request of me, up to half my kingdom, it shall be done.' Esther said in answer, 'What I ask and request of you is this. If I have won your majesty's favour, and if it please you, sire, to give me what I ask and to grant my request, will your majesty and Haman come tomorrow to the banquet which I shall prepare for you both? Tomorrow I will do as your majesty has said.'

So Haman went away that day in good spirits and well pleased with himself. Then he sent for his friends and his wife Zeresh and held forth to them how the king had promoted him. Haman said, 'Queen Esther invited no one but myself to accompany the king to the banquet which she had prepared; and she has invited me again tomorrow with the king. Yet all this means nothing to me so long as I see that Jew Mordecai in

六十一　計殺哈曼

以斯帖記

　　第三天以斯帖穿上朝服，站在國王禁宮內院裏，王看見以斯帖王后站在院子裏，他寵愛她就向她伸出了手裏的金杖。……國王對她說："你有什麼事嗎，以斯帖王后？"以斯帖說，"我想請陛下今日帶哈曼來赴我特為你而準備的筵席。"國王就下令召哈曼入宮，好讓以斯帖滿意。他和哈曼倆人一同赴以斯帖備下的宴席。席上王喝了酒對以斯帖說："不論你向我要什麼，哪怕是半壁江山，我都給你。"以斯帖答道："我只求你賜恩答應我的請求，就是請你同哈曼明日再來我這裏出席為你們兩人準備的筵席，明天我再按陛下的恩准提出要求好了。"

　　哈曼這天十分高興，心情愉快地回家去。他對他召來的朋友和妻子吹噓國王如何抬舉他，他說："以斯帖王后又邀了我一個人陪國王赴她的宴，而且明天又約了我同國王再去。只是

attendance at court.' Then his wife Zeresh and all his friends said to him, 'Let a gallows seventy-five feet high be set up, and recommend to the king in the morning to have Mordecai hanged upon it.

That night sleep eluded the king, so he ordered the chronicle of daily events to be brought; and it was read to him. Therein was recorded that Mordecai had given information about the two royal eunuchs among the keepers of the threshold who had plotted to lay hands on King Ahasuerus. Whereupon the king said, 'What honour or dignity has been conferred on Mordecai for this?' The king's courtiers who were in attendance told him that nothing had been done for Mordecai. Now Haman had just entered the outer court of the palace to recommend to the king that Mordecai should be hanged on the gallows which he had prepared for him. The king bade him enter and said to him, 'What should be done for the man whom the king wishes to honour?' Haman said to himself, 'Whom would the king wish to honour more than me?' And he said to the king. 'For the man whom the king wishes to honour, let there be brought royal robes which the king himself wears, and a horse which the king rides, with a royal crown upon its head. And let the robes and the horse be delivered to one of the king's most honourable officers, and let him attire the man whom the king wishes to honour and lead him mounted on the horse through the city square, calling out as he goes: "See what is done for the man whom the king wishes to honour."' Then the king said to Haman, 'Fetch the robes and the horse at once, as you have said, and do all this for Mordecai the Jew who is in attendance at court.'

So the king and Haman went to dine with Queen Esther. Again on that second day, over the wine, the king said, 'Whatever you ask of me will be given to you, Queen Esther.' Queen Esther answered 'My request and petition is that my own life and the lives of my people may be spared. For we have been sold, I and my people, to be destroyed, slain, and exterminated. Then King Ahasuerus said to Queen Esther,

猶太人末底改一天還是宮裏的人，這一切榮耀也不能解我心中之火。"他的妻子細利斯和朋友們對他說："那就吩咐人樹起一個七十五英尺高的絞架，明早請國王把末底改吊死在上面好了。"

那夜國王睡不着，就吩咐下人把日誌拿來讀給他聽。那裏記載了末底改曾報告那兩個看門的太監謀算他亞哈隨魯的事。聽到這裏，國王說："有沒有為給末底改榮譽和賞賜？"侍臣們說還沒有給末底改什麼賞賜。這時哈曼正好進到宮殿的外院裏想向國王提議把末底改吊死在他立起的絞架上。王叫他進來，對他說："對國王想賜予榮譽的人該做些什麼好呢？"哈曼心想："除去我，還有什麼人會得到國王的恩賜呢？"他就對王說："對國王要恩賜榮譽的人，可找一套國王穿的王袍和一匹國王騎的御馬。讓國王最尊崇的大臣拿去送去給那人，讓他把王袍給那人穿上，領那人騎着御馬在城中廣場走過，並呼喊道：'瞧，國王喜愛的人是得到這樣恩待的。'"國王就對哈曼說："那立刻按你說的去取王袍和御馬來，給宮中侍從猶太人末底改這種榮譽。……"

第二天國王同哈曼赴王后以斯帖的宴。酒宴上王說："以斯帖王后，無論你向我請求什麼，我都給你。"王后回答："我的懇求是請王上饒了我和我族人的性命，因為我同我族人都被出賣，要被毀滅、殺戮，一個不留。"亞哈隨魯王便問以斯帖

'Who is he, and where is he, who has presumed to do such a thing as this?' 'An adversary and an enemy,' said Esther, 'this wicked Haman.' At that Haman was dumbfounded in the presence of the king and the queen. The king rose from the banquet in a rage and went to the garden of the pavilion, while Haman remained where he was, to plead for his life with Queen Esther. When the king returned from the garden to the banqueting hall, Haman had flung himself across the couch on which Esther was reclining. The king exclaimed, 'Will he even assault the queen here in my presence?' Then Harbona, one of the eunuchs in attendance on the king, said, 'At Haman's house stands the gallows, seventy-five feet high, which he himself has prepared for Mordecai, who once served the king well.' 'Hang Haman on it', said the king. So they hanged him on the gallows that he himself had prepared for Mordecai.

王后："這人是誰？他在哪裏？誰要幹這種事情？""是一個反派分子，一個敵人，"以斯帖說，"就是惡人哈曼。"聽到這話，哈曼在王和王后面前嚇呆了。國王勃然起身，離席到御花園去了，哈曼留在席上哀求王后以斯帖救命。當國王從園中回到宴會廳裏時，哈曼正伏在以斯帖靠着的榻上。國王喊道："難道他還要當我的面凌辱王后麼？"這時一個太監哈波拿說："哈曼在家裏私設了一個七十五英尺高的絞架準備給末底改行刑，末底改是爲國王立過功的人。""那就把哈曼吊死在那上面吧。"王說。於是，哈曼就自作自受，被吊死在原來爲末底改準備的絞架上。

Job

There lived in the land of Uz a man of blameless and upright life named Job, who feared God and set his face against wrongdoing. He had seven sons and three daughters; and he owned seven thousand sheep and three thousand camels, five hundred yoke of oxen and five hundred asses, with a large number of slaves. Thus Job was the greatest man in all the East.

The day came when the members of the court of heaven took their places in the presence of the Lord, and Satan was there among them. The Lord asked him where he had been. 'Ranging over the earth', he said, 'from end to end.' Then the Lord asked Satan, 'Have you considered my servant Job? You will find no one like him on earth, a man of blameless and upright life, who fears God and sets his face against wrongdoing.' Satan answered the Lord, 'Has not Job good reason to be God-fearing? Have you not hedged him round on every side with your protection, him and his family and all his possessions? Whatever he does you have blessed, and his herds have increased beyong measure. But stretch out your hand and touch all that he has, and then he will curse you to your face.' Then the Lord said to Satan, 'So be it. All that he has is in your hands; only Job himself you must not touch.'

When the day came that Job's sons and daughters were eating and drinking in the eldest brother's house, a messenger came running to Job and said, 'The oxen were ploughing and the asses were grazing near them, when the Sabaeans

六十二　約伯受難

約伯記

　　烏斯地方有個耿直正派的人，名叫約伯。他敬畏上帝，因此從不做壞事。他有七子，三女，七千隻羊，三千匹駱駝，五百對牛和五百頭驢，還有大批奴婢。所以約伯成為東方最了不起的人。

　　一日天堂上神的眾子侍立在天主面前，撒旦也在其中。天主問撒旦去什麼地方了。他說："在世間各處走走，全都走遍了。"上帝問撒旦："你可曾留意過我的僕人約伯？世上再也找不到另一個像他那樣耿直正派、敬畏上帝、從不做壞事的人了。"撒旦對上帝說："約伯敬畏上帝並不是無緣無故的。你不是對他的家人和財產保護得十分周到嗎？你保祐他做的一切，他的牧羣繁殖得十分興旺。但你如果出手去觸犯他利益，他也要當面咒罵你的。"天主就對撒旦說："那我們就這樣辦，你可以隨意處置他的一切，只是不許傷害他本人。"

　　一天，約伯的子女們在長子家吃飯喝酒，一個人跑來給約伯報告說："咱們的牛在耕地，驢在吃草，忽然來了一些示巴

swooped down and carried them off, after putting the herdsmen to the sword; and I am the only one to escape and tell the tale.' While he was still speaking, another messenger arrived and said, 'God's fire flashed from heaven. It struck the sheep and the shepherds and burnt them up; and I am the only one to escape and tell the tale.' While he was still speaking, another arrived and said, 'The Chaldaeans, three bands of them, have made a raid on the camels and carried them off, after putting the drivers to the sword; and I am the only one to escape and tell the tale.' While this man was speaking, yet another arrived and said, 'Your sons and daughters were eating and drinking in the eldest brother's house, when suddenly a whirlwind swept across from the desert and struck the four corners of the house, and it fell on the young people and killed them; and I am the only one to escape and tell the tale.' At this Job stood up and rent his cloak; then he shaved his head and fell prostrate on the ground, saying:

Naked I came from the womb,
    naked I shall return whence I came.
    The Lord gives and the Lord takes away; blessed be the name of the Lord.

Throughout all this Job did not sin; he did not charge God with unreason.

Once again the day came when the members of the court of heaven took their places in the presence of the Lord, and Satan was there among them. The Lord asked him where he had been. Then the Lord asked Satan, 'You incited me to ruin Job without a cause, but his integrity is still unshaken.' Satan answered the Lord, 'There is nothing the man will grudge to save himself. But stretch out your hand and touch his bone and his flesh, and see if he will not curse you to your face.'

Then the Lord said to Satan, 'So be it. He is in your hands; but spare his life.' And Satan left the Lord's presence, and he smote Job with running sores from head to foot, so that he took a piece of a broken pot to scratch himself as he sat among the ashes. Then his wife said to him, 'Are you still unshaken

人，殺死了牧人，把牛、驢都拖走了。我是唯一死裏逃生回來報告的人。」說着，另一個報信的人來了，他說：「上帝之火從天而降，把咱們的羊和牧人都燒死了，我是唯一死裏逃生回來報告的人。」他說時又一個報信的人來了，他說：「迦勒底人分作三伙襲擊咱們的駱駝，殺死了趕駱駝的人，把駱駝搶走了。我是唯一死裏逃生回來報信的人。」這個人說着時，又來了一個報信的人，他說：「你的子女們在長兄家吃飯喝酒，突然從沙漠刮來一陣狂風，把房屋隅角吹倒了，屋子坍下來把你的子女都壓死了。我是唯一死裏逃生回來報告的人。」聽到這連串的惡耗，約伯站起來，撕裂衣袍，剃了髮，俯伏在地上說：「我從母腹赤裸來到世上。我也要一無所有地回到我來的地方。天主賜予我的，天主也可把它拿走。我要頌揚天主之名。」這整個過程中約伯沒有做任何不好的事，也沒有指責上帝的不公。

又到了天堂上神的眾子侍立在天主面前的日子了，撒旦也在其中。上帝問他去什麼地方了。又問他：「你引使我無故毀了約伯的一切，可他的耿直正派仍舊不變。」撒旦回答上帝：「這人到自己性命交關時就什麼都會做出來的。你要是出手傷他的骨和肉，他不當面罵你才怪呢？」

上帝就對撒旦說：「那我們就這樣辦！我任你處置他，但別殺死他就行。」撒旦離天主去了，他使約伯從頭到腳都長上疱，約伯只好坐在灰土中，用瓦片刮身上的瘡疥。他的妻子對

in your integrity? Curse God and die!' But he answered, 'You talk as any wicked fool of a woman might talk. If we accept good from God, shall we not accept evil?' Throughout all this, Job did not utter one sinful word.

When Job's three friends, Eliphaz of Teman, Bildad of Shuah, and Zophar of Naamah, heard of all these calamities which had overtaken him, they left their homes and arranged to come and condole with him and comfort him. But when they first saw him from a distance, they did not recognize him; and they wept aloud, rent their cloaks and tossed dust into the air over their heads. For seven days and seven nights they sat beside him on the ground, and none of them said a word to him; for they saw that his suffering was very great.

When the Lord had finished speaking to Job, he said to Eliphaz the Temanite, 'I am angry with you and your two friends, because you have not spoken as you ought about me, as my servant Job has done. So now take seven bulls and seven rams, go to my servant Job and offer a whole-offering for yourselves, and he will intercede for you.' The Lord showed favour to Job when he had interceded for his friends. So the Lord restored Job's fortunes and doubled all his possessions.

Furthermore, the Lord blessed the end of Job's life more than the beginning; and he had fourteen thousand head of small cattle and six thousand camels, a thousand yoke of oxen and as many she-asses.

Thereafter Job lived another hundred and forty years, he saw his sons and his grandsons to four generations, and died at a very great age.

他說：“你還堅持你的耿直正派麼？乾脆詛咒上帝，然後一死了事吧。”但約伯回答道：“你這話只有愚蠢的惡婦才說得出來。如果我們從天主處得到過賜福，那我們就也得承受災禍。”這整個過程中，約伯沒有說過一句褻瀆的話。

約伯的三個朋友，提縵人以利法、書亞人比勒達、拿瑪人瑣法，聽說落在約伯身上的這許多災禍，他們都離家前來看望和安慰約伯，和他分憂。但他們第一眼見到他時，都認不出他來了，他們不禁失聲痛哭，撕破衣裳，把灰土撒在頭頂。他們同約伯在地上並坐了七天七夜，也沒有跟他說話，因為他們看到約伯實在經受着極大的痛苦。

（七天後，約伯開始向上帝詛咒自己不該到這世上來，但求早死。並求上帝告訴他懲罰他的原因。他的三位友人開導他，還同他爭論起來。以利法指責約伯有罪，約伯說以利法冤枉了自己。最後天主和約伯對了話，並使他的身體康復。）

耶和華同約伯對話完畢就對提縵人以利法說：“我對你和你那兩個朋友生氣，因為你們歪曲了我，不像我僕人約伯那樣正確。因此，你們要拿七頭公牛和七隻公羊，到我僕人約伯那兒為你們自己獻上全牲燔祭。約伯會為你們求情禱告的。”約伯為朋友們求情禱告，天主恩待他。他使約伯重新得到財富，而且財產比先前多了一倍。

不止這樣，上帝還使約伯晚年比早先更好，他擁有一萬四千頭小牛、六千頭駱駝，一千對牛，和一千頭母驢。

從那時約伯又活了一百四十歲，他和兒孫五代同堂。他死時年紀已經很老很老了。

新約

New Testament

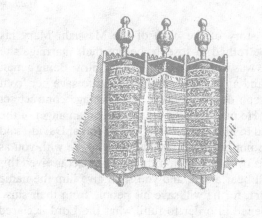

63   *The Birth of the Messiah*

Matthew

This is the story of the birth of the Messiah. Mary his mother was betrothed to Joseph; before their marriage she found that she was with child by the Holy Spirit. Being a man of principle, and at the same time wanting to save her from exposure, Joseph desired to have the marriage contract set aside quietly. He had resolved on this, when an angel of the Lord appeared to him in a dream. 'Joseph son of David,' said the angel, 'do not be afraid to take Mary home with you as your wife. It is by the Holy Spirit that she has conceived this child. She will bear a son; and you shall give him the name Jesus (Saviour), for he will save his people from their sins.' All this happened in order to fulfil what the Lord declared through the prophet: 'The virgin will conceive and bear a son, and he shall be called Emmanuel', a name which means 'God is with us'. Rising from sleep Joseph did as the angel had directed him; he took Mary home to be his wife, but had no intercourse with her until her son was born. And he named the child Jesus.

Jesus was born at bethlehem in Judaea during the reign of Herod. After his birth astrologers from the east arrived in Jerusalem, asking, 'Where is the child who is born to be king of the Jews? We observed the rising of his star, and we have come to pay him homage.' King Herod was greatly perturbed when he heard this; and so was the whole of Jerusalem. He called a meeting of the chief priests and lawyers of the Jewish people, and put before them the question: 'Where is it that

六十三　基督降生

馬太福音

現在講的是耶穌基督的降生。他母親馬利亞當時已經許配給約瑟，但還未過門，馬利亞發覺自己從聖靈懷了孕。約瑟是個正直的人，他不想公開羞辱她，便打算暗地把婚約解除算了。當他決心已定時，天主的使者在夢中向他顯靈說："大衞的子孫約瑟，你不用害怕，只管把馬利亞娶入門。她是從聖靈懷的孕。她將生個兒子，你要給他起名叫耶穌（救世主），因爲他將把自己的人民從罪惡中解救出來。"這一切之所以發生，是應驗了天主曾借先知之口講的話："將有童女懷孕生子，人要稱他爲以馬內利"，這名字意思就是"上帝與我們同在。"約瑟醒後，就遵循使者的吩咐，把馬利亞娶入門爲妻。但直至兒子降生，他一直都不跟馬利亞同房。他給兒子起名叫耶穌。

耶穌降生於猶太的伯利恒，當時是希律王當政。他出生後，有幾個占星學家從東方來到耶路撒冷，說："那個生下來要做猶太人之王的孩子在哪裏？我們看到他的星宿升起，特趕來拜謁他。"希律王聽後異常驚恐，耶路撒冷的全城居民也感到非常不安。希律王把祭司長和猶太人的法學家召集一起，問

the Messiah is to be born?' 'At Bethlehem in Judaea', they replied; and they referred him to the prophecy which reads: 'Bethlehem in the land of Judah, you are far from least in the eyes of the rulers of Judah; for out of you shall come a leader to be the shepherd of my people Israel.'

Herod next called the astrologers to meet him in private, and ascertained from them the time when the star had appeared. He then sent them on to Bethlehem, and said, 'Go and make a careful inquiry for the child. When you have found him, report to me, so that I may go myself and pay him homage.'

They set out at the king's bidding; and the star which they had seen at its rising went ahead of them until it stopped above the place where the child lay. At the sight of the star they were overjoyed. Entering the house, they saw the child with Mary his mother, and bowed to the ground in homage to him; then they opened their treasures and offered him gifts: gold, frankincense, and myrrh. And being warned in a dream not to go back to Herod, they returned home another way.

After they had gone, an angel of the Lord appeared to Joseph in a dream, and said to him, 'Rise up, take the child and his mother and escape with them to Egypt, and stay there until I tell you; for Herod is going to search for the child to do away with him.' So Joseph rose from sleep, and taking mother and child by night he went away with them to Egypt, and there he stayed till Herod's death. This was to fulfil what the Lord had declared through the prophet: 'I called my son out of Egypt.'

When Herod saw how the astrologers had tricked him he fell into a passion, and gave orders for the massacre of all children in Bethlehem and its neighbourhood, of the age of two years or less, corresponding with the time he had ascertained from the astrologers. So the words spoken through Jeremiah the prophet were fulfilled: 'A voice was heard in Rama, wailing and loud laments; it was Rachel weeping for her children, and refusing all consolation, because they were no more.'

道：“基督要降生在何處？”他們答道，“在猶太的伯利恒。”他們告訴他，先知預言說：“猶大地的伯利恒啊，你在猶大的統治者的眼裏，遠非是無關緊要的，因爲從這裏產生一位君王來帶領我們以色列人民。”

希律王私下又把占星學家召了來，問清楚那星是何時出現的。然後，便派他們到伯利恒去：“去仔細打聽一下那孩子的下落，找到後向我稟報，我好親自去拜謁他。”

占星學家們遵照希律王的命令起程去查訪。他們看到那顆升起的星一直在他們前邊移動，到了那孩子所在的地方的上空就停住了。他們看到這情況就十分高興。進屋後，他們看到那孩子正和他母親馬利亞在一起，便伏地拜見他；然後打開寶盒，把帶來的黃金、乳香和沒藥等禮品獻給他。占星學家們因爲在夢中得到指示說不要再回去見希律王，於是就從別的路徑返回家去。

他們走後，主的一個使者便在夢中向約瑟顯靈，對他說：“快起來，帶着孩子和他母親一起逃往埃及去吧。你們先住在那兒，以後我再告訴你們該怎麼辦；因爲希律王要尋找這孩子，要置他於死地。”約瑟醒來馬上起床，連夜帶着母子倆逃往埃及。他在那兒一直住到希律王死去。這就應驗了主借先知所講的話，“我把我的兒子召出了埃及。”

當希律得知自己受了占星學家的欺騙後，便怒不可遏地下令：按占星學家們指出的時間，凡是伯利恒城或其周圍地區的兩歲以內的孩子，全都要殺掉。這就應驗了主借先知耶利米所說的話：“在拉瑪，你會聽到號啕痛哭的聲音，這是拉結在哭她的孩子們，而且誰也勸不住，因爲她的兒女們再也不在人世了。”

The time came that Herod died; and an angel of the Lord appeared in a dream to Joseph in Egypt and said to him, 'Rise up, take the child and his mother, and go with them to the land of Israel, for the men who threatened the child's life are dead.' So he rose, took mother and child with him, and came to the land of Israel. Hearing, however, that Archelaus had succeeded his father Herod as king of Judaea, he was afraid to go there. And being warned by a dream, he withdrew to the region of Galilee; there he settled in a town called Nazareth. This was to fulfil the words spoken through the prophets: 'He shall be called a Nazarene '

希律終於死了。天主的使者便在埃及向約瑟夢中顯靈，說：“起來，帶着孩子和他母親去以色列吧，因爲要害孩子性命的人都已經死了。”約瑟便起來，帶着母子倆去以色列。但當他聽說亞基老接替他父親希律作了猶太王的消息後，便又不敢到那裏去。並按另一個夢中得到的告誡，他轉往加利利地區，在一座叫拿撒勒的城裏住下。這就應驗天主借先知們所說的：“他要被稱爲拿撒勒人了。”

About that time John the Baptist appeared as a preacher in the Judaean wilderness; his theme was: 'Repent; for the kingdom of Heaven is upon you!' It is of him that the prophet Isaiah spoke when he said, 'A voice crying aloud in the wilderness, "Prepare a way for the Lord; clear a straight path for him."'

John's clothing was a rough coat of camel's hair, with a leather belt round his waist, and his food was locusts and wild honey. They flocked to him from Jerusalem, from all Judaea, and the whole Jordan valley, and were baptized by him in the River Jordan, confessing their sins.

When he saw many of the Pharisees and Sadducees coming for baptism he said to them: 'You vipers' brood! Who warned you to escape from the coming retribution? Then prove your repentance by the fruit it bears; and do not presume to say to yourselves, "We have Abraham for our father." I tell you that God can make children for Abraham out of these stones here. Already the axe is laid to the roots of the trees; and every tree that fails to produce good fruit is cut down and thrown on the fire. I baptize you with water, for repentance; but the one who comes after me is mightier than I. I am not fit to take off his shoes. He will baptize you with the Holy Spirit and with fire. His shovel is ready in his hand and he will winnow his threshing-floor; the wheat he will gather into his granary, but he will burn the chaff on a fire that can never go out.'

Then Jesus arrived at the Jordan from Galilee, and came to

六十四　聖徒約翰

馬太福音

那時，聖徒約翰在猶太的曠野裏傳道，他說："你們懺悔吧，天國已臨近！"他就是以賽亞先知所說的"在曠野高聲呼叫'爲主修路，修一條筆直的路'"的那個人。

約翰身着粗陋的駱駝毛衣服，腰束皮帶，以蝗蟲和野蜜裹腹。耶路撒冷、猶太全境和約旦河谷一帶的人都紛紛來找約翰，坦誠懺悔，在約旦河裏接受他施洗。

約翰看到許多法利賽人和撒都該人也來受洗，便對他們說："你們這一伙毒蛇！誰教你們去逃避未來的報應呢？你們要作出善果來證明自己眞心悔改。不要心裏以爲'我們有亞伯拉罕爲我們的祖宗'。我告訴你們，上帝能從這些石頭中爲亞伯拉罕造出子孫來。現在斧子已放在樹根上，凡不結善果的樹，一律砍掉，扔進火裏燒了。我用水爲你們施洗，是叫你們悔改。繼我而來的那個人，能力比我大，我連給他脫鞋也不配。他將以聖靈和火爲你們施洗。他手拿簸箕，要揚淨打穀場的穀粒，把麥子收進穀倉裏，用永不熄滅之火把糠燒掉。"

這時，耶穌從加利利來到約旦，見到約翰後，便要受他的

John to be baptized by him. John tried to dissuade him. 'Do you come to me?' he said; 'I need rather to be baptized by you.' Jesus replied, 'Let it be so for the present; we do well to conform in this way with all that God requires.' John then allowed him to come. After baptism Jesus came up out of the water at once, and at that moment heaven opened; he saw the Spirit of God descending like a dove to alight upon him; and a voice from heaven was heard saying, 'This is my Son, my Beloved, on whom my favour rests.'

洗。約翰攔住他說："你來找我？我本應受你的洗。"耶穌答道："你暫讓我受你的洗，這樣，我們才能盡符神意。"於是，約翰便讓耶穌受了他的洗。耶穌受洗後，馬上從水中出來；這時，天忽然開了。他看到聖靈像鴿子一樣從天而降，落在了他身上。天上傳下一個聲音來說："這就是我所寵愛的愛子。"

65   *The Temptation by Satan*

Matthew

Jesus was then led away by the Spirit into the wilderness, to be tempted by the devil.

For forty days and nights he fasted, and at the end of them he was famished. The tempter approached him and said, 'If you are the Son of God, tell these stones to become bread.' Jesus answered, 'Scripture says, "Man cannot live on bread alone; he lives on every word that God utters."'

The devil then took him to the Holy City and set him on the parapet of the temple. 'If you are the Son of God,' he said, 'throw yourself down; for Scripture says, "He will put his angels in charge of you, and they will support you in their arms, for fear you should strike your foot against a stone."' Jesus answered him, 'Scripture says again, "You are not to put the Lord your God to the test."'

Once again, the devil took him to a very high mountain, and showed him all the kingdoms of the world in their glory. 'All these', he said, 'I will give you, if you will only fall down and do me homage.' But Jesus said, 'Begone, Satan! Scripture says, "You shall do homage to the Lord your God and worship him alone."'

Then the devil left him; and angels appeared and waited on him.

六十五　撒旦試探

馬太福音

耶穌被聖靈引到曠野，接受魔鬼撒旦的試探。

他四十晝夜齋戒禁食，感到飢餓難耐。魔鬼走近他，說道：“你若是聖子，就可叫這些石頭變成食物。”耶穌答道：“經書上講‘人活着不是光靠食物，而是要靠上帝講的每句話。’”

魔鬼就把他帶到聖城，讓他站在聖殿頂上，說：“你若是聖子，就跳下去，因爲經書上講‘主會吩咐他的使者用手托着你，免得你的腳碰到石頭上。’”耶穌答道：“可經書上還講‘不可試探你的上帝天主。’”

魔鬼又把他帶上了一座高山，把世上所有繁榮昌盛的國家指給他看，並說：“如果你肯向我拜服在地，我就把這一切全都賜給你。”但耶穌却說：“去吧，撒旦！經書上講‘你要敬拜你的天主上帝，而且只是崇拜他。’”

於是魔鬼便離耶穌而去；而主的衆使者就出來侍候他。

The next day again John was standing with two of his disciples when Jesus passed by. John looked towards him and said, 'There is the Lamb of God.' The two disciples heard him say this, and followed Jesus. When he turned and saw them following him, he asked, 'What are you looking for?' They said, 'Rabbi' (which means a teacher), 'where are you staying?' 'Come and see', he replied. So they went and saw where he was staying, and spent the rest of the day with him. It was then about four in the afternoon.

One of the two who followed Jesus after hearing what John said was Andrew, Simon Peter's brother. The first thing he did was to find his brother Simon. He said to him, 'We have found the Messiah' (which is the Hebrew for 'Christ'). He brought Simon to Jesus, who looked at him and said, 'You are Simon son of John. You shall be called Cephas' (that is, Peter, the Rock).

The next day Jesus decided to leave for Galilee. He met Philip, who, like Andrew and Peter, came from Bethsaida, and said to him, 'Follow me.' Philip went to find Nathanael, and told him, 'We have met the man spoken of by Moses in the Law, and by the prophets: it is Jesus son of Joseph, from Nazareth.' 'Nazareth!' Nathanael exclaimed; 'can anything good come from Nazareth?' Philip said, 'Come and see.' When Jesus saw Nathanael coming, he said, 'Here is an Israelite worthy of the name; there is nothing false in him.' Nathanael asked him, 'How do you come to know me?' Jesus

六十六　初收門徒

　　次日，約翰和他兩個門徒又站在那裏，這時耶穌從旁經過。約翰看着他說道："這就是上帝的羔羊。"兩個門徒聽了，便跟着耶穌走。耶穌轉身看到他們跟着他，便問道："你們要做什麼？"他們答道："拉比（猶太人用語：老師），你住在哪兒？"耶穌回答說："你們跟來看看吧。"他們便跟着他去看他的住處，當天便住在了那裏，此時已是午後近晚時分。

　　聽約翰的話跟從耶穌的這兩人中，一個名叫安得烈，是西門·彼得的弟弟。他先去找到了他哥哥西門，對他說："我們找到彌賽亞（希伯來語，意爲"基督"）了。"他便領西門去見基督。耶穌看見西門就說："你是約翰的兒子西門，你以後叫璣法（磐石之意）。"

　　第二天，耶穌決定去加利利。他遇到了腓力，對他說："跟隨我吧。"這腓力和安得烈、彼得都來自伯賽大。腓力去找到拿但業，說："我們遇到了摩西律法上寫的、衆先知提到的那個人了，他就是約瑟的兒子拿撒勒人耶穌。"拿但業喊道："拿撒勒！拿撒勒還會出什麼好事麼？"腓力說："那你來看看吧！"耶穌看到拿但業走來，就說："這是一個眞正的以色列人，他心胸坦誠，毫無虛詐。"拿但業問耶穌："你怎

replied, 'I saw you under the fig-tree before Philip spoke to you.' 'Rabbi,' said Nathanael, 'you are the Son of God; you are king of Israel.' Jesus answered, 'Is this the ground of your faith, that I told you I saw you under the fig-tree? You shall see greater things than that.' Then he added, 'In truth, in very truth I tell you all, you shall see heaven wide open, and God's angels ascending and descending upon the Son of Man.'

麼會知道我呢？"耶穌答道："腓力還未跟你說話，我就看到你在無花果樹下了。"拿但業說："拉比，你真是神的兒子，是以色列人之王。"耶穌答道："我說看到你在無花果樹下，你就已經信服我了？你還會看到比這更大的奇事呢。"接着，耶穌又說："我實實在在地告訴你們，你們將要看到天門大開，上帝的使者從天而降，落在人子的身上。"

67 To Turn Water into Wine

John

On the third day there was a wedding at Cana-in-Galilee. The mother of Jesus was there, and Jesus and his disciples were guests also. The wine gave out, so Jesus's mother said to him, 'They have no wine left.' He answered, 'Your concern, mother, is not mine. My hour has not yet come.' His mother said to the servants, 'Do whatever he tells you.' There were six stone water-jars standing near, of the kind used for Jewish rites of purification; each held from twenty to thirty gallons. Jesus said to the servants, 'Fill the jars with water', and they filled them to the brim. 'Now draw some off', he ordered, 'and take it to the steward of the feast' and they did so. The steward tasted the water now turned into wine, not knowing its source; though the servants who had drawn the water knew. He hailed the bridegroom and said, 'Everyone serves the best wine first, and waits until the guests have drunk freely before serving the poorer sort; but you have kept the best wine till now.'

六十七　變水爲酒

約翰福音

　　第三天，加利利的迦拿有一家人娶媳婦，設宴慶賀。耶穌的母親也赴宴，耶穌和他的門徒也應邀作客。酒喝完了，耶穌的母親便對他說："他們沒有酒了。"耶穌答道："母親，你講這事與我無關，現在還沒到要我的時候呢。"他母親就對佣人說："他讓你們幹什麼，你們就幹什麼。"那家擺着六個猶太人潔身禮用的石缸，每個缸可盛兩、三桶水。耶穌對佣人說："往缸裏倒滿水。"他們便把缸灌滿了水。耶穌吩咐道："現在舀出來給管宴席的送去。"他們照耶穌的吩咐做了。管宴席的嚐了嚐水變來的酒，却不知道是從哪兒來的，當然，舀水的人心裏清楚。管宴席的便把新郎叫來，對他說："人們待客總是先上好酒，等客人喝足了，再把次的拿上來。可你却把好酒留到現在才端出來。"

68   *Cleansing of the Temple*

John

After this he went down to Capernaum in company with his
mother, his brothers, and his disciples, but they did not stay
there long. As it was near the time of the Jewish Passover,
Jesus went up to Jerusalem. There he found in the temple the
dealers in cattle, sheep, and pigeons, and the money-changers
seated at their tables. Jesus made a whip of cords and drove
them out of the temple, sheep, cattle, and all. He upset the
tables of the money-changers, scattering their coins. Then he
turned on the dealers in pigeons: 'Take them out,' he said;
'you must not turn my Father's house into a market.' His disciples recalled the words of Scripture, 'Zeal for thy house will
destroy me.' The Jews challenged Jesus: 'What sign', they
asked, 'can you show as authority for your action?' 'Destroy
this temple,' Jesus replied, 'and in three days I will raise it
again.' They said, 'It has taken forty-six years to build this
temple. Are you going to raise it again in three days?' But the
temple he was speaking of was his body. After his resurrection his disciples recalled what he had said, and they believed
the Scripture and the words that Jesus had spoken.

While he was in Jerusalem for Passover many gave their
allegiance to him when they saw the signs that he performed.
But Jesus for his part would not trust himself to them. He
knew men so well, all of them, that he needed no evidence
from others about a man, for he himself could tell what was in
a man.

六十八　清潔聖殿

約翰福音

　　這件事以後，耶穌便和他的母親、兄弟和門徒一起到了迦百農，但他們在那裏並未住多久。因爲猶太人的逾越節快到了，耶穌便動身去耶路撒冷。到了耶路撒冷他看到聖殿裏有賣叫牛、羊、鴿子的，還有擺桌子兌換銀錢的，耶穌便用繩作鞭子，把牛、羊和人都趕出了聖殿。他又掀翻了兌換銀錢的人的桌子，使錢撒了一地。然後，他又對賣鴿子的說："把鴿子弄出去，不許你們把聖殿當做買賣市場！"他的門徒想起了經書上的話："我爲你的殿而心焦如焚。"那些猶太人難爲耶穌說："你能做些甚麼來顯示神迹給我們看看嗎？"他答道："你們拆毀聖殿，我三天之內要把它重建起來。"猶太人說："建造這殿用了四十六年，你三天之內能建得起來嗎？"但耶穌所講的聖殿是指他的身體(1)。在他復活之後，他的門徒們回想起了他曾講過的話，就更加相信聖經和耶穌的言語了。

　　耶穌在耶路撒冷過逾越節時，很多人都看到了他顯示的神迹，對他更爲篤信不疑。至於耶穌自己却不想把自己向他們交代清楚。他十分了解眾人，因此用不着別人向他說明誰是怎樣怎樣的，因爲他自己就知道人的內心是怎樣的。

———————

(1)　這裏指的是耶穌死後三日復活。

John

There was one of the Pharisees named Nicodemus, a member of the Jewish Council, who came to Jesus by night. 'Rabbi,' he said, 'we know that you are a teacher sent by God; no one could perform these signs of yours unless God were with him.' Jesus answered, 'In truth, in very truth I tell you, unless a man has been born over again he cannot see the kingdom of God.' 'But how is it possible', said Nicodemus, 'for a man to be born when he is old? Can he enter his mother's womb a second time and be born?' Jesus answered, 'In truth I tell you, no one can enter the kingdom of God without being born from water and spirit. Flesh can give birth only to flesh; it is spirit that gives birth to spirit. You ought not to be astonished, then, when I tell you that you must be born over again. The wind blows where it wills; you hear the sound of it, but you do not know where it comes from, or where it is going. So with everyone who is born from spirit.'

Nicodemus replied, 'How is this possible?' 'What!' said Jesus. 'Is this famous teacher of Israel ignorant of such things? In very truth I tell you, we speak of what we know, and testify to what we have seen, and yet you all reject our testimony. If you disbelieve me when I talk to you about things on earth, how are you to believe if I should talk about the things of heaven?

'No one ever went up into heaven except the one who came down from heaven, the Son of Man whose home is in heaven. This Son of Man must be lifted up as the serpent was lifted up

六十九　尼哥底母

約翰福音

　　有個法利賽人，名叫尼哥底母，是猶太人的一個官。他夜裏來見耶穌，說："拉比，我們知道你是上帝派來的教師，因為，若無上帝與你同在，你那些神迹是誰也行不了的。"耶穌答道："我實實在在地告訴你，人若不重生，就不能看到上帝之國。"尼哥底母問道："人已經老了，怎麼能重生呢？難道他能重入母腹，再次出生麼？"耶穌答道："我實在地告訴你，若非從水和聖靈生的，都不能進上帝之國。肉生的只能是肉身；聖靈生的才是靈。當我說你們必須重生時，你們不必驚愕。風隨意而行，你聽到風聲，却不知道它從何處來，往何處去。聖靈所生亦如此。"[1]

　　尼哥底母說道："怎能如此呢。"耶穌說："甚麼！你這以色列名師竟不知此種事？我實在地告訴你，我們講我們所知，證實我們所見。而你們竟拒絕接受我們的證言。我對你們講世上之事，你們尚且不信，若談天上之事，豈不更不信麼。

　　"除去那從天而降但家仍在上天的人子外，無人升過天。

―――――――――

[1]　"風"和"聖靈"在希臘文是同一詞，故語帶雙關。

by Moses in the wilderness, so that everyone who has faith in him may in him possess eternal life.

'God loved the world so much that he gave his only Son, that everyone who has faith in him may not die but have eternal life. It was not to judge the world that God sent his Son into the world, but that through him the world might be saved.

'The man who puts his faith in him does not come under judgement; but the unbeliever has already been judged in that he has not given his allegiance to God's only Son. Here lies the test: the light has come into the world, but men preferred darkness to light because their deeds were evil. Bad men all hate the light and avoid it, for fear their practices should be shown up. The honest man comes to the light so that it may be clearly seen that God is in all he does.'

像摩西在曠野裏高舉銅蛇一樣(1)，人子也必須被抬高舉起，使信奉他的人都會由他而獲得永生。

"上帝深愛世人，因此將自己獨子賜給世人，使所有信奉他者都不死而得永生。上帝差兒子到世上，並非去審判世人，而是通過他使世人得救。"

"信奉他的人不會被審判，而不信的人則已被判罪，因他不敬奉上帝的獨子。這是個考驗：光明來到世間，但世人因行為邪惡而不愛光明愛黑暗。惡人都恨光明而躲避它，是怕自己的邪行暴露出來。誠實者趨向光明，這就使人清楚看到他的行為都是上帝所贊同的。"

---

(1) 《民數記》中，蛇為患，摩西造銅蛇豎起，被蛇咬者一望銅蛇即可自癒。

John

A report now reached the Pharisees: 'Jesus is winning and baptizing more disciples than John'; although, in fact, it was only the disciples who were baptizing, and not Jesus himself. When Jesus learned this, he left Judaea and set out once more for Galilee. He had to pass through Samaria, and on his way came to a Samaritan town called Sychar, near the plot of ground which Jacob gave to his son Joseph and the spring called Jacob's well. It was about noon, and Jesus, tired after his journey, sat down by the well.

The disciples had gone away to the town to buy food. Meanwhile a Samaritan woman came to draw water. Jesus said to her, 'Give me a drink.' The Samaritan woman said, 'What! You, a Jew, ask a drink of me, a Samaritan woman?' (Jews and Samaritans, it should be noted, do not use vessels in common.) Jesus answered her, 'If only you knew what God gives, and who it is that is asking you for a drink, you would have asked him and he would have given you living water.' 'Sir,' the woman said, 'you have no bucket and this well is deep. How can you give me "living water"? Are you a greater man than Jacob our ancestor, who gave us the well, and drank from it himself, he and his sons, and his cattle too?' Jesus said, 'Everyone who drinks this water will be thirsty again, but whoever drinks the water that I shall give him will never suffer thirst any more. The water that I shall give him will be an inner spring always welling up for eternal life.' 'Sir,' said the woman, 'give me that water, and then I shall not be thirsty,

七十　叙加古井

約翰福音

　　法利賽人聽說，"耶穌施洗的門徒要比約翰的多"，而實際上是耶穌的門徒而不是耶穌自己施洗。耶穌知道此事，就離猶太地再次動身去加利利。由於要路經撒瑪利亞，他途中便到了撒瑪利亞的叙加城，這城離雅各給他兒子約瑟的那塊地不遠。那裏有口雅各井。時近中午，耶穌因旅途困乏，就坐在井旁休息。

　　耶穌的門徒進城去買食物。這時，一個撒瑪利亞的婦人來打水。耶穌對她說："給點水我喝吧。"那婦人說："什麼！你這猶太人怎麼能向我這個撒瑪利亞婦人要水喝呢？"（因猶太人和撒瑪利亞人從不共用器皿。）耶穌答道："你若知道上帝的恩賜以及向你要水喝的人是誰，你一定會求他，他也一定會給你活水的。""先生，"那婦人說，"你沒有桶而井又很深，你怎麼能給我'活水'呢？這口井是我們的祖先雅各留給我們的，他和他的兒子、牲畜都喝這口井裏的水。難道你比他還偉大嗎？"耶穌說："喝了這水的人，還會再感到口渴。而喝我的水的人，却永不再口渴了。我所賜的水則是一股身體內的清泉，直湧到永生。"婦人說："先生，那就請把那水賜給我吧，

nor have to come all this way to draw.'

Jesus replied, 'Go home, call your husband and come back.' She answered, 'I have no husband.' 'You are right', said Jesus, 'in saying that you have no husband, for, although you have had five husbands, the man with whom you are now living is not your husband; you told me the truth there.' 'Sir,' she replied, 'I can see that you are a prophet. Our fathers worshipped on this mountain, but you Jews say that the temple where God should be worshipped is in Jerusalem.' 'Believe me,' said Jesus, 'the time is coming when you will worship the Father neither on this mountain, nor in Jerusalem. You Samaritans worship without knowing what you worship, while we worship what we know. It is from the Jews that salvation comes. But the time approaches, indeed it is already here, when those who are real worshippers will worship the Father in spirit and in truth. Such are the worshippers whom the Father wants. God is spirit, and those who worship him must worship in spirit and in truth.' The woman answered, 'I know that Messiah' (that is Christ) 'is coming. When he comes he will tell us everything.' Jesus said, 'I am he, I who am speaking to you now.'

At that moment his disciples returned, and were astonished to find him talking with a woman; but none of them said, 'What do you want?' or, 'Why are you talking with her?' The woman put down her water-jar and went away to the town, where she said to the people, 'Come and see a man who has told me everything I ever did. Could this be the Messiah?' They came out of the town and made their way towards him.

Meanwhile the disciples were urging him, 'Rabbi, have something to eat.' But he said, 'I have food to eat of which you know nothing.' At this the disciples said to one another, 'Can someone have brought him food?' But Jesus said, 'It is meat and drink for me to do the will of him who sent me until I have finished his work.

'Do you not say, "Four months more and then comes harvest"? But look, I tell you, look round on the fields; they are

好叫我不再口渴，不用跑這麼遠來打水了。"

耶穌答道："回家去把你丈夫叫來。"婦人說："我沒有丈夫。"耶穌說："你說得對，你沒有丈夫，因為你已經有過五個丈夫，而現在和你一起的那個人不是你的丈夫。你說的倒是真話。"婦人答道："先生，我看得出你是個先知。我們的祖先都在這山上作禮拜，而你們猶太人却說，向上帝禮拜的地方應該在耶路撒冷。"耶穌說："你相信我吧，你們很快就不會在這山上也不會在耶路撒冷拜聖父了。你們撒瑪利亞人不知道自己拜的是甚麼，而我們却知道自己拜的是甚麼，因為救恩出自猶太人。時候將到，實際上已經到了，真誠崇拜的人要用心靈和誠實去拜聖父，因為聖父所要的就是這樣的崇拜者。上帝是神靈，要拜他的人必須用心靈和誠實去拜。"婦人答道："我知道彌賽亞（即基督）要來，他來了就會把一切都告訴我們。"耶穌說："現在和你說話的人就是他。"

這時，買東西的門徒們回來了，看見他正和一個婦人說話，都感到很奇怪。但他們誰也沒有問"你想怎樣？"或"你為何和她談話？"。那婦人放下水罐，進城去了，她對眾人說："你們快去看，有一個人把我的底細全都能講出來，莫非他就是基督？"於是眾人都出城往耶穌這裏走來。

這時，門徒們對耶穌說："拉比，吃點兒東西吧。"但耶穌說："我有東西吃，不過這東西你們是不知道的。"門徒們議論道："難道有人拿東西給他吃了？"耶穌說："我的飲食就是遵照差我來者的旨意，完成他的事。"

"你們不是講'離收割的時候還有四個月麼？'我告訴你們，看看周圍的田野吧。莊稼已經成熟，可以收割了。收割者得到

already white, ripe for harvest. The reaper is drawing his pay and gathering a crop for eternal life, so that sower and reaper may rejoice together. That is how the saying comes true: "One sows, and another reaps." I sent you to reap a crop for which you have not toiled. Others toiled and you have come in for the harvest of their toil.'

Many Samaritans of that town came to believe in him because of the woman's testimony: 'He told me everything I ever did.' So when these Samaritans had come to him they pressed him to stay with them; and he stayed there two days. Many more became believers because of what they heard from his own lips. They told the woman, 'It is no longer because of what you said that we believe, for we have heard him ourselves; and we know that this is in truth the Saviour of the word.'

酬勞，並積蓄五穀求永生。這樣，播種者和收割者可共享快樂。俗話說'前人種，後人收'，這話確實不假。我差你們去收穫你們沒有付出勞動的東西。別人要辛苦勞作，你們却坐享其成。"

城裏的許多人都信耶穌了，因為那婦人證實，"他把我的底細都能講出來。"於是，撒瑪利亞人來見耶穌時，都求他就在那裏住下。耶穌便在那裏住了兩天。聽過他親口講的話而成為他的信徒的人更多了。他們對那位婦人說："我們信他並不是因為聽了你說的事，而是由於我們親自聽了他講話。我們知道他是眞正的救世主。"

John

When the two days were over he set out for Galilee; for Jesus himself declared that a prophet is without honour in his own country. On his arrival in Galilee the Galileans gave him a welcome, because they had seen all that he did at the festival in Jerusalem; they had been at the festival themselves.

Once again he visited Cana-in-Galilee, where he had turned the water into wine. An officer in the royal service was there, whose son was lying ill at Capernaum. When he heard that Jesus had come from Judaea into Galilee, he came to him and begged him to go down and cure his son, who was at the point of death. Jesus said to him, 'Will none of you ever believe without seeing signs and portents?' The officer pleaded with him, 'Sir, come down before my boy dies.' Then Jesus said, 'Return home; your son will live.' The man believed what Jesus said and started for home. When he was on his way down his servants met him with the news, 'Your boy is going to live.' So he asked them what time it was when he began to recover. They said, 'Yesterday at one in the afternoon the fever left him.' The father noted that this was the exact time when Jesus had said to him, 'Your son will live', and he and all his household became believers.

This was now the second sign which Jesus performed after coming down from Judaea into Galilee.

Later on Jesus went up to Jerusalem for one of the Jewish festivals. Now at the Sheep-Pool in Jerusalem there is a place with five colonnades. Its name in the language of the Jews is

七十一　不藥而癒

約翰福音

　　兩天後耶穌動身去加利利，因爲他自己講過，一個先知在自己家鄉是不受尊敬的。他到加利利後受到人們熱情歡迎，因爲他們在耶路撒冷過逾越節時親眼看到耶穌所行的神迹。

　　耶穌再到加利利的迦拿，他以前曾在此變水爲酒。那兒有個大臣，他的兒子在迦百農患病。他聽到耶穌從猶太地來到了加利利，便來央求耶穌去爲他兒子治病，因爲他的兒子已病危。耶穌對他說："若非看見神迹奇事，你們總是不信。"大臣懇求說："先生，求你在我兒死前去一趟。"耶穌說："回家去吧，你的兒子就會好的。"這大臣相信耶穌的話，就動身回家。才在途中，他的僕人已帶着好消息來迎他，說："你的兒子已好些了。"他便問什麼時候開始好轉的。他們說："昨日下午一點就退燒了。"大臣一想，那正是耶穌對他說"你兒子就會好的"之時。因此，他們全家都信耶穌了。

　　這是耶穌從猶太地回加利利後施行的第二件神迹。

　　後來，耶穌去耶路撒冷過一個猶太人的節日。那兒，靠近羊門池旁有五個廊子的地方，希伯來語叫畢士大。廊下躺着許

Bethesda. In these colonnades there lay a crowd of sick people, blind, lame, and paralysed. Among them was a man who had been crippled for thirty-eight years. When Jesus saw him lying there and was aware that he had been ill a long time, he asked him, 'Do you want to recover?' 'Sir,' he replied, 'I have no one to put me in the pool when the water is disturbed, but while I am moving, someone else is in the pool before me.' Jesus answered, 'Rise to your feet, take up your bed and walk.' The man recovered instantly, took up his stretcher, and began to walk.

That day was a Sabbath. So the Jews said to the man who had been cured, 'It is the Sabbath. You are not allowed to carry your bed on the Sabbath.' He answered, 'The man who cured me said, "Take up your bed and walk."' They asked him, 'Who is the man who told you to take up your bed and walk?' But the cripple who had been cured did not know; for the place was crowded and Jesus had slipped away. A little later Jesus found him in the temple and said to him. 'Now that you are well again, leave your sinful ways, or you may suffer something worse.' The man went away and told the Jews that it was Jesus who had cured him.

It was works of this kind done on the Sabbath that stirred the Jews to persecute Jesus. He defended himself by saying, 'My Father has never yet ceased his work, and I am working too.' This made the Jews still more determined to kill him, because he was not only breaking the Sabbath, but, by calling God his own Father, he claimed equality with God.

To this charge Jesus replied, 'In truth, in very truth I tell you, the Son can do nothing by himself; he does only what he sees the Father doing: what the Father does, the Son does. For the Father loves the Son and shows him all his works, and will show greater yet, to fill you with wonder. As the Father raises the dead and gives them life, so the Son gives life to men, as he determines. And again, the Father does not judge anyone, but has given full jurisdiction to the Son; it is his will that all should pay the same honour to the Son as to the

多病人，有瞎子、瘸子和癱瘓的人。其中有個人已患殘疾38年。耶穌看到他躺在那兒，就知道他已病了好久，便問他："你想痊癒嗎？"病人答道："先生，天使把水攪動時，沒有人幫我浸入池裏，我自己爬去時，別人早已先下去了。"(1)耶穌說："你可以站起來，可以拿着舖蓋走了。"那人立時痊癒，拿起舖蓋，可以邁步行走了。

那天正是安息日，那些猶太人就對那被治癒的人說："今天是安息日，你是不能拿走舖蓋的。"(2)他答道："治癒我的那個人說'拿起你的舖蓋行走吧'。"那些猶太人便問他："說這話的是誰人？"但這人自己也不知道，因爲那地方人很多，耶穌早已悄悄走開。後來，耶穌在聖殿裏看到他，對他說："你已痊癒，以後要不做邪惡之事，否則，你會受苦更深。"那人就走了並告訴那些猶太人，是耶穌治好了他的病。

由於耶穌在安息日做這樣的事引起猶太人的反感，他們便要迫害他。耶穌據理說："我聖父從未中止過做事，我也一直在做事。"這就使得猶太人越發想要殺死他，因爲他不但褻瀆了安息日，而且稱上帝爲父，要和上帝平起平坐。

對他們的責難，耶穌答道："我實在地告訴你們，子基督自己是什麼事也做不了的。只有看着聖父怎樣做子才會做：聖父做什麼，子也做什麼。因爲聖父愛子，就把他做的一切都給子看，而且以後還要做出更偉大的事，叫你們感到驚奇。聖父叫死人復活，給他們以生命，子也就能按他的意願給人以生命。聖父不審判任何人，而是把審判全權交給子。他的意願是

---

(1) 據說天使會時常攪動池水，水動時誰先下去病即可癒。

(2) 猶太教認爲安息日諸事不宜做。

Father. To deny honour to the Son is to deny it to the Father who sent him.

'In very truth, anyone who gives heed to what I say and puts his trust in him who sent me had hold of eternal life, and does not come up for judgement, but has already passed from death to life. In truth, in very truth I tell you, a time is coming, indeed it is already here, when the dead shall hear the voice of the Son of God, and all who hear shall come to life. For as the Father has lifegiving power in himself, so has the Son, by the Father's gift.

'As Son of Man, he has also been given the right to pass judgement. Do not wonder at this, because the time is coming when all who are in the grave shall hear his voice and come out: those who have done right will rise to life; those who have done wrong will rise to hear their doom. I cannot act by myself; I judge as I am bidden, and my sentence is just, because my aim is not my own will, but the will of him who sent me.

要人像敬聖父一樣敬子。不敬子的，就是不敬差遣子來的聖父。

"我實在地告訴你們，任何人凡恭聽我的話又信仰那差我來者，都能獲得永生，不會被審判，而且已經出死復生了。我實在地告訴你們，時候就到或者說已到：死人會聽到聖子的聲音，而且聽到的就會復活。因爲聖父有使人復活之能力，子受聖父恩賜，也有此能力。"

"作爲人子，他亦被賜予審判權。你們不必對此驚奇，因這日子將來臨，到時墳墓中死者將聽到他的聲音而復出。行善者出而復活，作惡者出而受審。我自己並不可隨意行事。我只遵囑而作審判。而我的審判是公平合理的，因我並非按照自己意圖行事而是依據差遣我來者的旨意行事。"

John

Some time later Jesus withdrew to the farther shore of the Sea of Galilee (or Tiberias), and a large crowd of people followed who had seen the signs he performed in healing the sick. Then Jesus went up the hill-side and sat down with his disciples. It was near the time of Passover, the great Jewish festival. Raising his eyes and seeing a large crowd coming towards him, Jesus said to Philip, 'Where are we to buy bread to feed these people?' This he said to test him; Jesus himself knew what he meant to do. Philip replied, 'Twenty pounds would not buy enough bread for every one of them to have a little.' One of his disciples, Andrew, the brother of Simon Peter, said to him, 'There is a boy here who has five barley loaves and two fishes; but what is that among so many?' Jesus said, 'Make the people sit down.' There was plenty of grass there, so the men sat down, about five thousand of them. Then Jesus took the loaves, gave thanks, and distributed them to the people as they sat there. He did the same with the fishes, and they had as much as they wanted. When everyone had had enough, he said to his disciples, 'Collect the pieces left over, so that nothing may be lost.' This they did, and filled twelve baskets with the pieces left uneaten of the five barley loaves.

When the people saw the sign Jesus had performed, the word went round, 'Surely this must be the prophet that was to come into the world.' Jesus, aware that they meant to come and seize him to proclaim him king, withdrew again to the hills by himself.

七十二　五餅二魚

約翰福音

　　過了些時候，耶穌回到了加利利海，也就是提比哩亞海邊那裏。一大羣曾目睹他那妙手回春的神迹的人追隨着他。耶穌走上山坡，和他的門徒們一起坐下。那時候正接近猶太人的盛大節日逾越節。耶穌舉目看去，見許多人朝他走來，便對腓力說：“我們到何處買些餅食給這些人吃呢？”他說這話是爲了考考腓力，其實他已自有主意。腓力答道：“就是花二十兩銀子買餅也不夠每人吃一口的。”耶穌的一個門徒安德烈（就是西門·彼得的弟弟）對耶穌說：“這兒有個孩子，他有五個大麥餅和兩條魚；但分給這麼多人，也太少了。”耶穌說：“讓衆人坐下。”山坡上遍是草地，衆人便坐下來，大約有五千人。耶穌拿過餅來，先感謝神恩，然後把餅分給坐在那裏的衆人。魚也是這樣分了，衆人都可以要多少就分到多少。他們吃飽後耶穌對門徒們說：“把剩下的碎餅碎魚收集起來，不要糟蹋東西。”門徒照他的話做了，把衆人吃那五個大麥餅剩下的碎渣收拾起來，却整整裝滿十二籃。

　　衆人看到耶穌所行的神迹，大家都說道：“他肯定是那位來到世上的先知。”耶穌看到衆人有意要擁他稱王，便又退到山上去了。

Mark

So they came to the other side of the lake, into the country of the Gerasenes. As he stepped ashore, a man possessed by an unclean spirit came up to him from among the tombs where he had his dwelling. He could no longer be controlled; even chains were useless; he had often been fettered and chained up, but he had snapped his chains and broken the fetters. No one was strong enough to master him. And so, unceasingly, night and day, he would cry aloud among the tombs and on the hill-sides and cut himself with stones. When he saw Jesus in the distance, he ran and flung himself down before him, shouting loudly, 'What do you want with me, Jesus, son of the Most High God? In God's name do not torment me.' (For Jesus was already saying to him, 'Out unclean spirit, come out of this man!') Jesus asked him, 'What is your name?' 'My name is Legion,' he said, 'there are so many of us.' And he begged hard that Jesus would not send them out of the country.

Now there happened to be a large herd of pigs feeding on the hill-side, and the spirits begged him, 'Send us among the pigs and let us go into them.' He gave them leave; and the unclean spirits came out and went into the pigs; and the herd, of about two thousand, rushed over the edge into the lake and were drowned.

The men in charge of them took to their heels and carried the news to the town and country-side; and the people came out to see what had happened. They came to Jesus and saw

七十三 羣豬投水

馬可福音

　　耶穌和門徒渡湖到那邊的格拉森人居住的地方。耶穌一上岸，一個被污鬼附體的人便從他住的墳堆中走出來到他跟前。這人已沒有人能禁得住，就是用鐵鏈也沒有用。人們屢次用脚鐐和鐵鏈鎖住他，但鐵鏈被他掙斷了，脚鐐也被他砸碎了。誰也沒法強行制服他。他晝夜在墳堆間和山坡上大叫大喊，還用石塊砍自己。他遠遠看到了耶穌，便跑過去跪在了耶穌的面前，大叫道："至高上帝的兒子耶穌啊，你找我有什麼事？看在上帝的面上，不要再折磨我了。"（因爲耶穌已經對他講了："污鬼出來，從這人身上出來！"）耶穌問附在那人身上的污鬼："你叫什麼名字？"他答道："我叫羣。我們數目多得很。"然後，便苦苦懇求耶穌，不要叫他們離開那地方。

　　在山坡上，這時正好有一大羣豬在覓食，那些鬼便央求耶穌說："請你讓我們到豬羣裏去附到豬身上吧！"耶穌同意了，污鬼便跑出來附到豬羣身上。那些豬大概有兩千隻，都闖過山崖掉到湖裏淹死了。

　　放豬的人趕快跑了，把這消息告訴了城裏和鄉下的人。他們都出來看看是怎麼回事。來到耶穌那裏，他們看見那個曾被

the madman who had been possessed by the legion of devils, sitting there clothed and in his right mind; and they were afraid. The spectators told them how the madman had been cured and what had happened to the pigs. Then they begged Jesus to leave the district.

As he was stepping into the boat, the man who had been possessed begged to go with him. Jesus would not allow it, but said to him, 'Go home to your own folk and tell them what the Lord in his mercy has done for you.' The man went off and spread the news in the Ten Towns of all that Jesus had done for him; and they were all amazed.

羣鬼附體的瘋子正坐在那兒穿衣服，神經也正常，他們便感到害怕。那些目擊者告訴了他們這個瘋子如何被治癒和豬如何跳下山崖的經過。他們便請求耶穌離開那地方。

耶穌上船時，那個曾被污鬼附體的人懇求與耶穌同行。耶穌不許，並對他說：「回家去和家人團聚吧。告訴他們天主如何憐憫你、救了你。」那人便在十城逢人就講耶穌如何救了他，眾人聽後都感到非常驚奇。

Mark

As soon as Jesus had returned by boat to the other shore, a great crowd once more gathered round him. While he was by the lake-side, the president of one of the synagogues came up, Jairus by name, and, when he saw him, threw himself down at his feet and pleaded with him. 'My little daughter', he said, 'is at death's door. I beg you to come and lay your hands on her to cure her and save her life.' So Jesus went with him, accompanied by a great crowd which pressed upon him.

Among them was a woman who had suffered from haemorrhages for twelve years; and in spite of long treatment by many doctors, on which she had spent all she had, there had been no improvement; on the contrary, she had grown worse. She had heard what people were saying about Jesus, so she came up from behind in the crowd and touched his cloak; for she said to herself, 'If I touch even his clothes, I shall be cured.' And there and then the source of her haemorrhages dried up and she knew in herself that she was cured of her trouble. At the same time Jesus, aware that power had gone out of him, turned round in the crowd and asked, 'Who touched my clothes?' His disciples said to him, 'You see the crowd pressing upon you and yet you ask, "Who touched me?"' Meanwhile he was looking round to see who had done it. And the woman, trembling with fear when she grasped what had happened to her, came and fell at his feet and told him the whole truth. He said to her, 'My daughter, your faith has cured you. Go in peace, free for ever from this trouble.'

七十四 少女復甦

馬可福音

耶穌坐船回到湖那邊去。剛一抵岸，便又有許多人聚在他周圍。耶穌還在湖邊上，就有一個叫睚魯的會堂主持趕來見他。他一見到耶穌，便俯伏在他的腳前，懇求說："我的小女兒就要死了。求你給她行按手禮，讓聖靈治癒她，救她一命吧。"耶穌便同他前往，許多人擁着他們一起走。

眾人中有一個女人，患了十二年的血漏，受了好多苦。雖多方求醫，錢也花盡了，可病不但毫無起色，反而日漸沉重。她聽到眾人談論耶穌的神迹，便從眾人後面擠了上來摸摸耶穌的衣服。她心想："只要我摸摸他的衣服，病也肯定會好的。"她的血漏竟當時就停了，她感到身上的病已霍然而癒。這時，耶穌感到自己身上有一股能放了出去，便在人羣中轉過身來問道："誰摸我的衣服了？"門徒們說："眾人都擠擁你，你還問：'誰摸我來了？'"耶穌環視四周，看看是誰摸他。那女人見此情形，不由得滿心驚恐，便戰兢走上前去俯伏在他的腳前，吐露出全部實情。耶穌對她說："女兒，你的眞誠信仰救了你，安心地回去吧，你的病不會再犯的了。"

While he was still speaking, a message came from the president's house, 'Your daughter is dead; why trouble the Rabbi further?' But Jesus, overhearing the message as it was delivered, said to the president of the synagogue, 'Do not be afraid; only have faith.' After this he allowed no one to accompany him except Peter and James and James's brother John. They came to the president's house, where he found a great commotion, with loud crying and wailing. So he went in and said to them, 'Why this crying and commotion? The child is not dead: she is asleep'; and they only laughed at him. But after turning all the others out, he took the child's father and mother and his own companions and went in where the child was lying. Then, taking hold of her hand, he said to her, '*Talitha cum*', which means, 'Get up, my child.' Immediately the girl got up and walked about — she was twelve years old. At that they were beside themselves with amazement. He gave them strict orders to let no one hear about it, and told them to give her something to eat.

耶穌講話時，有人來向敎會會堂主持報信："你的女兒已經死了，用不着再麻煩拉比了。"耶穌聽見，便對那主持說："不要怕，要誠心堅信。"說完他不要別的人跟隨，只帶着彼得、雅各⑴和雅各的弟弟約翰前去。他們來到那主持的家，耶穌聽到抽泣聲、嚎哭聲亂成一片，他進去對他們說："亂哭亂喊什麼？孩子又不是死了，她祇不過是睡了。"衆人都嗤笑他。耶穌把他們全都推出屋外，然後把孩子的父母以及他的門徒們領進那女孩躺着的屋子。他握住女孩的手，對她說："大利大古米"，這話是阿拉姆語，翻譯過來就是"起來，孩子"。那個十二歲的女孩馬上站了起來，可以在屋裏走動了。看到這種情形，大家都感到萬分驚奇。耶穌切切囑咐他們，不要把此事告訴任何人。然後叫他們拿些東西給女孩吃。

⑴　James 是指雅各（Jacob）在新約裏的一個稱呼法。他是耶穌的一個門徒。

Luke

When he had finished addressing the people, he went to Capernaum. A centurion there had a servant whom he valued highly; this servant was ill and near to death. Hearing about Jesus, he sent some Jewish elders with the request that he would come and save his servant's life. They approached Jesus and pressed their petition earnestly: 'He deserves this favour from you,' they said, 'for he is a friend of our nation and it is he who built us our synagogue.' Jesus went with them; but when he was not far from the house, the centurion sent friends with this message: 'Do not trouble further, sir; it is not for me to have you under my roof, and that is why I did not presume to approach you in person. But say the word and my servant will be cured. I know, for in my position I am myself under orders, with soldiers under me. I say to one, "Go", and he goes; to another, "Come here", and he comes; and to my servant, "Do this", and he does it.' When Jesus heard this, he admired the man, and, turning to the crowd that was following him, he said, 'I tell you, nowhere, even in Israel, have I found faith like this.' And the messengers returned to the house and found the servant in good health.

Afterwards Jesus went to a town called Nain, accompanied by his disciples and a large crowd. As he approached the gate of the town he met a funeral. The dead man was the only son of his widowed mother; and many of the townspeople were there with her. When the Lord saw her his heart went out to her, and he said, 'Weep no more.' With that he stepped forward and laid his hand on the bier; and the bearers halted. Then he spoke: 'Young man, rise up!' The dead man sat up

七十五　在迦百農

路加福音

　　耶穌給聽道的人講完話後，就去了迦百農。那兒有個百人隊隊長，他重用的一個僕人生病快要死了。聽到耶穌所行的神迹，他就託幾位猶太長者去請耶穌來救他的僕人。他們來到耶穌那裏，懇切地對他說：“我們的百人隊隊長值得你賜他恩惠，因為他是我們的知心人，給我們建了會堂。”耶穌便和他們一同前往。快到那家時，百人隊隊長派了幾個朋友帶着他的口信來見耶穌，說：“先生，勞你親臨舍下，實在不敢當，當初我沒有親自去驚動你。就是只求你說一句話，我的僕人就會痊癒。我自己也是在人家手下做事，而士兵則在我手下當差。我對這個手下說‘去’，他就去，對那個說‘來’，他就來，對僕人說做這事，他就會應命而行。”聽了百人隊隊長的話，耶穌很讚賞他，便轉過身對衆人說，“我告訴你們，像這樣的誠篤，我即使在以色列也從未見過。”那些受託來見耶穌的人回到百人隊隊長家裏時，見那僕人已經痊癒了。

　　後來，耶穌在門徒們和許多人的陪同下，來到一座叫拿因的城鎮。走近城門時，他看到一家人在出殯。死者是個獨生子，母親是寡婦。城裏有許多人同她一起送殯。主看到那寡婦後，很同情她，便說：“不要哭了。”說完，上前去用手按住了棺架，抬棺的人便停住了。他說道：“年輕人，起來。”死

and began to speak; and Jesus gave him back to his mother. Deep awe fell upon them all, and they praised God. 'A great prophet has arisen among us', they said, and again, 'God has shown his care for his people.' The story of what he had done ran through all parts of Judaea and the whole neighbourhood.

John too was informed of all this by his disciples. Summoning two of their number he sent them to the Lord with this message: 'Are you the one who is to come, or are we to expect some other?' The messengers made their way to Jesus and said, 'John the Baptist has sent us to you: he asks, "Are you the one who is to come, or are we to expect some other?"' There and then he cured many sufferers from diseases, plagues, and evil spirits; and on many blind people he bestowed sight. Then he gave them his answer: 'Go', he said, 'and tell John what you have seen and heard: how the blind recover their sight, the lame walk, the lepers are made clean, the deaf hear, the dead are raised to life, the poor are hearing the good news — and happy is the man who does not find me a stumbling-block.'

After John's messengers had left, Jesus began to speak about him to the crowds: 'What was the spectacle that drew you to the wilderness? A reed-bed swept by the wind? No? Then what did you go out to see? A man dressed in silks and satins? Surely you must look in palaces for grand clothes and luxury. But what did you go out to see? A prophet? Yes indeed, and far more than a prophet. He is the man of whom Scripture says,

"Here is my herald, whom I send on ahead of you,
    and he will prepare your way before you."

I tell you, there is not a mother's son greater than John, and yet the least in the kingdom of God is greater than he.'

When they heard him, all the people, including the tax-gatherers, praised God, for they had accepted John's baptism; but the Pharisees and lawyers, who refused his baptism, had rejected God's purpose for themselves.

'How can I describe the people of this generation? What

者便坐起來並開口講話了。耶穌就把他交回他的母親。衆人不禁懍然敬畏，一齊讚頌上帝。他們說，"我們當中出了個偉大的先知"；又說，"上帝眷顧他的人民。"耶穌所行的神迹很快傳遍了猶太及其周圍的地方。

約翰的門徒把所有這些都告訴了約翰。他便叫了兩個門徒來，要他們去給主耶穌傳個口信："你是要來，還是我們要指望別人？"倆人便去見耶穌說："施洗約翰派我們來問你'要是你來，抑我們要指望別人？'"當時，耶穌在當地治癒了許多疫病纏身、惡鬼附體的人，還使不少盲人重見光明。他答道："你們回去把耳聞目睹的事都告訴約翰，如盲人復明，瘸子能行，患痲瘋的變得身光體潔，聾子復聰，死者復活，窮人得喜訊等。總之，凡不以我爲絆脚石者都得幸福。"

兩人走後，耶穌便向衆人談論起約翰來："你們曾去曠野，究竟要看什麼呢？看被風吹動的蘆葦叢？不？那你們去看什麼？去看一個身穿綢緞的人？你們只有在王宮裏才能看到錦衣與奢華。你們到底出去看什麼？看先知？確實，他比先知更偉大。他就是經書上講的那個人：

　　他是我遣在你前之使者，

　　他將在前爲你闢引道路。

我告訴你們，婦人生子未有大於約翰的，然而上帝國中最小者亦比他大。"

衆人和那些稅吏聽他講後，都齊聲稱頌上帝，因爲他們都接受過約翰的施洗。而那些拒受約翰施洗的法利賽人和律法師則得不到上帝賜給他們的恩惠。

"我如何描述這代人呢？他們像什麼？他們像坐在市場上的孩子，彼此叫道：

are they like? They are like children sitting in the market-place and shouting at each other,

"We piped for you and you would not dance."

"We wept and wailed, and you would not mourn."

For John the Baptist came neither eating bread nor drinking wine, and you say, "He is possessed." The Son of Man came eating and drinking, and you say, "Look at him! a glutton and a drinker, a friend of tax-gatherers and sinners!" And yet God's wisdom is proved right by all who are her children.'

One of the Pharisees invited him to eat with him; he went to the Pharisee's house and took his place at table. A woman who was living an immoral life in the town had learned that Jesus was at table in the Pharisee's house and had brought oil of myrrh in a small flask. She took her place behind him, by his feet, weeping. His feet were wetted with her tears and she wiped them with her hair, kissing them and anointing them with the myrrh. When his host the Pharisee saw this he said to himself, 'If this fellow were a real prophet, he would know who this woman is that touches him, and what sort of woman she is, a sinner.' Jesus took him up and said, 'Simon, I have something to say to you.' 'Speak on, Master', said he. 'Two men were in debt to a money-lender: one owed him five hundred silver pieces, the other fifty. As neither had anything to pay with he let them both off. Now, which will love him most?' Simon replied, 'I should think the one that was let off most.' 'You are right', said Jesus. Then turning to the woman, he said to Simon, 'You see this woman? I came to your house: you provided no water for my feet; but this woman has made my feet wet with her tears and wiped them with her hair. You gave me no kiss; but she has been kissing my feet ever since I came in. You did not anoint my head with oil; but she has anointed my feet with myrrh. And so, I tell you, her great love proves that her many sins have been forgiven; where little has been forgiven, little love is shown.' Then he said to her, 'Your sins are forgiven.' The other guests began to ask themselves, 'Who is this, that he can forgive sins?' But he said to the woman, 'Your faith has saved you; go in peace.'

'我們爲你們吹笛，而你們却不跳舞，

　我們哭泣哀號，你們却不哀傷。'
因爲施洗約翰來時，旣不吃餅，又沒飲酒，你們便說，'他被
鬼附體了。'人子來時，旣吃也喝，你們又說，'看那人貪飲好
食，與稅吏和罪人爲友！'然而，只要是上帝的孩子都可證明
上帝的智慧。"

　　有個法利賽人邀請耶穌去吃飯。耶穌便應邀上他家去。那
城裏有個不正派女人聽到耶穌在那個法利賽人家裏吃飯，她便
拿了一小瓶香膏，來到這家，坐在耶穌身後，靠近他的脚邊哭
泣。她的眼淚濕了耶穌的脚，她就用頭髮擦去脚上的淚水，吻
他的脚，然後又在上面塗上香膏。請耶穌吃飯的法利賽人見
了，心想："此人若是先知，一定知道摸他的這個女人是誰，
是個有罪的女人。"耶穌看出了法利賽人的心思，便說："西
門，我有句話要對你講。"西門答道："請講，老師。"耶穌
說："有個放債人有兩個債戶，一個欠他五百兩銀子，另一個
欠他五十兩。因爲他們誰也無力償還，放債人便都免去了他們
的債務。你說這兩人中誰最愛他？"西門答道："我想一定是
多受恩免的那個人了。"耶穌說："你說的對。"然後他轉向
那女人，又對西門說："你看到了這個女人嗎？我進你家時，
你沒有給我打洗脚水，而這個女人却用她的眼淚濕我的脚，然
後用頭髮把淚水擦乾；你沒有吻我，但這個女人自我進來後一
再吻我的脚；你沒有用油抹我的頭，但她却用香膏抹我的脚。
所以，我告訴你，她愛的深，因而她的罪就都被赦免了。而被
赦罪少的人，愛的就少。"然後，耶穌對她說："你的罪都被
赦免了。"同席的人心想："他是什麼人，竟能赦免罪孽？"但
耶穌却對那女人說："你的眞誠信仰救了你；安心地回去吧。"

Luke

Then Jesus, armed with the power of the Spirit, returned to Galilee; and reports about him spread through the whole country-side. He taught in their synagogues and all men sang his praises.

So he came to Nazareth, where he had been brought up, and went to synagogue on the Sabbath day as he regularly did. He stood up to read the lesson and was handed the scroll of the prophet Isaish. He opened the scroll and found the passage which says,

'The spirit of the Lord is upon me because he has anointed me;

he has sent me to announce good news to the poor,

to proclaim release for prisoners and recovery of sight for the blind;

to let the broken victims go free to proclaim the year of the Lord's favour.'

He rolled up the scroll, gave it back to the attendant, and sat down; and all eyes in the synagogue were fixed on him.

He began to speak: 'Today', he said, 'in your very hearing this text has come true.' There was a general stir of admiration; they were surprised that words of such grace should fall from his lips. 'Is not this Joseph's son?' they asked. Then Jesus said, 'No doubt you will quote the proverb to me, "Physician, heal yourself!", and say, "We have heard of all your doings at Capernaum; do the same here in your own

七十六　家鄉見棄

路加福音

　　耶穌帶聖靈的神力回到了加利利。他的聲名傳遍了城鄉各處。他在各個猶太敎會堂裏宣講道理，衆人對他交口稱譽。

　　耶穌來到拿撒勒，也就是他長大的地方，像通常那樣在安息日去會堂。他站起來要唸經書，這時有人把先知《以賽亞書》交給了他。他打開書，找到了下面這一段話：

　　　　"聖靈降在我身，因爲主塗油於我；

　　　　讓我傳福音於窮人，

　　　　着我宣告釋放虜囚，使盲人復明；

　　　　令受摧殘者得解放，

　　　　宣告爲上帝賜福之年。"

耶穌卷起書還給執事，然後坐下。會堂裏的人都看着他。

　　他開始講道："今天聽到的這段經文已經應驗了。"這引起一片讚嘆聲，同時衆人也感到驚奇，他會講出這樣的恩言。他們問道："這不是約瑟的兒子麼？"耶穌說："你們一定會向我引用一句俗語：'醫生，先治好自己的病吧！'又會說'我們已聽到你在迦百農所行的事，你在自己的家鄉也顯顯那些神迹

home town." I tell you this,' he went on: 'no prophet is recognized in his own country. There were many widows in Israel, you may be sure, in Elijah's time, when for three years and six months the skies never opened, and famine lay hard over the whole country; yet it was to none of those that Elijah was sent, but to a widow at Sarepta in the territory of Sidon. Again, in the time of the prophet Elisha there were many lepers in Israel, and not one of them was healed, but only Naaman, the Syrian.' At these words the whole congregation were infuriated. They leapt up, threw him out of the town, and took him to the brow of the hill on which it was built, meaning to hurl him over the edge. But he walked straight through them all, and went away.

Coming down to Capernaum, a town in Galilee, he taught the people on the Sabbath, and they were astounded at his teaching, for what he said had the note of authority. Now there was a man in the synagogue possessed by a devil, an unclean spirit. He shrieked at the top of his voice, 'What do you want with us, Jesus of Nazareth? Have you come to destroy us? I know who you are — the Holy One of God.' Jesus rebuked him: 'Be silent', he said, 'and come out of him.' Then the devil, after throwing the man down in front of the people, left him without doing him any injury. Amazement fell on them all and they said to one another: 'What is there in this man's words? He gives orders to the unclean spirits with authority and power, and out they go.' So the news spread, and he was the talk of the whole district.

On leaving the synagogue he went to Simon's house. Simon's mother-in-law was in the grip of a high fever; and they asked him to help her. He came and stood over her and rebuked the fever. It left her, and she got up at once and waited on them.

At sunset all who had friends suffering from one disease or another brought them to him; and he laid his hands on them one by one and cured them. Devils also came out of many of them, shouting, 'You are the Son of God.' But he rebuked

吧。'" 他接着說道："我告訴你們，沒有哪個先知在自己的家鄉被賞識的。我實話告訴你們，以利亞在世時，三年零六個月壞天氣，遍地都是饑荒。那時，以色列人中有許多寡婦。但上帝並沒有差以利亞去施恩於她們中的任何一個。而只是施恩於西頓的撒勒法的一個寡婦(1)。還有，先知以利沙在世時也是這樣。當時，以色列有許多人患大痲瘋，但沒有一個人被治好，只有叙利亞的乃縵被治癒。"聽到這話，會堂裏的眾人激怒起來。他們都站起來把耶穌推出城去，並把他帶到山崖邊（他們的城就建在這座山上），想把他推下去。但耶穌却能逕直穿過眾人而離去。

耶穌來到加利利的迦百農城，在安息日給眾人宣講道理。他們對他講的都感到驚奇，因為他的話裏顯出某種權威力量。會堂裏有個被污鬼附體的人高聲叫道："拿撒勒的耶穌，我們和你有何相干？你來是消滅我們的嗎？我知道你是誰，你是上帝基督。"耶穌斥責他道："住口，從他身內出來。"那污鬼把那人在眾人前摔倒，自己出來了，沒有傷害那人。眾人見了都十分驚訝，議論道："這個人的話可不一般，威嚴有力，叫污鬼出來污鬼就得出來。"這事傳開去後，耶穌的名聲在此無人不曉了。

從會堂一出來，耶穌就去了西門的家。西門的丈母娘正害熱病，他們求耶穌救她。耶穌站在她身旁，責令那熱病退走。熱就退了，她立刻站了起來可以招待他們了。

到日落時，眾人都把自己生病的親朋（不管什麼病）都帶到了耶穌那裏求治。耶穌把手放在他們身上，就把他們的病治癒了。鬼怪也都從他們一些人身上跑出來，喊道："你是聖

(1) 見五十三起死回生故事。

them and forbade them to speak, because they knew that he was the Messiah.

When day broke he went out and made his way to a lonely spot. But the people went in search of him, and when they came to where he was they pressed him not to leave them. But he said, 'I must give the good news of the kingdom of God to the other towns also, for that is what I was sent to do.' So he proclaimed the Gospel in the synagogues of Judaea.

子。"但耶穌斥責它們，不許它們說，因爲它們知道他就是基督。

天亮時，耶穌走出會堂去一個僻靜處。但衆人都追去找他，找到了便懇請他不要離開他們。但耶穌說："我也必須把上帝之國的福音傳給別的城鎮，因爲差我來的目的就是爲此。"就這樣，耶穌便在猶太地區的各個會堂裏傳道。

Luke

After this the Lord appointed a further seventy-two and sent them on ahead in pairs to every town and place he was going to visit himself. He said to them: 'The crop is heavy, but labourers are scarce; you must therefore beg the owner to send labourers to harvest his crop. Be on your way. And look, I am sending you like lambs among wolves. Carry no purse or pack, and travel barefoot. Exchange no greetings on the road. When you go into a house, let your first words be, "Peace to this house." If there is a man of peace there, your peace will rest upon him; if not, it will return and rest upon you. Stay in that one house, sharing their food and drink; for the worker earns his pay. Do not move from house to house. When you come into a town and they make you welcome, eat the food provided for you; heal the sick there, and say, "The kingdom of God has come close to you." When you enter a town and they do not make you welcome, go out into its streets and say, "The very dust of your town that clings to our feet we wipe off to your shame. Only take note of this: the kingdom of God has come close." I tell you, it will be more bearable for Sodom on the great Day than for that town.

'Alas for you, Chorazin! Alas for you, Bethsaida! If the miracles that were performed in you had been performed in Tyre and Sidon, they would have repented long ago, sitting in sackcloth and ashes. But it will be more bearable for Tyre and Sidon at the Judgement than for you. And as for you, Capernaum, will you be exalted to the skies? No, brought down to

七十七　遣徒傳道

路加福音

　　後來，耶穌又讓七十二個人，兩兩一組先到他自己要去的各城各地去。他對他們說：“莊稼很多，勞力很少，所以你們必須求種地的多派些人手去收割。你們去吧，不過要注意，我差你們去猶如把羊羔送入狼羣。不要帶錢囊和口袋，光腳而行，路上不要與人打招呼。無論走進哪一家，都要先說，‘願這一家平安’。如果那家有該得平安之人，你們的平安就會降他身上；否則，平安仍歸你們。住在那一家，和他們同吃同喝，因爲做工的人理應得到酬勞。不要從一家搬到另一家。如你們到某一個城鎮時受到接待，給什麼就吃什麼。要給那裏的病人治病，說：‘上帝之國已臨近你們了。’如你們到另一個城鎮，得不到接待，你們就在街上說：‘那怕就是你們城裏的塵土黏在我們脚上，我們也要當着你們的面就擦掉。要記住：上帝之國已經臨近了。’我告訴你們，審判日到來時，這樣的城鎮遭受的災難要比所多瑪遭受的厲害得多呢。

　　哥拉汛啊，你有禍了！伯賽大啊，你要遭難了！如果在你們中間行的奇迹被施行在推羅和西頓，他們早就披麻蒙灰、坐地悔改了。不過，審判日到來時，推羅和西頓遭受的災難要比你們受的輕得多。至於你，迦百農，你會升天嗎？不，你會被

the depths!

'Whoever listens to you listens to me; whoever rejects you rejects me. And whoever rejects me rejects the One who sent me.'

The seventy-two came back jubilant. 'In your name, Lord,' they said, 'even the devils submit to us.' He replied, 'I watched how Satan fell, like lightning, out of the sky. And now you see that I have given you the power to tread under-foot snakes and scorpions and all the forces of the enemy, and nothing will ever harm you. Nevertheless, what you should rejoice over is not that the spirits submit to you, but that your names are enrolled in heaven.'

At that moment Jesus exulted in the Holy Spirit and said, 'I thank thee, Father, Lord of heaven and earth, for hiding these things from the learned and wise, and revealing them to the simple. Yes, Father, such was thy choice.' Then turning to his disciples he said, 'Everything is entrusted to me by my Father; and no one knows who the Son is but the Father, or who the Father is but the Son, and those to whom the Son may choose to reveal him.'

Turning to his disciples in private he said, 'Happy the eyes that see what you are seeing! I tell you, many prophets and kings wished to see what you now see, yet never saw it; to hear what you hear, yet never heard it.'

On one occasion a lawyer came forward to put this test question to him: 'Master, what must I do to inherit eternal life?' Jesus said, 'What is written in the Law? What is your reading of it?' He replied, 'Love the Lord your God with all your heart, with all your soul, with all your strength, and with all your mind; and your neighbour as yourself.' 'That is the right answer,' said Jesus; 'do that and you will live.'

But he wanted to vindicate himself, so he said to Jesus, 'And who is my neighbour?' Jesus replied, 'A man was on his way from Jerusalem down to Jericho when he fell in with rob-bers, who stripped him, beat him, and went off leaving him half dead. It so happened that a priest was going down by the

推向地獄的。

"聽從你們的人就是聽從我；拒絕你們的人，也就是拒絕我。而拒絕我的人就是拒絕差我來的上帝。"

那七十二人歡歡喜喜地回來了。他們說："主啊，以你的名義，就連鬼都服了我們。"耶穌答道："我曾看到撒旦像閃電一樣從天落下。你們現在看到，我已給了你們力量去踐踏毒蛇、蝎子和所有的敵人，誰也不會傷害你們。不過，你們應當感到高興的不是制服了鬼怪，而是因你們的名字已登錄在天堂了。"

這時，耶穌為聖靈而感到喜悅，說："父啊，天地的主，我感謝你沒讓那些博學聰穎的人知曉這些事，而把它們顯示給純真的人。是的，父啊，這就是你的選擇。"然後，耶穌轉向門徒們說："父把一切交付了我；除去父，誰也不知子是誰；或除了子，以及子願意向其顯示的人外，誰也不知父是誰。"

耶穌轉身暗地對門徒們說："你們能看見現在所看見的，眼睛真是有福了。我告訴你們，過去許多先知和君王都想看到你們現在所看到的，但却未能如願；想聽到你們所聽到的，也沒有辦到。"

有一次，一個律法師提一個問題來試探耶穌："我主，我該做什麼才能獲得永生？"耶穌答道："律法上怎麼寫的？你怎麼唸的？"他答道："你要盡心、盡神、盡力、盡意地愛主，即你的上帝，還要像愛你自己那樣愛你的友鄰。"耶穌說："說得對，這樣做你就會獲得永生。"

但那人為表白自己，便對耶穌說："那誰是我的友鄰呢？"耶穌答道："一個人從耶路撒冷去耶利哥，途中遇上強盜。強盜剝去了他的衣服，把他打了個半死，然後丟下他走了。這時

same road; but when he saw him, he went past on the other side. So too a Levite came to the place, and when he saw him went past on the other side. But a Samaritan who was making the journey came upon him, and when he saw him was moved to pity. He went up and bandaged his wounds, bathing them with oil and wine. Then he lifted him on to his own beast, brought him to an inn, and looked after him there. Next day he produced two silver pieces and gave them to the innkeeper, and said, "Look after him; and if you spend any more, I will repay you on my way back." Which of these three do you think was neighbour to the man who fell into the hands of the robbers?' He answered, 'The one who showed him kindness.' Jesus said, 'Go and do as he did.'

While they were on their way Jesus came to a village where a woman named Martha made him welcome in her home. She had a sister, Mary, who seated herself at the Lord's feet and stayed there listening to his words. Now Martha was distracted by her many tasks, so she came to him and said, 'Lord, do you not care that my sister has left me to get on with the work by myself? Tell her to come and lend a hand.' But the Lord answered, 'Martha, Martha, you are fretting and fussing about so many things; but one thing is necessary. The part that Mary has chosen it best; and it shall not be taken away from her.

正好有個祭師從這路過，看到這受害人，便繞開走過去了。又走來一個利未人，看到受害人，也同樣繞路走過去了。但一個路過的撒瑪利亞人走來看到傷者，就動了惻隱之心。他上前用油和酒洗淨那人的傷口，給他包紮好，又扶他坐上了自己的牲口，把他帶到客店裏照料他。第二天，他拿出二両銀子交給店主，說：'好好照料他，若這些錢不夠，我回程時一定付還給你。'這三個人中，你看哪個是途中遇盜那人的友鄰呢？"那個律法師答道："當然是好心幫他的那個人。"耶穌說："那你就像他那樣去做吧。"

在他們的旅途中，耶穌進了一個村莊。一個叫馬大的女人在家中接待他。馬大有個妹妹叫瑪利亞，她坐在耶穌脚邊聽他講道。馬大事情很多忙不過來，就對耶穌說："主啊，你沒看到我妹妹就讓我一人幹活嗎？你叫她來幫我一下吧。"但耶穌答道："馬大啊，馬大，你爲許多事情煩惱忙亂，但有一件事是不可少的——聽講道。而瑪利亞則選上這大好事，你就別把她拉去幹活了。"

John

As he went on his way Jesus saw a man blind from his birth. His disciples put the question, 'Rabbi, who sinned, this man or his parents? Why was he born blind?' 'It is not that this man or his parents sinned,' Jesus answered; 'he was born blind so that God's power might be displayed in curing him. While daylight lasts we must carry on the work of him who sent me; night comes, when no one can work. While I am in the world I am the light of the world.'

With these words he spat on the ground and made a paste with the spittle; he spread it on the man's eyes, and said to him, 'Go and wash in the pool of Siloam.' (The name means 'sent'.)The man went away and washed, and when he returned he could see.

His neighbours and those who were accustomed to see him begging said, 'Is not this the man who used to sit and beg?' Others said, 'Yes, this is the man.' Others again said, 'No, but it is someone like him.' The man himself said, 'I am the man.' They asked him, 'How were your eyes opened?' He replied, 'The man called Jesus made a paste and smeared my eyes with it, and told me to go to Siloam and wash. I went and washed, and gained my sight.' 'Where is he?' they asked. He answered, 'I do not know.'

The man who had been blind was brought before the Pharisees. As it was a Sabbath day when Jesus made the paste and opened his eyes, the Pharisees now asked him by what means he had gained his sight. The man told them, 'He spread

七十八 瞽者復明

約翰福音

　　耶穌在傳道途中看到一個生來就瞎的人。門徒們問耶穌：
"先生，是這個人還是他的父母犯了罪？他爲什麼生來就是瞎
子？"耶穌答道："不是這個人，也不是他的父母犯了罪。他
生來就瞎，這樣上帝才能以治癒他而顯出神力。趁天還亮，我
們必須繼續做好上帝交給我的工作。黑夜一到，就沒有人能做
了。我在世上時，我就是世上的光明。"

　　說完這些耶穌便朝地上吐了口唾沫，並用唾沫和泥抹在那
瞎子的眼上，說："到西羅亞（這字意思是"奉差遣"）池子
裏去洗洗。"那人去洗了洗，回來時眼睛已能看見東西了。

　　他的鄰居和那些平常見他討飯的人說："這不是從前坐在
地上討飯的人嗎？"有人說："對，就是他。"又有人說："不，
很像他就是了。"那個人自己說："我就是那討飯的！"他們
便問他："你的眼睛是怎麼開了？"他答道："有一個叫耶穌
的人和泥抹在了我的眼上，叫我去西羅亞的池子裏洗一洗。我
去洗了，眼睛就復明了。"他們問道："他現在在哪兒？"他
回答說："我不知道。"

　　這原來眼瞎的人被帶到了法利賽人那裏。因爲耶穌和泥使
他眼開的那天是安息日，於是法利賽人便問他耶穌是用什麼辦

a paste on my eyes; then I washed, and now I can see.' Some of the Pharisees said, 'This fellow is no man of God: he does not keep the Sabbath.' Others said, 'How could such signs come from a sinful man?' So they took different sides. Then they continued to question him: 'What have you to say about him? It was your eyes he opened.' He answered, 'He is a prophet.'

The Jews would not believe that the man had been blind and had gained his sight, until they had summoned his parents and questioned them: 'Is this man your son? Do you say that he was born blind? How is it that he can see now?' The parents replied, 'We know that he is our son and that he was born blind. But how it is that he can now see, or who opened his eyes, we do not know. Ask him; he is of age; he will speak for himself.' His parents gave this answer because they were afraid of the Jews; for the Jewish authorities had already agreed that anyone who acknowledged Jesus as Messiah should be banned from the synagogue. That is why the parents said, 'He is of age; ask him.'

So for the second time they summoned the man who had been blind, and said, 'Speak the truth before God. We know that this fellow is a sinner.' 'Whether or not he is a sinner, I do not know', the man replied. 'All I know is this: once I was blind, now I can see.' 'What did he do to you?' they asked. 'How did he open your eyes?' 'I have told you already', he retorted, 'but you took no notice. Why do you want to hear it again? Do you also want to become his disciples?' Then they became abusive. 'You are that man's disciple,' they said, 'but we are disciples of Moses. We know that God spoke to Moses, but as for this fellow, we do not know where he comes from.'

The man replied, 'What an extraordinary thing! Here is a man who has opened my eyes, yet you do not know where he comes from! It is common knowledge that God does not listen to sinners; he listens to anyone who is devout and obeys his will. To open the eyes of a man born blind — it is unheard of

法使他重見光明的。那人告訴他們：“他和泥抹在我的眼上，我去池子裏一洗，現在就看得見了。”有些法利賽人說：“這個人不是上帝派來的，因爲他不守安息日。”另一些人說：“可一個罪人又怎能行這種神迹呢？”他們意見分歧，就又繼續盤問那人：“旣然他使你復明，你說他是個什麼人？”他答道：“他是個先知。”

那些猶太人還不相信他原先是個瞎子，後來才復明的。他們找來他的父母親問道：“這是你們的兒子嗎？他是不是生來就眼瞎？怎麼現在能看得見了？”他父母答道：“他是我們的兒子，而且生來就是瞎子，至於他是怎麼復明的，或者是誰開了他的眼，我們不知道。他已成人，你們問他吧。他自己會講的。”他父母這樣回答是因爲他們害怕猶太人；因爲猶太人中的掌權的人已經說過，凡是承認耶穌是救世主的，都要被逐出猶太教會堂。因此，他父母才說“他已成人，你們問他吧。”

法利賽人再把那個原先眼瞎的人叫了來，對他說：“你在上帝面前要講眞話。我們知道，那傢伙是個罪人。”那人說道：“他是否罪人，我不知道。我只知道，我過去眼瞎，而如今能看見東西了。”他們問他“他給你做了什麼了？他怎樣使你復明的？”那人負氣答道：“我已經告訴你們了，可你們不聽。爲什麼又要叫我講呢？難道你們也想做他的門徒？”他們就罵道：“你才是那人的門徒呢。我們是摩西的門徒。我們只知上帝對摩西講話。至於這個傢伙，我們却不知他來自何處。”

那人答道：“他能使我復明，你們還不知他來自何處？這眞是個怪事！誰都知道，上帝是不聽罪人的話的，只聽那些虔誠而又遵他旨意的人的話。從創世以來，還從未聽說過生來就

since time began. If that man had not come from God he could have done nothing.' 'Who are you to give us lessons', they retorted, 'born and bred in sin as you are?' Then they expelled him from the synagogue.

Jesus heard that they had expelled him. When he found him he asked, 'Have you faith in the Son of Man?' The man answered, 'Tell me who he is, sir, that I should put my faith in him.' 'You have seen him,' said Jesus; 'indeed, it is he who is speaking to you.' 'Lord, I believe', he said, and bowed before him.

Jesus said, 'It is for judgement that I have come into this world — to give sight to the sightless and to make blind those who see.' Some Pharisees in his company asked, 'Do you mean that we are blind?' 'If you were blind,' said Jesus, 'you would not be guilty, but because you say "We see", your guilt remains.

瞎的人眼睛會復明的。那人若非上帝所遣就決不能行此神迹。"那些人申斥他道："像你這樣一個在罪孽中生養的人，還有資格教訓我們？"於是便把他趕出了猶太教會堂。

耶穌聽到了他們把那復明的人趕出會堂的消息。所以見到他時便問他："你堅信上帝的兒子嗎？"那人答道："先生，誰是上帝的兒子，好讓我信奉他呢？"耶穌說："你已經看到了他，現在和你講話的就是他。"那人說："主啊，我信了。"他就向耶穌叩拜。

耶穌說："我是為了公正才到這世上來的——叫瞎子復明，使看得見的人視而不見。"在他近旁的一些法利賽人問道："你是說我們也是瞎的嗎？"耶穌說："你們若是瞎的，也就沒罪了。但因為你們說'我們能看見'，所以你們的罪還在。"

Matthew

Six days later Jesus took Peter, James, and John the brother of James, and led them up a high mountain where they were alone; and in their presence he was transfigured; his face shone like the sun, and his clothes became white as the light. And they saw Moses and Elijah appear, conversing with him. Then Peter spoke: 'Lord,' he said, 'how good it is that we are here! If you wish it, I will make three shelters here, one for you, one for Moses, and one for Elijah.' While he was still speaking, a bright cloud suddenly overshadowed them, and a voice called from the cloud: 'This is my Son, my Beloved, on whom my favour rests; listen to him.' At the sound of the voice the disciples fell on their faces in terror. Jesus then came up to them, touched them, and said, 'Stand up; do not be afraid.' And when they raised their eyes they saw no one, but only Jesus.

On their way down the mountain, Jesus enjoined them not to tell anyone of the vision until the Son of Man had been raised from the dead. The disciples put a question to him: 'Why then do our teachers say that Elijah must come first?' He replied, 'Yes, Elijah will come and set everything right. But I tell you that Elijah has already come, and they failed to recognize him, and worked their will upon him; and in the same way the Son of Man is to suffer at their hands.' Then the disciples understood that he meant John the Baptist.

When they returned to the crowd, a man came up to Jesus, fell on his knees before him, and said, 'Have pity, sir, on my

七十九　高山顯聖

馬太福音

　　六天之後，耶穌帶着彼得、雅各和雅各的弟弟約翰上一座無人的高山去。耶穌當着他們的面改變了形象。他的面龐亮如旭日，衣服潔白如光。他們又看到摩西和以利亞出現，同耶穌講話。彼得對耶穌說："主啊，我們在此多好。你若願意，我就在此搭三座棚，一座與你，一座與摩西，一座與以利亞。"正講着，突然有一朵明亮雲彩遮住他們，有個聲音從雲中傳下："這是我愛子，我喜歡他。你們要聽從他。"各門徒聽見都驚恐地俯伏地上。耶穌走近他們拍拍他們說："起來吧，不要怕。"他們抬頭一看，已沒有其他人，只見耶穌一人了。

　　下山途中，耶穌吩咐他們，在人子還未復活前，不要把看到的告訴別人。門徒們問他："爲何我們的先生說以利亞必須先來？"耶穌答道："以利亞要來並匡正萬事，但我告訴你們，以利亞已來了，只是人們沒有認出他，並隨意強加於他。人子也要像他那樣受他們的迫害。"門徒們這才明白他指的是聖徒約翰。

　　他們回到衆人那裏時，有個人走到耶穌近前，跪下說：

son: he is an epileptic and has bad fits, and he keeps falling about, often into the fire, often into water. I brought him to your disciples, but they could not cure him.' Jesus answered, 'What an unbelieving and perverse generation! How long shall I be with you? How long must I endure you? Bring him here to me.' Jesus then spoke sternly to the boy; the devil left him, and from that moment he was cured.

Afterwards the disciples came to Jesus and asked him privately, 'Why could not we cast it out?' He answered, 'Your faith is too small. I tell you this: if you have faith no bigger even than a mustard-seed, you will say to this mountain, "Move from here to there!", and it will move; nothing will prove impossible for you.'

They were going about together in Galilee when Jesus said to them, 'The Son of Man is to be given up into the power of men, and they will kill him; then on the third day he will be raised again.' And they were filled with grief.

On their arrival at Capernaum the collectors of the temple-tax came up to Peter and asked, 'Does your master not pay temple-tax?' 'He does', said Peter. When he went indoors Jesus forestalled him by asking, 'What do you think about this, Simon? From whom do earthly monarchs collect tax or toll? From their own people, or from aliens?' 'From aliens', said Peter. 'Why then,' said Jesus, 'their own people are exempt! But as we do not want to cause offence, go and cast a line in the lake; take the first fish that comes to the hook, open its mouth, and you will find a silver coin; take that and pay it in; it will meet the tax for us both.'

"先生，可憐可憐我兒子吧。他的癲癇病發得很厲害，經常跌倒，有時跌進火裏，有時掉入水中。我帶他到了你的門徒那兒，但他們治不好他。"耶穌說道："你們這些不信仰又墮落的一代！我要在這兒呆到幾時呢？我還要容忍你們到幾時呢？把他帶到我這兒來。"然後，耶穌對孩子嚴厲地講了些話，鬼就離開了他身體，從此也就痊癒了。

那些門徒走近耶穌細聲問道："為什麼我們趕不走那鬼呢？"耶穌答道："你們的虔誠信仰太小。我告訴你們，你們的信仰只要有芥菜籽那麼大。那你們對這座山說：'從這移到那！'山也就會移去的。世上也沒有你們做不到的事了。"

他們在加利利傳道時，耶穌對門徒們說："人子就要被送交到眾人手裏，他們將殺害他。而到第三天，他却得復活。"門徒們聽了感到十分傷心。

他們到了迦百農，稅吏來見彼得說："你們的主不納稅嗎？"彼得答道："納的。"進屋後，耶穌就問："西門(1)，你認為怎樣？世上的君王向誰徵收關卡稅？向他自己的百姓呢，還是向外人？"彼得答道："向外人。"耶穌說："既然如此，那他們的百姓就可豁免了。但我們不想觸犯他們，那就去湖邊垂釣吧。把最先釣到的魚拿來，打開牠的嘴，你就會看到有一個銀幣。你把它交給他們，就夠付我們倆人的稅金了。"

---

(1) "西門"是彼得的原名。

Matthew

(1)

And now a man came up and asked Jesus, 'Master, what good must I do to gain eternal life?'... Jesus said: 'One alone is good. But if you wish to enter into life, keep the commandments.' 'Which commandments?' he asked. Jesus answered, 'Do not murder; do not commit adultery; do not steal; do not give false evidence; honour your father and mother; and love your neighbour as yourself.' The young man answered, 'I have kept all these. Where do I still fall short?' Jesus said to him, 'If you wish to go the whole way, go, sell your possessions, and give to the poor, and then you will have riches in heaven; and come, follow me.' When the young man heard this, he went away with a heavy heart; for he was a man of great wealth.

Jesus said to his disciples, 'I tell you this: a rich man will find it hard to enter the kingdom of Heaven. I repeat, it is easier for a camel to pass through the eye of a needle than for a rich man to enter the kingdom of God.' The disciples were amazed to hear this. 'Then who can be saved?' they asked. Jesus looked at them, and said, 'For men this is impossible; but everything is possible for God.'

(2)

Jesus said, 'Listen to another parable. There was a land-owner who planted a vineyard: he put a wall round it, hewed out a winepress, and built a watch-tower; then he let it out to vine-growers and went abroad. When the vintage season

八十 寓言闡理

馬太福音

（一）

一個人來見耶穌，問他：“主啊，我該做什麼善事才得永生？”耶穌說：“你若想獲得永生，那就遵守誡命。”那人問道：“什麼誡命？”耶穌答道：“不可殺人、奸淫、偷盜和做僞證。應該孝敬父母，愛人如己。”那個年輕人答道：“這一切我都遵守了，還欠缺什麼呢？”耶穌對他說：“如果想做個完人，那就去變賣你的財產，把錢都分給窮人。這樣，在天國你就會有很多財富。而且還須追隨我。”那年輕人聽後，垂頭喪氣地走了，因爲他有很多財產。

耶穌對門徒說：“我告訴你們，富人進天國是很難的。我再說一遍，富人進天國，比駱駝鑽針眼還難！”門徒聽後，都感驚奇，便問道：“那麼誰能得救呢？”耶穌看看他們說：“人是不能，但上帝萬事皆能。”

（二）

耶穌說：“你們再聽一個比喩。有個葡萄園主，種了一片葡萄園。他在園四周圍上圍牆，在裏面挖了個榨酒池，蓋了一座瞭望樓，然後把它租給了佃戶，自己就到國外去了。收穫季

approached, he sent his servants to the tenants to collect the produce due to him. But they took his servants and thrashed one, killed another, and stoned a third. Again, he sent other servants, this time a larger number; and they did the same to them. At last he sent to them his son. "They will respect my son", he said. But when they saw the son the tenants said to one another, "This is the heir; come on, let us kill him, and get his inheritance." And they took him, flung him out of the vineyard, and killed him. When the owner of the vineyard comes, how do you think he will deal with those tenants?' 'He will bring those bad men to a bad end', they answered, 'and hand the vineyard over to other tenants, who will let him have his share of the crop when the season comes.' Then Jesus said to them, 'Have you never read in the scriptures: "The stone which the builders rejected has become the main corner-stone. This is the Lord's doing, and it is wonderful in our eyes"? Therefore, I tell you, the kingdom of God will be taken away from you, and given to a nation that yields the proper fruit.'

節臨近時，他派了幾個僕人到佃戶那兒去收他該收的一份葡萄。佃戶抓住了他們，痛打了一個，殺了一個，又用石頭砸死了一個。後來那園主又派了些僕人去，人數比先前還多。佃戶還是照樣對付他們。最後，那園主把他的兒子派了去。他說：'他們會尊敬我的兒子的。'但佃戶一看到他的兒子，便商議道：'這是他的嗣子，來，我們殺了他，奪了他的產業。'他們抓住他的兒子，把他扔出葡萄園殺死了。園主回來了，你們認為他會怎樣處置這些佃戶呢？"門徒們答道："他會剪除那些壞人，把園子另租給那些會按時交葡萄的佃戶。"耶穌對他們說："經上寫着，'匠人所棄的石頭已成了主要的基石，這是上帝所做的，這是使人感到驚奇的，這些話難道你們沒有讀過嗎？所以，我告訴你們，上帝之國必從你們手中拿去，賜給那些能生產好果實的民族。"

Luke

Another time, the tax-gatherers and other bad characters were all crowding in to listen to him; and the Pharisees and the doctors of the law began grumbling among themselves: 'This fellow', they said, 'welcomes sinners and eats with them.' He answered them with this parable: 'If one of you has a hundred sheep and loses one of them, does he not leave the ninety-nine in the open pasture and go after the missing one until he has found it? How delighted he is then! He lifts it on to his shoulders, and home he goes to call his friends and neighbours together. "Rejoice with me!" he cries. "I have found my lost sheep." In the same way, I tell you, there will be greater joy in heaven over one sinner who repents than over ninety-nine righteous people who do not need to repent.

Again he said: 'There was once a man who had two sons: and the younger said to his father, "Father, give me my share of the property." So he divided his estate between them. A few days later the younger son turned the whole of his share into cash and left home for a distant country, where he squandered it in reckless living. He had spent it all. So he went and attached himself to one of the local landowners, who sent him on to his farm to mind the pigs. He would have been glad to fill his belly with the pods that the pigs were eating: and no one gave him anything. Then he came to his senses and said, "I will set off and go to my father."

'While he was still a long way off his father saw him, and his heart went out to him. He ran to meet him, flung his arms

八十一　浪子回頭

路加福音

又有一次，一些稅吏和罪人擠近耶穌在聽他講道。那些法利賽人和律法師在下面嘟囔說："這個人款待罪人，又和他們一起吃飯。"耶穌便講了一則寓言回答他們的責難："假如你們誰有一百隻羊，丟了一隻，難道他不先讓那九十九隻羊呆在牧場，自己去尋找那隻迷途的羊嗎？找到後，他會多麼高興！他把牠背着回家，然後把朋友和鄰居都請來。喊道：'你們替我高興吧！我找到了那隻丟失的羊了。'同樣，我告訴你們：在天上，一個悔改了的罪人帶來的喜悅比九十九個無須悔改的正人君子使人感到的喜悅還要大呢！

耶穌又說道："從前，有一個人有兩個兒子。小兒子對他說：'父親，把我應得的那份產業交給我吧。'那人就把產業分給了自己的兩個兒子。幾天以後，小兒子把他分得的產業賣了錢，到遠方去了。在那兒他揮霍無度，縱情享受，把錢全都花光了。於是，他去投靠當地的一個地主，地主就讓他放豬。因為沒有人給他東西吃，他恨不得拿豬吃的豆莢充飢。這樣他終於醒悟了，說：'我要回家找我父親去。'離家還很遠，他的父親就看見了他，心情十分激動。他跑向兒子，伸出雙臂擁抱他，

round him, and kissed him. The son said, "Father, I have sinned, against God and against you; I am no longer fit to be called your son." But the father said to his servants, "Quick! fetch a robe, my best one, and put it on him; put a ring on his finger and shoes on his feet. Bring the fatted calf and kill it, and let us have a feast to celebrate the day. For this son of mine was dead and has come back to life; he was lost and is found."

'Now the elder son was out on the farm; and on his way back, as he approached the house, he heard music and dancing. He called one of the servants and asked what it meant. The servant told him, "Your brother has come home, and your father has killed the fatted calf because he has him back safe and sound." But he was angry and refused to go in. His father came out and pleaded with him; but he retorted. "You know how I have slaved for you all these years; I never once disobeyed your orders; and you never gave me so much as a kid, for a feast with my friends. But now that this son of yours turns up, after running through your money with his women, you kill the fatted calf for him." "My boy," said the father, "you are always with me, and everything I have is yours. How could we help celebrating this happy day? Your brother here was dead and has come back to life, was lost and is found."'

親吻他。兒子說：'父親，我得罪了上帝，也得罪了你，不配做你的兒子。'但他父親却對僕人說：'快去把我那件最好的袍子拿來給他穿上。給他戴上戒指，穿上鞋。把那隻肥牛犢牽來宰了，設宴慶賀。因爲我這個兒子就像死而復生，失而復得！'

　　"這時，大兒子在田裏幹活。幹完回家。快到家時，便聽到一片鼓樂聲。他問一個僕人那是怎麼回事。僕人告訴他：'你弟弟回來了。他平安歸來，你父親宰了頭肥牛犢爲他慶賀。'大兒子很生氣，拒不進屋。他父親出來勸他。大兒子說：'我盡心服侍你這麼多年，從未違背過你的意願，可你連隻羊羔都沒有給過我，好叫我和朋友們吃一頓。而這個拿你的錢在外面和女人胡混的兒子一回來，你就爲他宰肥牛犢慶賀。'他父親說：'孩子，你是一直和我在一起，我所有的一切都是你的。你這個弟弟死而復生，失而復得，我們能不慶賀一下這個好日子嗎？'"

Luke

Jesus said, 'There was once a rich man, who dressed in purple and the finest linen, and feasted in great magnificence every day. At his gate, covered with sores, lay a poor man named Lazarus, who would have been glad to satisfy his hunger with the scraps from the rich man's table. Even the dogs used to come and lick his sores. One day the poor man died and was carried away by the angels to be with Abraham. The rich man also died and was buried, and in Hades, where he was in torment, he looked up; and there, far away, was Abraham with Lazarus close beside him. "Abraham, my father," he called out, "take pity on me! Send Lazarus to dip the tip of his finger in water, to cool my tongue, for I am in agony in this fire." But Abraham said, "Remember, my child, that all the good things fell to you while you were alive, and all the bad to Lazarus; now he has his consolation here and it is you who are in agony. But that is not all: there is a great chasm fixed between us; no one from our side who wants to reach you can cross it, and none may pass from your side to us." "Then, father," he replied, "will you send him to my father's house, where I have five brothers, to warn them, so that they too may not come to this place of torment?" But Abraham said, "They have Moses and the prophets; let them listen to them." "No, father Abraham," he replied, "but if someone from the dead visits them, they will repent." Abraham answered, "If they do not listen to Moses and the prophets they will pay no heed even if someone should rise from the dead."'

八十二　寓言再囑

路加福音

　　耶穌說：“從前有個財主，身穿紫色細蔴布衣袍，每日花天酒地。他的大門口躺着一個叫拉撒路的窮人，靠財主宴席的殘羹剩飯充飢。他渾身瘡疥，有時狗也來舔他的瘡。一天，這個窮人死了，他被天使帶到亞伯拉罕那裏。後來，那個財主也死了葬掉。他在陰間受苦，當他舉頭遠遠看見亞伯拉罕和緊靠着他身邊的拉撒路。他喊道：‘我祖亞伯拉罕，可憐可憐我吧。請打發拉撒路來，用手指蘸點兒水，凉凉我的舌頭，因爲我在這地獄火中受罪極了。’但亞伯拉罕說道：‘我的孩子，想想你生前享過的福、拉撒路受的罪吧。如今他在這裏得到安慰，而你則要受痛苦。不僅如此，我們之間隔有一道深淵，我們這邊的人要越過它到你們那兒是去不了的，你們那邊的人要過來也不可能。’財主說：‘我祖，旣然如此，那就請你打發拉撒路到我父親家去，告訴我的五個兄弟，免得他們以後也來這兒受罪。’亞伯拉罕說：‘讓他們聽摩西和先知的話吧。’財主說：‘不，我祖，要有一個死而復生的人去見他們，他們才會悔改的。’ 亞伯拉罕說：‘如果他們不聽摩西和先知的話，即使有個死而復生的人也不管用，因爲他們不會聽勸告的。’”

Matthew

That same day Jesus went out and sat by the lake-side, where so many people gathered round him that he had to get into a boat. He sat there, and all the people stood on the shore. He spoke to them in parables, at some length.

(1)

He said, 'The kingdom of Heaven is like this. There was once a landowner who went out early one morning to hire labourers for his vineyard; and after agreeing to pay them the usual day's wage he sent them off to work. Going out three hours later he saw some more men standing idle in the market-place. "Go and join the others in the vineyard," he said, "and I will pay you a fair wage"; so off they went. At midday he went out again, and at three in the afternoon, and made the same arrangement as before. An hour before sunset he went out and found another group standing there; so he said to them, "Why are you standing about like this all day with nothing to do?" "Because no one has hired us", they replied; so he told them, "Go and join the others in the vineyard." When evening fell, the owner of the vineyard said to his steward, "Call the labourers and give them their pay, beginning with those who came last and ending with the first." Those who had started work an hour before sunset came forward, and were paid the full day's wage. When it was the turn of the men who had come first, they expected something extra, but were paid the same amount as the others. As they took it, they grumbled at their employer: "These late-comers have

八十三　天國奧秘

馬太福音

那一天，耶穌走出門去坐在湖邊。許多人圍着他，他只好坐到船上，衆人則站在岸上。他用比喻向他們講了許多道理：

（一）

他說：“天國就像這樣：有個莊園主一大早出去僱人到他的葡萄園做工。他和僱工講好通常的工價後，便讓他們去幹活。三個小時後，他看見市場上還有很多人站着沒事幹，便對他們說：‘到葡萄園和那些人一起幹吧，我會給你們公道的工錢。’他們便進園去了。他在正午和下午三點時又出去兩趟，又像先前那樣僱了一些人進園去。天黑前一小時，他出去還看見有人站在那兒，便對他們說：‘你們幹嗎整天站在這兒不幹活兒呢？’他們答道：‘因爲沒有人請我們。’他對他們說：‘你們也進葡萄園一起幹活吧。’到了晚上，園主對管事的說：‘把工人都叫來，發他們工錢，後來的先發，先來的後發。’天黑前一小時進園的工人上前來，領到一整天的工錢。輪到那些先進園幹活的人了，他們以爲工錢要比晚來的多一點，誰知發的工錢竟是一樣的。他們拿到工錢後，就對僱主不滿：‘我們頭頂

done only one hour's work, yet you have put them on a level with us, who have sweated the whole day long in the blazing sun!" The owner turned to one of them and said, "My friend, I am not being unfair to you. You agreed on the usual wage for the day, did you not? Take your pay and go home. I choose to pay the last man the same as you. Surely I am free to do what I like with my own money. Why be jealous because I am kind?" Thus will the last be first, and the first last.'

(2)

Jesus said, 'When that day comes, the kingdom of Heaven will be like this. There were ten girls, who took their lamps and went out to meet the bridegroom. Five of them were foolish, and five prudent; when the foolish ones took their lamps, they took no oil with them, but the others took flasks of oil with their lamps. As the bridegroom was late in coming they all dozed off to sleep. But a midnight a cry was heard: "Here is the bridegroom! Come out to meet him." With that the girls all got up and trimmed their lamps. The foolish said to the prudent, "Our lamps are going out; give us some of your oil." "No," they said; "there will never be enough for all of us. You had better go to the shop and buy some for yourselves." While they were away the bridegroom arrived; those who were ready went in with him to the wedding; and the door was shut. And then the other five came back. "Sir, sir," they cried, "open the door for us." But he answered, "I declare, I do not know you." Keep awake then; for you never know the day or the hour.'

(3)

Jesus said, 'It is like a man going abroad, who called his servants and put his capital in their hands; to one he gave five bags of gold, to another two, to another one, each according to his capacity. Then he left the country. The man who had the five bags went at once and employed them in business, and made a profit of five bags, and the man who had the two bags made two. But the man who had been given one bag of gold went off and dug a hole in the ground, and hid his mas-

烈日、汗流浹背地幹了一整天，而那些最後來的只幹了一小時，可工錢却和我們一樣多！'僱主對他們的一個人說：'朋友，我並沒有虧待你。你當初不是同意拿通常一日的工錢嗎？拿工錢回家吧。至於我給後來的人一樣多的工錢，是因爲這是我自己的錢，我愛怎麼用，就怎麼用。我做好人，你爲什麼要妒忌呢？'因而，在後的將要在前，在前的則要在後了。"

（二）

耶穌說："當那天來臨時，天國就像這樣：十個童女拿着燈去迎接新郎。其中五個愚蠢，五個精明。愚蠢的拿着燈，却未備油；聰明的拿着燈，在盞上備了油。由於新郎來晚了，童女都打盹睡着了。半夜時，有人喊道：'新郎來了，快出去迎接。'童女聽到後便起來收拾燈。愚蠢的對聰明的說：'我們的燈沒油了，把你們的油給我們點兒吧。'聰明的答道，'不行，這點油不夠我們大伙兒用的。你們最好自己去舖子裏買些吧。'她們出去買油時，新郎到了。做好了準備的那五個童女便和新郎一起進去赴喜宴，同時關上了門。一會兒，那五個愚蠢的童女回來了，她們叫道：'先生，先生，給我們開門。'但新郎却說：'我說，我不認識你們。'所以，你們一定要警醒，因爲你們不知道究竟何時何日會有甚麼事發生。"

（三）

耶穌說："天國就像這樣：一個人到外國去。他把幾個僕人叫來，把產業交給他們。他按照各人的才幹，給他們金子。這個人五袋，那個人兩袋，第三個人一袋。然後，他就離開了家鄉。那得了五袋金子的人馬上用這筆錢去做買賣，淨賺了五袋金子。那得兩袋金子的也淨賺了兩袋。而那得一袋金子的人

ter's money. A long time afterwards their master returned, and proceeded to settle accounts with them. The man who had been given the five bags of gold came and produced the five he had made: "Master," he said, "you left five bags with me; look, I have made five more." "Well done, my good and trusty servant!" said the master. "You have proved trustworthy in a small way; I will now put you in charge of something big. Come and share your master's delight." The man with the two bags then came and said, "Master, you left two bags with me; look, I have made two more." "Well done, my good and trusty servant!" said the master. "You have proved trustworthy in a small way; I will now put you in charge of something big. Come and share your master's delight." Then the man who had been given one bag came and said, "Master, I knew you to be a hard man: you reap where you have not sown, you gather where you have not scattered; so I was afraid, and I went and hid your gold in the ground. Here it is — you have what belongs to you." "You lazy rascal!" said the master. "You knew that I reap where I have not sown, and gather where I have not scattered? Then you ought to have put my money on deposit, and on my return I should have got it back with interest. Take the bag of gold from him, and give it to the one with the ten bags. For the man who has will always be given more, till he has enough and to spare; and the man who has not will forfeit even what he has. Fling the useless servant out into the dark, the place of wailing and grinding of teeth!'"

却挖了個坑，把錢埋了起來。過了很久，主人回來了，便和他們結算賬目。那領了五袋金子的人連本帶利帶了來，說：'主人，你給了我五袋金子，你看，我又賺了五袋。'主人說：'好，你真是個善良可靠的僕人！你既在小事上靠得住，我現在叫你管些大事。你可以和主人一起分享快樂了。'然後，那領了兩袋金子的人上前說道：'主人，你給了我兩袋金子，看，我又賺了兩袋。'主人說：'好，你真是個善良可靠的僕人！你既在小事上靠得住，我現在叫你管些大事。你可以和主人一起分享快樂了。'最後，那個領了一袋金子的人對主人說：'主人，我知道你是個狠心的人，你不播種要收割，不撒種要收穫。我害怕了，便去把你的金子埋在地裏。你看，你給我的金子在這兒。'主人說：'你這個懶傢伙！你既知道我不播種就收割，不撒種要收穫，那你就該拿我的錢去放債，等我回來時，連本帶利還給我。把那一袋金子拿回來，給那個有十袋金子的人。凡有的，還要多給他，使他有餘；凡沒有的，連他原有的，也要失去。把這個無用的僕人丟在外邊的黑暗處，叫他切齒哀號去吧！'

There was a man named Lazarus who had fallen ill. His home was at Bethany, the village of Mary and her sister Martha. (This Mary, whose brother Lazarus had fallen ill, was the woman who anointed the Lord with ointment and wiped his feet with her hair.) The sisters sent a message to him: 'Sir, you should know that your friend lies ill.' When Jesus heard this he said, 'This illness will not end in death; it has come for the glory of God, to bring glory to the Son of God.'

After this, he said to his disciples, 'Let us go back to Judaea.' 'Rabbi,' his disciples said, 'it is not long since the Jews there were wanting to stone you. Are you going there again?'

Jesus said, 'Our friend Lazarus has fallen asleep, but I shall go and wake him.' The disciples said, 'Master, if he has fallen asleep he will recover.' Then Jesus spoke out plainly: 'Lazarus is dead. I am glad not to have been there; it will be for your good and for the good of your faith. But let us go to him.'

On his arrival Jesus found that Lazarus had already been four days in the tomb. Bethany was just under two miles from Jerusalem, and many of the people had come from the city to Martha and Mary to condole with them on their brother's death. As soon as she heard that Jesus was on his way, Martha went to meet him, while Mary stayed at home.

Martha said to Jesus, 'If you had been here, sir, my brother

八十四 伯大尼村

約翰福音

　　有個叫拉撒路的人生了病。他住在伯大尼，就是馬利亞和她姐姐馬大的村莊（馬利亞就是那個用香膏抹主，用頭髮擦他腳的馬利亞，患病的拉撒路就是她弟弟）。她姊妹倆派人來告訴耶穌："主啊，你知道你的朋友病了吧。"耶穌聽後說道："這病不至於死的，它因上帝的榮耀而起，也會給聖子帶來榮耀的。"……

　　這事之後，他對門徒們說："我們回猶大去吧。"門徒說："拉比，那兒的猶太人不久前還要拿石頭打你呢，你還要到那兒去？"耶穌說："我們的朋友拉撒路睡着了，我要去叫醒他。"門徒們說："主啊，如果他睡着了，他就會痊癒的。"耶穌就逕直告訴他們："拉撒路是死了。當時我不在那兒倒合適。因爲這對你們有好處，這事會使你們信服。我們先到他那兒去吧。"

　　耶穌到伯大尼時，拉撒路已埋葬了四天。伯大尼離耶路撒冷只有兩英里地，所以有許多猶太人從耶路撒冷來看馬大和馬利亞，就拉撒路的死向她們表示慰問。馬大一聽說耶穌來了，馬上就去迎接他，而馬利亞則留在家裏。

　　馬大對耶穌說："主啊，如果你當時在這兒，我的弟弟肯

would not have died. Even now I know that whatever you ask of God, God will grant you.' Jesus said, 'Your brother will rise again.' 'I know that he will rise again', said Martha, 'at the resurrection on the last day.' Jesus said, 'I am the resurrection and I am life. If a man has faith in me, even though he die, he shall come to life; and no one who is alive and has faith shall ever die. Do you believe this?' 'Lord, I do,' she answered; 'I now believe that you are the Messiah, the Son of God who was to come into the world.'

With these words she went to call her sister Mary, and taking her aside, she said, 'The Master is here; he is asking for you.' When Mary heard this she rose up quickly and went to him.

So Mary came to the place where Jesus was. As soon as she caught sight of him she fell at his feet and said, 'O sir, if you had only been here my brother would not have died.' When Jesus saw her weeping and the Jews her companions weeping, he sighed heavily and was deeply moved. 'Where have you laid him?' he asked. They replied, 'Come and see, sir.' Jesus wept. The Jews said, 'How dearly he must have loved him!' But some of them said, 'Could not this man, who opened the blind man's eyes, have done something to keep Lazarus from dying?'

Jesus again sighed deeply; then he went over to the tomb. It was a cave, with a stone placed against it. Jesus said, 'Take away the stone.' Martha, the dead man's sister, said to him, 'Sir, by now there will be a stench; he has been there four days.' Jesus said, 'Did I not tell you that if you have faith you will see the glory of God?' So they removed the stone.

Then Jesus looked upwards and said, 'Father, I thank thee; thou hast heard me. I knew already that thou always hearest me, but I spoke for the sake of the people standing round, that they might believe that thou didst send me.'

Then he raised his voice in a great cry: 'Lazarus, come forth.' The dead man came out, his hands and feet swathed in linen bands, his face wrapped in a cloth. Jesus said, 'Loose

定死不了。即使現在，我也知道，無論你向上帝求什麼，上帝也會賜給你的。"耶穌說："你弟弟會復活的。"馬大說："我知道在最後審判日人類復活時，他會復活。"耶穌說："復活在我，生命也在我。信我的人，即使死了，也會復活。而信我的活人，必定永遠不死。你信我的話嗎？"馬大答道："主啊，我信。我現在相信你是基督，是要降臨塵世的上帝之子。"

馬大說完便回去找她妹妹說："主來啦，他找你呢。"馬利亞聽了就趕快起來到耶穌那裏去。

馬利亞來到耶穌那裏。她一看見他，便俯伏在他的脚前，說："主啊，你若早在這兒，我弟弟就不會死了。"耶穌看到她和同來的猶太人都哭泣，也感到很悲痛，深深嘆了口氣說："你們把他葬於何處？"他們答道："請主來看吧。"耶穌也流了淚。那些猶太人說："他多麼愛這個拉撒路啊！"有個人說："他既能使盲人重見光明，難道就不能使拉撒路不死嗎？"

耶穌又深深嘆了口氣，然後向那墓走去。這墓穴前放着一塊石頭。耶穌說："把石頭挪開。"死者的姐姐馬大對他說："主啊，他現在已經腐臭了，他已經死了四天了。"耶穌說："我不是對你說過嗎？只要心誠，你就會看到上帝的榮耀的事。"衆人就把石頭移開了。

耶穌舉目朝天說："聖父啊，我感謝你，你已聽到我的聲音。我知道你總會傾聽我。但我說這話，是爲了使這裏周圍的人，相信我是你差遣來的。"

接着耶穌高聲叫喚："拉撒路，出來吧。"那死人便從墳墓出來，手脚裹着蔴布，臉上也包着布。耶穌說："解開它，

him; let him go.'

Now many of the Jews who had come to visit Mary and had seen what Jesus did, put their faith in him. But some of them went off to the Pharisees and reported what he had done.

Thereupon the chief priests and the Pharisees convened a meeting of the Council. 'What action are we taking?' they said. 'This man is performing many signs. If we leave him alone like this the whole populace will believe in him. Then the Romans will come and sweep away our temple and our nation.' But one of them, Caiaphas, who was High Priest that year, said, 'You know nothing whatever; you do not use your judement; it is more to your interest that one man should die for the people, than that the whole nation should be destroyed.' He did not say this of his own accord, but as the High Priest in office that year, he was prophesying that Jesus would die for the nation — would die not for the nation alone but to gather together the scattered children of God. So from that day on they plotted his death.

叫他走吧。"

不少來看望馬利亞的猶太人見到耶穌所行的奇事，便都信了他。其中也有人去見法利賽人，把耶穌行的神迹告訴他們。

祭司長和法利賽人聚起來議論道："我們該怎麼辦呢？這個人行了許多神迹，若由他這樣下去，所有的人都會信他了。羅馬人也就會摧毀我們的廟宇，踐踏我們的百姓的。"其中有一個人叫該亞法，是那一年度的大祭司，他說："你們什麼也不懂，也不動動腦子。爲了人民寧可讓一個人死，也不可使全國遭殃。這樣才符合你們的利益。"他說這話不是出於本意，而是因爲他是本年度的大祭司，所以預言耶穌要替這一國人民死。不但要替這一國人民死，還要將上帝的四散的子民，聚集歸一。於是，從那一天起，他們便策劃謀害耶穌。

Matthew

They were now nearing Jerusalem; and when they reached Bethphage at the Mount of Olives, Jesus sent two disciples with these instructions: 'Go to the village opposite, where you will at once find a donkey tethered with her foal beside her; untie them, and bring them to me. If anyone speaks to you, say, "Our Master needs them"; and he will let you take them at once.' This was to fulfil the prophecy which says, 'Tell the daughter of Zion, "Here is your king, who comes to you in gentleness, riding on an ass, riding on the foal of a beast of burden."'

The disciples went and did as Jesus had directed, and brought the donkey and her foal; they laid their cloaks on them and Jesus mounted. Crowds of people carpeted the road with their cloaks, and some cut branches from the trees to spread in his path. Then the crowd that went ahead and the others that came behind raised the shout: 'Hosanna to the Son of David! Blessings on him who comes in the name of the Lord! Hosanna in the heavens!'

When he entered Jerusalem the whole city went wild with excitement. 'Who is this?' people asked, and the crowd replied, 'This is the prophet Jesus, from Nazareth in Galilee.'

八十五　騎驢進京

馬太福音

　　耶穌及其門徒們快到耶路撒冷了。他們到了橄欖山的伯法其，耶穌吩咐兩個門徒說：“你們到對面那村裏去，必定會看到一匹驢栓在那兒，旁邊還有一匹驢駒。解開韁繩，把牠們牽到我這兒來。如果有人問你們，就說：‘我主人要用’，他就會讓你們牽來的。”這是要應驗先知的話：“告訴錫安的居民(1)，‘這就是你們的王，騎着驢，騎着驢駒，親切地看你們來了。’”

　　門徒便照耶穌的吩咐，去把驢和驢駒牽了來。他們把自己的衣服鋪在驢背上，耶穌便騎了上去。人們爭相把衣服鋪在路上，還有些人把砍下的樹枝也鋪在路上。前呼後擁的人羣高喊：“和散拿(2)歸於大衞之子！奉主之名而來的人，願主賜福！讚美天國！”

　　耶穌進入耶路撒冷，全城居民為之哄動。有些人問道：“他是誰？”人們答：“他是由加利利的拿撒勒來的先知耶穌。”

----

(1) 原文為“daughter”，但這裏意思是“人們”。

(2) 和散那（Hosanna）這詞在“新約”裏只出現在耶穌進耶路撒冷這節裏。它是一個祈使詞語，意思是：O, Save!這字後來引入希臘語，已被人們接受為一種讚美的表示。

Jesus then went into the temple and drove out all who were buying and selling in the temple precincts; he upset the tables of the money-changers and the seats of the dealers in pigeons; and said to them, 'Scripture says, "My house shall be called a house of prayer"; but you are making it a robbers' cave.'

In the temple blind men and cripples came to him, and he healed them. The chief priests and doctors of the law saw the wonderful things he did, and heard the boys in the temple shouting, 'Hosanna to the Son of David!', and they asked him indignantly, 'Do you hear what they are saying?' Jesus answered, 'I do; have you never read that text, "Thou hast made children and babies at the breast sound aloud thy praise"?' Then he left them and went out of the city to Bethany, where he spent the night.

Next morning on his way to the city he felt hungry; and seeing a fig-tree at the roadside he went up to it, but found nothing on it but leaves. He said to the tree, 'You shall never bear fruit any more!'; and the tree withered away at once. The disciples were amazed at the sight. 'How is it', they asked, 'that the tree has withered so suddenly?' Jesus answered them, 'I tell you this: if only you have faith and have no doubts, you will do what had been done to the fig-tree; and more than that, you need only say to this mountain, "Be lifted from your place and hurled into the sea", and what you say will be done. And whatever you pray for in faith you will receive.'

He entered the temple, and the chief priests and elders of the nation came to him with the question: 'By what authority are you acting like this? Who gave you this authority?' Jesus replied, 'I have a question to ask you too; answer it, and I will tell you by what authority I act. The baptism of John: was it from God, or from men?' This set them arguing among themselves: 'If we say, "from God", he will say, "Then why did you not believe him?" But if we say, "from men", we are afraid of the people, for they all take John for a prophet.' So they answered, 'We do not know.' And Jesus said: 'Then neither will I tell you by what authority I act.'

耶穌進入神殿，把在殿裏做買賣的人都趕出去，並掀翻了兌換銀錢人的桌子和賣鴿子人的櫈子，對他們說，"經書上講，'我的殿是禱告之殿'，而你們却把它變成了藏污納垢的地方。"

殿裏的瞎子和瘸子來找耶穌，他治癒了他們。祭司長和律法師看到了他所行的奇蹟，又聽到孩子們在殿裏喊："和散拿歸於大衞之子！"便氣憤地問耶穌："你聽見這些人的話了嗎？"耶穌答道："聽見了。經書上講'你使幼童乳嬰對你衷心高唱贊歌'，你們沒有讀過麼？"於是，他離開他們出城前往伯大尼，並在那兒過夜。

第二天早晨回城時，耶穌感到有點餓。看到路旁有棵無花果樹，便走到樹跟前。但他發現樹上只有葉子，並無果實。就對樹說："你永遠不會再結果實了！"那樹馬上枯萎了。門徒們看到後很驚奇，便問："這樹爲何突然枯萎了？"耶穌答道："我告訴你們，你們若堅信不疑，就能做出我對無花果樹所做之事。即使你們對這座山說，'你從此處挪開，投入海中'，山也就會投入海中。只要有信念，無論你們祈求何物，都會得到的。"

耶穌進了聖殿，祭司長和那些長老便來問他："你靠誰的權能做到這些事？誰給了你這些權能？"耶穌答道："我也有個問題問你們。你們回答後，我再告訴你們我是靠何種權能做事的：約翰的施洗是來自上帝，還是人？"這使他們彼此爭議起來，衆說不一："我們若說'來自上帝'，他必會講，'那你們爲何不信上帝？'若說'來自人'，那我們就會害怕百姓，因爲他們奉約翰爲先知。"於是他們答道："不知道。"耶穌說："那我也不告訴你們我是靠何種權能做事的。"

As he was leaving the Temple, one of his disciples exclaimed, 'Look, Master, what huge stones! What fine buildings!' Jesus said to him, 'You see these great buildings? Not one stone will be left upon another; all will be thrown down.'

When he was sitting on the Mount of Olives facing the temple he was questioned privately by Peter, James, John, and Andrew. 'Tell us,' they said, 'when will this happen? What will be the sign when the fulfilment of all this is at hand?'

Jesus began: 'Take care that no one misleads you. Many will come claiming my name, and saying, "I am he"; and many will be misled by them.

'When you hear the noise of battle near at hand and the news of battles far away, do not be alarmed. Such things are bound to happen; but the end is still to come. For nation will make war upon nation, kingdom upon kingdom; there will be earthquakes in many places; there will be famines. With these things the birth-pangs of the new age begin.

'As for you, be on your guard. You will be handed over to the courts. You will be flogged in synagogues. You will be summoned to appear before governors and kings on my account to testify in their presence. But before the end the Gospel must be proclaimed to all nations. So when you are arrested and taken away, do not worry beforehand about what you will say, but when the time comes say whatever is given you to say; for it is not you who will be speaking, but the

八十六　人子再來

耶穌離開聖殿時，他的一個門徒喊道："看，我主！何等巨大的石塊！何等壯觀的廟宇！"耶穌對他說："你看到這宏大的廟宇了麼？將來不會再有這樣疊起的石頭建築了，所有的東西都會傾倒的。"

當耶穌坐在面對聖殿的橄欖山上時，彼得、雅各、約翰和安得烈暗地問道："請告訴我們，這事何時發生？到來之前又有何預兆？"

他答道："要當心有人迷惑你們，許多人會冒我之名，說：'我就是他'。許多人會被他們引入迷途。

"你們聽到附近的戰鬥廝殺聲和遠方的戰事消息時，不要驚慌。這些事總要發生，只是末日還未到。民族會與民族相爭，一國會向另一國開戰；很多地方要發生地震，要鬧飢荒。這些都顯示災難的開始。

"你們務必當心。你們將被交付審判，在會堂裏受到鞭笞。你們會因爲我而被召到官長和國王的面前作證。但在末日來臨之前，你們必須把福音書傳給萬國之民。因此，在人們抓你們入牢之前，不要預先考慮該講什麼，而一旦真的被抓了，賜給你們什麼話，你們就講什麼話，因爲說話的已不是你們自

Holy Spirit. Brother will betray brother to death, and the father his child; children will turn against their parents and send them to their death. All will hate you for your allegiance to me; but the man who holds out to the end will be saved.

'But when you see "the abomination of desolation" usurping a place which is not his (let the reader understand), then those who are in Judaea must take to the hills. If a man is on the roof, he must not come down into the house to fetch anything out; if in the field, he must not turn back for his coat. Alas for women with child in those days, and for those who have children at the breast! Pray that it may not come in winter. For those days will bring distress such as never has been until now since the beginning of the world which God created — and will never be again. If the Lord had not cut short that time of troubles, no living thing could survive. However, for the sake of his own, whom he has chosen, he has cut short the time.

'Then, if anyone says to you, "Look, here is the Messiah", or, "Look, there he is", do not believe it. Improstors will come claiming to be messiahs or prophets, and they will produce signs and wonders to mislead God's chosen, if such a thing were possible. But you be on your guard; I have forewarned you of it all.

'But in those days, after that distress, the sun will be darkened, the moon will not give her light; the stars will come falling from the sky, the celestial powers will be shaken. Then they will see the Son of Man coming in the clouds with great power and glory, and he will send out the angels and gather his chosen from the four winds, from the farthest bounds of earth to the farthest bounds of heaven.

'Learn a lesson from the fig-tree. When its tender shoots appear and are breaking into leaf, you know that summer is near. In the same way, when you see all this happening, you may know that the end is near, at the very door. I tell you this: the present generation will live to see it all. Heaven and earth will pass away; my words will never pass away.

己，而是聖靈。兄弟將互相殘殺，父要置子於死地，兒女會逆殺父母。眾人會因你們忠於我而憎恨你們，只有堅持到底之人才能得救。

"但當你們看到'可憎的破壞者'强佔不該佔的地方時（讓讀經的人明白），在猶大的人要逃到山上去，在房上的人不能下來入屋取物，在田裏的人也不要回家取衣。在此期間，懷孕和餵奶婦女都不好過。你們應該祈求不要讓這些事在冬天來臨。因在那時來臨，必成大災難。自上帝創造萬物至今，如此大災難也是空前絕後的。若非天主減少那些災難日子，任何生靈都不會得救。只是為他選的子民，上帝才把那些日子縮短。"

"那時如有人對你們說：'看，救世主在這兒'或'看，救世主在那兒'，你們不要相信。將有假救主、假先知製造一些神迹奇事去把上帝選擇的子民引入迷途。你們要當心，要發生的事我都已預先告訴你們。

"災難過後，太陽要變黑，月亮也無光，星辰要從天墜落，整個天宇也為它震動。那時，他們將會看到能力巨大、榮耀無比的人子駕着祥雲從天而降。他將派遣天使，把他選擇的子民從四面八方、天涯海角都召來。

"你們可從無花果樹得到教訓。樹枝發芽長葉時，你們就知夏天臨近。同樣，你們看到所有這一切發生時，也知道末日來臨，近在咫尺了。我告訴你們，這一代人會看到所有這些事發生。天和地都可逝去，而我的話却永不消逝。

'But about that day or that hour no one knows, not even the angels in heaven, not even the Son; only the Father.

'Be alert, be wakeful. You do not know when the moment comes.It is like a man away from home: he has left his house and put his servants in charge, each with his own work to do, and he has ordered the door-keeper to stay awake. Keep awake, then, for you do not know when the master of the house is coming. Evening or midnight, cock-crow or early dawn — if he comes suddenly, he must not find you asleep. And what I say to you, I say to everyone: Keep awake.'

"至於是何日何時，無人可知，連天使和人子亦不知，唯有聖父才知道。

"你們要警覺，要警醒，因爲你們不知那日何時來臨。猶如離家游子把家事交由僕人掌管，令各盡其責，又囑咐看門人警醒。所以，你們要經常要警醒，因爲你們不知家主人何時回來。假如他在晚上、半夜、鷄鳴時分，或淸晨突然回來，別讓他看到你們在睡覺。我對你們也就是對衆人要說：要經常警醒。"

Mark

Now the festival of Passover and Unleavened Bread was only two days off; and the chief priests and the doctors of the law were trying to devise some cunning plan to seize him and put him to death. 'It must not be during the festival,' they said, 'or we should have rioting among the people.'

Jesus was at Bethany, in the house of Simon the leper. As he sat at table, a woman came in carrying a small bottle of very costly perfume, pure oil of nard. She broke it open and poured the oil over his head. Some of those present said to one another angrily, 'Why this waste? The perfume might have been sold for thirty pounds and the money given to the poor'; and they turned upon her with fury. But Jesus said, 'Let her alone. Why must you make trouble for her? It is a fine thing she has done for me. You have the poor among you always, and you can help them whenever you like; but you will not always have me. She has done what lay in her power; she is beforehand with anointing my body for burial. I tell you this: wherever in all the world the Gospel is proclaimed, what she has done will be told as her memorial.'

Then Judas Iscariot, one of the Twelve, went to the chief priests to betray him to them. When they heard what he had come for, they were greatly pleased, and promised him money; and he began to look for a good opportunity to betray him.

Now on the first day of Unleavened Bread, when the Passover lambs were being slaughtered, his disciples said to him,

八十七　最後晚餐

馬可福音

　　過兩天就到逾越節和除酵節。祭司長和律法師策劃施詭計捉拿耶穌並殺害他。他們說：“這事不能在節日幹，否則，百姓會發生騷亂。”

　　耶穌在伯大尼的生大痲瘋的西門家裏吃飯時，有個婦人拿來一瓶很貴的眞哪噠香膏，打開它澆在了耶穌的頭上。席上有些人見了很生氣，說：“爲何要浪費呢？這香膏可賣三百第納里(1)來賙濟窮人的。”他們就怒氣冲冲地指責她。但耶穌却說：“由她吧，爲何要指責她呢？她對我做的是件好事。你們中總有不少窮人，你們隨時都可幫助他們。但我却不會常和你們在一起。她已盡她所能做了。她是爲我的安葬而預先塗膏於我。我告訴你們，無論在何地傳播福音，也要把她所行的這事講給人們聽來紀念她。”

　　十二門徒中有個叫猶大的加略人去見祭司長，說要出賣耶穌給他們。聽到他的來意後，他們非常高興，答應給他賞錢。於是，他開始尋找機會，出賣耶穌。

　　除酵節的第一天，也就是宰逾越節羊羔的那一天，門徒們

---

(1)　原文是古羅馬銀幣300 denarii 約等於30 pounds。

'Where would you like us to go and prepare for your Passover supper?' So he sent out two of his disciples with these instructions: 'Go into the city, and a man will meet you carrying a jar of water. Follow him, and when he enters a house give this message to the householder: "The Master says, 'Where is the room reserved for me to eat the Passover with my disciples?'" He will show you a large room upstairs, set out in readiness. Make the preparations for us there.' Then the disciples went off, and when they came into the city they found everything just as he had told them. So they prepared for Passover.

In the evening he came to the house with the Twelve. As they sat at supper Jesus said, 'I tell you this: one of you will betray me — one who is eating with me.' At this they were dismayed; and one by one they said to him, 'Not I, surely?' 'It is one of the Twelve', he said, 'who is dipping into the same bowl with me. The Son of Man is going the way appointed for him in the scriptures; but alas for that man by whom the Son of Man is betrayed! It would be better for that man if he had never been born.'

During supper he took bread, and having said the blessing he broke it and gave it to them, with the words: 'Take this; this is my body.' Then he took a cup, and having offered thanks to God he gave it to them; and they all drank from it. And he said, 'This is my blood, the blood of the covenant, shed for many. I tell you this: never again shall I drink from the fruit of the vine until that day when I drink it new in the kingdom of God.'

After singing the Passover Hymn, they went out to the Mount of Olives. And Jesus said, 'You will all fall from your faith; for it stands written: "I will strike the shepherd down and the sheep will be scattered." Nevertheless, after I am raised again I will go on before you into Galilee.' Peter answered, 'Everyone else may fall away, but I will not.' Jesus said, 'I tell you this: today, this very night, before the cock crows twice, you yourself will disown me three times.' But he insisted and repeated: 'Even if I must die with you, I will

對耶穌說："你要我們到哪兒去給你預備逾越節宴席呢？"耶穌便打發兩個門徒說："你們進城去，會遇到一個手拿水罐的人，你們就跟着他。他走進一家後，你們就對那家的主人說：'我主問，我和門徒們要吃逾越節宴席的屋子在哪兒呢？'他會引你們到樓上一間預備停當的大屋子，你們就在那兒爲我們準備。"門徒便走了。進城後，發現一切都如耶穌所說的一樣。於是他們就在那兒準備逾越節的宴席。

到了晚上，耶穌和十二門徒來到了那人的家。他們坐下吃時，耶穌說："我告訴你們，你們中間有一個正和我一起吃飯的人要出賣我了。"他們聽後都感到十分驚愕，一個接一個地問耶穌："不是我吧？"耶穌說："是你們當中和我同蘸一個盤子吃飯的那個人。人子就要像經書上安排的那樣逝去。但那個出賣人子的人就要遭難了。那人如果並未生存過，那就好了。"

他們吃飯時，耶穌拿起麵包先謝主賜食，然後把麵包分給衆人。他說："吃吧，這是我的身體。"然後他又拿起一杯葡萄汁先謝主賜食後，遞給他們，他們每人都喝了。耶穌說："這是我的血，是我立約爲衆人而流的血。我告訴你們，在我於上帝之國喝到新的葡萄汁的日子之前，我再也不喝這葡萄汁了。"

唱完逾越節讚美詩後，他們便離開那人家去橄欖山。耶穌說："你們都會背棄信仰，因爲經書上講：'我要把牧人擊倒在地，使羊羣四散'。不過，我復活之後，要在你們之前進入加利利。"彼得說："別人會背棄信仰，我決不會。"耶穌說："我告訴你，就在今夜鷄叫兩遍之前，你自己就會有三次不認我。"但彼得堅持說："即使我和你同死，也決不會不認你。"

never disown you.' And they all said the same.

When they reached a place called Gethsemane, he said to his disciples, 'Sit here while I pray.' And he took Peter and James and John with him. Horror and dismay came over him, and he said to them, 'My heart is ready to break with grief; stop here, and stay awake.' Then he went forward a little, threw himself on the ground, and prayed·that, if it were possible, this hour might pass him by. 'Abba, Father,' he said, 'all things are possible to thee; take this cup away from me. Yet not what I will, but what thou wilt.'

He came back and found them asleep; and he said to Peter, 'Asleep, Simon? Were you not able to stay awake for one hour? Stay awake, all of you; and pray that you may be spared the test. The spirit is willing, but the flesh is weak.' Once more he went away and prayed. On his return he found them asleep again, for their eyes were heavy; and they did not know how to answer him.

The third time he came and said to them, 'Still sleeping? Still taking your ease? Enough! The hour has come. The Son of Man is betrayed to sinful men. Up, let us go forward! My betrayer is upon us.'

其他的門徒也都這樣說。

　　當他們到達一個叫客西馬尼的地方後，耶穌對門徒講：
“你們坐在這兒，等我禱告。”他便帶着彼得、雅各和約翰同
去。他感到恐懼和憂傷，便對他們說：“我傷心得心都碎了。
你們在這兒等着，不要睡。”他向前走了幾步，俯伏在地，禱
告說：如果可能，便叫那時刻過去。他說，“天父，我父啊，
你萬事皆能，求你把這杯子拿走吧。不過，不是依從我的意
思，而要遵從你的意願。”

　　耶穌回來後，發現幾個門徒睡着了。他對彼得說：“西
門，睡着了嗎？你難道不能儆醒一會麼？你們都不要睡，要禱
告，這樣才能免遭考驗。你們的心靈雖然願意，可肉體却很虛
弱。”於是他再次去禱告。回來時，耶穌發現他們又睡着了，
因爲他們睏得睜不開眼，也不知如何回答他。

　　耶穌第三次回來，對他們說：“還睡嗎？還在享安逸麼？
夠了！時候到了。人子已被出賣給罪人們。起來！我們往前
走！出賣我的人已經到了。”

Matthew

(1)

While he was still speaking, Judas, one of the Twelve, appeared; with him was a great crowd armed with swords and cudgels, sent by the chief priests and the elders of the nation. The traitor gave them this sign: 'The one I kiss is your man; seize him'; and stepping forward at once, he said, 'Hail, Rabbi!', and kissed him. Jesus replied, 'Friend, do what you are here to do.' They then came forward, seized Jesus, and held him fast.

Jesus was led off under arrest to the house of Caiaphas the High Priest, where the lawyers and elders were assembled. Peter followed him at a distance till he came to the High Priest's courtyard, and going in he sat down there among the attendants, meaning to see the end of it all.

The chief priests and the whole Council tried to find some allegation against Jesus on which a death-sentence could be based; but they failed to find one, though many came forward with false evidence.... The High Priest then said, 'By the living God I charge you to tell us: Are you the Messiah, the Son of God?' Jesus replied, 'The words are yours. But I tell you this: from now on, you will see the Son of Man seated at the right hand of God and coming on the clouds of heaven.' At these words the High Priest tore his robes and exclaimed, 'Blasphemy! Need we call further witnesses? You have heard the blasphemy. What is your opinion?' 'He is guilty,' they answered; 'he should die.'

八十八 耶穌之死

馬太福音

（一）

耶穌話還沒完，十二門徒之一的猶大來了。和他同來的許多人都帶着刀、棒，他們是祭司長和長老派來的。那出賣耶穌的叛徒先給他們一個暗號："我吻的那人就是你們要抓的，你們便上去抓住他。"他逕直走到耶穌跟前，說："給拉比請安。"然後吻了他。耶穌答道："朋友，做你來此要做的事吧。"於是，他們擁上前抓住耶穌。

抓耶穌的人把他帶到了大祭司該亞法那裏。那些律法師和長老都已聚集在那裏。彼得在後邊遠遠地跟着耶穌進入大祭司的院子。進去後他便坐在差役中間，想看看事情如何結局。

祭司長和全公會企圖尋找些藉口控告耶穌，以治他死罪。儘管許多人作偽證，但他們還是沒有一個真實的證據。祭司長說："我以永生的上帝起誓，要你告訴我們，你是不是基督、上帝的兒子？"耶穌答道："那是你講的。而我要告訴你們，從今以後，你們會看到人子坐在上帝的右邊，駕雲從天而降。"祭司長聽後，就撕開耶穌的衣服，叫道："太狂妄了！難道我們還需要別的證據嗎？你們都聽到了他的僭妄的話了。你們以為如何？"他們答道："他有罪，應該處死。"

Then they spat in his face and struck him with their fists; and others said, as they beat him, 'Now, Messiah, if you are a prophet, tell us who hit you.'

Meanwhile Peter was sitting outside in the courtyard when a serving-maid accosted him and said, 'You were there too with Jesus the Galilean.' Peter denied it in face of them all. 'I do not know what you mean', he said. He then went out to the gateway, where another girl, seeing him, said to the people there, 'This fellow was with Jesus of Nazareth.' Once again he denied it, saying with an oath, 'I do not know the man.' Shortly afterwards the bystanders came up and said to Peter, 'Surely you are another of them; your accent gives you away!' At this he broke into curses and declared with an oath: 'I do not know the man.' At that moment a cock crew; and Peter remembered how Jesus had said, 'Before the cock crows you will disown me three times.' He went outside, and wept bitterly.

When Judas the traitor saw that Jesus had been condemned, he was seized with remorse, and returned the thirty silver pieces to the chief priests and elders. 'I have sinned,' he said; 'I have brought an innocent man to his death.' But they said, 'What is that to us? See to that yourself.' So he threw the money down in the temple and left them, and went and hanged himself.

Taking up the money, the chief priests argued: 'This cannot be put into the temple fund; it is blood-money.' So after conferring they used it to buy the Potter's Field, as a burial-place for foreigners. This explains the name 'Blood Acre', by which that field has been known ever since.

(2)

From Caiaphas Jesus was led into the Governor's head quarters....

Pilate now took Jesus and had him flogged; and the soldiers plaited a crown of thorns and placed it on his head, and robed him in a purple cloak. Then time after time they came up to him, crying, 'Hail, King of the Jews!', and struck him on the face.

他們便向耶穌臉上吐唾沫，用拳頭打他。一些人邊打邊說：“基督，你若是先知，那你就告訴我們打你的人是誰吧。”

這時，彼得正坐在外面的院子裏。有個使女上前對他說：“你也是和那加利利人耶穌同伙的。”彼得在眾人面前否認說：“我不懂你的意思。”他便走到門口。門口的另一個女子看到他，便對眾人說：“這個人和拿撒勒人耶穌是一伙的。”彼得又否認，並起誓說：“我不認識他。”不一會兒，旁觀的人來對他說：“你的確是他們一伙的，你的口音也說明這一點。”彼得賭咒發誓說：“我不認識那個人。”這時，鷄叫了。彼得想起了耶穌的話，“鷄叫以前，你會三次不認我。”彼得走了出去，失聲痛哭。

當出賣耶穌的猶大看到耶穌被定罪，良心感到不安，於是就把那三十塊銀幣還給那些祭司長和長老，說：“我有罪，我令無辜者致死。”但他們却說：“這事與我們有何相干？你自己承担一切吧。”猶大便把銀幣丟在殿裏，離開他們，出去上吊死了。

祭司長拿起那些錢，說：“這是血錢，不要放入廟庫裏。”他們商量後便用那錢買了一塊公共墓地，以埋葬外鄉人。這就是流傳至今的那塊“血地”的來由。

（二）

約翰福音

眾人把耶穌從該亞法家裏，解往總督衙門。

（總督）彼拉多叫人捉住耶穌用鞭子抽打他。士兵用荆棘編了個冠冕，戴在耶穌頭上，並給他穿上紫袍。他們一次又一次地走向耶穌，挖苦道：“恭喜你啦！猶太人之王！”又狠打他的臉。

Once more Pilate came out and said to the Jews, 'Here he is; I am bringing him out to let you know that I find no case against him.' The Jews answered, 'We have a law; and by that law he ought to die, because he has claimed to be Son of God.'

Pilate tried hard to release him; but the Jews kept shouting, 'If you let this man go, you are no friend to Caesar; any man who claims to be a king is defying Caesar. Away with him! Away with him! Crucify him!' 'Crucify your king?' said Pilate. 'We have no king but Caesar', the Jews replied. Then at last, to satisfy them, he handed Jesus over to be crucified.

Jesus was now taken in charge and, carrying his own cross, went out to the Place of the Skull, as it is called (or, in the Jews' language, 'Golgotha'), where they crucified him, and with him two others, one on the right, one on the left, and Jesus between them.

And Pilate wrote an inscription to be fastened to the cross; it read, 'Jesus of Nazareth King of the Jews.'

The soldiers, having crucified Jesus, took possession of his clothes, and divided them into four parts, one for each soldier, leaving out the tunic. The tunic was seamless, woven in one piece throughout; so they said to one another, 'We must not tear this; let us toss for it'; and thus the text of Scripture came true: 'They shared my garments among them, and cast lots for my clothing.'

Jesus saw his mother, with the disciple whom he loved standing beside her. He said to her, 'Mother, there is your son'; and to the disciple, 'There is your mother'; and from that moment the disciple took her into his home.

After that, Jesus, aware that all had now come to its appointed end, said in fulfilment of Scripture, 'I thirst.' A jar stood there full of sour wine; so they soaked a sponge with the wine, fixed it on marjoram, and held it up to his lips. Having

彼拉多又出去對猶太人說："他出來了，我帶他來是要告訴你們我找不出他有什麼罪。"猶太人說："我們有律法。依法他是該被處死的，因爲他擅自稱是上帝的兒子。"

　　彼拉多很想釋放耶穌，但猶太人却不停地高喊："你若放這人，你就不是凱撒的朋友。凡是自稱爲王的都是背叛凱撒的。幹掉他！幹掉他！把他釘在十字架上！"彼拉多問："要把你們的王釘在十字架上麼？"他們答道："除了凱撒，我們沒有別的王。"最後，彼拉多答應了他們的要求，把耶穌交給他們去釘在十字架上。

　　耶穌被他們帶了去。他身背自己的十字架，到了一個叫髑髏地的地方（希伯來語叫各各他）。猶太人在那兒把他釘在了十字架上，此外還有兩個人跟他一樣，被釘在左右兩邊，耶穌被釘在中間。

　　彼拉多寫了一塊牌子釘在十字架上。牌上的字是"拿撒勒人耶穌—猶太人之王。"

　　幾個士兵把耶穌釘在十字架上後，便脫下他的外衣，分成了四份，每人拿一份，賸下一件內衣。耶穌的內衣沒有接縫，是上下一片織成的。他們就商議道："我們不要撕破它，還是抓閹吧。"這就應驗了經書上說的："他們瓜分了我的外衣，還爲我的衣服抓閹。"

　　耶穌看到他母親和站在她身旁的他所鍾愛的一個門徒，便對他母親說："母親，那是你的兒子了。"然後他又對那門徒說："這是你的母親了。"從此，那門徒就把她接到自己家中。

　　之後，耶穌看到諸事均已安排停當，爲了使經書上的話應驗，便說："我渴了。"那兒正好有一滿罐醋，他們便用海棉蘸了些醋，綁在牛膝草上，送到他唇邊。耶穌喝完醋，便說：

received the wine, he said, 'It is accomplished!' He bowed his head and gave up his spirit.

Because it was the eve of Passover, the Jews were anxious that the bodies should not remain on the cross for the coming Sabbath, since that Sabbath was a day of great solemnity; so they requested Pilate to have the legs broken and the bodies taken down. The soldiers accordingly came to the first of his fellow-victims and to the second, and broke their legs; but when they came to Jesus, they found that he was already dead, so they did not break his legs. But one of the soldiers stabbed his side with a lance, and at once there was a flow of blood and water. This happened in fulfilment of the text of Scripture: 'No bone of his shall be broken.' And another text says, 'They shall look on him whom they pierced.'

After that, Pilate was approached by Joseph of Arimathaea, disciple of Jesus, but a secret disciple for fear of the Jews, who asked to be allowed to remove the body of Jesus. They took the body of Jesus and wrapped it, with the spices, in strips of linen cloth according to Jewish burial-customs. Now at the place where he had been crucified there was a garden, and in the garden a new tomb, not yet used for burial. There, because the tomb was near at hand and it was the eve of the Jewish Sabbath, they laid Jesus.

"事成了。"頭便垂下，靈魂付與上帝了。

　　由於已是逾越節前夕，而即將到來的安息日又是個大節日，猶太人唯恐屍體在安息日還留在十字架上，他們就請彼拉多叫人打斷死者的腿，把屍體取下來。士兵們便把和耶穌同死的兩個人的腿打斷了。但當他們來到耶穌跟前時，發現他已經死了，就沒有打斷他的腿。但却有一個士兵用槍尖扎了耶穌的肋部，於是馬上就有血和水流了出來。而這就應驗了經書上講的："他的骨頭一根也沒有折斷。"另一處講："他們要仰望自己所扎的人。"

　　這事以後，有個亞利馬太人約瑟來見彼拉多。約瑟是耶穌的一個門徒，因爲懼怕猶太人，所以只是暗地作了他的門徒。他求彼拉多允許他把耶穌的屍體領去。他們依照猶太人的殯葬習俗，把耶穌的身體用香料和長條蔴布裹好。而在耶穌被釘十字架的地方，有一座園子，園子裏有一新墓穴，還沒有葬人。因爲就在近處，加上那天是猶太人安息日的前夕，他們就把耶穌安葬在那裏了。

John

Early on the sunday morning, while it was still dark, Mary of Magdala came to the tomb. She saw that the stone had been moved away from the entrance, and ran to Simon Peter and the other disciple, the one whom Jesus loved. 'They have taken the Lord out of his tomb,' she cried, 'and we do not know where they have laid him.' So Peter and the other set out and made their way to the tomb. When they reached the tomb, Simon Peter went into the tomb first and saw the linen wrappings lying, and the napkin which had been over his head, not lying with the wrappings but rolled together in a place by itself.

So the disciples went home again; but Mary stood at the tomb outside, weeping. As she wept, she peered into the tomb; and she saw two angels in white sitting there, one at the head, and one at the feet, where the body of Jesus had lain. They said to her, 'Why are you weeping?' She answered, 'They have taken my Lord away, and I do not know where they have laid him.' With these words she turned round and saw Jesus standing there, but did not recognize him. Jesus said to her, 'Why are you weeping? Who is it you are looking for?' Thinking it was the gardener, she said, 'If it is you, sir, who removed him, tell me where you have laid him, and I will take him away.' Jesus said, 'Mary!' She turned to him and said, 'Rabbuni!' (which is Hebrew for 'My Master'). Jesus said, 'Do not cling to me, for I have not yet ascended to the Father. But go to my brothers, and tell them that I am now ascending to my

八十九　救主復活

約翰福音

七日的第一天清晨，天還未亮，抹大拉的馬利亞便來到了耶穌的墓前。她看到石頭已從墓門被移開，她便跑去見西門・彼得和耶穌的另一個愛徒。她叫道：“他們把主從墓裏弄走了，我們不知道他被放在何處。”彼得和那個門徒便立刻朝墓地走去。他們到了墓地，彼得先進入墓裏，他看到蔴布還在那兒，但耶穌生前的裹頭布却沒有和蔴布在一起，而是被捲起放在一旁了。

這兩個門徒回去了。但馬利亞却站在墳墓外抽泣。她邊哭邊朝墓裏看。她看到兩個身着白衣的天使坐在原來安放耶穌遺體的地方，一個在頭那邊，一個在脚這邊。他們問：“你哭什麼呢？”她答道：“他們把我主弄走了，我不知他被安放在何處。”說着她轉身就看到耶穌站在那兒，但她認不出他來。耶穌問她：“你哭什麼呢？你在找誰呢？”馬利亞以爲他是管園子的，就說：“先生，若是你把他搬動的，請告訴我你把他放在哪兒了，我好去領走他。”耶穌說：“馬利亞。”馬利亞轉過身來說：“拉波尼（希伯來語的意思是我主）。”耶穌：“不要挨近我，因我還未升天去見聖父。你往我兄弟那兒去，告訴

Father and your Father, my God and your God.' Mary of Magdala went to the disciples with her news: 'I have seen the Lord!' she said, and gave them his message.

Late that Sunday evening, when the disciples were together behind locked doors, for fear of the Jews, Jesus came and stood among them. 'Peace be with you!' he said, and then showed them his hands and his side. So when the disciples saw the Lord, they were filled with joy.

One of the Twelve, Thomas, that is 'the Twin', was not with the rest when Jesus came. So the disciples told him, 'We have seen the Lord.' He said, 'Unless I see the mark of the nails on his hands, unless I put my finger into the place where the nails were, and my hand into his side, I will not believe it.'

A week later his disciples were again in the room, and Thomas was with them. Although the doors were locked, Jesus came and stood among them, saying, 'Peace be with you!' Then he said to Thomas, 'Reach your finger here; see my hands. Reach your hand here and put it into my side. Be unbelieving no longer, but believe.' Thomas said, 'My Lord and my God!' Jesus said, 'Because you have seen me you have found faith. Happy are they who never saw me and yet have found faith.'

Some time later, Jesus showed himself to his disciples once again, by the Sea of Tiberias, and in this way. Simon Peter and Thomas 'the Twin' were together with Nathanael of Cana-in-Galilee. The sons of Zebedee and two other disciples were also there. Simon Peter said, 'I am going out fishing.' 'We will go with you', said the others. So they started and got into the boat. But that night they caught nothing.

Morning came, and there stood Jesus on the beach, but the disciples did not know that it was Jesus. He called out to them, 'Friends, have you caught anything?' They answered 'No.' He said, 'Shoot the net to starboard, and you will make a catch.' They did so, and found they could not haul the net aboard, there were so many fish in it. Then the disciple whom Jesus loved said to Peter, 'It is the Lord!' When Simon Peter

他們我要升天去見我聖父，也是你的聖父，去見我的上帝，也是你的上帝。"抹大拉的馬利亞就去對門徒們說："我看到主了。"她還把主講的話告訴他們。

七日頭一天的夜裏，門徒們因懼怕猶太人，便把門關上。耶穌却又來站在他們中間說："願你們平安"，然後又把手和肋部給他們看。門徒們看到主，心裏非常高興。

十二門徒中有個被稱爲"孿生"的多馬，耶穌來時，他正好不在。於是門徒們便告訴他："我們看到主了。"他說："我只有看到他手上的釘痕，用手指摸到那些釘痕和他的肋部傷痕，我才相信。"

七天以後，門徒們又聚在那屋裏，多馬也在。儘管門是栓着的，耶穌仍然進了來，站在他們中間說："願你們平安。"然後，他對多馬說："把手指伸過來摸摸我的手；把手伸過來，摸摸我的肋部。不要再疑惑而應該相信。"多馬說："我的主，我的上帝！"耶穌說："你是看到了我才信的。那些沒有見到我而堅信的人都會快樂的。"

以後不久，耶穌又再次在提比哩亞海邊向門徒們顯現。此事是這樣：西門·彼得和被稱爲"孿生"的多馬與加利利的迦拿人拿担業在一起。西庇大的兩個兒子和另外兩個門徒也在那裏。西門·彼得說："我要去打魚"。衆人說："我們和你一起去。"於是他們就出發了，上了一條船。但那一夜，他們什麼魚也沒打着。

早晨時分，耶穌站在岸上，但門徒們不知那就是耶穌。他向他們喊道："朋友，有什麼收穫嗎？"他們說沒有。他說："把網撒在船的右側，你們就會打到魚的。"他們就把網撒向右側，却覺得重得拉不上來，因爲網中的魚太多了。耶穌的愛

heard that, he wrapped his coat about him (for he had stripped) and plunged into the sea. The rest of them came on in the boat, towing the net full of fish; for they were not far from land, only about a hundred yards.

When they came ashore, they saw a charcoal fire there, with fish laid on it, and some bread. Jesus said, 'Bring some of your catch.' Simon Peter went aboard and dragged the net to land, full of big fish, a hundred and fifty-three of them; and yet, many as they were, the net was not torn. Jesus said, 'Come and have breakfast.' None of the disciples dared to ask 'Who are you?' They knew it was the Lord. Jesus now came up, took the bread, and gave it to them, and the fish in the same way.

This makes the third time that Jesus appeared to his disciples after his resurrection from the dead.

徒就對彼得說："那是主。"彼得正光着身子，一聽是主，趕忙披上一件外衣，跳入海中往岸上游。其餘的門徒駕着那拖着滿滿的一網魚的船回到岸上，他們離岸並不遠，只有一百碼左右。

他們上岸後，看到有堆炭火，上面有魚和一些麵包。耶穌說："把你們打的魚拿幾條來。"彼得上船把網拉到岸上。網裏都是大魚，共計一百五十三條。魚雖多但網却沒有破。耶穌說："來吃早飯吧。"門徒們誰也不敢問："你是誰？"因為他們知道他就是主。耶穌走上前拿了餅和魚分給他們吃。

這是耶穌復活後第三次向門徒顯靈。

Acts

In the first part of my work, Theophilus, I wrote of all that Jesus did and taught from the beginning until the day when, after giving instructions through the Holy Spirit to the apostles whom he had chosen, he was taken up to heaven. He showed himself to these men after his death, and gave ample proof that he was alive: over a period of forty days he appeared to them and taught them about the kingdom of God.

So, when they were all together, they asked him, 'Lord, is this the time when you are to establish once again the sovereignty of Israel?' He answered, 'It is not for you to know about dates or times, which the Father has set within his own control. But you will receive power when the Holy Spirit comes upon you; and you will bear witness for me in Jerusalem, and all over Judaea and Samaria, and away to the ends of the earth.'

When he had said this, as they watched, he was lifted up, and a cloud removed him from their sight. As he was going, and as they were gazing intently into the sky, all at once there stood beside them two men in white who said, 'Men of Galilee, why stand there looking up into the sky? This Jesus, who has been taken away from you up to heaven, will come in the same way as you have seen him go.'

九十　門徒聚會

使徒行傳

提阿非羅(1)啊，我已在本書的第一部分寫了耶穌從一開始到他在以聖靈去教導他選的門徒後被接上天的全部事迹和教導。他死後向門徒顯靈，用大量證據表明他仍然活着：在四十多天的時間裏，他多次出現在他們面前，把上帝之國的事告訴他們。

因此，門徒們一起聚會時，便問耶穌："主啊，你要復興以色列國，就在此時嗎？"他答道："聖父自己掌握的時日，不是你們該知道的。但當聖靈降臨你們身上時，你們就會變得有能力。你們將在耶路撒冷、猶太全境、撒馬利亞直至天涯海角，爲我作見證。"

他說完後，門徒們看到他徐徐升起，一朵祥雲接他而去，便不見了。耶穌去時，衆門徒都仰天看着他。這時，突然有兩個白衣人站在他身邊，說，"加利利人，你們爲何站在這兒仰望天空呢？離你們升天去的耶穌，如你們所見怎樣接上天去，也就會怎樣再回來的。"

---

(1)　提阿非羅(Theophilus)意思是"上帝所愛的"，可能指的是贊助聖經印行的一個人。

Then they returned to Jerusalem from the hill called Olivet, Entering the city they went to the room upstairs where they were lodging: Peter and John and James and Andrew, Philip and Thomas, Bartholomew and Matthew, James son of Alphaeus and Simon the Zealot, and Judas son of James. All these were constantly at prayer together, and with them a group of women, including Mary the mother of Jesus, and his brothers.

It was during this time that Peter stood up before the assembled brother-hood, about one hundred and twenty in all, and said: 'My friends, the prophecy in Scripture was bound to come true, which the Holy Spirit, through the mouth of David, uttered about Judas who acted as guide to those who arrested Jesus. For he was one of our number and had his place in this ministry.' Peter continued, 'The text I have in mind is in the Book of Psalms: "Let his homestead fall desolate; let there be none to inhabit it"; and again, "Let another take over his charge." Therefore one of those who bore us company all the while we had the Lord Jesus with us, coming and going, from John's ministry of baptism until the day when he was taken up from us — one of those must now join us as a witness to his resurrection.'

Two names were put forward: Joseph, who was known as Barsabbas, and bore the added name of Justus; and Matthias. They drew lots and the lot fell on Matthias, who was then assigned a place among the twelve apostles.

While the day of Pentecost was running its course they were all together in one place, when suddenly there came from the sky a noise like that of a strong driving wind, which filled the whole house where they were sitting. And there appeared to them tongues like flames of fire, dispersed among them and resting on each one. And they were all filled with the Holy Spirit and began to talk in other tongues, as the Spirit gave them power of utterance.

Now there were living in Jerusalem devout Jews drawn from every nation under heaven; and at this sound the crowd

他們於是離開橄欖山⑴回耶路撒冷。進城後，門徒們便上他們住處樓上的一個房間，那兒有彼得、約翰、雅各、安得烈、腓力、多馬、巴多羅買、馬太、亞勒腓的兒子雅各、奮銳黨⑵的西門和雅可的兒子猶大。這些人和一些婦女，如耶穌的母親馬利亞等以及他的兄弟們，經常在一起作禱告。

這時聚在這兒的約有一百二十人，彼得站起來對他們說："朋友，在經書中聖靈借大衞之口預言，領人捉拿耶穌的是猶大，這話是完全應驗的。他本是我們中的一員，並且得了使徒的職分。"他接着說："我記得《詩篇》上講，'願他的家宅變爲荒野，無人居住'，又說'願別人獲得他的職分。'因此，我們要從由約翰施洗起直至耶穌升天時止一直和我們一起跟隨耶穌的人中選出一個使徒，讓他和我們一起作耶穌復活的見証。"

衆門徒推舉出兩個人：一是被稱爲巴撒巴，又稱爲猶士都的約瑟，另一個是馬提亞。於是衆人便以抽簽抽出了馬提亞。他便成了十二門徒中的一個。

五旬節到了，門徒們又聚在一起。忽然從天上傳下聲音，好似一陣疾風掠過，在他們坐着的屋中迴响。又有像焰火一樣的舌頭顯現，並紛落在每個人的頭上。他們就都被聖靈充滿，並以聖靈賜與的言語能力，講起各種語言來。

那時，來自世上各國的虔誠的猶太人，都住在耶路撒冷。

⑴ Olivet 是 Olives 的另一個拼法。

⑵ 奮銳黨(the Zealot)是猶太人反抗羅馬統治者的組織。

gathered, all bewildered because each one heard his own language spoken. They were and amazed perplexed, saying to one another, 'What can this mean?' Others said contemptuously, 'They have been drinking!'

But Peter stood up with the Eleven, raised his voice, and addressed them: 'Fellow Jews, and all you who live in Jerusalem, mark this and give me a hearing. These men are not drunk, as you imagine; for it is only nine in the morning. No, this is what the prophet spoke of: "God says, 'This will happen in the last days: I will pour out upon everyone a portion of my spirit; and your sons and daughters shall prophesy; and I will show portents in the sky above, and signs on the earth below — blood and fire and drifting smoke. The sun shall be turned to darkness, and the moon to blood, before that great, resplendent day, the day of the Lord, shall come. And then, everyone who invokes the name of the Lord shall be saved.'"

'Men of Israel, listen to me: I speak of Jesus of Nazareth, a man singled out by God and made known to you through miracles, portents, and signs, which God worked among you through him, as you well know. When he had been given up to you, by the deliberate will and plan of God, you used heathen men to crucify and kill him. But God raised him to life again, setting him free from the pangs of death, because it could not be that death should keep him in its grip.'

When they heard this they were cut to the heart, and said to Peter and the apostles, 'Friends, what are we to do?' 'Repent,' said Peter, 'repent and be baptized, everyone of you, in the name of Jesus the Messiah for the forgiveness of your sins; and you will receive the gift of the Holy Spirit. Then those who accepted his word were baptized, and some three thousand were added to their number that day.

They met constantly to hear the apostles teach, and to share the common life, to break bread, and to pray. A sense of awe was everywhere, and many marvels and signs were brought about through the apostles. All whose faith had drawn them

聽到響聲後，他們都聚集過來。聽見門徒們用他們各自不同語言說話，都感到大惑不解。他們困惑地議論說："這是什麼意思？"也有人輕蔑地說："他們是喝糊塗了。"

彼得和十一個使徒站起來，他提高聲音說道："你們猶太人和一切住在耶路撒冷的人，注意聽我講。這些人並非如你們所想的那樣喝醉了，因為現在只不過是早上九點。其實這是先知講到的：上帝說：'在最後審判的日子裏，我要用我的靈灌注給每個人，你們的兒女會作出預言。在天上我要顯出奇迹，在地上我要顯示神迹，有血、有火、有煙霧。日要變黑，月要變血紅，這些都要在天主的偉大顯現日之前出現。因此，凡祈求天主保佑的都會得救。'

"以色列人哪，聽我講。你們都知道，上帝通過他選定的拿撒勒人耶穌在你們中間作出神迹奇事。他按照上帝的意旨和安排被交給你們，你們却借異教人的手，把他釘死在十字架上。但上帝使他免遭死亡的痛若，使他復活了，因為死亡本來是奈何他不得的。"

他們聽後，都感到痛心疾首，便對彼得和其他使徒們說："朋友，我們該怎麼辦呢？"彼得說："悔改。你們每人都要悔改，並要以耶穌基督的名義受洗，使罪過得以赦免。你們也會得到聖靈的恩賜。"於是，那些信他的話的人便受了洗。那一天就增加了信徒大約三千人。

信徒們時常聚會來聆聽使徒的教誨，彼此交往、共用聖餐和進行祈禱。處處都呈現出一種使人敬畏的氣氛；使徒們又行

together held everything in common: they would sell their property and possessions and make a general distribution as the need of each required. With one mind they kept up their daily attendance at the temple, and, breaking bread in private houses, shared their meals with unaffected joy, as they praised God and enjoyed the favour of the whole people. And day by day the Lord added to their number those whom he was saving.

了許多神迹奇事。信的人都聚在一處，凡物公用。他們還變賣了田產家業，分給所需的人。他們同心同德，天天去殿裏聚會，在家中共用聖餐，高高興興地一同吃飯，他們頌揚上帝，得到全民的喜愛。這樣主就使得救的人一天天增加了。

Next day the Jewish rulers, elders, and doctors of the law met in Jerusalem. There were present Annas the High Priest, Caiaphas, Jonathan, Alexander, and all who were of the high-priestly family. They brought the apostles before the court and began the examination. 'By what power', they asked, 'or by what name have such men as you done this?' Then Peter, filled with the Holy Spirit, answered, 'Rulers of the people and elders, if the question put to us today is about help given to a sick man, and we are asked by what means he was cured, here is the answer, for all of you and for all the people of Israel: it was by the name of Jesus Christ of Nazareth, whom you crucified, whom God raised from the dead; it is by his name that this man stands here before you fit and well.'

Now as they observed the boldness of Peter and John, and noted that they were untrained laymen, they began to wonder, then recognized them as former companions of Jesus. 'What are we to do with these men?' they said; 'for it is common knowledge in Jerusalem that a notable miracle has come about through them; and we cannot deny it. But to stop this from spreading further among the people, we had better caution them never again to speak to anyone in this name.'

The court repeated the caution and discharged them. They could not see how they were to punish them, because the people were all giving glory to God for what had happened.

九十一　天佑神助

使徒行傳

（祭司長和守殿官對使徒教導人民並以耶穌為例宣講復活感到非常惱怒。他們就捉住這些使徒，把他們關在獄中。）

第二天，猶太官吏、長老和律法師們便聚在耶路撒冷。他們當中有大祭司亞那以及該亞法、約翰、亞歷山大和他們的親族。他們把使徒帶上堂來進行審問："你們憑什麼權力、以什麼名義作這些事？"那充滿了聖靈的彼得答道："人民的官長和長老們，如果要問我們如何治病及以何治病，我們對你們以及所有以色列人的答覆是：我們是以被你們釘在十字架上、後來被上帝復活的拿撒勒人耶穌的名行這事的，正是以他的名，病人才能治癒，健康地站在你們面前。"

那些人見到彼得和約翰果敢無畏，又見他們以前只不過是毫無學問的小民，他們都感到驚訝，才確信他們原是耶穌的門徒。他們說："該如何處置這兩個人呢？因為全耶路撒冷的人都知道，是他們行的這奇迹，對此我們也無法否認。為了不使這事在民間進一步傳播，我們最好禁止他們再用這個名義講道。"

這些人重申一遍禁令後，便把他們釋放了。他們想不出方法懲罰他們，因為百姓都為見到神迹而頌揚上帝。

The whole body of believers was united in heart and soul. Not a man of them claimed any of his possessions as his own, but everything was held in common, while the apostles bore witness with great power to the resurrection of the Lord Jesus. They were all held in high esteem; for they had never a needy person among them, because all who had property in land or houses sold it, brought the proceeds of the sale, and laid the money at the feet of the apostles; it was then distributed to any who stood in need.

But there was another man, called Ananias, with his wife Sapphira, who sold a property. With the full knowledge of his wife he kept back part of the purchase-money, and part he brought and laid at the apostles' feet. But Peter said, 'Ananias, how was it that Satan so possessed your mind that you lied to the Holy Spirit, and kept back part of the price of the land? You have lied not to men but to God.' When Ananias heard these words he dropped dead.

About three hours passed, and then his wife came in, unaware of what had happened. Peter turned to her and said, 'Tell me, were you paid such and such a price for the land?' 'Yes,' she said, 'that was the price.' Then Peter said, 'Why did you both conspire to put the Spirit of the Lord to the test? Hark! there at the door are the footsteps of those who buried your husband; and they will carry you away.' And suddenly she dropped dead at his feet.

They used to meet by common consent in Solomon's Portico, no one from outside their number venturing to join with them. But people in general spoke highly of them, and more than that, numbers of men and women were added to their ranks as believers in the Lord. In the end the sick were actually carried out into the streets and laid there on beds and stretchers, so that even the shadow of Peter might fall on one or another as he passed by.

Then the High Priest and his colleagues, the Sadducean party as it then was, were goaded into action by jealousy. They proceeded to arrest the apostles, and put them offical

所有信徒都是一心一意，沒有人把自己的東西認爲只屬於自己，而認爲應該大家享用。而使徒們則顯出巨大的能力作爲主耶穌復活的見證。他們都很受尊重，誰也不缺食少用，因爲人人都把田產房屋賣掉，把得來的錢奉獻在使徒的跟前。這些錢則分給需要資助的人。

　　但也有一個叫亞拿尼亞的人，他和妻子撒非喇賣了田產。他把那錢私自留下一部分，只把其餘一部分錢拿給使徒。這事他妻子也完全知道。彼得對他說："亞拿尼亞，你爲何讓撒旦迷住心竅去欺哄聖靈，私自留下一部分賣田的錢呢？你不是在欺騙別人，而是在欺騙上帝。"亞拿尼亞聽後馬上倒地身亡。

　　大約三小時後，他的妻子來了，還不知道剛才發生的事。彼得對她說："告訴我，你們賣田的錢都交出來了麼？"她答道："是的，就賣了這些。"彼得說："你們夫妻倆爲何合謀來試探主的神靈？聽着！埋葬你丈夫的人已臨門，他們還要把你也抬走。"那婦人馬上就倒斃在彼得的腳下。

　　使徒經常相約聚在所羅門的廊下，外人誰也不會貿然加入他們行列。但人們都很敬重他們，而且，信主的男男女女越來越多。後來甚至有人把病人用床和担架抬到大街上，指望彼得走過時，他的影子會照到他們中的什麼人身上。

　　因此，祭司長和那些撒都該教門的人都心懷妒忌。他們便採取行動，把使徒抓起來關在監裏。但天主派使者在夜裏開了

custody. But an angel of the Lord opened the prison doors during the night, brought them out, and said, 'Go, take your place in the temple and speak to the people, and tell them about this new life and all it means.' Accordingly they entered the temple at daybreak and went on with their teaching.

When the High Priest arrived with his colleagues, they sent to the jail to fetch the prisoners. But the police who went to the prison failed to find them there, so they returned and reported, 'We found the jail securely locked at every point, with the warders at their posts by the doors, but when we opened them we found no one inside.' Then a man arrived with the report, 'Look! the men you put in prison are there in the temple teaching the people.' At that the Controller went off with the police and fetched them, but without using force for fear of being stoned by the people.

So they brought them and stood them before the Council; and the High Priest began his examination. 'We expressly ordered you', he said, 'to desist from teaching in that name; and what has happened?' Peter replied for himself and the apostles: 'We must obey God rather than men. The God of our fathers raised up Jesus whom you had done to death by hanging him on a gibbet.'

This touched them on the raw, and they wanted to put them to death. But a member of the Council rose to his feet, a Pharisee called Gamaliel, a teacher of the law held in high regard by all the people. He moved that the men be put outside for a while. Then he said, 'Men of Israel, be cautious in deciding what to do with these men. For if this idea of theirs or its execution is of human origin, it will collapse; but if it is from God, you will never be able to put them down, and you risk finding yourselves at war with God.'

They took his advice. They sent for the apostles and had them flogged; then they ordered them to give up speaking in the name of Jesus, and discharged them. So the apostles went out from the Council rejoicing that they had been found worthy to suffer indignity for the sake of the Name. And

監門，把他們領出來，說："回到殿裏去，向人們講解新生命的道理。"於是，他們便在天亮時去殿裏繼續講道。

（第二天）當祭司長和他們的同事叫人到獄中提使徒們上堂時，差役發覺使徒都不在監裏了，便回去稟報："監獄把守得嚴嚴實實，獄卒還在門外把守着，但打開監門，裏邊却沒有人了。"這時，有個人來稟報說："你們原來關在監裏的人正在殿裏給人們講道呢。"守殿官聽後，馬上帶領差役去抓人，只是不敢用暴力，因爲害怕人們會用石頭打他們。他們把使徒帶到公會前站着。祭司長開始審問道："我們已明令你們不許以那人的名傳道，怎麼還不聽？"彼得代使徒們說："我們必須遵從上帝，而不是凡人。你們在木架上釘死耶穌，但他已被我們列祖的神復活了。"

這些話觸到了公會的人的痛處，他們便要殺害使徒們。但有一個叫迦瑪列的法利賽人，是人們敬重的教法師。他站起來吩咐差役把使徒暫且帶出外面。然後說："以色列人哪，怎樣對待這些人，要愼重考慮才好。……因爲，他們的想法和所爲若出於人意，是必然失敗的；但若來自上帝，那你們想壓制也壓制不了，而且搞不好還會與上帝爲敵。"

公會的人聽從他的勸告。他們叫人把使徒帶來，鞭笞懲戒，命令他們今後不許以耶穌的名講道，然後釋放他們。使徒

every day they went steadily on with their teaching in the temple and in private houses, telling the good news of Jesus the Messiah.

們離開公會，以能爲耶穌之名受辱而感到高興。他們堅持每天在殿裏或人們家中講道，傳播耶穌基督的福音。

Acts

Meanwhile Saul was still breathing murderous threats against the disciples of the Lord. He went to the High Priest and applied for letters to the synagogues at Damascus authorizing him to arrest anyone he found, men or women, who followed the new way, and bring them to Jerusalem. While he was still on the road and nearing Damascus, suddenly a light flashed from the sky all around him. He fell to the ground and heard a voice saying, 'Saul, Saul, why do you persecute me?' 'Tell me, Lord,' he said, 'who you are.' The voice answered, 'I am Jesus, whom you are persecuting. But get up and go into the city, and you will be told what you have to do.' Meanwhile the men who were travelling with him stood speechless; they heard the voice but could see no one. Saul got up from the gound, but when he opened his eyes he could not see; so they led him by the hand and brought him into Damascus. He was blind for three days, and took no food or drink.

There was a disciple in Damascus named Ananias. He had a vision in which he heard the voice of the Lord: 'Ananias!' 'Here I am, Lord', he answered. The Lord said to him, 'Go at once to Straight Street, to the house of Judas, and ask for a man from Tarsus named Saul. You will find him at prayer; he has had a vision of a man named Ananias coming in and laying his hands on him to restore his sight.' Ananias answered, 'Lord, I have often heard about this man and all the harm he has done to thy people in Jerusalem. And he is here with authority from the chief priests to arrest all who invoke thy

九十二　棄暗投明

使徒行傳

　　掃羅(1)一直在恐嚇主的門徒，揚言要殺死他們。他去見祭司長，請求發文書給大馬色的各個會堂，使他有權查找信道的人。查到後不論男女，一律押回耶路撒冷。當他走近大馬色的途中，突然天上閃出一道強光，把他團團罩住。他仆倒地上，聽見一個聲音對他說：「掃羅，掃羅，你爲何逼迫我？」掃羅說：「主啊，請告訴我你是誰。」那聲音說：「我就是你一直在逼迫的耶穌。起來進城去，就會有人告訴你該做什麼。」當時和他同行的人都呆在那裏說不出話來。他們聽到聲音却看不到人。掃羅從地上爬起來，他睜眼要看，眼睛却看不見東西了。那些人便拉着他的手，領他進了大馬色。整整三天他都看不見東西，不吃也不喝。

　　大馬色那兒有一個門徒叫亞拿尼亞。主顯聖對他說：「亞拿尼亞！」他說：「主啊，我在這兒。」主對他講：「馬上去直街，到猶大的家裏去見一個從大數來的名叫掃羅的人，你會見到他在禱告。我已向他顯靈說有個叫亞拿尼亞的人會走來把手按在他頭上，使他恢復視力。」亞拿尼亞答道：「主啊，我常聽人講，這個人是在耶路撒冷迫害你的人。他現在又有祭司

————————————

(1) 掃羅是一個原先狂熱迫害耶穌門徒的人。

name.' But the Lord said to him, 'You must go, for this man is my chosen instrument to bring my name before the nations and their kings, and before the people of Israel. I myself will show him all that he must go through for my name's sake.'

So Ananias went. He entered the house, laid his hands on him and said, 'Saul, my brother, the Lord Jesus, who appeared to you on your way here, has sent me to you so that you may recover your sight, and be filled with the Holy Spirit.' And immediately it seemed that scales fell from his eyes, and he regained his sight. Thereupon he was baptized, and afterwards he took food and his strength returned.

He stayed some time with the disciples in Damascus. Soon he was proclaiming Jesus publicly in the synagogues: 'This', he said, 'is the Son of God.' All who heard were astounded. 'Is not this the man', they said, 'who was in Jerusalem trying to destroy those who invoke this name? Did he not come here for the sole purpose of arresting them and taking them to the chief priests?' But Saul grew more and more forceful, and silenced the Jews of Damascus with his cogent proofs that Jesus was the Messiah.

As the days mounted up, the Jews hatched a plot against his life; but their plans became known to Saul. They kept watch on the city gates day and night so that they might murder him; but his converts took him one night and let him down by the wall, lowering him in a basket.

When he reached Jerusalem he tried to join the body of disciples there; but they were all afraid of him, because they did not believe that he was really a convert. Barnabas, however, took him by the hand and introduced him to the apostles. He described to them how Saul had seen the Lord on his journey, and heard his voice, and how he had spoken out boldly in the name of Jesus at Damascus. Saul now stayed with them, moving about freely in Jerusalem. He spoke out boldly and openly in the name of the Lord, talking and debating with the Greek-speaking Jews. But they planned to murder him, and when the brethren learned of this they escorted him to Caesarea and saw him off to Tarsus.

長給他權力去抓那些祈求你保佑的人呢。」但主對他說：「你只管去，因為這人是我挑選的工具，要在外邦人及其君王和以色列人面前宣揚我的名。我自己也要指示他，為了我的名，他必須經受許多考驗。」

亞拿尼亞便遵囑前往。他進了那家，把手按在掃羅頭上說：「掃羅兄弟，在你來此路上向你顯聖的主就是耶穌，他打發我來並讓聖靈充滿你身使你重見光明。」立刻，掃羅的眼睛彷彿有些鱗片掉了下來，他的雙眼復明了。他於是受了洗。進食之後，體力又恢復了。

掃羅和大馬色的門徒們同住了些日子。接着，他就在各會堂裏公開宣傳耶穌，說：「他就是聖子。」聽到的人都很詫異。他們說：「在耶路撒冷要殺耶穌信徒的，不就是這人麼？他不是來這兒為了抓信徒去見祭司長的麼？」但掃羅勁頭越來越足，並以令人信服的証據說明耶穌就是基督，這就使得大馬色的猶太人無話可說。

過了些日子，猶太人便策劃要謀害掃羅。但他們的陰謀被掃羅知道了。他們日夜在城門口守候，伺機暗害他。但一天夜裏，掃羅的門徒們用繩子把他從城牆上縋下去，讓他走掉了。

掃羅抵達耶路撒冷後，便想和那裏的信徒建立聯系。但他們害怕他，不信他眞的也成了門徒。只有巴拿巴拉着他的手，引他去見使徒們，向他們介紹掃羅在路上見到主、聽到主的聲音以及他如何在大馬色以耶穌的名大膽傳道的事蹟。於是，掃羅便和使徒們在一起，可以在耶路撒冷自由活動。他以耶穌之名大膽傳道，和說希臘語的猶太人討論辯駁。他們就策劃要殺害他。他的同胞們知道後，便護送他去該撒利亞，並讓他再轉去大數。

Meanwhile the church, throughout Judaea, Galilee, and Samaria, was left in peace to build up its strength. In the fear of the Lord, upheld by the Holy Spirit, it held on its way and grew in numbers.

In Joppa there was a disciple named Tabitha (in Greek, Dorcas, meaning a gazelle), who filled her days with acts of kindness and charity. At that time she fell ill and died; and they washed her body and laid it in a room upstairs. As Lydda was near Joppa, the disciples, who had heard that Peter was there, sent two men to him with the urgent request, 'Please come over to us without delay.' Peter thereupon went off with them. When he arrived they took him upstairs to the room, where all the widows came and stood round him in tears showing him the shirts and coats that Dorcas used to make while she was with them. Peter sent them all outside, and knelt down and prayed. Then, turning towards the body, he said, 'Get up, Tabitha.' She opened her eyes, saw Peter, and sat up. The news spread all over Joppa, and many came to believe in the Lord. Peter stayed on in Joppa for some time with one Simon, a tanner.

At Caesarea there was a man named Cornelius, a centurion in the Italian Cohort, as it was called. He was a religious man, and he and his whole family joined in the worship of God. He gave generously to help the Jewish people, and was regular in his prayers to God. One day about three in the afternoon he had a vision in which he clearly saw an angel of God, who

九十三 恩澤外邦

使徒行傳

那時，整個猶太、加利利和撒瑪利亞的教會都平安順利，影響日增。因爲人們崇敬天主，又得聖靈激勵，教會日益發展，信徒也越來越多了。

約伯有個叫大比大（希臘語爲多加，意思是羚羊）的女信徒，一生行善施濟。這時她因病死去。人們把她的遺體洗淨，停放在樓上的房間裏。呂大離約帕不遠，信徒們聽說彼得在呂大，便派了兩個人趕去見他，央求他道："請馬上到我們那兒去吧。"彼得便跟他們去了。到那裏人們領他上樓，那裏聚集了一些寡婦，她們圍在四周哭泣，還把多加生前做的衣衫給他看。彼得讓她們都出去，然後便跪下祈禱。過了一會兒，他轉身朝那死人說："起來吧，大比大。"大比大睜開了眼，看到彼得便坐了起來。這消息傳遍了約帕，於是很多人都信了基督。後來，彼得在約帕的一個鞣皮匠西門的家裏住了些日子。

該撒利亞有個叫哥尼流的人，是被稱爲意大利營的百人隊隊長。他是個虔誠的人，全家都信奉上帝。他爲人慷慨，多方賙濟猶太人民，常常向上帝禱告。一天，日頭偏西時分，他清楚地看到上帝的一個使者顯靈，並走進他的屋子說："你的禱

came into his room and said, 'Your prayers and acts of charity have gone up to heaven to speak for you before God. And now send to Joppa for a man named Simon, also called Peter: he is lodging with another Simon, a tanner, whose house is by the sea.' So when the angel who was speaking to him had gone, he summoned two of his servants and a military orderly who was a religious man, told them the whole story, and sent them to Joppa.

The day after that, Peter arrived at Caesarea. Cornelius was expecting them and had called together his relatives and close friends. When Peter arrived, Cornelius came to meet him, and bowed to the ground in deep reverence. But Peter raised him to his feet and said, 'Stand up; I am a man like anyone else.' Still talking with him he went in and found a large gathering. He said to them, 'I need not tell you that a Jew is forbidden by his religion to visit or associate with a man of another race; yet God has shown me clearly that I must not call any man profane of unclean. That is why I came here without demur when you sent for me. May I ask what was your reason for sending?'

Cornelius said, 'Four days ago, just about this time, I was in the house here saying the afternoon prayers, when suddenly a man in shining robes stood before me. He said: "Cornelius, your prayer has been heard and your acts of charity remembered before God. Send to Joppa, then, to Simon Peter, and ask him to come. He is lodging in the house of Simon the tanner, by the sea." So I sent to you there and then; it was kind of you to come. And now we are all met here before God, to hear all that the Lord has ordered you to say.'

Peter began: 'I now see how true it is that God has no favourites, but that in every nation the man who is god-fearing and does what is right is acceptable to him. He sent his word to the Israelites and gave the good news of peace through Jesus Christ, who is Lord of all. I need not tell you what happened lately all over the land of the Jews, starting from Galilee after the baptism proclaimed by John. You

告和善行已達上天，神已知道。你現在應派人到約帕去，把那又名彼得的西門請來。他住在另一個也叫西門的鞋皮匠家裏，房子就在海邊上。"天使說完離去後，哥尼流叫了兩個僕人和一個常侍候他的虔誠的待衞來，把剛才的事告訴他們，並派他們前往約帕。

第三天，彼得來到該撒利亞。哥尼流已經請來親朋，一起恭候他。彼得一到，哥尼流便迎上前去，俯伏在地，向他叩拜。彼得扶起他，說："快起來，我只是一個普通人。"邊講邊走進屋子，他看到那兒已有很多人，便對他們說："你們知道，依照教義，猶太人是不許和外邦人親近來往的。但上帝已明確指示我，不能把任何人都看做是世俗不潔的。所以，你們一請我，我便欣然而至。請問，你們叫我有什麼事呢？"

哥尼流說："四天之前的這個時候，我正在家中做午後禱告，突然，一個身着閃閃發光的袍子的人站在我面前。他說：'哥尼流，你的禱告已蒙垂聽，你的善行已稟告上帝。你派人到約帕去，請西門（彼得）來。他住在海邊一個鞋皮匠西門的家裏。'所以我就立刻派人去請你，你竟然賞光駕臨。現在，我們都聚在上帝面前，聆聽主吩咐你講的話。"

彼得就說："我現在眞的看到，上帝不會偏愛，凡是崇敬主而又行正義的人，不論是何國何邦的，上帝都可悅納。他宣道給以色列人，並通過衆生之主耶穌傳播和平福音。你們都知道，自約翰宣傳洗禮後，從加利利起，上帝的道已傳遍了猶太

know about Jesus of Nazareth, how God anointed him with the Holy Spirit and with power. He went about doing good and healing all who were oppressed by the devil, for God was with him. And we can bear witness to all that he did in the Jewish country-side and in Jerusalem. He was put to death by hanging on a gibbet; but God raised him to life on the third day, and allowed him to appear, not to the whole people, but to witnesses whom God had chosen in advance — to us, who ate and drank with him after he rose from the dead. He commanded us to proclaim him to the poeple, and affirm that he is the one who has been designated by God as judge of the living and the dead. It is to him that all the prophets testify, declaring that everyone who trusts in him receives forgiveness of sins through his name.'

Peter was still speaking when the Holy Spirit came upon all who were listening to the message. The believers who had come with Peter, men of Jewish birth, were astonished that the gift of the Holy Spirit should have been poured out even on Gentiles. For they could hear them speaking in tongues of ecstasy and acclaiming the greatness of God. Then Peter spoke: 'Is anyone prepared to withhold the water for baptism from these persons, who have received the Holy Spirit just as we did ourselves?' Then he ordered them to be baptized in the name of Jesus Christ. After that they asked him to stay on with them for a time.

全境。你們也知道，上帝是怎樣以聖靈和神力施膏於拿撒勒人耶穌的。他周遊四方，廣行善事，治好所有被魔鬼附體的人，因爲上帝與他同在。他在猶太地和耶路撒冷行道，我們都可作見証。但他却被釘在十字架上而死。上帝在第三天使他復活，並讓他顯靈，不是顯靈於衆人，而是顯靈於上帝先選好的人，也就是我們這些在他復活後與他飲食與共的人。他囑咐我們向衆人宣示他，證明他是上帝選定的可裁定生死的主。衆先知爲他作見證，宣告凡是信奉他的人，必會因其名而獲赦罪。"

彼得講話時，聖靈降在所有聽道者的身上。那些和彼得同來的信奉割禮的人，看到聖靈的恩賜也傾注在外邦人的身上，便感到十分詫異。因爲他們聽到這些外邦人用他們自己的語言盛讚上帝的偉大。於是彼得說："這些人和我們一樣接受聖靈，誰能禁止用水給他們施洗呢？"他就吩咐以耶穌基督的名爲他們施洗。這事以後，他們便留彼得住下一個時期。

Acts

There were at Antioch, in the congregation there, certain prophets and teachers: Barnabas, Simeon called Niger, Lucius of Cyrene, Manaen, who had been at the court of Prince Herod, and Saul. While they were keeping a fast and offering worship to the Lord, the Holy Spirit said, 'Set Barnabas and Saul apart for me, to do the work to which I have called them.' Then, after further fasting and prayer, they laid their hands on them and let them go.

They went through the whole island as far as Paphos, and there they came upon a sorcerer, a Jew who posed as a prophet, Bar-Jesus by name. He was in the retinue of the Governor, Sergius Paulus, an intelligent man, who had sent for Barnabas and Saul and wanted to hear the word of God. This Elymas the sorcerer (so his name may be translated) opposed them trying to turn the Governor away from the Faith. But Saul, also known as Paul, filled with the Holy Spirit, fixed his eyes on him and said, 'You swindler, you rascal, son of the devil and enemy of all goodness, will you never stop falsifying the straight ways of the Lord? Look now, the hand of the Lord strikes: you shall be blind, and for a time you shall not see the sunlight.' Instantly mist and darkness came over him and he groped about for someone to lead him by the hand. When the Governor saw what had happened he became a believer, deeply impressed by what he learned about the Lord.

At Iconium similarly they went into the Jewish synagogue

九十四　廣出傳道

使徒行傳

　　在安提阿的教會裏有幾位先知和教師，他們就是巴拿巴，又稱爲尼結的西面、古利奈人路求、曾在希律王宮廷供職的馬念以及掃羅。他們齋戒和參拜天主時，聖靈說："派巴拿巴和掃羅去做我要他們做的事。"於是，齋戒禱告完後，他們便用手按在二人頭上求神垂降，然後打發他們去了。

　　他們（到撒拉米後，）經過全島，到了帕弗，在那兒遇到了一個假冒先知的猶太術士，名叫巴耶穌。此人是總督士求・保羅的扈從，而士求・保羅却是個通情達理之人，他請巴拿巴和掃羅來講上帝之道。但那術士以呂馬(1)（意即"行法術"）則反對他們，極力阻止總督去信他們。但掃羅（亦即保羅）(2)聖靈在身，便盯着他說："你這個騙子、惡棍、魔鬼的兒子、衆善的仇敵，你還不停止歪曲主的正道麽？看，主已給你打擊，你的眼要瞎一段時間，看不見陽光。"那假先知頓覺眼前一片昏黑，摸着求人引領他了。總督看到這奇事後，對主的道更加深信不疑而成了主的信徒。

　　在以哥念，他們二人也進猶太人的會堂講道，因此，許多

----

(1)　以呂馬（Elymas）就是巴耶穌（Bar-Jesus）。

(2)　Paul（保羅）原名 Saul（掃羅）。

and spoke to such purpose that a large body both of Jews and Gentiles became believers. But the unconverted Jews stirred up the Gentiles and poisoned their minds against the Christians. For some time Paul and Barnabas stayed on and spoke boldly and openly in reliance on the Lord; and he confirmed the message of his grace by causing signs and miracles to be worked at their hands. The mass of the townspeople were divided, some siding with the Jews, others with the apostles. But when a move was made'by Gentiles and Jews together, with the connivance of the city authorities, to maltreat them and stone them, they got wind of it and made their escape to the Lycaonian cities of Lystra and Derbe and the surrounding country, where they continued to spread the good news.

At Lystra sat a crippled man, lame from birth, who had never walked in his life. This man listened while Paul was speaking. Paul fixed his eyes on him and saw that he had the faith to be cured, so he said to him in a loud voice, 'Stand up straight on your feet'; and he sprang up and started to walk. When the crowds saw what Paul had done, they shouted, in their native Lycaonian, 'The gods have come down to us in human form.' And they called Barnabas Jupiter, and Paul they called Mercury, because he was the spokesman. And the priest of Jupiter, whose temple was just outside the city, brought oxen and garlands to the gates, and he and all the people were about to offer sacrifice.

But when the apostles Barnabas and Paul heard of it, they tore their clothes and rushed into the crowd shouting, 'Men, what is this that you are doing? We are only human beings, no less mortal than you. The good news we bring tells you to turn from these follies to the living God, who made heaven and earth and sea and everything in them.

With these words they barely managed to prevent the crowd from offering sacrifice to them.

Then Jews from Antioch and Iconium came on the scene and won over the crowds. They stoned Paul, and dragged him out of the city, thinking him dead. The converts formed a ring

猶太人和外邦人都成了信徒。但那些不信的猶太人則煽動外邦人，使他們憎恨基督徒。保羅和巴拿巴在那裏住下，靠主進行公開的傳道。主通過他們的手，行使神迹奇事，以證明他的恩威。城裏的人就分成兩派，一些人附從猶太人，另一些人則追隨使徒。當一些外邦人和猶太人在該城官吏的慫恿下企圖侮辱並用石擊兩個使徒時，他們聽到了風聲，便逃往呂高尼的路司得和特庇城及其周圍一帶，在那裏繼續傳播福音。

在路司得城，有個生來就瘸的人。他只能坐着，從不會走路。他聽保羅講道時，保羅凝視着他，見他心誠可治，便大聲對他說："站立起來吧。"那人便一下子站了起來，並且能走路了。衆人看見保羅行這奇事，便用呂高尼話高喊："天神借着人體降臨到我們中間了。"他們便稱巴拿巴爲朱庇特，叫保羅爲墨丘利[1]，因爲保羅爲天神傳信。城外朱庇特廟的祭司牽着牛、拿着花環來到門前，要和衆人一道向使徒獻祭。

巴拿巴、保羅聽到後，感到十分不安，他們撕開衣服跑到衆人中間喊道："諸君，你們這是幹什麼啦！我們和你們一樣，都是普通人。我們向你們宣講福音，是叫你們摒棄那些愚行，歸向那創造天地、海洋和萬物的永生的上帝。

說完這些話後，他們才勉强勸住衆人，不向他們獻祭。

後來有些來自安提阿和以哥念的猶太人在那裏拉攏衆人。他們用石頭擲保羅，以爲他死了，便把他拖到了城外。門徒們

---

[1] Mercury 是"諸神的使神"。

round him, and he got to his feet and went into the city. Next day he left with Barnabas for Derbe.

After bringing the good news to that town, where they gained many converts, they returned to Lystra, then to Iconium, and then to Antioch, heartening the converts and encouraging them to be true to their religion. The warned them that to enter the kingdom of God we must pass through many hardships. They also appointed elders for them in each congregation, and with prayer and fasting committed them to the Lord in whom they had put their faith.

Then they passed through Pisidia and came into Pamphylia. When they had given the message at Perga, they went down to Attalia, and from there set sail for Antioch, where they had originally been commended to the grace of God for the task which they had now completed. When they arrived and had called the congregation together, they reported all that God had done through them, and how he had thrown open the gates of faith to the Gentiles. And they stayed for some time with the discipled there.

圍着他，他却沒事地站了起來，進城去了。第二天，他和巴拿巴到特庇去了。

他們對特庇城的居民傳了福音，使許多人信了道之後，又回到路司得、以哥念和安提阿，鼓勵門徒要恆守所信之道。他們告誡門徒說，要進上帝之國必需經歷千辛萬苦。兩人又在各教會中選立長老，又禁食禱告，把他們託付給他們信奉的主。

然後，掃羅和巴拿巴經過彼西底，來到旁非利亞。在別加講完道後，又到了亞大利，再從那兒乘船到達安提阿，這安提阿就是當初他們蒙受神恩，受託去做上帝要他們做的事情的地方。現在他們已完成了任務。他們到後，便聚集會衆，講述了上帝通過他們所行的事以及上帝是怎樣爲外邦人廣開信道之門的。二人就在那兒和門徒們住了一些日子。

It was about this time that king Herod attacked certain members of the church. He beheaded James, the brother of John, and then, when he saw that the Jews approved, proceeded to arrest Peter also. This happened during the festival of Unleavened Bread. Having secured him, he put him in prison under a military guard, four squads of four men each, meaning to produce him in public after Passover. So Peter was kept in prison under constant watch, while the church kept praying fervently for him to God.

On the very night before Herod had planned to bring him forward, Peter was asleep between two soldiers, secured by two chains, while outside the doors sentries kept guard over the prison. All at once an angel of the Lord stood there, and the cell was ablaze with light. He tapped Peter on the shoulder and woke him. 'Quick! Get up', he said, and the chains fell away from his wrists. The angel then said to him, 'Do up your belt and put your sandals on'. He did so. 'Now wrap your cloak round you and follow me.' He followed him out, with no idea that the angel's intervention was real: he thought it was just a vision. But they passed the first guard-post, then the second, and reached the iron gate leading out into the city, which opened for them of its own accord. And so they came out and walked the length of one street; and the angel left him.

Then Peter came to himself. 'Now I know it is true,' he said; 'the Lord has sent his angel and rescued me from Herod's

九十五　惡貫滿盈

在這期間，希律王迫害教會中的一些人。他把約翰的哥哥雅各斬首；他看到猶太人都贊同這樣做，便又抓捕了彼得。當時正值除酵節。希律抓到彼得後，把他關在監裏，派四組士兵看守，每組四人，準備待逾越節過後，再把他提交公衆審判。彼得被囚在監裏，士兵看管很嚴，而教會則熱切地爲他禱告上帝。

在希律王準備把他提堂的前夜，彼得給兩條鎖鏈捆着，睡在兩個士兵中間，門口還有人看守。突然，主的一個使者出現在那裏，使整個囚室亮如白晝。天使輕輕拍拍彼得的肩膀叫醒他，說：“快起來！”於是，鐵鏈便從他手腕上脫落了。天使又對他說：“束上腰帶，穿上鞋。”彼得照辦了。“披好外衣跟我走。”彼得便跟隨天使走出了牢房，他絲毫沒想到天使這樣做是眞事，還以爲只是一種幻像。他們過了第一道崗哨又過了第二道崗哨，然後來到那個臨街的鐵門。鐵門自己開啟，他們便出了監獄。走過一條街，那天使就離他而去了。

這時，彼得方才醒悟過來，心想：“現在我知道這是眞的了。是主派天使救我擺脫希律的毒手和猶太人的圖謀的。”明

clutches and from all that the Jewish people were expecting.'
When he realized how things stood, he made for the house of
Mary, the mother of John Mark, where a large company was
at prayer. He knocked at the outer door and a maid called
Rhoda came to answer it. She recognized Peter's voice and
was so overjoyed that instead of opening the door she ran in
and announced that Peter was standing outside. 'You are
crazy', they told her; but she insisted that it was so. Then they
said, 'It must be his guardian angel.'

Meanwhile Peter went on knocking, and when they opened
the door and saw him, they were astounded. With a movement of the hand he signed to them to keep quiet, and told
them how the Lord had brought him out of prison. 'Report
this to James and the members of the church', he said. Then
he left the house and went off elsewhere.

When morning came, there was consternation among the
soldiers: what could have become of Peter? Herod made close
search, but failed to find him, so he interrogated the guards
and ordered their execution.

Afterwards he left Judaea to reside for a time at Caesarea.
He had for some time been furiously angry with the people of
Tyre and Sidon, who now by common agreement presented
themselves at his court. There they won over Blastus the royal
chamberlain, and sued for peace, because their country drew
its supplies from the king's territory. So, on an appointed day,
attired in his royal robes and seated on the rostrum, Herod
harangued them; and the populace shouted back, 'It is a god
speaking, not a man!' Instantly an angel of the Lord struck
him down, because he had usurped the honour due to God;
he was eaten up with worms and died.

Meanwhile the word of God continued to grow and spread.

Barnabas and Saul, their task fulfilled, returned from
Jerusalem, taking John Mark with them.

白了是甚麼一回事，他便往約翰‧馬可的母親馬利亞的家走去。當時，許多人在屋裏禱告。彼得敲敲大門，一個叫羅大的女僕應聲來開門。她聽出了彼得的聲音，便顧不得開門，驚喜地跑進屋告訴眾人彼得已回到門外了。眾人道：“你瘋了。”但她堅決說這是真的。他們說：“那準是保護他的天使吧。”

這時彼得在繼續敲門。眾人開門看果真是他，都非常驚愕。彼得擺了擺手，示意叫他們不要張聲，然後告訴他們主是如何把他領出了監獄的。他說：“請把這事告訴雅各和眾信徒。”說完，他便離開那家到別處去了。

天亮以後，士兵們驚惶失措，不知彼得哪兒去了。希律四處搜查，也沒找到，便審問看守人並把他們處死。

後來，希律離開了猶太，暫時住在該撒利亞。有一段時間，他對推羅、西頓的人非常生氣。這些人商量好前來宮廷見他。他們買通了希律的內侍伯拉斯都，向希律求和，因為他們要靠他的國土才獲得糧食。在約定之日，希律穿上朝服坐在王位上，把他們訓斥了一頓。那些民眾喊道：“這是神而不是人在講話。”由於他篡用了上帝的榮耀，主的天使馬上把他擊倒在地。他便遭萬蟲噬咬而死了。

此時上帝之道已日漸興盛並廣泛傳播。巴拿巴和掃羅做完了他們的事後，便帶着約翰‧馬可從耶路撒冷回來了。

He went on to Derbe and to Lystra, and there he found a disciple named Timothy, the son of a Jewish Christian mother and a Gentile father. He was well spoken of by the Christians at Lystra and Iconium, and Paul wanted to have him in his company when he left the place. So he took him and circumcised him, out of consideration for the Jews who lived in those parts; for they all knew that his father was a Gentile. As they made their way from town to town they handed on the decisions taken by the apostles and elders in Jerusalem and enjoined their observance. And so, day by day, the congregations grew stronger in faith and increased in numbers.

They travelled through the Phrygian and Galatian region, because they were prevented by the Holy Spirit from delivering the message in the province of Asia; and when they approached the Mysian border they tried to enter Bithynia; but the Spirit of Jesus would not allow them, so they traversed Mysia and reached the coast at Troas. During the night a vision came to Paul: a Macedonian stood there appealing to

九十六　獄卒信主

使徒行傳

　　保羅到了特庇，又去到路司得。那兒有個叫提摩太的門徒，他母親是個猶太基督徒，而他父親却是個希利尼人[1]。路司得和以哥念的兄弟們都交口稱讚提摩太，因此，保羅離開時便想帶他同去。保羅接受了他，但考慮到那些地方的猶太人都知道提摩太的父親不是猶太人，便給他行了割禮。他們途經各城時，讓門徒們遵守耶路撒冷的使徒和長老所定的戒律。於是，各地教會信道益篤，人數日增。

　　由於聖靈禁止他們在亞西亞講道，他們便行經弗呂家和加拉大一帶地方。靠近每西亞[2]邊界時，他們想去庇推尼，但耶穌的靈却不許。他們便越過每西亞，到達特羅亞[3]的海邊。夜間一個幻像出現在保羅面前：一個馬其頓人站着央求他說：

---

(1)　Gentile 這字的意思是："除猶太人以外的人"。但提摩太（Timothy）的父親根據記載是個 Greek，這裏就譯爲希利尼人。

(2)　每西亞（Mysia）是亞洲西北部的一個地區。當時在羅馬的亞洲管轄區（the Province of Asia）內。

(3)　特羅亞（Troas）是每西亞境內的一個海港。這裏的海，指的是愛琴海（Aegean Sea）。

him and saying, 'Come across to Macedonia and help us.' After he had seen this vision we at once set about getting a passage to Macedonia, concluding that God had called us to bring them the good news.

So we sailed from Troas and made a straight run to Samothrace, the next day to Neapoils, and from there to Philippi, a city of the first rank in that district of Macedonia, and a Roman colony. Here we stayed for some days, and on the Sabbath day we went outside the city gate by the river-side, where we thought there would be a place of prayer, and sat down and talked to the women who had gathered there. One of them named Lydia, a dealer in purple fabric from the city of Thyatira, who was a worshipper of God, was listening, and the Lord opened her heart to respond to what Paul said. She was baptized, and her household with her, and then she said to us, 'If you have judged me to be a believer in the Lord, I beg you to come and stay in my house.' And she insisted on our going.

Once, when we were on our way to the place of prayer, we met a slave-girl who was possessed by an oracular spirit and brought large profits to her owners by telling fortunes. She followed Paul and the rest of us, shouting, 'These men are servants of the Supreme God, and are declaring to you a way of salvation.' She did this day after day, until Paul could bear it no longer. Rounding on the spirit he said, 'I command you in the name of Jesus Christ to come out of her', and it went out there and then.

When the girl's owners saw that their hope of gain had gone, they seized Paul and Silas and dragged them to the city authorities in the main square; and bringing them before the magistrates, they said, 'These men are causing a disturbance in our city; they are Jews; they are advocating customs which it is illegal for us Romans to adopt and follow.' The mob joined in the attack; and the magistrates tore off the prisoners' clothes and ordered them to be flogged. After giving them a severe beating they flung them into prison and ordered the

"請你來馬其頓幫幫我們吧。"保羅看到這異像後，我們（他們）(1)立即出發去馬其頓。認為是神召我們（他們）去那裏傳播福音的。

我們（他們）乘船離開了特羅亞，直抵撒摩特喇。第二天，去了尼亞波利，然後再從那兒抵達腓立比，這是入馬其頓境內的第一座城鎮，又是羅馬人的駐防地。我們（他們）在那裏住了幾天。在安息日那天，出城到河邊找個供禱告的地方。我們（他們）在河邊坐下，對聚在那裏的婦女講道。婦女中有個叫呂底亞的推雅推喇城人，是來這裏販賣紫色布匹的。她敬奉上帝，認真聽道。主便開導她使她傾聽保羅講道。她和她全家便都受了洗，然後，她對我們（他們）說："你們若認我是主的信徒，就請你們來我家住吧。"她堅持要我們（他們）去。

一次，我們（他們）在去那禱告處的路上遇到了一個女奴，她被巫鬼附體，靠算命使她的主人大發橫財。她跟在保羅他們後頭，高喊道："這些人是至高無上的上帝的僕人，對你們講得救之道來了。"她一連幾天都這樣，弄得保羅不耐煩，他便轉身對那巫鬼說："我以耶穌基督之名，命令你從她身上出來。"那鬼馬上便跑掉了。

女奴的主人看到靠她弄錢的指望沒了，便抓住保羅和西拉，拉他們到市上去見官。見到官長後，說："這些猶太人在我們城裏製造混亂。他們信奉的那一套是我們羅馬人所不可接受和效法的。"一些人聽後也攻擊責罵他們。於是官長就吩咐剝去他們的衣服，加以鞭打。痛打一頓後，命令把他們下囚，

_____

(1) 從這裏開始，原文在人稱上有不統一處，因此用括號把正確的人稱加在後面。後面就不一一加註了。

jailer to keep them under close guard. In view of these orders, he put them in the inner prison and secured their feet in the stocks.

About midnight Paul and Silas, at their prayers, were singing praises to God, and the other prisoners were listening, when suddenly there was such a violent earthquake that the foundations of the jail were shaken; all the doors burst open and all the prisoners found their fetters unfastened. The jailer woke up to see the prison doors wide open, and assuming that the prisoners had escaped, drew his sword intending to kill himself. But Paul shouted, 'Do yourself no harm; we are all here.' The jailer called for lights, rushed in and threw himself down before Paul and Silas, trembling with fear. He then escorted them out and said, 'Masters, what must I do to be saved?' They said, 'Put your trust in the Lord Jesus, and you will be saved, you and your household.' Then they spoke the word of the Lord to him and to everyone in his house. At that late hour of the night he took them and washed their wounds; and immediately afterwards he and his whole family were baptized. He brought them into his house, set out a meal, and rejoiced with his whole household in his newfound faith in God.

When daylight came the magistrates sent their officers with instructions to release the men. The jailer reported the message to Paul: 'The magistrates have sent word that you are to be released. So now you may go free, and blessings on your journey.' But Paul said to the officers: 'They gave us a public flogging, though we are Roman citizens and have not been found guilty; they threw us into prison, and are they now to smuggle us out privately? No indeed! Let them come in person and escort us out.' The officers reported his words. The magistrates were alarmed to hear that they were Roman citizens, and came and apologized to them. Then they escorted them out and requested them to go away from the city. On leaving the prison, they went to Lydia's house, where they met their fellow-Chirstians, and spoke words of encouragement to them; then they departed.

並吩咐獄卒嚴加看守。獄卒奉命把他們關在內監裏，並上了足枷。

到午夜時，保羅和西拉在做禱告、唱詩讚頌上帝，其他囚犯在聽着。忽然，大地猛烈震動，監獄的地基震得搖搖晃晃。監門都震開了，眾囚犯身上的鐐銬都脫落了。獄卒驚醒過來看到監門大開，以爲囚徒都跑光了，便欲拔刀自刎。保羅喝止他們道：「不要傷害自己。我們全都在這兒呢。」獄卒叫人拿來燈火，跑進監裏戰戰兢兢地一頭拜倒在保羅、西拉面前。這獄卒把他們送出來，問道：「我主！我該作什麼才能得救？」二人說：「只要信奉主耶穌，你和你全家便會得救。」他們又把天主之道講給他和他全家人聽。就在那深夜時分，獄卒領他們去洗滌好傷口，他和他的全家人就都受了洗。獄卒把他們帶回家裏，弄飯菜給他們吃。他和他全家因信了上帝而感到滿懷喜悅。

天亮後，官長派手下的人來釋放兩人。獄卒便告知保羅說：「官長派人來說要釋放你們。現在你們可以走了，祝你們一路平安。」但保羅卻對那些來人說：「我們是羅馬公民，並無犯罪。但他們都當眾鞭打我們，把我們囚在監裏。現在，他們想偷偷地趕我們走，那怎麼行！叫他們親自來，把我們請出去才行。」差役便把保羅的話回稟了官長。官長一聽他們是羅馬公民，大驚失色，便來向他們賠不是，然後把二人送了出來，請他們離開那城。一離開監獄，二人便去了呂底亞的家。在那兒，他們會見了那些基督徒，說了些勉勵的話，便上路去了。

Acts

When the disturbance had ceased, Paul sent for the disciples and, after encouraging them, said good-bye and set out on his journey to Macedonia. He travelled through those parts of the country, often speaking words of encouragement to the Christians there, and so came into Greece. When he had spent three months there and was on the point of embarking for Syria, a plot was laid against him by the Jews, so he decided to return by way of Macedonia. He was accompanied by Sopater son of Pyrrhus, from Beroea, the Thessalonians Aristarchus and Secundus, Gaius the Doberian and Timothy, and the Asians Tychicus and Trophimus. These went ahead and waited for us at Troas; we ourselves set sail from Philippi after the Passover season, and in five days reached them at Troas, where we spent a week.

On the Saturday night, in our assembly for the breaking of bread, Paul, who was to leave next day, addressed them, and went on speaking until midnight. Now there were many lamps in the upper room where we were assembled; and a youth named Eutychus, who was sitting on the window-ledge, grew

九十七　保羅囑託

使徒行傳

　　（以佛所城的）騷亂停息之後，保羅便叫衆門徒來，說了些勉勵的話，然後便與他們告別，動身前往馬其頓。他在沿途經過的地方都勉勵那兒的門徒。後來他到了希臘，在那兒住了三個月。在他就要乘船回叙利亞時，猶太人密謀要殺害他，所以他決定經由馬其頓回去。同行的有庇哩亞人華羅斯的兒子所巴特、帖撒羅尼迦人亞里達古和西公都、特庇人該猶和提摩太以及亞細亞人推基古、特羅非摩。這些人先走，在特羅亞等我們（他們）[1]。我們（他們）自己則在除酵節[2]後，從腓立比乘船啟程。五天後，我們（他們）到了特羅亞，和在那兒等着的人相會，並在那裏住了一週。

　　禮拜六晚上，大家聚在一起共用聖餐。保羅因次日要啟程，便給他們講道，直至半夜。我們（他們）聚會的那座樓上，有許多燈燭。有個少年人名叫猶推古，坐在窗台上聽講。

---

[1] "我們"（we）在這故事裏，同前面出現過的一樣，造成了人稱上的混亂。譯者在按照原文翻譯的同時，根據不同的上下文，用括弧在它後面注明了其應該的含義。有的地方就省略掉，沒譯出來。

[2] 這兒說的 "Passover season" 實際上指的是除酵節的日子（the days of Unleavened Bread）。

more and more sleepy as Paul went on talking. At last he was completely overcome by sleep, fell from the third storey to the ground, and was picked up for dead. Paul went down, threw himself upon him, seizing him in his arms, and said to them, 'Stop this commotion; there is still life in him.' He then went upstairs, broke bread and ate, and after much conversation, which lasted until dawn, he departed. And they took the boy away alive and were immensely comforted.

We went ahead to the ship and sailed for Assos, where we were to take Paul aboard. He had made this arrangement, as he was going to travel by road. When he met us at Assos, we took him aboard and went on to Mitylene. Next day we sailed from there and arrived opposite Chios, and on the second day we made Samos. On the following day we reached Miletus. For Paul had decided to pass by Ephesus and so avoid having to spend time in the province of Asia; he was eager to be in Jerusalem, if he possibly could, on the day of Pentecost. He did, however, send from Miletus to Ephesus and summon the elders of the congregation; and when they joined him, he spoke as follows:

'You know how, from the day that I first set foot in the province of Asia, for the whole time that I was with you, I served the Lord in all humility amid the sorrows and trials that came upon me through the machinations of the Jews. You know that I kept back nothing that was for your good: I delivered the message to you; I taught you, in public and in your homes; with Jews and Gentiles alike I insisted on repentance before God and trust in our Lord Jesus. And now, as you see, I am on my way to Jerusalem, under the constraint of the Spirit. Of what will befall me there I know nothing, except that in city after city the Holy Spirit assures me that imprisonment and hardships await me. For myself, I set no store by lift; I only want to finish the race, and complete the task which the Lord Jesus assigned to me, of bearing my testimony to the gospel of God's grace.

'One word more: I have gone about among you proclaim-

保羅講的時間很長，這少年人越來越感到睏倦。最後他完全睡着了，便從三樓掉了下去。人們抱起他時，他已死了。保羅下樓搶過去抱起他，對衆人說：「你們不用担心，他的靈魂還在身上。」說罷他就回到樓上去進聖餐，又和別人談話，直至天亮才離開。衆人高高興興地把那活過來的少年帶回去了。

我們（使徒們）先乘船前往亞朔，在那兒再接保羅上船。這是他的安排，因爲他要從陸路前往。在亞朔會合後，我們（他們）和他乘船去達米推利尼。第二天我們（他們）又離開了那裏，到了對面的基阿。第三天，船在撒摩靠岸。第四天，抵達米利都。因爲保羅已決定要繞過以弗所，以免在亞細亞省躭擱。他急於盡量在五旬齋節趕到耶路撒冷，不過他還是從米利都派人到以弗所去，請教會的長老們來。他們來後，保羅便對他們說：

「自到亞細亞後，我一直和你們在一起。你們知道，我雖屢遭猶太人加害，憂患交加，但却始終謙恭事主。你們也知道，凡對你們有益之事，我從未有所保留，總會告訴你們。或在大衆面前，或在你們各自的家裏，我一直在教導你們。對猶太人和希利尼人，我都同樣要他們在上帝面前悔改，信奉我主耶穌。你們現在看到，在聖靈的催促下，我要到耶路撒冷去。我不知道在那裏會遇到什麼事，但聖靈已在各城鎮向我指明，等待的是監禁和苦難。我並不以一己性命爲憂，只想走完我的途程，盡我從主耶穌所領受的天職，去爲上帝恩惠的福音作證明。

「再者，我一直在你們之中宣揚天國之道，但現在我知

ing the Kingdom, but now I know that none of you will see my face again. That being so, I here and now declare that no man's fate can be laid at my door; for I have kept back nothing; I have disclosed to you the whole purpose of God. Keep watch over yourselves and over all the flock of which the Holy Spirit has given you charge, as shepherds of the church of the Lord, which he won for himself by his own blood. I know that when I am gone, savage wolves will come in among you and will not spare the flock. Even from your own body there will be men coming forward who will distort the truth to induce the disciples to break away and follow them. So be on the alert; remember how for three years, night and day, I never ceased to counsel each of you, and how I wept over you.

'And now I commend you to God and to his gracious word, which has power to build you up and give you your heritage among all who are dedicated to him. I have not wanted anyone's money or clothes for myself; you all know that these hands of mine earned enough for the needs of myself and my companions. I showed you that it is our duty to help the weak in this way, by hard work, and that we should keep in mind the words of the Lord Jesus, who himself said, "Happiness lies more in giving than in receiving."'

As he finished speaking, he knelt down with them all and prayed. Then there were loud cries of sorrow from them all, as they folded Paul in their arms and kissed him. What distressed them most was his saying that they would never see his face agian. So they escorted him to his ship.

道，以後你們誰也見不到我了。因此，我此時此地向你們講明，你們中間無論何人死亡，罪都不在我身上。這是因為我對你們從未保留任何不講的事，我已把上帝的全部旨意告訴了你們。聖靈既然讓你們負責，你們自己就要小心謹慎，也要悉心照管信徒們，當好主的教會的牧羊人，而這正是他用自己的血換來的。我知道，我去之後，必有兇狠的狼來到你們之中而且不會放過徒眾。就是在你們中間，也會有人出來篡改真道，引誘門徒跟他們走。所以，你們一定要警惕，不要辜負我三年來日日夜夜勸導你們、為你們而難過的苦心。

　　"現在，我要把你們託付給上帝及其恩道。這道能成就你們，能使你們以及所有忠心事神的人同得基業。我沒有貪圖過別人的錢財衣物。你們都知道，我憑雙手掙得我和我的同伴之所需。我已給你們指出，應該扶助弱小，要牢記主耶穌的話：'施捨比受用更有福。'"

　　說完這些話後，保羅便跪下同眾人一起禱告。眾人摟著保羅親吻他，失聲痛哭。最使他們傷心的是保羅講的那句話，即眾人以後再也見不到他了。就這樣，他們送他上船去了。

We made the passage from Tyre and reached Ptolemais. Next day we left and came to Caesarea. We went to the home of Philip the evangelist, who was one of the Seven, and stayed with him. When we had been there several days, a prophet named Agabus arrived from Judaea. He came to us, took Paul's belt, bound his own feet and hands with it, and said, 'These are the words of the Holy Spirit: Thus will the Jews in Jerusalem bind the man to whom this belt belongs, and hand him over to the Gentiles.' When we heard this, we and the local people begged and implored Paul to abandon his visit to Jerusalem. Then Paul gave his answer: 'Why all these tears? Why are you trying to weaken my resolution? For my part I am ready not merely to be bound but even to die at Jerusalem for the name of the Lord Jesus.'

At the end of our stay we packed our baggage and took the road up to Jerusalem.

Next day Paul paid a visit to James; we were with him, and all the elders attended. He greeted them, and then described in detail all that God had done among the Gentiles through his ministry. When they heard this, they gave praise to God. Then they said to Paul: 'You see, brother, how many thousands of converts we have among the Jews, all of them staunch upholders of the Law. Now they have been given certain information about you: it is said that you teach all the

九十八　知難而進

使徒行傳

我們（保羅一行）⑴從推羅乘船來到了多利靈。第二天，我們（他們）離開那裏去該撒利亞，到了傳福音的七執事之一腓利的家，在他那裏住下。住了幾天，有個叫亞迦布的先知從猶太來到該撒利亞。他見我們（他們）後，就用保羅的腰帶捆住自己的手腳，說：“聖靈講，耶路撒冷的猶太人也要這樣捆綁這腰帶的主人，並把他交給外邦人。”聽到這話後，我們（使徒們）和當地人都哀勸保羅不要去耶路撒冷。保羅答道：“你們哭什麼呢？爲何要動搖我的決心？爲了主耶穌之名，我不僅準備受綁，甚至還準備死在耶路撒冷。”

我們（他們）在那裏住的最後幾天便收拾好行裝，啟程赴耶路撒冷。

到了耶路撒冷的第二天，保羅去見雅各。我們（他們）和他同去，長老們也在那裏。保羅向大家問了安，然後便把自己如何在外邦人中傳上帝之道的事仔細講給他們聽。他們聽後，讚美上帝，對保羅說：“兄弟，我們在猶太人中的信徒眞是成千上萬，他們都是崇奉律法的。如今他們聽人說，你教導所有

⑴　這裏出現的“我們”（we）與前文的處理方法一樣。

Jews in the gentile world to turn their backs on Moses, telling them to give up circumcising their children and following our way of life. What is the position, then? You must therefore do as we tell you. We have four men here who are under a vow; take them with you and go through the ritual of purification with them, paying their expenses, after which they may shave their heads. Then everyone will know that there is nothing in the stories they were told about you, but that you are a practising Jew and keep the Law yourself.... So Paul took the four men, and next day, after going through the ritual of purification with them, he went into the temple to give notice of the date when the period of purification would end and the offering be made for each one of them.

But just before the seven days were up, the Jews from the province of Asia saw him in the temple. They stirred up the whole crowd, and seized him.

The whole city was in a turmoil, and people came running from all directions. While they were clamouring for his death, a report reached the officer commanding the cohort, that all Jerusalem was in an uproar. He immediately took a force of soldiers with their centurions and came down on the rioters at the double. The commandant stepped forward, arrested him, and ordered him to be taken into barracks.

Just before Paul was taken into the barracks he said to the commandant, 'I am a Jew, a Tarsian from Cilicia, a citizen of no mean city. I ask your permission to speak to the people.' When permission had been given, Paul stood on the steps and with a gesture called for the attention of the people. As soon as quiet was restored, he addressed them in the Jewish language:

'I am a trueborn Jew,' he said, 'a native of Tarsus in Cilicia. I was brought up in this city, and as a pupil of Gamaliel I was thoroughly trained in every point of our ancestral law. And so I began to persecute this movement to the death, arresting its followers, men and women alike, and putting them in chains. For this I have as witnesses the High Priest and the whole

在外邦的猶太人背離摩西，告訴他們不要給孩子行割禮，也不要遵守我們的條規。這可不大好辦。你按我們的辦法去做吧：我們這兒有四個人決意要行潔身禮，你帶他們去並和他們一起行潔身禮，替他們付規費，他們就可以剃了頭。這樣，人們就會知道，以前關於你的傳言都是假的。你是個循規蹈矩、遵守律法的人。"於是，第二天保羅便帶着那四個人一起行了潔身禮，然後進殿報明潔淨的日期已滿，只等祭司為他們各人獻祭。

七日將完時，來自亞細亞的猶太人看到保羅在殿裏，便煽動眾人捉住他。

全城騷動起來，人們從四方八面跑了來。他們正高喊要殺保羅時，有人給營裏的千人隊隊長(1)報信說，耶路撒冷全城都亂了。千人隊隊長馬上帶了幾個百人隊隊長和一隊士兵趕到了騷亂現場。千人隊隊長上前抓住保羅，吩咐手下把保羅帶回營房。

進營房前保羅對千人隊隊長說："我是猶太人，生在基利家的大數，並非無名小城的人。我請你准許我和百姓說話。"千人隊隊長答應了，保羅便站在台階上，向百姓擺了擺手，讓他們仔細聽他講。百姓靜下來後，他便使用希伯來語對他們說："我原是猶太人，在基利家的大數出生，在這城裏長大。我完全是按照我們祖先的法規在迦瑪列的門下受教。我也曾扼殺過這道的傳播，把信道的男女抓進監獄。此事祭司長和眾長老都

---

(1) Cohort 在古羅馬實際是只有300—600人的一個步兵大隊。

Council of Elders. I was given letters from them to our fellow-Jews at Damascus, and had started out to bring the Christians there to Jerusalem as prisoners for punishment; and this is what happened. I was on the road and nearing Damascus, when suddenly about midday a great light flashed from the sky all around me, and I fell to the ground. Then I heard a voice saying to me, "Saul, Saul, why do you persecute me?" I answered, "Tell me, Lord, who you are." "I am Jesus of Nazareth," he said, "whom you are persecuting." "What shall I do, Lord?" I said, and the Lord replied, "Get up and continue your journey to Damascus; there you will be told of all the tasks that are laid upon you." As I had been blinded by the brilliance of that light, my companions led me by the hand, and so I came to Damascus.

'There, a man called Ananias, a devout observer of the Law and well spoken of by all the Jews of the place, came and stood before me and said, "Saul, my brother, recover your sight." Instantly I recovered my sight and saw him. He went on: "The God of our fathers appointed you to know his will and to see the Righteous One and to hear his very voice, because you are to be his witness before the world, and testify to what you have seen and heard."

'After my return to Jerusalem, I was praying in the temple when I fell into a trance and saw him there, speaking to me. "Make haste", he said, "and leave Jerusalem without delay, for they will not accept your testimony about me."'

Up to this point they had given him a hearing; but now they began shouting, 'Down with him! A scoundrel like that is better dead!' And as they were yelling and waving their cloaks and flinging dust in the air, the commandant ordered him to be brought into the barracks and gave instructions to examine him by flogging. But when they tied him up for the lash, Paul said to the centurion who was standing there, 'Can you legally flog a man who is a Roman citizen, and moreover has not been found guilty?' When the centurion heard this, he went and reported it to the commandant, and the commandant

可爲我作證。我曾拿着祭司長老們給猶太弟兄的信函前往大馬色，要把那裏的基督徒抓到耶路撒冷下獄懲處。但當我離大馬色不遠時，中午時分，天上忽然降下一道亮光降到了我身邊，我仆倒在地。這時，一個聲音對我說：'掃羅，掃羅，你爲何迫害我？'我答道：'主啊，請告訴我你是誰？'他說：'我就是你迫害的拿撒勒人耶穌。'我說：'主啊，我該怎麼辦？'主答道：'起來，仍然到大馬色去。那兒會有人告訴你該怎麼辦的。'因爲那耀眼的光使我一時失明，同行的人便拉着我的手引我到大馬色去。

"城裏有個叫亞拿尼亞的人，他虔誠地遵奉律法，在當地猶太人中享有很高的聲譽。他站在我面前說：'掃羅兄弟，你可以看見了。'我的雙眼立時復明，看見他了。他繼續說：'我們先祖的神選上你，讓你懂得他的旨意，得見那義人，聆聽他的聲音，因爲你得把你的所見所聞這些事向世人傳達，爲他作證。'

"我後來回到了耶路撒冷。在殿裏祈禱時，我在幻像中看見主對我說：'趕快離開此地，不可遲延，因爲他們不會接受你爲我做的見證。'"

衆人一直在聽，但到這裏便開始喊叫："幹掉他！這樣的惡人最好處死！"那些人高聲叫嚷，揮動衣服，把塵土撒向空中。千人隊隊長便吩咐手下把保羅關入營房，鞭打拷問。他們用皮條把保羅捆上，保羅便對在那的百人隊隊長說："我是羅馬公民，又未犯罪，你們這樣鞭笞我合法嗎？"聽到這話，那

himself was alarmed when he realized that Paul was a Roman citizen and that he had put him in irons.

The following day, wishing to be quite sure what charge the Jews were bringing against Paul, he released him and ordered the chief priests and the entire Council to assemble.

百人隊隊長便去報告給千人隊隊長聽。千人隊隊長知道保羅是羅馬公民，而自己還用鐵鏈捆綁他，心裏倒害怕起來了。

第二天，千人隊隊長想弄清楚猶太人究竟控告保羅甚麼罪狀，就先放開保羅的捆綁，並叫祭司長和全公會的人前來會審。

Acts

After spending eight or ten days at most in Jerusalem, he went down to Caesarea, and next day he took his seat in court and ordered Paul to be brought up. When he appeared, the Jews who had come down from Jerusalem stood round bringing many grave charges, which they were unable to prove. Paul's plea was: 'I have committed no offence, either against the Jewish law, or against the temple, or against the Emperor.' Festus, anxious to ingratiate himself with the Jews, turned to Paul and asked, 'Are you willing to go up to Jerusalem and stand trial on these charges before me there?' But Paul said, 'I am now standing before the Emperor's tribunal, and that is where I must be tried.... I appeal to Caesar!' Then Festus, after conferring with his advisers, replied, 'You have appealed to Caesar: to Caesar you shall go.'

After an interval of some days King Agrippa and Bernice arrived at Caesarea on a courtesy visit to Fesuts. They spent several days there, and during this time Festus laid Paul's case before the king.... Agrippa said to Festus, 'I should rather

九十九　保羅自辯

使徒行傳

（保羅被誣，關在監獄裏兩年之久。直到非斯都代替腓力斯任總督後，保羅的案子才再得到審理。）

非斯都在耶路撒冷住了八到十天左右，便回到了該撒利亞。第二天開庭，他吩咐把保羅帶上來。保羅來到，那些從耶路撒冷來的猶太人站到他四周圍，指控他犯有許多重罪，但都提不出甚麼根據。保羅申訴說：“無論是猶太人的律法，或是聖殿、或是羅馬皇帝，我都沒有冒犯過。”非都斯渴望討好猶太人，便問保羅：“你願去耶路撒冷那兒讓我審斷此案麼？”保羅說：“我現在站在皇帝凱撒的堂前，這就是我應當受審的地方。……我要上告凱撒！”非斯都和顧問們商議後說：“你既然要上告凱撒，那你就到凱撒那兒去吧。”

過了些日子，亞基帕王(1)和百尼基(2)來到該撒利亞，向非斯都作禮節性訪問。他們在那兒住了幾天，其間，非斯都把保羅的事告訴了亞基帕王……。亞基帕對非斯都說：“我倒想聽

---

(1)　亞基帕王（Herod Agrippa）：這裏指的是小亞基帕王（H.Agrippa Ⅱ）。

(2)　百尼基（Bernice）是他的同胞姐妹。

like to hear the man myself.'

So next day Agrippa and Bernice came in full state and entered the audience-chamber accompanied by high-ranking officers and prominent citizens; and on the orders of Festus Paul was brought up. Then Festus said, '…But I have nothing definite about him to put in writing for our Sovereign. Accordingly I have brought him up before you all and particularly before you, King Agrippa, so that as a result of this preliminary inquiry I may have something to report. There is no sense, it seems to me, in sending on a prisoner without indicating the charges against him.'

Agrippa said to Paul, 'You have our permission to speak for yourself.' Then Paul stretched out his hand and began his defence:

'I consider myself fortunate, King Agrippa, that it is before you that I am to make my defence today upon all the charges brought against me by the Jews, particularly as you are expert in all Jewish matters, both our customs and our disputes. And therefore I beg you to give me a patient hearing.

'My life from my youth up, the life I led from the beginning among my people and in Jerusalem, is familiar to all Jews. Indeed they have known me long enough and could testify, if they only would, that I belonged to the strictest group in our religion: I lived as a Pharisee. And it is for a hope kindled by God's promise to our forefathers that I stand in the dock today. Our twelve tribes hope to see the fulfilment of that promise, worshipping with intense devotion day and night; and for this very hope I am impeached, and impeached by Jews, Your Majesty. Why is it considered incredible among you that God should raise dead men to life?

'I myself once thought it my duty to work actively against the name of Jesus of Nazareth; and I did so in Jerusalem. It was I who imprisoned many of God's people by authority obtained from the chief priests; and when they were condemned to death, my vote was cast against them. In all the synagogues I tried by repeated punishment to make them

聽這個人講些什麼。"

第二天，亞基帕和百尼基一行，威風凜凜地在千人隊隊長和城中顯貴的陪同下，來到公堂。非斯都吩咐把保羅帶上堂來。然後，非斯都說："……但關於此人，我沒有什麼確實的事可奏明主上，因此，我把他帶到你們面前，特意帶到你亞基帕王面前，爲的是在查問之後，有所陳奏。在我看來，解送囚犯而不指明其罪狀，是不合理的。"

亞基帕對保羅說："我們准許你爲自己申訴。"於是保羅便伸手申辯道：

"亞基帕王啊，我有幸能在你面前對猶太人強加於我的指控作辯。尤其有幸的是，你熟諳猶太人的規習和他們的爭論。所以，請你耐心聽我講來。

"自幼年時起，我在羣衆中以及在耶路撒冷爲人如何，猶太人都十分清楚。他們非常了解我，因些，如果他們願意，就能證實我屬於我們教中最嚴緊的教派，是個法利賽人。我現在站在這裏受審，是因爲要希望得到上帝給我們先祖的許諾，我們十二支派日夜忠心奉神就是指望得到這許諾。陛下，正因如此我就被猶太人一再指責控告。上帝叫死人復活，你們爲何看作是不可信的呢？

"我自己也曾以猛烈攻擊拿撒勒人耶穌爲己任。我在耶路撒冷就是這樣做的。是我從祭司長請得權柄，監禁過許多聖徒，並贊成把他們處死。在各個會堂，我也屢次用刑來強迫他

renounce their faith; indeed my fury rose to such a pitch that I extended my persecution to foreign cities....

'And so, King Agrippa, I did not disobey the heavenly vision. I turned first to the inhabitants of Damascus, and then to Jerusalem and all the country of Judaea, and to the Gentiles, and sounded the call to repent and turn to God, and to prove their repentance by deeds. That is why the Jews seized me in the temple and tried to do away with me. But I had God's help, and so to this very day I stand and testify to great and small alike. I assert nothing beyond what was foretold by the prophets and by Moses: that the Messiah must suffer, and that he, the first to rise from the dead, would announce the dawn to Israel and to the Gentiles.'

While Paul was thus making his defence, Festus shouted at the top of his voice, 'Paul, you are raving; too much study is driving you mad.' 'I am not mad, Your Excellency,' said Paul; 'what I am saying is sober truth. The king is well versed in these matters, and to him I can speak freely. I do not believe that he can be unaware of any of these facts, for this has been no hole-and-corner business. King Agrippa, do you believe the prophets? I know you do.' Agrippa said to Paul, 'You think it will not take much to win me over and make a Christian of me.' 'Much or little,' said Paul, 'I wish to God that not only you, but all those also who are listening to me today, might become what I am, apart from these chains.'

With that the king rose, and with him the Governor, Bernice, and the rest of the company, and after they had withdrawn they talked it over. 'This man', they said, 'is doing nothing that deserves death or imprisonment.' Agrippa said to Festus, 'The fellow could have been discharged, if he had not appealed to the Emperor.'

們放棄自己的信仰。我這樣惱恨他們，以至不惜追到外邦去迫害他們。（保羅接着講了他在去大馬色途中遇到主耶穌顯靈之事。）

"亞基帕王啊，我並沒有違背那從天而降的顯靈指示，先在大馬色，後又在耶路撒冷、猶太全境以及外邦，我都勸勉衆人悔改，歸向上帝，用行動改過。因而被猶太人在聖殿拿住，他們並要殺我。然而，蒙上帝相助，今天我才能在不論尊卑的人們面前作證。我所講的並未超出先知和摩西的預言，即基督必須受難，而且第一個復活，去把光明之道帶給以色列和外邦的人們。"

保羅這樣申辯時，非斯都大聲喊道："保羅，你發瘋了。你的學問過多，反使你瘋狂了。"保羅說："大人，我沒有瘋，說的都是實話。亞基帕王深通事理，我才大胆直言。我不信他對這些事一無所知，因爲這不是在背地裏幹的。亞基帕王啊，你信先知麼？我想你是信的。"亞基帕對保羅說："你以爲稍加勸說，就會使我成爲一個基督徒麼？"保羅說："勸說不論多少，我向上帝所求的，不只是你一人，而是今天聽我講的所有人，他們都會成爲像我一樣的人，只是不帶這些鎖鏈。"

於是，王、總督、百尼基和同坐之人都起來退席。他們議論此事說："這個人並未犯什麼該處死或囚禁之罪。"亞基帕對非斯都說："如果這人不曾要上告皇帝，本是可以釋放的。"

Acts

When it was decided that we should sail for Italy, Paul and some other prisoners were handed over to a centurion named Julius, of the Augustan Cohort.

There the centurion found an Alexandrian vessel bound for Italy and put us aboard. As the wind continued against us, we struggled on to a place called Fair Havens, not far from the town of Lasea.

By now much time had been lost, the Fast was already over, and it was risky to go on with the voyage. Paul therefore gave them this advice: 'I can see, gentlemen," he said, 'that this voyage will be disastrous: it will mean grave loss, loss not only of ship and cargo but also of life.' But the centurion paid more attention to the captain and to the owner of the ship than to what Paul said. So when a southerly breeze sprang up, they thought that their purpose was as good as achieved, and, weighing anchor, they sailed along the coast of Crete hugging the land. But before very long a fierce wind tore down from the landward side. It caught the ship and, as it was impossible to keep head to wind, we had to give way and run before it. Next day, as we were making very heavy weather, they began to lighten the ship; and on the third day they jettisoned the ship's gear with their own hands. For days on end there was no sign of either sun or stars, a great storm was raging, and our last hopes of coming through alive began to fade.

When they had gone for a long time without food, Paul stood up among them and said, 'You should have taken my

一百　苦盡甘來

非斯都決定叫我們（他們）乘船去意大利後，便將保羅和其他囚犯交給御營裏一個叫猶流的百人隊隊長。

百人隊隊長在那兒找到了一艘開往意大利的亞歷山大的船，讓大家上了船。因爲逆風，我們（他們）好不容易才抵達離拉西亞城不遠的佳澳。

在海上旅行多日，又過了禁食的節期，而繼續航行又很危險，於是保羅便勸衆人道："諸位，我看此次航行，凶多吉少，不僅船和貨物要遭受重大損失，恐怕連我們的性命也難保。"但百人隊隊長不信保羅的話，只聽信船長和船主的。因此，當有一天微微起了南風，他們覺得很合意，於是便起錨沿着革哩底海岸航行。行不多時，狂風從陸上猛吹過來。船被吹得搖搖晃晃，無法迎風行駛，只好任風颺去。第二天，因爲風高浪急，他們便把貨物拋入海中。第三天，他們又動手扔掉船上的器具。一連多日都看不到太陽和星辰，只見狂風掀起滔天巨浪，得救的指望越來越渺茫了。

他們已有很長時間未吃東西了。保羅站起來說："諸位，

advice, gentlemen, not to sail from Crete; then you would have avoided this damage and loss. But now I urge you not to lose heart; not a single life will be lost, only the ship. For last night there stood by me an angel of the God whose I am and whom I worship. "Do not be afraid, Paul," he said; "it is ordained that you shall appear before the Emperor; and, be assured, God has granted you the lives of all who are sailing with you." So keep up your courage: I trust in God that it will turn out as I have been told; though we have to be cast ashore on some island.'

The fourteenth night came and we were still drifting in the Sea of Adria.

When day broke they could not recognize the land, but they noticed a bay with sandy beach, on which they planned, if possible, to run the ship ashore. The soldiers thought they had better kill the prisoners for fear that any should swim away and escape; but the centurion wanted to bring Paul safely through and prevented them from carrying out their plan. He gave orders that those who could swim should jump overboard first and get to land; the rest were to follow, some on planks, some on parts of the ship. And thus it was that all came safely to land.

Once we had made our way to safety we identified the island as Malta. The rough islanders treated us with uncommon kindness: because it was cold and had started to rain, they lit a bonfire and made us all welcome. Paul had got together an armful of sticks and put them on the fire, when a viper, driven out by the heat, fastened on his hand. The islanders, seeing the snake hanging on to his hand, said to one another, 'The man must be a murderer; he may have escaped from the sea, but divine justice has not let him live.' Paul, however, shook off the snake into the fire and was none the worse. They still expected that any moment he would swell up or drop down dead, but after waiting a long time without seeing anything extraordinary happen to him, they changed their minds and now said, 'He is a god.'

你們本該聽我的勸告，不駛離革哩底。那樣，就不會遭受今天這樣的損失了。不過，現在你們也不必喪氣，船雖然保不住，但你們誰也不會喪命的。因為我所敬拜的上帝的使者昨夜站在我身邊說：'保羅，不要怕。你注定要見到皇帝的面。你放心，神已把同船人的性命交託給你了。'所以，鼓起勇氣來吧，我相信上帝會用事實驗證他對我講的話的。不過，我們的船會撞破在某個島上的。"

到了第十四天夜間，船仍在亞底亞海面上隨風飄流。

天亮之後，他們都不認識這個是甚麼地方，只看見一個有沙灘的海灣，便商量能否把船開進去。士兵們恐怕囚徒游水逃脫，便想將他們全部殺死。但百人隊隊長想把保羅安全帶到目的地，便阻止了他們這樣做。他吩咐會游泳的人先跳下水游上岸，其餘的人或伏在木板上，或借助船上的可漂浮物上岸。這樣，大家都平安上了岸。

我們（大家）平安上岸後，才知那島叫米利大。住在島上的土人待我們非常熱情。因當時天氣寒冷，又下起雨來，他們便升起了火招待我們。保羅揀了一抱柴加到火上，這時，一條蛇受不了火烤，竄了出來，咬住保羅的手。土人看到那蛇懸在他手上，便議論道："這人準是個兇手，他在海上脫了險，但天理卻不容他活着！"但保羅卻絲毫無損，一揮手就把蛇甩到火裏。土人在想，他早晚會中毒腫脹，倒地而死的。但等了許久見保羅依然無恙，便改變了想法，說："他準是個神。"

In the neighbourhood of that place there were lands belonging to the chief magistrate of the island, whose name was Publius. He took us in and entertained us hospitably for three days. It so happened that this man's father was in bed suffering from recurrent bouts of fever and dysentery. Paul visited him and, after prayer, laid his hands upon him and healed him; whereupon the other sick people on the island came also and were cured. They honoured us with many marks of respect, and when we were leaving they put on board provision for our needs.

Three months had passed when we set sail in a ship which had wintered in the island. And so to Rome....

When we entered Rome Paul was allowed to lodge by himself with a soldier in charge of him. Three days later he called together the local Jewish leaders; and when they were assembled, he said to them: 'My brothers, I, who never did anything against our people or the customs of our forefathers, am here as a prisoner; I was handed over to the Romans at Jerusalem. They examined me and would have liked to release me because there was no capital charge against me; but the Jews objected, and I had no option but to appeal to the Emperor.' They replied, 'We have had no communication from Judaea, nor has any countryman of ours arrived with any report or gossip to your discredit. We should like to hear from you what your views are.'

So they fixed a day, and came in large numbers as his guests. He dealt at length with the whole matter; he spoke urgently of the kingdom of God and sought to convince them about Jesus by appealing to the Law of Moses and the prophets....

He stayed there two full years at his own expense, with a welcome for all who came to him, proclaiming the kingdom of God and teaching the facts about the Lord Jesus Christ quite openly and without hindrance.

離那地方不遠，有一片屬於該島長部百流的田產。他把我們（大家）接到家裏，殷勤款待三日。部百流的父親當時正因患熱病和痢疾，臥床起不來。保羅去看他，作禱告並把手按在他身上，治好了他。於是島上的其他病人也來求醫，保羅也把他們治好了。島上居民對我們（他們）千恩萬謝，十分尊敬。離別時，他們還把許多用品送到船上。

過了三個月，我們（他們）上了一艘停靠在那島過冬的船。便到羅馬去了。

進羅馬後，保羅被允准和一個看守他的兵士另住一處。三天後，保羅便把當地的猶太人首領請來。他們來後，保羅對他們說："弟兄們，我雖從未做過違反本國人民的利益和先祖的條規的事，但如今却被囚在此。我是在耶路撒冷被交到羅馬人手裏的。他們審問過我，也願意釋放我，因爲我沒有犯任何死罪。但猶太人不幹，我只得上告皇帝。"那些猶太人首領說："我們沒有收到猶太的信件，也沒有任何弟兄來這兒報告或談論過你有什麼不好。我們倒願聽聽你的看法。"

於是，他們商定了個日子；那一天，許多人都來了。保羅向他們仔細講述了事情的始末。他熱切地給他們講上帝之國的道，並引用摩西律法和先知書使衆人信奉耶穌。

保羅在租來的房子裏住了整整兩年。凡來見他的，他都熱情接待，大胆地向他們講上帝之國的道，宣傳主耶穌基督的事迹，也沒有什麼人來干涉他。

Bibliography 參考書目

(1) Samuel Sandmel: "The New English Bible", Oxford Study Edition, New York Oxford University Press, 1792.

(2) 科西多斯夫斯基（波蘭）著，張會森、陳啓民譯《聖經故事集》，新華社出版，1984。

(3) 張久宣編《聖經故事》，中國社會科學出版社，1982。

(4) 《新舊約全書》（官話和合譯本），上海聖書公會印發，1928。

(5) Rev. James L. Dow M.A.: "Collins Gem Dictionary of the Bible", William Collins Sons & Co. Ltd., London and Glasgow, 1974.

(6) The Gideons International "The Holy Bible" (The Authorised King James Version) National Publishing Company, Nashville, Tennessee, 1975.

(7) 王佐良、李賦寧、周珏良、劉承沛："英國文選名篇選注"，商務印書館，1983——張谷若："The English Bible" pp.191—217。